TEXAS PARKS
& CAMPGROUNDS

LONE ★ STAR
TRAVEL ★ GUIDE

TO

TEXAS PARKS
& CAMPGROUNDS

Fifth Edition

GEORGE OXFORD MILLER

A Lone Star Guide

TAYLOR TRADE PUBLISHING
Lanham • New York • Boulder • Toronto • Plymouth, UK

"Blessed is the spot, and the house, and the place, and the city, and the heart, and the mountain, and the refuge, and the cave, and the valley, and the land, and the sea, and the island, and the meadow where mention of God hath been made, and His praise glorified."*
—Bahá'u'lláh

This book is dedicated to my children, Koda and Heather, and to those who love the outdoors and are committed to preserving its natural condition for future generations.

Published by Taylor Trade Publishing
A Lone Star Guide
An imprint of The Rowman & Littlefield Publishing Group, Inc.
4501 Forbes Boulevard, Suite 200
Lanham, MD 20706

Distributed by NATIONAL BOOK NETWORK

First Taylor Trade Publishing Edition 2003

ISBN 978-1-58979-397-2
LCCN: 2004209706

∞™ The paper used in this publication meets the minimum requirements of American National Standard for Information Sciences—Permanence of Paper for Printed Library Materials, ANSI/NISO Z39.48-1992.

Manufactured in the United States of America.

* From the writings of Bahá'u'lláh. This passage appears on page 1 of *Bahá'i Prayers*, copyright © 1954, 1982, National Spiritual Assembly of the Bahá'is of the United States. Reprinted with permission.

CONTENTS

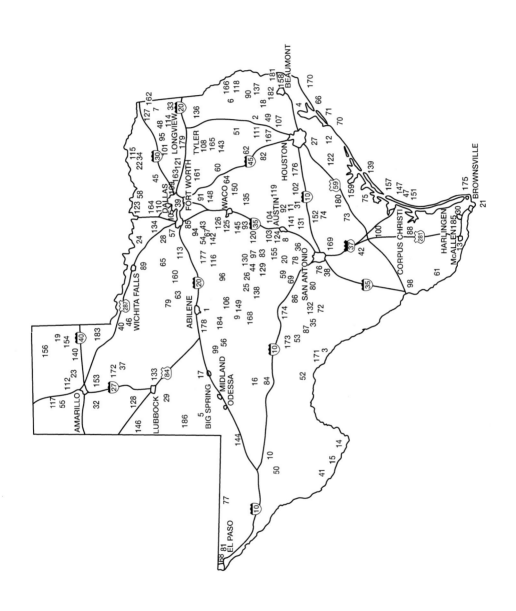

Texas Parks and Campgrounds

1. Abilene State Park
2. Alabama-Coushatta Indian Reservation
3. Amistad National Recreation Area
4. Anahuac Parks
5. Andrews:
   Florey Park
   Municipal Trailer Park
6. Angelina National Forest
7. Atlanta State Park
8. Austin: Emma Long Municipal Park
9. Ballinger
   City Park
   Lake Park
10. Balmorhea State Park
11. Bastrop State Park
12. Bay City: Riverside Park
13. Bentsen-Rio Grande Valley State Park
    World Birding Center Headquarters
14. Big Bend National Park
15. Big Bend Ranch State Park
16. Big Lake: Reagan County Park
17. Big Spring:
    Comanche Trail Park
    Moss Creek Lake Park
18. Big Thicket National Preserve
19. Black Kettle National Grassland
    Lake Marvin Recreation Area
20. Blanco State Park
21. Boca Chica Beach/USFWS Chica Tract
22. Bonham State Park
23. Borger: Huber Park
24. Bowie City Parks
25. Brady: Lake Brady Park
26. Brady: Richards Park
27. Brazos Bend State Park
28. Bridgeport: Wise County Park
29. Brownfield: Coleman Park
30. Brownsville: Adolph Thomae Jr. Park
31. Buescher State Park
32. Buffalo Lake National Wildlife Refuge
33. Caddo Lake State Park
34. Caddo National Grasslands
35. Camp Wood: Wes Cooksey Park
36. Canyon Lake
37. Caprock Canyons State Park and Trailway
38. Castroville Regional Park
39. Cedar Hill State Park
40. Childress: Baylor/Childress Lakes
41. Chinati Mountains State Natural Area
42. Choke Canyon State Park
43. Cleburne State Park
44. Colorado Bend State Park
45. Cooper Lake State Park
46. Copper Breaks State Park
47. Corpus Christi: Padre Balli Park
48. Daingerfield State Park
49. Davis Hill State Park
50. Davis Mountains State Park
51. Davy Crockett National Forest
52. Devils River State Natural Area
53. Devil's Sinkhole State Natural Area
54. Dinosaur Valley State Park
55. Dumas: Texoma Park
56. E. V. Spence Reservoir
57. Eagle Mountain Lake State Park
58. Eisenhower State Park
59. Enchanted Rock State Natural Area
60. Fairfield Lake State Park
61. Falcon State Park
62. Fort Boggy State Park
63. Fort Griffin State Historic Site
64. Fort Parker State Park
65. Fort Richardson State Park and Historic
    Site and Lost Creek Reservoir State
    Trailway
66. Fort Travis Seashore Park
67. Fossil Rim Ranch Wildlife Center
68. Franklin Mountains State Park
69. Fredericksburg: Lady Bird Johnson
    Municipal Park
70. Freeport:
    Quintana Beach County Park
    San Luis County Park
71. Galveston Island State Park
72. Garner State Park
73. Goliad State Park
74. Gonzales:
    Independence Park
    J. B. Wells Park
    Lake Wood Recreation Area
75. Goose Island State Park
76. Government Canyon State Natural Area
77. Guadalupe Mountains National Park
78. Guadalupe River State Park and Honey
    Creek State Natural Area
79. Haskell City Park
80. Hill Country State Natural Area
81. Hueco Tanks State Historic Site
82. Huntsville State Park
83. Inks Lake State Park
84. Iraan: City Parks
85. Joe Pool Lake, Lloyd Park
86. Kerrville-Schreiner Park
87. Kickapoo Cavern State Park
88. Kingsville: Kaufer-Hubert Memorial Park
    and SeaWind RV Resort
89. Lake Arrowhead State Park
90. Lake B. A. Steinhagen, "Dam B"
91. Lake Bardwell
92. Lake Bastrop Recreation Area
93. Lake Belton
94. Lake Benbrook
95. Lake Bob Sandlin State Park
96. Lake Brownwood State Park
97. Lake Buchanan
    Black Rock Park
    Canyon of the Eagles Lodge and Nature
    Park
98. Lake Casa Blanca International State Park
99. Lake Colorado City State Park
100. Lake Corpus Christi State Park
101. Lake Cypress Springs
102. Lake Fayette
103. Lake Georgetown
104. Lake Granger
105. Lake Grapevine
106. Lake Hords Creek
107. Lake Houston Park
108. Lake Jacksonville Park
109. Lake Lavon
110. Lake Lewisville
111. Lake Livingston State Park
     Wolf Creek Park
112. Lake Meredith National Recreation Area
     and Alibates Flint Quarries National
     Monument
113. Lake Mineral Wells State Park and Trailway
114. Lake O' the Pines
115. Lake Pat Mayse
116. Lake Proctor
117. Lake Rita Blanca City Park
118. Lake Sam Rayburn
119. Lake Somerville (Corps of Engineers
     Parks)
     Lake Somerville State Park
120. Lake Stillhouse Hollow
121. Lake Tawakoni State Park
     Wind Point Park
122. Lake Texana:
     Brackenridge Plantation Campground
     Mustang Wilderness Park
     Lake Texana State Park
123. Lake Texoma
124. Lake Travis:
     Arkansas Bend Park
     Cypress Creek Park
     Pace Bend Park
     Sandy Creek Park
125. Lake Waco
126. Lake Whitney (Corps of Engineers Parks)
     Lake Whitney State Park
127. Lake Wright Patman

INTRODUCTION

For people who like the great outdoors, Texas has a lot to offer. Each year almost 10 million people visit the 123 parks in the state park system and millions more enjoy the national parks and preserves and the many city and county parks, hike and bike trails, and greenbelts. To help you explore and enjoy the state's vast outdoor resources, this book describes more than 400 public parks with camping facilities. In addition, historical parks and nature preserves without camping are also described.

The immense size of Texas gives it more than just impressive numbers, it gives it diversity—there is something for everyone. From the dense pine-hardwood forests of East Texas to the 8,000-foot-high mountains and Chihuahuan Desert west of the Pecos, Texas has a phenomenal diversity of natural habitats. In addition to the flat coastal prairies and a crescent-shaped coastline, this state includes the rocky hill country of Central Texas, the broad prairies of the Panhandle, and a subtropical climate in the lush Rio Grande Valley in the south. The Big Thicket, the most ecologically diverse woodlands in North America, and Big Bend National Park, a million acres of unspoiled wilderness that encompasses an entire mountain range, are two examples of Texas' rich natural heritage.

The diversity of habitats in Texas and its southern locale make camping enjoyable throughout the year, not just in the spring and summer. In the winter, visitors from the north flock to the salubrious climate of South Texas by the tens of thousands. Spring and fall are delightful just about anywhere in the state. The mountains offer a respite from the simmering summer heat, and despite unpredictable weather in the winter, we often find Big Bend National Park warm and sunny in December and January.

Texas encompasses ten distinct vegetational zones, each with its own characteristic plant and animal communities. The Piney Woods, Gulf Coast Prairies and Marshes, Post Oak Savanna, and Blackland Prairies make up the eastern half of the state. South Texas is mostly plains or brush country. Central Texas includes the Edwards Plateau and the Cross Timbers and Prairies. The Panhandle has the Rolling Plains and the High Plains, also called the Llano Estacado, or Staked Plains. In West Texas, the Trans-Pecos includes mountain ranges and desert flats.

The diversity found in Texas is due, in part, to its size, 276,000 square miles or 7.5 percent of the land area of the United States. To say that Texas is large is an understatement. Anyone traveling across the state, which stretches 830 miles from Beaumont to El Paso and 780 miles between Brownsville and Amarillo, can identify with the old saying, "The sun has riz, the sun has set, and here we is, in Texas yet."

No matter where you go, however, you will be close to some public camping facility. This guidebook provides information to help you decide where to spend your vacation and how to better understand and enjoy the area upon arriving. We explain the ecological and historical significance of each major area and present the facilities available and noteworthy nearby attractions. Our hope is that this book will enhance your outdoor experience and make your vacation, whether a weekend or extended holiday, more meaningful and enjoyable.

WHAT IS INCLUDED IN THIS BOOK

This book includes all state parks, national parks, national forests, and U.S. Army Corps of Engineers parks with public camping facilities. Many of the state parks that do not have campgrounds are mentioned in the relevant descriptions under "Nearby Attractions" and in the section on historical parks.

In addition, we include many noncommercial, nonprofit, and concession-operated parks and nature preserves that have recreational interest. As resources, we used a statewide outdoor recreation inventory compiled by the Texas Parks and Wildlife Department (TPWD), as well as questionnaires mailed to each park. We visited all the state and national parks and forests and the majority of the Corps of Engineers reservoirs, but not all of the county and regional parks. We relied on the questionnaires obtained from the parks not visited to determine whether or not to include them. If the park was very small and had few facilities, we omitted it from the book. However, we did include a few parks that, though they had minimal camping facilities, were interesting places to visit as natural areas or that provided a good overnight stop.

We did not include the hundreds of privately owned campgrounds and RV parks existing across the state. They are adequately listed in directories published regularly by Woodalls and other commercial directories. Refer to the bibliography for those books.

HOW TO USE THE BOOK

For ease of reference, each campground is designated by number on a map of the state. The campgrounds are listed in the text in alphabetical order. If you desire to visit a specific area, find the campground numbers on the map, and refer to the detailed information found in the text. Alternatively, the vacationer could first read the comprehensive descriptions, decide on an interesting spot, and locate it on the map by its map number. Once you have visited a park and are ready to move on, use the map to select your next stop—attractive and interesting areas are available in every direction.

Besides providing a list of the numbers and types of campsites and recreational facilities, each write-up describes features of special interest to the visitor. The ecological and historical significance of the park is discussed, and nearby attractions are usually noted. This will help you plan your trip around, say, spring dogwood blooms or songbird migration, summer wildflowers, fall hiking, and winter hunting. Knowledge of the camping facilities, recreational opportunities, and natural attractions should greatly enhance vacation planning. Refer to the appendixes for lists of parks with cabins and motels and group facilities.

Before you load up your car or van, take advantage of the websites and phone numbers listed in this book. With our ever-increasing population, park campgrounds fill quickly, especially near metropolitan areas. Go online or call ahead for reservations and current conditions. Use this book to help you make the best use of your limited vacation time. Use the listed websites to download trail maps, brochures, bird lists, the latest scheduled activities.

PRESERVING FOR THE FUTURE

Texas has been tamed. The outdoor experience in Texas has changed vastly in the last two or three generations. Our forefathers, and mothers, saw vast herds of bison ranging across the Texas plains, and piney woods so dense that they repelled Indians and whites alike. Now, the prairies have been converted into farmland, cities, and suburbs. In large areas of West Texas, desert brush now grows on overgrazed land where vast grasslands once held the precious soil in place. The deep piney woods have been logged to such an extent that only 10 percent of the Big Thicket remains. The waterways of Texas have been impounded and channelized, and the underground water reservoirs have almost been pumped dry.

When Texas joined the Union, it retained possession of its vast land resources. Unfortunately, the money-poor but land-rich state gave away practically all of its inherent wealth. The citizens of Texas themselves raised the funds to buy Big Bend National Park and donated it to the federal government. The state park system, since its beginning in 1923, has preserved some of Texas' most scenic areas.

The report "Texas Parks & Wildlife for the 21st Century," commissioned by the department in 2002, advised that the state needed to acquire an additional 1,428,117 acres of state parkland by 2030 to maintain the targeted 55 acres of regional parkland for every 1,000 residents. Yet TPWD ignores its own recommendation and channels the majority of its budget to the largest land holders in the state. In 1999, the department spent $2.4 million on landowner assistance programs to help ranchers and landowners develop conservation practices. In contrast, TPWD spent only $300,000 on actual land acquisition in 2001.

The Nature Conservancy and more than 35 other nonprofit land trust groups are racing developers, speculators, and industry to preserve unique areas that once lost can never be replaced. The Nature Conservancy alone has purchased more than 250,000 acres of the state's pristine areas to preserve for future generations. The group has identified more than 500 critical areas that still need protection.

Will the outdoor experiences of our children and grandchildren be as dramatically different as ours is from our parents, not to mention our grandparents? We hope that our descendents will know more than freeways, strip malls, and crowded picnic parks. As population pressures increase, the preservation of portions of our irreplaceable natural heritage becomes more imperative.

CAMPING ETIQUETTE

With more and more people using our natural areas, each recreationist's actions must reflect a basic consideration for others. This goes beyond simply obeying the rules concerning quiet times in the evening and not littering the campsites and trails. Each of us must consider not only the individual's impact on the natural condition of an area but also our collective impact. For instance, the scenic Twin Falls area in Pedernales Falls State Park had to be closed because overuse was compacting the soil so much that the bald cypress trees were dying.

Common violations of the outdoor ethic include gathering firewood in public parks, chopping off live limbs for firewood, picking flowers, and cutting across switchbacks on mountain trails. Each of those actions may seem harmless when done once, but they are devastating when repeated continually by dozens of park users. The results are denuded trees and unsightly scars caused by erosion along the trails.

The goals of preserving wilderness, scenic beauty, and sensitive ecological areas while providing outdoor recreation for thousands, even millions, of people can be mutually exclusive if we are not aware of our individual responsibilities. Our personal impact on our environment, whether in a neighborhood park or on a remote trail, must be as neutral as possible. Better yet, we can often have a positive impact by picking up litter and assisting in the preservation of natural areas.

PERSONAL COMMENTS

We occasionally have included our own editorial comments on the suitability of some areas for camping. For some of the county and regional parks that we visited, we have added a few words about the quality of the areas. A few of the smaller local parks have exceptionally good facilities, but many have minimally adequate facilities and can be thought of as little more than overnight stopping places.

In general, in our years of camping in Texas, we have found the campgrounds to be pleasant and our fellow campers to be friendly and helpful. However, in an unsupervised park, people driving in for a late-night beer-drinking party can be loud, inconsiderate, and threatening. In parks likely to be a locally popular party spot, it is advisable to camp in a supervised area or in a section of the park where the campers outnumber the day users. More and more of the parks around lakes now lock the gates to the camping areas at night to avoid such problems. The state parks are supposed to be closed to all except campers after 10 p.m., but the gates are usually open all night. We have experienced late-night harassment only in parks that were close to large cities or in the Panhandle where small-town youths presumably have little to do after dark but cruise the parks. After a sleepless night at Lake Meredith, we questioned park personnel the next day to find that the park budget didn't provide for adequate supervision of the grounds. The next night, at Fort Griffin, we were relieved to see the park ranger make his rounds several times before we went to sleep.

RESERVATIONS

Most camp sites in national parks and national forests are first come, first serve, though some parks allow a portion of campsites to be reserved during peak seasons. Federal recreation facilities, including national, Corps of Engineers, and national forest parks use ReserveAmerica.com online and/or the interagency National Recreation Reservation Service, 877-444-6777, www.recreation.gov, to handle all reservations. Golden Age and Golden Access discounts may apply for basic fees. Check the park entries in this book for specifics. A processing fee is charged if using the reservation system.

Texas State Park campsites, cabins, day-use facilities, tours, and activities can be reserved up to 11 months in advance. Popular parks and ones near cities often book up far in advance. You can check availability and make reservations through the TPWD centralized reservations system (www.tpwd.state.tx.us/business/park_reservations). Contact by phone (512-389-8900 during working hours, M–F 8 a.m.–5 p.m.), email (customer.service@tpwd.state.tx.us) or fax (512-389-8959). Reservation forms for faxing can be downloaded from the TPWD website in PDF form. Internet reservations can be emailed or made online at the link above. The TPWD and its partner ReserveAmerica.com accept Master Card, VISA, and Discover, or you can mail a check or money order to TPWD Reservation Center, PO Box 17488, Austin, TX, 78760-7488.

STATE PARK FEES

Per-person entrance fees range from $1 to $5 with children under 13 free. In addition, some parks charge extra facility, activity, land use, lake use, boat, fishing, and group sponsored fees. Camping varies from $4–$9 for primitive sites, $6–$12 for sites with water nearby, $9–$16 for RV sites with water and electricity, $10–$17 for RV sites with water, electric, and sewer hookups, $15–$32 for screened shelters, and $35–$100 for cabins. Activity fees cover special activities such as rock climbing and tours. Some parks with lakes charge for boats, per fishing pole, and any object placed in the water, such as a swim float. An excess vehicle overnight fee applies when more that two vehicles, counting trailers, use a designated campsite. Historical parks may charge for museum entrance and tours. Some parks charge higher rates with minimum stay requirements during holidays and peak visitation periods, and some offer premium, preferred facilities at increased prices.

The Texas State Parks Pass costs $60 per person for one year and allows entrance for all passengers in the same vehicle with the pass holder. Families that regularly travel to state parks in more than one vehicle can purchase a two-card membership that provides two personalized pass cards for $75. Separate names must be on each card, and both must be residents of the same household. Members receive advance notice of park events in the Texas Conservation Passport Journal. Texas residents over 65 can obtain a Texas Parklands Passport good for 50 percent discount in entry fee. Residents with disabilities may be eligible for a reduced entry fee. For more information on state park fees, call TPWD information, 800-792-1112.

STATE PARKS

The 123 state-owned parks in Texas are classified as state parks, natural areas, historical parks and partnership parks. As of spring 2009, about 10 of the parks were unopened or open only for limited use until funding and/or master plans can be developed, another 5 are undeveloped beaches with no facilities, and 32 are day-use only. Hurricanes Rita (2005) and Ike (2008) damaged facilities, campgrounds, and trails in numerous coastal and east Texas state, federal, and county parks that may take a decade to fully restore. Call to check status of facilities. So Texas has approximately 80 state-operated parks with developed camping facilities. State parks preserve areas of outstanding ecological or geological importance and offer noteworthy recreational opportunities. Except for a few undeveloped parks and beaches, they all provide tent and RV camping facilities and restrooms with hot-water showers.

The designation "recreation area," used for some state and national facilities, indicates that the main attraction of the park is not as a natural area. In Texas, the term is generally used for parks that are built on man-made reservoirs or on the Gulf Coast. Boating and fishing, rather than hiking and exploring nature, are the dominant forms of recreation at those parks.

State historical parks are just what the term implies, areas where a particular aspect of Texas history has been preserved and displayed. Some parks not designated as historic do, nevertheless, have interesting exhibits on Texas' past.

The "natural area" designation indicates that the state is maintaining a biologically unique area in a natural condition, while still allowing camping and hiking in restricted areas. This book describes each park's natural environment, nature trails, and backpacking opportunities, as well as camping and recreation facilities.

Parks in the state system generally have the best camping facilities of any public parks in Texas. In recent years, many of the older parks have upgraded their facilities, installing modern restrooms with hot showers, and many now have recently added sewage hookups to the RV sites.

We were disappointed to discover that few state parks have interpretive exhibits or ranger-led programs. The historical parks, such as Goliad and the forts, have historical structures and displays, but in many of the parks, little information is available on the ecological and historical importance of the area. Some notable exceptions are the wonderful exhibits at Seminole Canyon, Dinosaur Valley, Brazos Bend, Enchanted Rock, and Lost Maples. In our write-ups, we have noted whether the park has interpretive exhibits.

Many state parks have free bird lists and trail-guide brochures available. Some do not display their pamphlets; you have to ask for them. Interpretation of the natural habitats of the state parks has a low priority for funding in Texas. In many parks, the supervisor has to act as park manager, security guard, ticket taker, phone answerer, and perform a variety of other time-consuming jobs. Since this guidebook was first published in 1984, the state has added more than 30 new parks; however, the number of employees has not increased proportionally. Please, let your state representative know if you would like to see more emphasis on interpretation in your state parks.

Few public parks have adequate facilities for people confined to wheelchairs. However, a few state parks have installed special camping pads and nature trails for wheelchair access. The best facilities are at the state parks. A Texas Parks and Wildlife brochure lists parks with facilities for the handicapped. Inquire at any state park for a copy.

NATIONAL PARKS

Texas has two national parks—Guadalupe Mountains and Big Bend; Padre Island National Seashore; the Big Thicket National Preserve; two national recreation areas—Amistad and Lake Meredith; and two national historical parks—Missions, in San Antonio, and Lyndon B. Johnson. The National Park Service operates these facilities. The national recreation areas are impounded reservoirs, which attract those interested in fishing and water sports. In contrast, the national parks, preserve, and national seashore are rare areas of fascinating ecological diversity. They provide superb opportunities to learn about the natural vegetation and wildlife of Texas and to experience the wilderness that once covered this vast state.

The national parks in Texas have few exhibits. Most have pamphlets on the vegetation and wildlife of the areas. Refer to the write-ups on the parks for information about the ecology and history of these unique areas. For general information on National Park Service Parks on the Internet, see www.nps.gov/parks.html.

STATE FORESTS

Texas has five state forests—Fairchild, near Rusk; Jones, near Conroe; Kirby, near Woodville; Masterson, near Buna; and Siecke, near Kirbyville—all located in the piney woods of East Texas. The forests, varying from 600 to 2,900 acres, are managed by the Texas Forest Service as part of the Texas A&M University System to study modern forestry techniques. Picnicking, hiking, nature study, and limited fishing are allowed. Since camping is prohibited in state forests, they are not included in this book. For information on hiking in state forests, see the Texas Forest website, http://txforestservice.tamu.edu/.

The woodlands of East Texas include longleaf, shortleaf, and loblolly pines; a wide variety of oaks, hickory, magnolia, beech, sweetgum, and American holly; and numerous species of understory trees, shrubs, vines, wildflowers, and mushrooms. Dwarf palmetto, bald cypress, and water tupelo thrive in the lush swamplands. Many birds make their home in the forests, including the large pileated woodpecker, the rare red-cockaded woodpecker, the brown-headed nuthatch, and many warblers and vireos. See the bibliography for field guides to the trees, wildflowers, reptiles, birds, and amphibians of this luxuriant area of the state.

NATIONAL FORESTS

Texas has four national forests operated by the U.S. Forest Service: Angelina, Davy Crockett, Sabine, and Sam Houston. All are managed from a central office in Lufkin. Camping facilities in the national forests are not as well-developed as in the state parks in Texas. Many camping areas have only primitive sites with a water hydrant nearby and pit toilets. Some have flush toilets and cold showers. None of the national forest parks have electric hookups. For information on the Internet, see www.southern region.fs.fed.us/texas/.

The four national forests, each covering more than 150,000 acres, have private land scattered throughout their boundaries. The U.S. Forest Service manages them with a multiple-use philosophy that includes lumbering, grazing, oil production, hunting, and recreation. The timber is managed primarily to maximize pine growth. Portions of the forests are clear-cut and seeded with pine trees; other areas are selectively logged, with the hardwoods culled and mature pines removed for market. Timber is sold to private logging operations, and there is occasional poaching of timber. The trees are considered a cash crop, such as corn, and the land is managed to produce the maximum yield.

The woodlands you see today may have been logged two or three times. Sections thousands of acres in extent are now pine plantations that are as ecologically barren as a wheat field. Fortunately, a few areas have been set aside to preserve the rich diversity of plant and animal life for this and future generations to enjoy.

Deer and squirrel hunting are popular activities in the fall. During deer season in November and December, camping is permitted only in designated campgrounds. At other times, camping is permitted throughout the forests, unless posted otherwise. Hikers are advised to wear regulation orange hunting vests or other highly visible apparel during hunting season.

Logging operations, hunting, and off-road-vehicle use are not conducive to enjoying a quiet walk in the woods. However, the national forests have plenty of areas that allow you to get away from it all. The Lone Star Hiking Trail traverses 140 miles of the Sam Houston National Forest. Developed with the assistance of the Houston Group of the Lone Star Chapter of the Sierra Club, the trail offers hikers a rare opportunity to explore the forest. Refer to the descriptions of individual forests for information on other hiking trails in the Davy Crockett National Forest.

The national forest trails and regulations often are abused by thoughtless users. Policing the forests is difficult, to say the least, because of the vast area and the limited number of rangers.

NATIONAL GRASSLANDS

The U.S. Forest Service operates four national grasslands in Texas: Caddo, Lyndon B. Johnson, Black Kettle, and McClellan Creek. The grasslands are available for public hunting and fishing. The few camping areas available have minimal facilities.

During the thirties, millions of acres of valuable farmland in a vast area, including much of Kansas, Oklahoma, North Texas, and the Panhandle, became a wasteland. Decades of poor soil-conservation practices in the dry central and southwestern prairies left the soil denuded of vegetation. The thirties brought year after year of drought and howling winds. The ravaged area became known as the Dust Bowl. By the end of the decade, more than 20 million acres had lost two to five inches of topsoil, and thousands of farmers in five states had deserted their land.

In the mid-thirties, the federal government began purchasing eroded cropland for rehabilitation. The national grasslands, scattered from Texas to Montana, became a part of the restoration program. At one time the home of bison, prairie dogs, and longhorns, the grasslands today provide pastures for cattle, lakes for fishing, and woods for hunting.

ARMY CORPS OF ENGINEERS RESERVOIRS

Texas has virtually no naturally occurring lakes, but man-made reservoirs abound throughout the state, particularly in the northern and eastern portions. The U.S. Army Corps of Engineers has impounded every major river and stream in the state. Even Caddo Lake, which was originally formed by a natural logjam, has been dammed. The Corps of Engineers home page, www.swf-wc.usace.army.mil/index.htm, lists information on selected lakes.

The reservoirs serve the two main functions of flood control and storage for the water normally carried to the Gulf of Mexico by rivers and streams. A reservoir is designed to be filled to a level below its maximum capacity; this extra capacity is necessary for flood protection. Each year, dams on Texas rivers and streams prevent millions of dollars in flood damage. Some of the dams also provide hydroelectric power.

A few of the reservoirs were built adjacent to natural areas that offer interesting habitats for exploration. However, most of the lakes we visited were extensively cleared of natural vegetation and did not offer much of interest to the nature lover. Nonetheless, many of the lakes provide pleasant relief from the hot summer temperatures. Lakes near large towns may receive as many as five million visitors annually.

Many of the lakes have campgrounds, day-use parks, and wildlife management areas where hunting is allowed. For ease of reference, a matrix itemizing the camping facilities accompanies each write-up. Fishing and water sports are the dominant recreational activities at the reservoirs. All have boat ramps; many have fishing piers and marinas. Campgrounds vary from primitive, with pit toilets and a few water hydrants, to concessionaire-operated parks with full RV hookups, flush toilets, and hot showers.

Parks with high visitation have suffered from vandalism and rude and rowdy visitors. Many of the parks now have full-time gate attendants that lock the gates at 10 p.m. We applaud that security precaution and encourage park users to continue the tradition of politeness that makes camping so enjoyable.

Most of the state has little naturally occurring surface water. Municipalities, agriculture, and industry must depend on ground water or impounded streams and rivers. Surface water is cheaper and easier to obtain than ground water, so many Texas cities rely on reservoirs for their water supply. In West Texas, some towns, such as Coleman, resorted to importing water by train before a local reservoir was built.

Many of the lakes in Texas were built for flood protection and have prevented millions of dollars worth of damage. However, harnessing a river has many ramifications beyond preventing floods and providing a source of water. Those dependent on the land, both humans and wildlife, must pay the price. While providing downstream flood protection, a reservoir destroys many thousands of acres above the dam. That has resulted in the destruction of entire towns, important archaeological sites, prime farmland, and a major loss of wildlife habitat.

Over the years, silt, which normally would have been deposited in floodplains and deltas, accumulates behind the dam. After several decades, the silt can build up to such high levels that protection from flooding is severely limited. The problem can be particularly acute in shallow lakes, and most Texas reservoirs averaged only 10 to 15 feet deep when formed.

While the trapped water supplies an immediate need for local towns, the lake, by exposing a larger surface area to the sun, increases water loss due to evaporation. In West Texas the rate of evaporation may be ten times greater than the annual rainfall. In addition, the change in the speed of water flow, the increased temperature, and reduced oxygen content of the water makes it an inhospitable habitat for many native fish.

One of the greatest economical and environmental problems created by impounding Texas rivers is the detrimental effect on the bays and estuaries. To the inland user, every drop that reaches the ocean is a wasted drop. To coastal fish and wildlife, fresh water means life. With less fresh water entering the bays, the estuaries and marshes become increasingly saline. The marshes can become more than twice as salty as the ocean, particularly in periods of drought. These delicate areas are some of the most biologically productive habitat in the state and the nursery grounds for fish that support a multimillion-dollar fishing industry. The health of the coastal fisheries depends on the health of the estuaries, which depends on an adequate inflow of fresh water from the rivers.

USEFUL TELEPHONE NUMBERS AND INTERNET WEB SITES

TELEPHONE NUMBERS

Texas state park information
Texas Parks and Wildlife Department, 1-800-792-1112.

State park reservations for campsites and park tours
512-389-8900.

Commercial campgrounds information
Texas Association of Campground Owners, 1-800-657-6555.

State highway map and Travel Guide with listings of cities, calendar of events, and parks
  800-8888-TEX.

Corps of Engineers and National Forest reservations at selected locations
  National Recreation Reservations System, toll-free 1-877-444-6777.

Sabine National Forest reservations and information
  866-235-1750.

FEDERAL WEB SITES

National parks and seashores:
  www.nps.gov/parks.html

U.S. Forest Service and National Grasslands in Texas:
  www.southernregion.fs.fed.us/texas/

U.S. Army Corps of Engineers-operated lakes in Texas:
  www.swf-wc.usace.army.mil/index.htm

U.S. Fish and Wildlife Service:
  http://southwest.fws.gov/refuges/

To reserve selected campsites at Corps of Engineers lakes and National Forests:
  www.reserve.usa

STATE WEB SITES

Texas Parks and Wildlife—all state park facilities, seasonal events, tours
  www.tpwd.state.tx.us

Texas Department of Commerce—comprehensive information about places, events, tours, and areas of interest
  www.traveltex.com

Wild Texas home page lists parks, nature, and travel information
  www.wildtexas.com

Lower Colorado River Authority parks (Travis County)
  www.lcra.org/lands/parks.html

Texas State Forests
  http://txforestservice.tamu.edu/

Texas Historical Commission—information on sixteen historic sites.
  www.thc.state.tx.us/hsites/hsdefault.shtml

TEXAS PARKS AND CAMPGROUNDS

1. ABILENE STATE PARK

LOCATION

Taylor County. 16 miles south of Abilene on FM 89.
Mailing address: 150 Park Road 32, Tuscola, Texas 79562.
Phone: 325-572-3204. For all state park reservations, call the
centralized reservations system, 512-389-8900, or
www.ReserveAmerica.com online. Call the state park information
number, 800-792-1112, for information and fee updates.

FACILITIES

Fees: entrance, facility, activity use; subject to change. Seasonal rates half
price December – February, weekly discounts available. Special group
packages available, 512-389-8900 or the park 325-572-3204.

Camping: 3 tent campsites ($8/night). 12 tent only campsites with water
($10/night), 35 campsites with electric and water hookups in the Wagon
Circle Group Trailer overflow camping area, no picnic tables or fire
rings ($10/night). 41 campsites with electric and water hookups ($15/
night). 3 campsites with electric, water, and sewer hookups ($18/night).
8 screened shelters ($18/night). 3 yurts (year-round recreational tent)
with double/single bunk bed with mattresses, foldout sofa, a microwave,
& a nightstand, outside picnic table, fire ring, water spigot, one ADA accessible unit ($40/night). Modern restrooms, trailer dump station.

Day-Use Facilities: 2 group recreation halls with a kitchen, capacity 50
people ($80/day). Swimming pool open during summer.

Recreation: picnic areas and playgrounds, 1-mile hiking trail, swimming and wading pools (summer only), fishing and boating in nearby Lake Abilene, state longhorn herd, Texas State Park Store. Open 7 days a week year-round except for Pecan Grove, which is closed December through February.

WEATHER

July high averages 95 degrees, January low 31 degrees.

MAIN ATTRACTIONS

The heavily wooded drainage of Elm Creek provides a scenic contrast to the semiarid prairie grasslands of the surrounding area. The dense groves of trees provide a pleasant setting for picnicking and camping. The park swimming pool is open in the summer, and fishing is popular on the 675-acre Lake Abilene, which borders the park. A trail loops around the campgrounds and along Elm Creek. A portion of the state longhorn herd is maintained in the park.

PLANTS AND ANIMALS

The 490-acre park is located in an area known since pioneer times as Buffalo Gap, named for the many bison that moved through the natural pass between two flat-topped buttes northeast of the park. The hills form the Callahan Divide, separating the headwaters of the Brazos and the Colorado rivers.

The Callahan Divide is characterized by lowlands broken by mesas up to 400 feet high. The hills are capped with Comanchean limestones and underlaid with soft sandstones and shales. The limestones, resistant to weathering in the dry climate of West Texas, have prevented the buttes from eroding away. The red clay soil of the park is the result of the weathering of the shales.

The Permian sedimentary layers beneath the lowlands of the area were deposited in shallow seas 280 million years ago. These same geologic formations are 6,000 feet beneath the surface farther west and have yielded some of the richest oil fields in Texas.

The forested areas of the park are composed of Ashe juniper, live oak, and mesquite trees; yuccas and prickly pear cacti are scattered through the grassy savannas. Groves of pecan trees shade the banks of Elm Creek. Soaptree, elm, Texas oak, and hackberry trees grow in the creek drainage. Poison ivy is common throughout the camping and picnic grounds—arriving in the park late one night, we mistakenly pitched our tent in the midst of a patch!

The most common wildlife in the park are armadillos, squirrels, and rabbits. Deer, raccoons, skunks, and coyotes also occur. Many species of birds are attracted to the groves of trees.

HISTORY

The dense woodlands surrounding Elm Creek have attracted both wildlife and humans since early times. The southern herds of bison passed through the divide, giving the area the name "Buffalo Gap"; today the settlement of Buffalo Gap is popular for its restaurants and its Historical Village, which has a number of original and facsimile pioneer buildings. Tonkawa and Comanche Indians lived in the area, and artifacts are often found in the vicinity of the park.

In the 1870s, in an attempt to eradicate a major food source for the Indians, buffalo hunters were encouraged to eliminate the massive herds of bison, selling their hides for $2 each. Soon cattle dominated the grasslands and great drives passed through the gap. In 1858, the Butterfield State Route from St. Louis to San Francisco passed near the park. When the Texas and Pacific Railroad reached Abilene in 1880, the town became the county seat and the center of activity in the area.

2. ALABAMA-COUSHATTA INDIAN RESERVATION

LOCATION

Polk County. 17 miles east of Livingston on U.S. 190.
Mailing address: Route 3, Box 640, Livingston, Texas 77351.
Phone: 936-563-1221, 800-926-9038. Tribal website www.alabama-coushatta.com

FACILITIES

Fees: entrance, facility; subject to change.

Camping: 24 RV/tent sites with water and electricity ($15), 49 RV sites with full hookups ($20), 20 pull-through RV with water and electricity ($15), 40 primitive tent sites ($10), cabin for 6 with kitchen, dining, living areas ($100), cabin for 4 with kitchen ($75), 2 cabins for 2 ($40), tipi for 6, ground cloth required ($40).

Recreation: picnic areas, covered pavilion, hiking and nature trails, lake swimming, bathhouse, fishing.

MAIN ATTRACTIONS

At the campgrounds surrounding the 26-acre Lake Tombigbee, fishing, swimming, and canoeing are popular activities. Except on a 2-hour hiking trail, hiking outside the tourist area is not permitted.

The reservation, located in the Big Thicket, encompasses 4,600 acres. The Big Thicket is biologically unique and has the greatest plant and animal diversity of any area in North America. See the write-up of that area for a description.

HISTORY

The first historical record of the Alabama and Coushatta tribes comes from 1541, when they were attacked by Hernando de Soto in what is now Mississippi. These peaceful Indians lived in accord with the French during the French occupation of the area, which ended in 1763. In 1807, a group of Alabama Indians and the Coushatta tribe established a village on the Trinity River in Texas.

The Indians fled into Louisiana rather than side with either Texas or Mexico during the Revolution. When they returned, their lands had been preempted by white settlers. Finally, in 1854, the state legislature purchased 1,280 acres as the initial unit of the reservation, to be held by the Indians "inalienable forever."

3. AMISTAD NATIONAL RECREATION AREA

LOCATION

Val Verde County. Northwest of Del Rio on U.S. 90 and U.S. 277. Visitor Information Center: 10 miles north of Del Rio on Hwy 90W across from Three Rivers RV Park. Open 8 a.m.–5 p.m. Mailing address: 4121 Veterans Blvd., Del Rio, TX 78840-9350. Phone: 830-775-7491. E-mail: amis_interpretation@nps.gov. Internet: www.nps.gov/amis.

FACILITIES

Camping: Amistad has primitive camping, with no water and is accessible only by boat, anywhere along the shore below the 1,144-foot contour line except in restricted areas. Camping is on a first-come basis, except in the commercial campgrounds.

There are campsites with tables, grills, and chemical toilets but no water at San Pedro Flats off U.S. 90 on the south shore, Old 277 North Campground off U.S. 277 on the north shore, Spur 406 Campground off U.S. 90 on the north shore, and Governors Landing off U.S. 90 on the south shore. Camping fees, $4–$8.

Group camping is available at Rock Quarry, Old 277 North, and San Pedro Flats campgrounds. Reservations are accepted for groups.

Commercial campgrounds are at Diablo East off U.S. 90 on the south shore, Rough Canyon, 830-775-8779, off U.S. 277 to RR 2, and the Pecos River off U.S. 90.

Roadrunners live in the rock hills around Amistad reservoir.

There is a trailer dump station at Diablo East service road.

The camping facilities at Amistad are primitive and the terrain rocky and hilly, yet more than a million people a year visit the lake. We recommend the facilities primarily for those interested in fishing and water sports or for winter visitors looking for RV campgrounds with a mild climate.

Recreation: picnicking, nature trails, swimming in Amistad Reservoir, fishing, boating, marinas at Diablo East and Rough Canyon, hunting, pavilion at Rough Canyon, amphitheaters at Governors Landing and Spur 454, stores at Diablo East and Rough Canyon. Fishing in the Mexican waters of the reservoir requires a Mexican fishing license, about $25/week, but not a boat permit, from the Mexico National Aquaculture and Fishing Commission (CONAPESCA) in San Diego, CA. For online application forms, see www.conapescasandiego.org, or call 619-233-4324.

MAIN ATTRACTIONS

Amistad Reservoir was formed on the Rio Grande by a cooperative effort between Mexico and the United States. The immense lake covers 67,000 acres about half of the year and has 850 miles of shoreline. The

AMISTAD NATIONAL RECREATION AREA

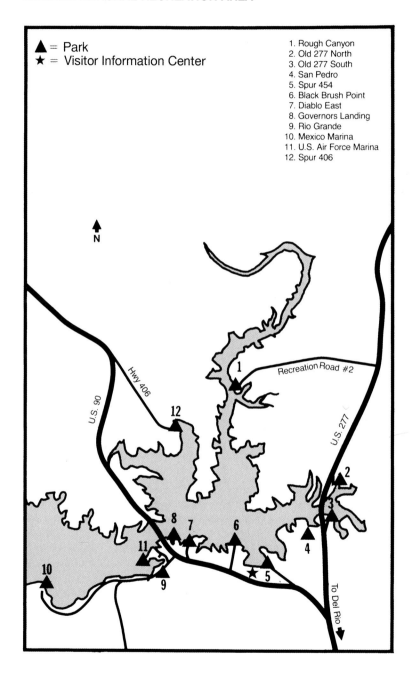

▲ = Park
★ = Visitor Information Center

1. Rough Canyon
2. Old 277 North
3. Old 277 South
4. San Pedro
5. Spur 454
6. Black Brush Point
7. Diablo East
8. Governors Landing
9. Rio Grande
10. Mexico Marina
11. U.S. Air Force Marina
12. Spur 406

reservoir provides water-oriented activities in a semiarid environment. Fishing for channel catfish, yellow catfish, crappie, and sunfish is reportedly best in spring and early summer. Call or see the park website for hunting seasons and regulations.

PLANTS AND ANIMALS

The Amistad Dam impounds the Rio Grande just below its confluence with the Devils and Pecos rivers. The reservoir extends 25 miles into Devils Canyon, 14 miles up the Pecos, and 74 miles up the Rio Grande. The lake stands in stark contrast to the semiarid environment of the chaparral-covered hillsides. The vegetation of the dry rocky terrain is mainly thorny blackbrush acacia, guajillo, yucca, mesquite, and sotol. Wildlife adapted to the harsh environment includes javelinas, white-tailed deer, jackrabbits, rock squirrels, raccoons, and many reptiles, especially rattlesnakes, king snakes, and lizards.

The temperature in the summer can surpass 100 degrees; sunburn and heat exhaustion can develop rapidly under those conditions. Freezing weather with violent windstorms may occur from December to February. Thunderstorms are common, accounting for the 18 inches of rain received annually. Campers, hikers, and boaters should take adequate precautions to protect themselves from the elements.

HISTORY

Indian artifacts dating back 12,000 years have been found in the area. The rising water of the lake inundated many archaeological sites. However, the nearby Seminole Canyon State Historical Park preserves some excellent examples of Indian pictographs.

The building of the railroad across West Texas, with Irish and Chinese labor, and the activities of the legendary Judge Roy Bean highlighted the colorful period around the turn of the century. The story of the railroad and early ranching is presented at Seminole Canyon State Historical Park, and Judge Roy Bean's role in taming the West is portrayed at the Judge Roy Bean Visitor Center in Langtry.

4. ANAHUAC PARKS

Chambers County. Mailing address: P. O. Box PP, Anahuac, TX 77514. Phone: 409-267-3041. These seven parks have restrooms, drinking water unless noted, electricity unless noted, RV and/or primitive camping sites that are often merely open space within the park. Hurricane Ike in 2008 caused considerable area-wide damage. Call to check condition of park facilities.

Cedar Hill Park: Facilities: grills, covered pavilion, fishing, birding, nature trails, boardwalk, picnic area, no electricity.

Double Bayou Park: From Anahuac, east on TX 61 to FM 562, south for 7 miles, west 0.5 miles on Eagle Ferry Rd. Facilities: 30 acres on Double Bayou with covered pavilion, fishing, picnic area, playground. On the Anahuac Loop of the Great Texas Coastal Birding Trail.

Fort Anahuac Park: On Main St., Anahuac. Facilities: 40 acres on Trinity Bay with birding walk and tower, boat ramp, covered pavilion, fishing, birding, ball fields, lighted fishing pier, nature trail, picnic area, restrooms with showers. On the Anahuac Loop of the Great Texas Coastal Birding Trail.

Hugo Point Park and Boat Ramp: Facilities: covered pavilion, grills, electricity, fishing, birding, nature trails, boardwalk, picnic area, no water.

J.J. Mayes Wildlife Trace: Wallisville Lake Project, IH-10 (milepost 805/806), 40 miles east of Houston, Trinity River boat ramp exit. NO CAMPING FACILITIES. This 4-mile auto/nature trail is designed for bird and other wildlife viewing. Includes 2.5-mile walking trail with an 0.8-mile handicapped accessible loop and 1,000-foot boardwalk, observation decks and tower, picnic areas, pavilion, visitor center with restrooms. The 23,000-acre Wallisville Lake Project is a site partner of the Gulf Coast Bird Observatory and on the Anahuac Loop of the Great Texas Coastal Birding Trail. U.S. Army Corps of Engineers, Galveston Dist., P.O. Box 293, Wallisville, TX 77597, 409-389-2285, www.swg. usace.army.mil/items/Wallisville.

Job Beason Park: From Anahuac, FM 563 south to Eagle Rd., south 4.7 miles to W. Bayshore Rd, south 0.5 miles to Double Bayou. Facilities: 12 acres with playground, fishing, boat ramp.

McCollum Park: IH-10 exit FM 3180, south 10 miles to McCollum Rd., east 1 mile. Facilities: primitive camping on Trinity Bay, covered pavilion, fishing, birding, nature trails, picnic area, playground.

Whites Park: From IH-10, exit TX 61, south .1 mile. Facilities: 83 acres on Turtle Bayou with 15 pull-through RV/tent sites, cold showers, community building, covered pavilion, grills, fishing, equestrian area. On the Anahuac Loop of the Great Texas Coastal Birding Trail.

5. ANDREWS: FLOREY PARK

Andrews County. 65 miles west of Big Spring on TX 176 to Andrews, 10 miles north on U.S. 385. Mailing address: 5969 NE CR 1011, Andrews, TX 79714. Phone: 432-524-1401. Camping: 200 pull-through RV/tent sites with water and electricity, 52 sites with full hookups, 7-day limit. Fees charged. Recreation: picnic areas and playgrounds, pavilion, recreation hall (must be reserved). Open all year.

ANDREWS: MUNICIPAL TRAILER PARK

Andrews County. Behind Chamber of Commerce building at 700 West Broadway (TX 176 west). Mailing address: Chamber of Commerce, 700 West Broadway, Andrews, TX 79714. Phone: 432-523-2695. Camping: 12 pull-through RV/tent sites with water, electricity, sewage. No restrooms. No fees, no reservations, 3-day limit. Fishing, playground, prairie dog town. Open all year.

6. ANGELINA NATIONAL FOREST

LOCATION

Surrounds Sam Rayburn Reservoir, east of Lufkin on U.S. 69 to Zavalla.
Mailing address: 111 Walnut Ridge Road, Zavalla, TX 75980.
Phone: 936-897-1068. Internet: www.fs.fed.us/r8/texas/.

FACILITIES

(Some trails and campgrounds suffered damage from Hurricane Rita and may be closed indefinitely. Call for current status of facilities.) Angelina offers 5 parks campgrounds. Campsites cannot be reserved. Primitive camping at no charge is allowed anywhere in the national forest, except when hunting or logging is in progress. Some campgrounds are free, fees vary at others.

Dogwood blossoms decorate the Angelina National Forest trails in the spring.

As no map of the forest is included here, the following directions are given to those parks that have campgrounds. Write the headquarters for maps and further details.

Bouton Lake: 8 miles southeast of Zavalla on TX 63, 7.7 miles south on FSR 303. 12-acre lake with 7 tent sites, no water, pit toilets, hiking; 936-897-1068. Fees charged.

Boykin Springs: 11 miles southeast of Zavalla on TX 63, 2.5 miles south on FSR 313. 9-acre lake with 33 back-in RV/tent sites, flush toilets, showers, picnic shelters, bathhouse, lake swimming on 10-acre lake, hiking; 936-897-1068. Fees charged.

Caney Creek: 4 miles southeast of Zavalla on TX 63, 6.5 miles east on FM 2743. See map for Lake Sam Rayburn. On Sam Rayburn Reservoir with 123 back-in RV/tent sites with water, flush toilets, cold showers, trailer dump station, bathhouse, picnic shelters, lake swimming, fishing boat ramp; 936-897-1068. Fees charged.

Harvey Creek: 3.5 miles southeast of Broaddus on FM 83, 5 miles south on FM 2390. See map for Lake Sam Rayburn. On Sam Rayburn Reservoir with 19 RV/tent sites, primitive tent camping, flush toilets, showers; 936-275-2762. Fees charged.

Sandy Creek: 17.5 miles southeast of Zavalla on TX 63, 3 miles north on FSR 333. See map for Lake Sam Rayburn. On Sam Rayburn reservoir with 10 back-in RV/tent sites, no water, pit toilets, picnic shelter, boat launch, no swimming; 936-897-1068. Fees charged.

Townsend: about 13 miles northeast of Zavalla on TX 147, turn north on FM 1277 about 3 miles to FM 2923, west to park. On Sam Rayburn Reservoir with primitive camping, no water, chemical toilets; Operated by San Augustine County, 936-275-2762. Fees charged.

Sawmill Hiking Trail: The 5.5-mile trail connects Bouton Lake and Boykin Springs with 0.75 mile spur that leads to the historic Aldridge Sawmill site. White painted rectangular markings, about head high, mark the

Campground	water	fee area	flush toilets	season	showers	boating	fishing	swimming	trails
Bouton Lake				all		•	•		•
Boykin Springs	•	•	•	all	•	•	•	•	•
Caney Creek	•	•	•	all	•	•	•		•
Sandy Creek		•		all		•	•		
Townsend		•		all		•	•		

trail. Hikers can see the Neches River from several points along the trail. Portions of the trail follow an old tramway once used as a rail line to haul logs to the sawmills.

Aldridge Sawmill Historic Site: The sawmill, closed in 1923, includes the abandoned shells of the mill, power plant, fuel building, and a dry kiln, various concrete foundations, the mill pond, and portions of the old railroad tram. Directions: From Lufkin follow Highway 69 south to Zavalla; turn left (east) on Highway 63 and follow 13 miles to Boykin Springs road; turn right (south) for 1.5 miles to fork; bear left onto dirt road and follow 3 miles to Aldridge.

MAIN ATTRACTIONS

The Angelina National Forest covers 154,916 acres of mixed pine-hardwood forests in Angelina, Jasper, Nacogdoches, and San Augustine counties. Sam Rayburn Reservoir, with the national forest along its shores, is popular for fishing, camping, picnicking, and water sports. At Bouton Lake and Boykin Springs, only boats with electric motors are allowed. Horseback riding is popular on the dirt roads in the forest and the Upland Islands Wilderness Area. Contact USFS headquarters for a forest map.

HIKING

From Bouton Lake, the 5.5-mile Sawmill Hiking Trail follows the winding Neches River, crosses several creeks, passes two abandoned sawmills, and parallels Boykin Creek to Boykin Springs Campground. The bottomlands are filled with a great diversity of hardwoods, including bald cypress, tupelo, oaks, ironwood, and elm. Magnolia and dogwood trees decorate the woods each spring with their fragrant white flowers.

Deer hunting is allowed in the forest during November and December. Hikers as well as hunters should wear regulation orange vests.

7. ATLANTA STATE PARK

LOCATION

Cass County. 20 miles south of Texarkana on U.S. 59 to Queen City, 7 miles west on FM 96, 2 miles north on FM 1154 to PR 42. Mailing address: 927 Park Rd. 32, Atlanta, TX 75551. Phone: 903-796-6476. For all state park reservations, call the centralized reservations system, 512-389-8900, or www.ReserveAmerica.com online. Call the state park information number, 800-792-1112, for information and fee updates.

FACILITIES

Fees: entrance, facility; subject to change. Senior discount available for camping from October – March.

Camping: 44 RV/tent sites with water, electricity ($12), 17 RV/tent sites with full hookups ($14/night), 5 primitive sites ($10/night), modern restrooms, trailer dump station. Fees charged.

Recreation: picnic areas, playgrounds, group picnic pavilion, sport courts, 3.5-mile hiking trail, 1.2-mile nature/interpretive trail, boat ramp, fish-cleaning station, lake swimming and water sports, amphitheater, Texas State Park Store.

WEATHER

July high averages 90 degrees, January low 32 degrees.

MAIN ATTRACTIONS

The densely wooded park is located on the 20,300-acre Wright Patman Lake. Water sports and fishing for bass, crappie, and catfish are popular activities. A trail leads through the beautiful oak and pine woodlands and along the shoreline, and high bluffs at the picnic area overlook the lake.

PLANTS AND ANIMALS

The high ridges and stream drainages forming the 1,475-acre park are wooded with a wide variety of trees. Shortleaf and loblolly pines and white oaks are dominant; flowering dogwood, red buckeye, sassafras, sweetgum, viburnum, river birch, and red maple trees are also present.

In the spring, the snow-white blossoms of the dogwoods and the crimson flowers of the buckeyes add color to the campgrounds and the picnic area. Mayapples blanket the forest floor before the deciduous trees are fully leafed out, and delicate purple oxalis flowers are scattered throughout the park.

Many herons, egrets, and waterfowl frequent the large reservoir. Rough-winged swallows and kingfishers make their nest burrows near the picnic area in the eroding bluffs of the old bank of the Sulphur River. The wave action of the lake and variable water levels have caused dangerous undercutting of the once scenic bluffs, and recent cave-ins are evident.

HISTORY

When Europeans first explored East Texas in the 1500s, they encountered the Caddo Indian Confederation, a group of several tribes that were highly developed culturally. The Caddos lived in villages with well-constructed houses and grew corn, five types of beans, sunflowers, and pumpkins. They collected fruit, chestnuts, and pecans and hunted deer, bison, and small animals.

The Smithsonian Institution, conducting archaeological excavations in the park, has uncovered graves, artifacts, and a house or village site. Unfortunately, at the time of writing there was no information available in the park for the visitor regarding either the excavations or the plants and animals common to the park.

8. AUSTIN: EMMA LONG METROPOLITAN PARK

Travis County. 6 miles northwest of Austin on FM 2222, 4 miles west on City Park Rd. to Lake Austin. Mailing address: 1706 City Park Rd., Austin, Texas 78730-4201. Phone: 512-346-1831. Camping: 20 campsites with water and electricity, 46 with tables and water nearby; flush toilets, showers. Fees charged, no reservations. Park gates open 7 a.m. to 10 p.m. Recreation: Only 70 of the 1,142 acres of the rugged oak-juniper Hill Country park have been developed. With 1 mile of waterfront on Lake Austin and a 350-foot sandy beach, swimming, boating, and skiing are popular. Facilities include a picnic area and group shelter, designated swimming area, boat ramp, motorcross track, archery range, volleyball courts, nature trails. Expect crowed conditions in the summer. Lake Austin is a good birdwatching area—the endangered golden-cheeked warbler nests in the hills in the spring.

Emma Long Metropolitan Park preserves woodlands along the shore of Lake Austin.

9. BALLINGER CITY PARK

Runnels County. 35 miles northeast of San Angelo on U.S. 67, on the eastern edge of Ballinger. Mailing address: Box 497, Ballinger, Texas 76821-0497. Phone: 325-365-3511. Camping: 16 pull-through sites with water and electricity, flush toilets, cold-water showers, trailer dump station. Fees charged ($9/night) subject to change. No reservations. Recreation: picnic areas and playgrounds, swimming pool (summer only), swimming in Elm Creek, fishing, pavilion. Open all year.

BALLINGER LAKE PARK

Runnels County. 5 miles west of Ballinger on eastern shore of 6,050-acre municipal lake. Mailing address: Box 497, Ballinger, Texas 76821-0497. Phone: 325-365-5411. Camping: 10 pull-through sites with water and electricity, trailer dump station, flush toilets, picnic tables, wheelchair accessible. Fees charged ($9/night) subject to change. Open all year, no reservations. Recreation: lake swimming, boat ramp, fishing. Lake stocked with bass, crappie, walleye, catfish.

10. BALMORHEA STATE PARK

LOCATION

Reeves County. 56 miles west of Fort Stockton on IH-10, south on TX 17, at the head of San Solomon Springs. Mailing address: Box 15, Toyahvale, Texas 79786. Phone: 432-375-2370. For all state park reservations, call the centralized reservations system, 512-389-8900, or www.ReserveAmerica.com online. Call the state park information number, 800-792-1112, for information and fee updates.

FACILITIES

Fees: entrance, facility, activity use; subject to change. WiFi available (user fee).

Camping: 6 RV/tent sites with water ($11/night), 16 RV/tent sites with electric and water ($14 per night), 12 RV/tent sites with electric, water, cable TV ($17/night). Modern restrooms, showers, trailer dump station. San Solomon Spring Courts, 18 motel rooms, non-smoking ($55–$75 double occupancy). Additional adults $7, children 12 years of age and under free.

Recreation: picnic areas, playgrounds, recreation hall with kitchen, swimming pool, bathhouse, scuba, concessions (summer), native plant gardens, wetlands exhibit, Texas State Park Store with tube rentals. Air tank refills are locally available.

MAIN ATTRACTIONS

San Solomon Springs has been the main attraction of the area for centuries—artifacts found indicate that Indian groups relied on the springs long before the Europeans arrived. In the 1930s, the Civilian Conservation Corps constructed the swimming pool around the springs as well as the motel and concession buildings. The pool, at a near constant temperature of 74 degrees, is 1.75 acres in size and 25 feet deep in places; it is one of the largest spring-fed pools in the nation. Its clear water, fed at a rate of 22 million to 26 million gallons daily, and abundant fish life make it ideal for snorkeling and scuba diving.

The nearby Fort Davis National Historic Site, Davis Mountains State Park, and Davis Mountains Skyline Drive, leading to McDonald Observatory, are accessible from the city of Fort Davis, located 30 miles south of the park. Lake Balmorhea, 3 miles southeast of Balmorhea, offers boating and fishing.

PLANTS AND ANIMALS

Very little of the original vegetation remains, because of the use of the surrounding land and modification of the springs. What was once desert grassland has been farmed and grazed and replaced by such thorny shrubs as mesquite, lotebush, catclaw acacia, and native mimosa. The springs and drainages formerly supported cattails, sedges, rushes, reeds, and salt grass. Now the springs and channelized drainages are shaded by large cottonwood, ash, sycamore, and hackberry trees.

The springs are famous for two rare and endangered species of fish. The Comanche Springs pupfish and the Pecos mosquito fish, only a few inches long, can be seen in the drainage canals. Many minnows, perch, and catfish inhabit the cool, clear depths of the pool.

The springs are an oasis surrounded by irrigated farmland and shrubby desert vegetation. Mule deer, white-tailed deer, bobcats, javelinas, skunks, raccoons, porcupines, and coyotes can be seen in and around the park by the alert visitor, primarily at dawn and dusk. Many birds are attracted to the large trees, especially during spring and fall migrations. The colorful vermilion flycatcher, the greater roadrunner, quail, hawks, herons, and ducks frequent the life-supporting springs.

When San Soloman Springs was impounded during the Depression to create the swimming pool and channelized for irrigation, the ciénega, or desert wetland, disappeared. Fortunately, the endangered Comanche Springs pupfish and Pecos gambusia managed to survive in the canals. Finally, in 1996, after extraordinary efforts, a small version of the original ciénega was resurrected. Once again the tiny, endangered fishes swim with Mexican tetra, channel catfish, roundnose minnows, red crayfish, blotched water snakes, and soft-shell turtles. A window in the small dam that maintains a three-acre marsh affords a glimpse of the below-water life. Visitors can view the variety of birds and wildlife attracted to the desert wetland from an observation deck overlooking the marsh.

11. BASTROP STATE PARK

LOCATION

Bastrop County. 1.5 miles east of Bastrop on TX 21. Also accessible via PR 1 from BuescherState Park. Mailing address: Box 518, Bastrop, Texas 78602. Phone: 512-321-2101. For all state park reservations, call the centralized reservations system, 512-389-8900, or www.ReserveAmerica.com online. Call the state park information number, 800-792-1112, for information and fee updates.

FACILITIES

Fees: entrance, facility, activity use; subject to change. Wireless Internet available (user fee). Weekly and monthly rates available November–February. WiFi available (user fee).

Camping: 35 RV/tent sites with full hookups ($17/night), 19 RV/tent sites with water and electricity ($15/night), 16 tent sites with tent pad and water ($12/night), 7 walk-in (60 yards) tent sites with tent pad and water nearby ($12), 50 primitive backpack sites with minimum 1-mile hike on 8.5-mile loop trail ($10/night), youth group camp with primitive sites 200 yards from trailhead (capacity 50, $50–$75), group camp with dining hall and 4 barracks with ac/heat (capacity 80, $250/night), 13 cabins on small lake with A/C, fireplace, kitchen with stove, microwave, refrigerator, outside grill, full bathroom (2–8 people, $65–$150/night). Campgrounds have modern restrooms, showers, trailer dump station.

Recreation: picnic areas, playgrounds, 60' × 100' swimming pool (summer), 18-hole, 6,152-yard golf course and pro shop, fishing, hiking, mountain biking, scenic drive, nature tours, Texas State Park Store.

WEATHER

July high averages 96 degrees, January low 38 degrees.

MAIN ATTRACTIONS

Bastrop State Park covers 3,503 acres of the Central Texas loblolly pine forest. This forest is separated from the East Texas Piney Woods by post oak woodlands and by what used to be prairie grasslands but is now ranchland and farmland. Known as the Lost Pines, this remnant forest was probably connected to East Texas forests during the last ice age, about 10,000 years ago, when Texas was wetter and cooler. The area from Bastrop to Buescher state parks preserves 7 percent of the Central Texas pines.

HIKING

The Lost Pines Trail makes an 8.5-mile loop through the forest, with an additional 3.5 miles of trails connecting the campgrounds. Backpacking is permitted along the trail, but no bikes. The 12-mile Park Road 1C connects Bastrop and Buescher State Parks, creating a scenic auto or bike ride through the rolling hills and Lost Pines of Central Texas. This ride is part of the MS-150 bike race from Houston to Austin.

PLANTS AND ANIMALS

The pine forest hosts a wide variety of plants and animals not commonly seen in other parts of Central Texas. Yaupon holly, wax myrtle, farkleberry bushes, and mushrooms thrive in the shade of the towering pines. Alum Creek, with fern-covered banks, winds its way through the park.

More than 200 species of birds have been sighted in the park. Red-shouldered hawks nest in the area, and pileated and red-headed woodpeckers are occasionally seen. The Central Texas population of pine warblers is found in the woods. Some of the birds, plants, mammals, and reptiles are at the western limit of their range. A checklist of birds is available. One of the largest colonies of the endangered Houston toad (*Bufo houstonensis*) occurs in the park and is the focus of ongoing studies.

The aromatic piney woods of Bastrop seem out of place among the surrounding deciduous woodlands. The pines would not be able to survive on the area's 35 inches of annual rain without the sandstone aquifer underlying the forest. Two sandstone formations, the Carrizo and Recklaw, form the aquifer. Holding water like a giant sponge, they enable the pines to thrive in an otherwise unsuitably dry habitat.

The red stone fence and buildings in the park were built from local sandstone. Iron oxides in the sandstone account for the red and yellow colors of the rocks and sandy soil. Rain leaches the iron out of the soil into the creeks and discolors the water.

Just outside the park entrance, an abrupt change from pines and oaks to mesquite trees indicates the contact between the Carrizo sandstone, which forms sandy soil, and the Sabinetown shale, which weathers into a clay soil.

HISTORY

The town of Bastrop, one of the earliest settlements in Texas, is 1.5 miles west of the park on TX 21. The town was settled by William Barton,

Josiah Wilbarger, and Reuben Hornsby in 1829. Originally called Mina, the town was renamed in 1837 in honor of the Baron de Bastrop, who helped Stephen Austin in his negotiations with the Mexican government to allow colonists into the area.

Early industry in Bastrop included lignite mining, lumbering, and brick making. As the cost of other fuels has risen in recent years, plans for strip-mining the lignite near Bastrop to fuel an electrical power plant are being considered.

The cabins, swimming pool, bathhouse, roads, and golf course in the park were constructed in the thirties by the Civilian Conservation Corps.

12. BAY CITY: RIVERSIDE PARK

Matagorda County. South from Bay City 3 miles on TX 60, southwest 1.6 miles on FM 2668. Mailing Address: 7330 FM 2668, Bay City, TX 77414. Phone: 979-245-0340, fax 979-323-1695. Email: riversidepark@cityofbaycity.org. Located on the Colorado River.

Camping: 40 pull-through RV/tent sites with full hookups ($18/night), 34 sites with water and electricity ($15/night). Modern restrooms, showers, trailer dump station, group pavilion (100-car capacity). Fees: entrance, facility, weekly and monthly rates available.

Recreation: picnic pavilion, river swimming, fishing, boat ramp, laundry, grocery store, jogging trail. Adjacent to 18-hole Gary Player-designed Rio Colorado Golf Course (979-244-2955).

13. BENTSEN-RIO GRANDE STATE PARK—
WORLD BIRDING CENTER HEADQUARTERS

LOCATION

Hidalgo County. 7 miles west of McAllen on Expressway 83 to Bentsen Palm Dr. , then south on Bentsen Palm Dr. (FM 2062) to park. Mailing address: 2800 S. Bentsen Palm Drive (FM 2962), Mission, TX 78572. Phone: 956-585-1107. Rare Bird Alert: 956-584-2731. Reservations and information: 956-584-9156. For all state park reservations, call the centralized reservations system, 512-389-8900, or www.ReserveAmerica.com online. Call the state park information number, 800-792-1112, for information and fee updates.

FACILITIES

Fees: entrance, facility, activity use; subject to change. WiFi available (user fee).

Green jays and other subtropical birds flock to the feeders at Bentsen-Rio Grande Valley State Park.

Camping: 10 primitive sites 50 yards from road, access to trailhead by tram or bike, water in nearby picnic area, restrooms with showers about 1,000 yards away. Park hours 6 a.m.–10 p.m. Tram operates 8:30 a.m.–4:30 p.m.

Recreation: wildlife viewing, bike rental, tram tours, guided bird walks, guided nature hikes and programs, fishing, picnic areas, group shelter gift shop, café (8 a.m.–1 p.m. Wednesday–Sunday).

WEATHER

July high averages 95 degrees, January low 48 degrees.

MAIN ATTRACTIONS

The 760-acre park, donated by the Bentsen family in 1944, borders the Rio Grande and includes two resacas, or oxbow lakes. The subtropical climate, proximity to Mexico, and pristine habitat surrounded by cabbage and onion fields makes the park an island refuge for wildlife, especially birds. Many of the bird species occur in few other places in the United States. The unique confluence in the thorn-brush woodlands of temperate

and subtropical birdlife, as well as migrating raptors and neotropical songbirds, attracts bird watchers from across the nation. With more than 400
species of birds throughout the Lower Rio Grande Valley, the area rates as
one of the top 10 birdwatching locations in North America.

Recognizing the ecological, and increasingly economical, importance of preserving the lower valley woodland habitat, state agencies,
nonprofits, and cities have worked for decades to create a network of
preserves to complement the federal national wildlife refuge system. The
World Birding Center, whose headquarters are located in the state park,
coordinates a network of nine birding sites along the 120-miles between
Roma and South Padre Island. For detailed information about the nine
sites, please see page 291.

The 2,088-acre Santa Ana National Wildlife Refuge, another popular
must-see refuge for birdwatchers, is 30 miles southeast of Bentsen-Rio
Grande Valley State Park via U.S. 83 to Alamo, then 7.5 miles south on
FM 907. The refuge operates an interpretive wildlife tram November-
April, has 19 miles of self-guided nature trails, wildlife observation blinds,
7 miles of paved roads open to bikes, and a visitor center with exhibits
and a bookstore. For information, call 956-784-7500, www.fws.gov.

HIKING

The free tram takes visitors into the park (8:30 a.m.–4:30 p.m.) with
frequent stops at trails and observation points. The 1.8-mile Rio Grande
Trail loops through riparian woodlands to a wildlife viewing tower and
observation deck. The one-way 0.7-mile Resaca Vieja trail, 0.3-mile
Green Jay trail, and 0.4-mile Kiskadee trail connect to observation decks
and are wheelchair accessible. Bikes are allowed on park roads.

PLANTS AND ANIMALS

Like a biological island, the park is surrounded by cultivated farmland.
Except in a few protected sanctuaries, the plants and animals once native
to the deep alluvial soil of the lower Rio Grande plains have been displaced by cabbage patches, onion fields, and citrus groves—today, the
fertile Rio Grande Valley is one of the most productive farming areas in
North America. To step into the park is to step into a bygone era of lush,
subtropical vegetation and abundant wildlife.

The rich soil formed by the Rio Grande's deposits of sand and clay
supports a wide variety of plants. Subtropical vegetation thrives in the
mild climate, where freezing temperatures are very rare. The two dominant plant communities native to the area are the dry brushlands and the
rich riparian woodlands.

The Valley's moderate rainfall, high temperatures, and rapidly draining
soils create arid conditions favoring drought-resistant species. Thorny
shrubs form an impenetrable brush woodland. Examples of plant and
animal communities found in this habitat are identified along the nature trails and in the park interpretive center. The small thorny bushes

include lotebush, guayacan with its feathery foliage, catclaw acacia, brazilwood or bluewood, and the aromatic lime prickly ash.

Woodlands parallel the river and surround the resacas, where moisture is more abundant. Cedar elms and hackberry trees are common, as are the anaqua with its sandpapery leaves and the Texas ebony with its thick black seedpods. Rio Grande ash and willow trees prosper along the waterways.

Bentsen-Rio Grande Valley is famous among bird-watchers from across the nation; more than 200 species of birds have been recorded in the limited confines of the park. Nineteen species, including the green jay and the chachalaca, can be seen in the United States only in South Texas. Ask for a checklist of the birds and other wildlife at the park entrance. A large number and variety of migrating birds spend their winters along the Rio Grande Delta, and occasionally a rare Mexican species will unexpectedly appear in the park. However, the most common winter birds throughout the Valley are the snowbirds, retirees who flee the northern chill and flock to the warm climate here.

Mammals common to the park include raccoons, opossums, coyotes, striped skunks, and armadillos. Bobcats are frequently sighted at dawn and dusk, and the tropical jaguarundi and ocelot occur, but rarely.

HISTORY

The lower Rio Grande Valley abounds with historical significance. The city of Mission was named after the small mission, La Lomita Chapel, located 3 miles south on FM 1016. The chapel was established in 1824 by priests of the oblate order.

The early priests may have been the first to plant citrus trees in the Valley. Now Mission, considered the home of the famous ruby red grapefruit, is the location of more than 30 citrus-processing plants.

14. BIG BEND NATIONAL PARK

LOCATION

Brewster County. Headquarters: 70 miles south of Marathon on U.S. 385
or 100 miles south of Alpine on TX 118.
Mailing address: Headquarters, P.O. Box 129, Big Bend National Park, Texas 79834. Phone: 432-477-2251. Weather information: 432-477-1183. Internet: www.nps.gov/bibe.

FACILITIES

Fees: admission ($20/vehicle for 7-day pass), camping, river use. Annual, senior, and interagency passes cover admission and discount camping fees. Fees subject to change.

Casa Grande towers over the Basin Campground in the Chisos Mountains.

Camping: Big Bend offers primitive camping in designated backcountry sites, no water or facilities. Backcountry permits ($10) must be obtained in person at park visitor centers. A limited number of campsites in Rio Grande Village ($26 and up/night) and the Chisos Basin ($14/night) campgrounds can be reserved between November 15–April 15. Reservations may be made up to 180 days in advance by visiting www.recreation .gov or by calling 877-444-6777. The national park cannot make reservations. Privately owned RV parks operate near Study Butte outside the park's western edge. The campgrounds are usually full Thanksgiving to Christmas and spring break (March, April).

The Chisos Basin Campground has 60 campsites with water nearby, modern restrooms but no showers, and a trailer dump station. Trailers over 20 feet long are not recommended. The Chisos Mountains Lodge has motel rooms, cabins, and a restaurant; reservations are recommended.

Cottonwood Campground, near Santa Elena Canyon, has 35 campsites with water nearby and chemical toilets.

Rio Grande Village has 100 campsites with water nearby; 25 trailer sites with water, electricity, and sewage hookups; group campgrounds with water nearby; modern restrooms with pay showers, a laundromat, and a trailer dump station.

BIG BEND NATIONAL PARK

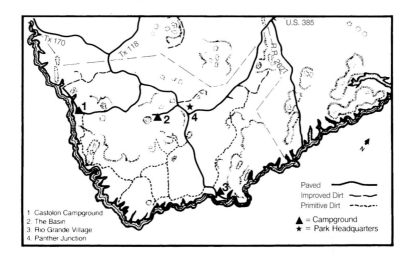

Chisos Mountains Lodge: reservations 432-477-2291, Big Bend National Park, Basin Rural Station, Big Bend National Park, TX 79834. www.chisosmountainslodge.com/. Motel rooms and cottages begin at $100/night.

Recreation: picnicking, hiking and nature trails, interpretive exhibits with trail-guide booklets and animal checklists, swimming in the Rio Grande, fishing in the Rio Grande, canoeing and rafting in the Rio Grande (permit required), amphitheaters at the Basin and Rio Grande Village, restaurant and coffee shop at the Basin, park headquarters and service station at Panther Junction, gasoline at Rio Grande Village, stores at the Basin, Rio Grande Village, and Castolon.

WEATHER

July high averages 93 degrees, January low 35 degrees. Temperatures run 5 to 10 degrees warmer in the desert and 5 to 10 degrees cooler in the mountains.

MAIN ATTRACTIONS

Big Bend National Park is large—1,256 square miles—so large that the visitor should begin by touring the park headquarters at Panther Junction. Exhibits and ranger-led programs help explain the park's unique geology, cacti and other plants, wildlife, and history. Guidebooks are essential to understanding and enjoying the park: particularly helpful are the "Road Guide," "Backcountry Road Guide," and "Hiker's Guide." Books on the wildflowers and cacti and guides to various nature trails are also sold. After visiting the park more than twenty times in as many years, I still find that Big Bend is one of my favorite spots.

Big Bend is situated in a large crook, or bend, in the Rio Grande, which forms the 107-mile southern boundary of the park and occupies 801,163 acres of the Chihuahuan Desert. But the park offers more than desert scenery. The Chisos Mountains, with mile-high peaks, are completely surrounded by the park. The rugged mountains provide the visitor unparalleled vistas both of the desert below and of distant peaks in Mexico. There are many hiking trails—varying from easy to strenuous—in the mountains. When conditions are right, the evenings provide some of the most beautiful sunsets in the West.

The desert has its own special charm, especially in the cooler months of the year. Secluded canyons offer surprises to the explorer, and springs often provide glimpses of desert wildlife. In the early spring, wildflowers are scattered across the seemingly barren desert floor, if there has been ample rainfall. By April, the cacti begin to bloom. Many of the delicate blossoms may last only one day.

The third scenic wonder in the park, after the desert and the mountains, is the Rio Grande. The river has cut three spectacular canyons, with sheer walls up to 1,500 feet high. Santa Elena, to the west, is the most impressive. Here, the river has sliced a snakelike gorge across a mesa that towers above the desert basin. Boquillas Canyon is near Rio Grande Village on the eastern side of the park. Mariscal Canyon, midway between the other canyons, is accessible only by boat or four-wheel-drive vehicle.

Big Bend and the surrounding area are rich in legends and lore of the Indians, the Spanish, and the early settlers. Numerous books have been written about the rugged pioneers who mined, ranched, farmed, and hid out in this remote section of Texas. Many of the place-names in the park are reminders of heroes and events of past days.

HIKING

The park's *Hikers Guide* booklet describes more than 40 trails that cover 150 miles and vary from easy day hikes to strenuous backpacking adventures. Several of the most popular are described here.

The Lost Mine, Window, and South Rim trails have trailheads in the Basin. The trail to Lost Mine Peak is 4.8 miles round trip, ascends 1,250 feet, and is rated medium difficulty. The view from the top is breathtaking, though some say the climb is more so! The Window Trail, another medium-difficulty hike of 5.2 miles round trip, leads down an oak-lined canyon to the point where Oak Creek plunges over a cliff to the desert below. The South Rim Trail is a strenuous 14-mile hike suitable only for those in good physical shape. There are other trails branching from the South Rim Trail, including ones to Emory Peak, Boot Canyon, Juniper Canyon, and Blue Creek.

Eight self-guided trails have signs and pamphlets explaining significant ecological and historical facts. These trails are suitable for almost

A 3-foot-tall species of bluebonnet grows in Big Bend.

everyone, and the easy walking provides an excellent opportunity for exploring the park. Also, pullouts along the roadsides have interpretive exhibits relating interesting geological and historical events.

PLANTS AND ANIMALS

The park has a wide variety of ecosystems, including desert, mountain, and riparian environments. In addition, desert springs, mountain slopes, and protected canyons provide specialized habitats for rare plants and animals. The mountains are a biological island surrounded by inhospitable desert. A small grove of aspen trees, a rarity in Texas, grows near the top of Emory Peak, while just a few miles away, creosote bushes cover the parched desert floor.

Water is the limiting factor in the desert—the river is like a green ribbon stretched through the arid land. Trees, cane, and an often impenetrable shrubby growth parallel the life-giving river. Desert springs also support rich vegetation. Cottonwood trees and rare columbine flowers find a home around pools and streams formed by runoff from the mountains.

Mule deer, javelinas, coyotes, desert cottontails, and blacktail jack-rabbits are commonly seen in the desert. Foxes, bobcats, and mountain lions are occasionally reported, especially near the springs. Beavers live along the river, white-tailed deer are seen in the mountains, and skunks are common camp guests throughout the park. Nocturnal ringtails and badgers may be seen on the back roads at night.

Birdlife is abundant, with several species occurring in the United States only in the park. The Colima warbler can be seen only in Boot Canyon in the Chisos Mountains, and the Lucifer hummingbird builds its delicate nests on ocotillos in the desert. Thirteen other hummers have been sighted in the park, making one of the largest concentrations of hummingbirds in the state. Other rare birds include the golden eagle, peregrine falcon, painted redstart, and varied bunting.

The vegetation in much of the park is different from that of a hundred years ago. When ranchers moved into the area around the turn of the century, what is now rocky soil supporting only scrub brush was a desert grassland. Old photographs show horses and cattle standing in deep grass. Even the driest part of the park, Tornillo Flat, was covered with grass. But, as in most of Texas, many ranches were stocked with too many cattle and sheep and the land was overgrazed. When the park was acquired in 1944, more than 40,000 head of stock were removed from the area.

Insufficient vegetation allowed wind and rain to strip away the topsoil, leaving the barren, rocky slopes as we see them today. With the scanty rain running off into the washes and rivers instead of soaking into the ground, springs dried up and creeks stopped flowing. Large cottonwood stumps can still be seen along the dry wash that was once Terlingua Creek. The beavers are gone, and so are the farmers. Terlingua Abaja, once a farming community, is now a cluster of tumbling adobe ruins on a gravelly hillside.

The weather at Big Bend can be, and often is, quite rugged. Desert temperatures in the summer exceed 100 degrees, and in the mountains gusts of wind will rock RVs and test the durability of a tent. From late fall to early spring, blue northers may drop temperatures 20 to 30 degrees in less than an hour, causing misery for those caught on the trail. However, except in the summer, the climate is generally pleasant, and many retirees journey to the park for their winter vacation. Even in the summer, hiking and camping are pleasant at higher elevations of the Chisos Mountains. Peak visitation occurs during March and April, college spring break, and Thanksgiving. At these times, expect the park and private campgrounds and motels to be filled to capacity.

Big Bend is a textbook example of geological processes—many universities from across the nation annually bring classes to the park during spring break. The mountains, canyons, and desert provide classic examples of igneous, metamorphic, and sedimentary rocks, of faulting and folding, weathering and erosion. Fossils are common in some strata, varying from tiny sea organisms to crocodilelike creatures with six-foot skulls to the world's largest flying reptile. Guidebooks are available for those with specific interests in geology.

15. BIG BEND RANCH STATE PARK

LOCATION

Brewster and Presidio counties. Extends 60 miles along Rio Grande and north of TX 170 between Lajitas and Fort Leaton State Historical Park.
Mailing address: P.O. Box 2319, Presidio, TX 79845. Phone: Administrative office (Presido) 432-229-3416, Sauceda headquarters 432-358-4444. Contact points: Fort Leaton State Historic Site (4 miles east of Presidio on FM 170), 432-229-3613; Barton Warnock Environmental Education Center, 432-424-3327 (1 mile east of Lajitas on FM 170). Mailing address: P O Box 2319, Presidio, TX 79845. A 36-mile gravel road leads to the Sauceda HQ. For all state park reservations, call the centralized reservations system, 512-389-8900, or www.ReserveAmerica.com online. Call the state park information number, 800-792-1112, for information and fee updates.

PARK USE ZONES

The state park is divided into three zones according to accessibility, facilities provided, and activities permitted.

Front Country Zone: within ¼ mile either side of designated 2WD roads. All street legal and licensed vehicles permitted in this zone. Camping only at designated locations.

Primitive Road Zone: within ¼ mile either side of designated 4WD or 2WD high-clearance roads. Motorized vehicle access to this zone restricted to street legal and licensed vehicles with at least four functional wheels. Camping only at designated campsites.

Backcountry Zones: more than ¼ mile from publicly accessible roads. Twenty separate zones defined. Only non-motorized travel allowed, cross-country travel permitted.

FACILITIES

Fees: entrance ($3/person), camping ($5–$8/night), facility use fees; fees subject to change. No gas or groceries available in park, limited cell phone service. WiFi available at Sauceda HQ (user fee).

Camping: Backcountry road conditions may prohibit RVs and motor homes from entering. Camping areas with composting toilets located along River Road (FM 170) at Colorado Canyon, Madera (Monilla) Canyon and Grassy Banks River Access, 2 group camping areas (Contrabando and Arenosa) along River Road. Inside park, 55 primitive car camping sites with picnic table, fire ring, and tent pads on 2WD all-access, 2WD high-clearance, or 4WD roads. Check with HQ for road conditions. Primitive backcountry camping permitted anywhere ¾ mile from trailheads or roads, ¼ mile from existing campsites, 300 feet from water or historic sites. Equestrian group campgrounds available. Call Sauceda headquarters, 432-358-4444, for campsite and backcountry reservations. Showers and restrooms available by the Sauceda visitor center. Meals available at the Sauceda Bunkhouse Kitchen with prior arrangements.

Lodging at Sauceda Headquarters: The Big House, a three bedroom lodge with kitchen, accommodates 8 ($100/room, double; $50 per extra person, $25 for children 12 years of age or less). Sauceda Bunkhouse accommodates 30, men on one side, women on the other, $25/person. Call 432-229-3416 for reservations. Meals available with prior arrangements. Presidio, Lajitas, Study Butte offer a limited selection of motels.

Recreation: picnic areas along River Road, backpacking, river rafting, mountain biking, guided 4WD and horseback tours, mountain bike rentals and horseback tours at Sauceda HQ, park programs, Texas Longhorn Herd with semiannual roundup, birding (300+ species), stargazing (millions).

Airstrip: Big Bend Ranch paved airstrip 3TE3, 103-56-11.7030 W, 28-28-10.6840 N, Elevation: 4,240 feet, Length: 5,500 feet.

Barton Warnock Environmental Education Center: Located east of Lajitas on TX 170, the center offers geological, ecological, and historical displays of the area. The botanical gardens provide an opportunity to learn the desert vegetation and see cacti in bloom. A book store sells guidebooks, trail maps, and other related materials. Admission is charged to the museum sections. Hours 8:00 a.m. to 4:30 p.m.

MAIN ATTRACTIONS

With one purchase, the state doubled the total acreage in the state park system. This 280,280-acre park covers some of the most remote, rugged, and beautiful country in west Texas. It includes the Solitario, a crater-like geological uplift more than 5 miles in diameter. The unusual formation reveals a concentric sequence of rock strata spanning 500 million years. The park borders the Rio Grande and harbors scenic waterfalls, Indian pictographs, rare plants, mesas, mountains, scenic vistas, hidden canyons, caves, and volcanic formations. The trails and river corridor provide excellent opportunities for bird watching (300+ species), wildlife observations (cougars, javelina, deer), scenic photography, and studying the cacti and other plants adapted to the rugged Chihuahuan Desert. Several developed landings on the river provided access for boating and fishing.

The 36-mile gravel road to the Sauceda HQ normally is passable to all vehicles, but if you have a large rig, check road conditions with the park since washouts occur. The road continues another 8 miles to the Solitario overlook

The 60-mile drive on TX 170 through the park between Presidio and Lajitas can be an adventure in itself. The road parallels the Rio Grande, climbs steep, winding grades to dramatic viewpoints above the river, and traverses numerous low-water crossings prone to flooding after thunderstorms. In addition to the frequent pullouts, you can stop for photography, or to soak up the vistas, or to eat a leisurely lunch at the Tepee roadside park at Madera Canyon.

The park is home to a portion of the Texas Longhorn Herd. Each April and October, 25 weekend wranglers can sign up for an authentic, three-day roundup. Participants mount up and help drive the herd from the ranch's remote pastures to the stock pens at Sauceda Headquarters, then brand and vaccinate the calves. The cattle drive is the park's most popular program.

HIKING AND BIKING

Old stock, wagon, and jeep trails crisscross the ridges and canyons of the park, which was a cattle and goat ranch after the Indians were driven out in the 1870s. The park, 22 miles by 29 miles wide, has constructed miles of trails and will ultimately establish a system with 65 routes and 236 miles of interconnected trails. Six trailheads lead into the interior from TX 170 and dozens of trailheads depart from interior roads.

Exploring the old roads and new trails of the park offers an intimate way to experience the rugged beauty of the desert mountains and canyons. Trails lead to desert springs, narrow canyons, expansive vistas, historic ruins, pictographs, waterfalls, mountaintops, and through dramatic examples of volcanism, erosion, and tectonic forces. Loops make for exciting day hikes or you can sample the solitude of the desert mountains and canyons on extended overnight adventures.

Many of the primitive campgrounds are located at trailheads accessible by vehicles and provide a convenient base for exploring the backcountry. Several campgrounds provide equestrian facilities and access to multi-use trails. Even if you don't drive all the way into Sauceda headquarters, you can explore the park from trailheads on FM 170.

The 4-mile one-way Rancherias Canyon trail leaves from the Rancherias West Trailhead on FM 170. The trail leads up the drainage to an 80-foot pour-off. Water and trees in the canyon add to the scenic beauty and the chance to see birds and other wildlife.

The 19-mile Rancherias Loop Trail begins at the same trailhead. It climbs out of the canyon and meanders along mesas and ridges, past historic ruins, springs, examples of the volcanism that created the rugged landscape, and breathtaking vistas of the desert mountains, including the 8,000-foot peaks across the river in Mexico. About 2.5 miles of FM 170 separate the east and west trailheads of the loop.

The one-mile roundtrip Closed Canyon Trial leads from FM 170 between the two Rancherias trailheads. This easy hike enters a canyon so narrow you can almost touch both sides at places. The knife of erosion sliced through walls of compacted ash (tuff) and created a winding corridor that leads to a shadowy adventure.

The 25-mile Contrabando Trail, is named after smugglers who, depending on the decade, brought cattle, candelilla wax, and liquor across the border to avoid customs taxes. The multi-use trail (hike, bike, horse) begins at the Barton Warnock Environmental Education Center. A side loop connects from another trailhead 7.5 miles west on FM 170. The network includes a number of loops suitable for various levels of fitness. It circles the red rock Lajitas Mesa and Contrabando Dome, follows creeks with historic waterholes, and gives hikers a true taste of the Chihuahua Desert. Trailside exhibits that interpret the area's mining and ranching heritage.

Hiking and biking in the desert presents many potentially dangerous situations. Overheating even in mild temperatures can occur rapidly, so always take plenty of water, a gallon per day in the summer. Steep trails with sharp, loose rocks, thorny vegetation, and poisonous snakes can cause injury in an area where the closest hospital is more than a hundred miles away in Alpine.

RAFTING

One of the most popular rafting trips in the Big Bend area is through Colorado Canyon. The nine-mile float is an easy day trip and can be arranged through several outfitters in Lajitas and Terlingua. The river, with Class II and III rapids, is not considered dangerous during normal flow. Obtain permits for private trips and check on river conditions at the Barton Warnock Center or Fort Leaton. The park has certified three commercial tour companies that offer a variety of rafting, mountain biking, hiking/camping, nature, and multi-sport tours.

Big Bend River Tours, PO Box 317 Terlingua, TX 79852, 800-545-4240, 432-371-3033, rapids317@hotmail.com, www.bigbendrivertours.com.

Far Flung Outdoor Center, P.O. Box 377, 1 Adventure Lane, Farm Road 170, Terlingua, TX, 79852, 800-839-7238, info@ffoc.net, www.ffoc.net.

Desert Sports, PO Box 448 Terlingua, TX, 79852, 888-989-6900, 432-371-2727, info@desertsportstx.com, www.desertsportstx.com.

16. BIG LAKE: REAGAN COUNTY PARK

Reagan County. Within city on Utah Ave. Mailing address: Box 100, Big Lake, TX 76932. Phone: 325-884-2376. Facilities: 50 acres with 75 pull-through RV/tent sites with water and electricity, modern restrooms, trailer dump station, picnic tables, swimming pool, sports courts. Fees charged.

17. BIG SPRING: COMANCHE TRAIL PARK

Howard County. In Big Spring, 4 miles south of IH-20 on U.S. 87. Mailing address: City Parks Department, 310 Nolan, Big Spring, Texas 79720. Phone: 432-264-2376 or 866-430-7100, Internet: www.mybigspring.com/Recreation/Parks.htm. Camping: pads only, water nearby, flush toilets. Recreation: picnic pavilion, playgrounds, swimming pool, golf, tennis, hike/bike trails.

BIG SPRING: MOSS CREEK LAKE PARK

Howard County. 7.5 miles east of Big Spring on IH-20, 5 miles south on Moss Lake Rd. Mailing address: 10000 E. Moss Lake Rd., Big Spring, TX 79720. Phone: 432-393-5246, 866-430-7100, Internet: www.mybigspring .com/Recreation/MossLake.htm. Camping: pull-through RV/tent sites with full hookups and with water and electricity only, 26 sites with shelters, flush toilets, dump station. Recreation: 2 pavilions with electricity, playground, beach swimming area, boat ramp, dock, fishing, dirt bike course, trails, store. Fees charged.

18. BIG THICKET NATIONAL PRESERVE

LOCATION

Mailing address: Visitor Center and Information, 6044 FM 420, Kountze, TX 77625. Phone: 409-951-6725. Visitor Center directions: from Beaumont 8 miles north on U.S. Highway 69-287 to Kountze, east on FM 420 and follow the signs to the visitor center. Hours: 9:00 a.m. to 5:00 p.m., daily. Closed Thanksgiving, Christmas, and New Year's Day. Internet: www.nps.gov/bith.

FACILITIES

Camping: Only primitive backcountry camping in designated areas is allowed. Write for maps and permits. Public campgrounds in the area include the Alabama-Coushatta Indian Reservation, Lake B. A. Steinhagen, Martin Dies, Jr., State Park, Village Creek State Park, and Lake Livingston State Park.

Recreation: ranger programs, a self-guided auto tour, hiking, bird-watching, photography, nature study, canoeing.

Note: Mosquitoes can be serious any time of the year, so unless you enjoy donating blood, take repellent on your outings.

Slow-flowing creeks in the Big Thicket reflect trees like mirrors.

MAIN ATTRACTIONS

The United Nations designated the Big Thicket National Preserve as a UNESCO Biosphere Reserve and a Globally Important Bird Area. The preserve includes 9 land units and 6 water corridors separate units and river corridors with a total of 97,000 acres. Begin your exploration of this unique wilderness at the visitor center in the Turkey Creek Unit just north of Kountze. The center has exhibits, maps, information and a ranger on duty. A self-guided nature trail leads through the deep woods, along scenic Village Creek, by sloughs with waist-high cypress knees, and across pine-covered ridges.

Eight hiking trails, varying from 18 miles to ¼ mile, lead through the various habitats of the Big Thicket. The tails follow the creeks and climb the pine-scented ridges to let the hiker sample the wildness of the deep woods that makes the Big Thicket so special. You can take a 1.7-mile, 2.4-mile, or .5 mile loops on the 15-mile-long Turkey Creek Trail system, accessible from four trailheads. The trail passes through pine uplands, mixed forests, floodplains, and baygalls.

The Kirby Nature Trail System in the southern end of the Turkey Creek Unit, has a 1.7-mile inner loop and a 2.4-mile outer loop through

BIG THICKET NATIONAL PRESERVE

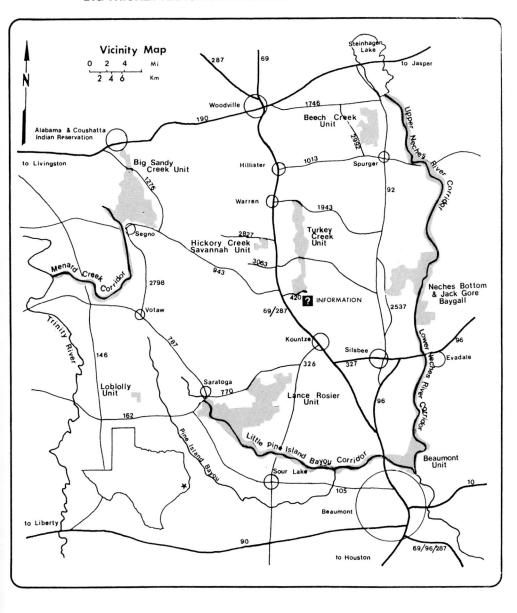

hardwood-pines woodlands, bald cypress swamps, and along Village Creek. The quarter-mile Pitcher Plant Trail on the northeast side of the Turkey Creek Unit shows visitors rare carnivorous plants.

You can also see carnivorous plants on the Sundew Trail in the Hickory Creek Unit. A ⅙-mile outer loop and .8-mile inner loop, mostly on a boardwalk, pass through a longleaf pine wetland savanna with pitcher plants, sundews, and a large variety of flowers. The Pitcher Plant and Sundew trails are ADA accessible.

Another short loop, the 1-mile Beech Woods Trail, gives you the majestic experience of hiking through a mature beech-magnolia-loblolly pine forest with trees that tower into the sky. (This trail is closed from the opening day of fall hunting season until the second Sunday in January. Call 409-951-6725 for specific dates.) The 5.4-mile Woodlands Trail winds through the Big Sandy Unit with shorter loops of 3.3 and 4.5 miles available. The trail crosses between dense hardwood stands and reclaimed pasture land.

The 1.5-mile loop Beaver Slide Trail in the southeast corner of the Big Sandy Creek Unit circles several ponds formed by old beaver dams. Horses and mountain bikes can use the 18-mile-long loop Big Sandy Creek Horse/Bike Trail accessible near Dallardsville. The trail crosses upland pine forests and beech-magnolia-loblolly pine slopes before entering a floodplain forest of basket oak, sweetgum, hornbeam, and holly. (This trail is closed from the opening day of fall hunting season until the second Sunday in January. Call 409-951-6725 for specific dates.)

If you have ever floated down one of the peaceful, primeval waterways of the Big Thicket, you know why canoeing is one of the most popular activities in the preserve. The river corridor units preserve beautiful wilderness stretches of Village Creek, Pine Island Bayou, and the Neches River. Canoers can float 93 miles on the Neches River between Lake B. A. Steinhagen and Beaumont, 49 miles on Pine Island Bayou, and 37 miles on Village Creek. Camping is permitted on the sandbars and within preserve boundaries with a permit. A canoe trip planner and maps are available. Park rangers often lead canoe outings. Several canoe liveries operate in the area.

A 75-mile auto tour takes you through seven different plant communities and shows you why the Big Thicket is considered the biological crossroads of North America. At the stops, you can explore deep mature forests, a sandhill plant community, a wet baygall community with acid-loving plants, a cypress slough, a pitcher plant savanna, a climax pine forest with a thick carpet of pine needles, and wetlands abounding with carnivorous sundews.

PLANTS AND ANIMALS

The first settlers discovered three million acres of dense forests, swamps, marshes, bogs, and sloughs laced with meandering streams and bayous. They bypassed the trackless region, leaving it to bears, beavers, panthers, and outlaws. Later, businessmen saw money in the giant pines and hardwoods and began chipping away at the seemingly endless acres of woodlands. Now powerful tree-crushing machines level thousands of acres of forest annually. Less than a tenth of the original Big Thicket remains. Monocultures of pine trees now grow where the richest diversity of plant life in North America once existed. Each of the scattered units of the national preserve represents examples of the diverse plant communities that make this area special.

Four major plant provinces converge in the Big Thicket, making it one of the richest biological regions on the continent. Cacti typical of the Southwest deserts grow on xeric sandhills, while bog-loving plants also found in Florida swamps grow a few yards away. In the dense woodlands of the Thicket, one finds a majestic interplay of tree species from northern, eastern, and southern forests. Grasses, mushrooms, vines, shrubs, and herbs mingle like an intricately composed symphony, as do mammals, reptiles, amphibians, and birds. Forty kinds of orchids grow in the Big Thicket, and 1,000 kinds of fungi. Three hundred species of birds make their way through the canopy of trees. Beavers cut a silent v across the slow-moving sloughs, the drumming of pileated woodpeckers resounds through the pine-oak forests, and mosquitoes remind visitors that the idyllic forest exacts a price from those with romantic visions of Walden Pond.

Concerned citizens organized the Big Thicket Association a number of years ago to raise funds and influence legislation for the preservation of the rapidly diminishing mixed pine-hardwood forests in East Texas. The result was the establishment of the national preserve. The association still is active in preserving lands not included in the national preserve. The Big Thicket Museum is operated by the association as part of its program of educating the public about this significant natural area. The museum, closed on Mondays, is in Saratoga and has plant and animal exhibits and information.

19. BLACK KETTLE NATIONAL GRASSLAND: LAKE MARVIN RECREATION AREA

LOCATION

Hemphill County. 12 miles east of Canadian on FM 2266
Mailing address: Route 1, Box 55-B, Cheyenne, Oklahoma, 73628-9725. Phone: 580-497-2143. Internet: www.fs.fed.us/r3/cibola/districts/black.shtml.

FACILITIES

Camping: 20 RV/tent sites, some with water (fee charged), some with water nearby (free), vault toilets, open all year.

Recreation: picnicking, hiking trails, fishing, boating.

MAIN ATTRACTIONS

The 575-acre national grasslands were purchased by the U.S. Department of the Interior in the thirties in an effort to restore eroded, agriculturally abused land to productivity. Fishing and boating on 63-acre Lake Marvin are the main attractions of this park, located in the farthest reaches of the Texas Panhandle. Open grasslands, marshes, and woodlands provide homes for deer, turkeys, rabbits, and beavers. The quarter-mile Big Tree Trail leads to a large cottonwood tree used by early pioneers as a landmark. A Watchable Wildlife Trail leads to a lakeside viewing platform, where ducks and waterfowl are abundant in the winter.

Many eastern species of birds reach their western breeding limit along the lake and the adjoining Canadian River. Nesting birds at this park include the northern oriole, wood duck, barred owl, and least tern.

20. BLANCO STATE PARK

LOCATION

Blanco County. 42 miles west of Austin on U.S. 290, 8 miles south on U.S. 281 to Blanco, on the Blanco River.
Mailing address: Box 493, Blanco, Texas 78606. Phone: 830-833-4333. For all state park reservations, call the centralized reservations system, 512-389-8900, or www.ReserveAmerica.com online. Call the state park information number, 800-792-1112, for information and fee updates.

FACILITIES

Fees: entrance, facility, activity use; subject to change.

Camping: 16 back-in RV/tent sites with full hookups, 12 with water, electricity; 7 screened shelters, modern restrooms with showers, trailer dump station. Fees charged.

Recreation: picnic areas and playgrounds, swimming in the Blanco River, fishing, boating (electric motors only), pavilion with kitchen, ¾-mile loop trail, Texas State Park Store.

WEATHER

July high averages 86 degrees, January low 46 degrees.

MAIN ATTRACTIONS

The shaded banks of the Blanco River provide the perfect setting for picnicking, camping, and family recreation. There is swimming in the river, and a three-foot-deep wading pool is filled as the water cascades over a small picturesque spillway. This park, as are all parks in and near cities, is heavily used by local inhabitants.

The 105-acre park, located in the city of Blanco, consists of a narrow corridor along the Blanco River. A small dam impounds the river in the park, and much of the well-kept shore is shaded with large oaks. Because of modifications of the natural environment, the native vegetation is not especially representative of Hill Country rivers.

Lyndon B. Johnson National Historical Park, with a reconstructed 1880-period ranch and exhibits, is 14 miles north in Johnson City. And Lyndon B. Johnson State Historic Site is 15 miles northwest near Stonewall. The park features bus tours of the LBJ Ranch, a working pioneer farm, bison and longhorns, and a swimming pool.

21. BOCA CHICA BEACH / USFWS BOCA CHICA TRACT

LOCATION

Cameron County. Undeveloped beach. 22.5 miles east of Brownsville at end of TX 4. Mailing address: Brownsville Convention and Visitors Bureau, 650 FM 802 Brownsville, TX 78520. Phone: 956-546-3721, 800-626-2639. Email: visinfo@brownsville.org. Internet: www.brownsville.org. Administered by the Lower Rio Grande Valley National Wildlife Refuge, Route 2 Box 202A, Alamo, TX 78516, 956-784-7521, www.fws.gov/southwest/refuges/texas/lrgv.html.

FACILITIES

Undeveloped with no facilities, no water, no fees, no gates. Vehicles permitted on beach but be cautious of soft sand. This area is not staffed or patrolled and overnight use is not advised due to security reasons.

WEATHER

July high averages 93 degrees, January low 51 degrees.

MAIN ATTRACTION

If you love isolated beaches, you're not alone, but you can be at Boca Chica. While the crowds cavort on the beaches across the bay on South Padre, gulls and a few beachcombers and anglers stroll the wind- and wave-swept beaches in this undeveloped park. Storms have long inhibited development and left the beach for the use and abuse of natural forces and humans.

PLANTS AND ANIMALS

The Rio Grande ends its long journey to the sea in Boca Chica Bay. Unfortunately, upstream dams trap most of the silt that formed Padre Island and the other barrier islands, and they are slowly eroding. The park preserves 1,055 acres of beaches and bays in the Boca Chica Subdelta and includes the Mesa de Gavilan (a flat upland about 5 feet above sea level), the south shore of South Bay, the west shore of Boca Chica Bay, and the flat, sandy, northern end of Boca Chica Island. Low, active sand dunes anchored with vegetation and bare sand flats cover most of the area. Vegetation consists of low, shrubby, salt-tolerant grasses and herbs with yucca and prickly pear on the slightly higher elevations.

Large numbers of endangered and threatened shorebirds, gulls, and terns nest and winter on the beaches and bays of the park. Look for brown pelicans, reddish egrets, roseate spoonbills, osprey, white-tailed kites, Aplomado falcons, snowy plovers, least and sooty terns, black skimmers, Chihuahua ravens, and Cassin's, Botteri's, and seaside sparrows. The area serves as a major winter ground for endangered peregrine falcons and piping plovers. Dolphins frequently swim the offshore waters near the beach. South Bay serves as a hypersaline nursery area for many marine shellfish and fin fish.

Boca Chica Beach is one of four stops on the Boca Chica Loop of the Great Texas Coastal Birding Tail, a popular bird viewing area, especially during winter migration. This section of the trail extends from Brownsville to the end of Texas 4 at the mouth of the Rio Grande and includes the Audubon Sabal Palm Sanctuary (www.audubon.org/local/sanctuary/sabal). The 557-acre sanctuary, open 7 a.m.–5 p.m. daily except Thanksgiving, Christmas, and New Year's, preserves the largest remaining Texas Sabal Palm woodland in Texas. The forest once

Scenic dunes border the beach at Boca Chica State Park.

covered 40,000 areas along the Rio Grande corridor but was cleared for agriculture.

HISTORY

In addition to a rich flora and fauna, Boca Chica Bay has a rich history dating back to the first European explorers. In 1519, Alonso Alvarez de Pineda sailed up the Rio de los Palmos (Rio Grande) and traded with friendly Coahuiltecan natives. About 2,500 Indians lived in 40 pueblos between the mouth of the Rio Grande and present-day Brownsville. After a succession of slave raids, the natives repelled further visits.

In 1846, General U. S. Grant crossed through the park on his way back from fighting in Mexico. A year later, Robert E. Lee crossed the tract several times. The last battle of the Civil War was fought at Palmito Hill in the park. On May 11, 1865, 250 Union soldiers crossed Boca Chica Bay and joined 50 troops at Palmito Hill. The next day 190 Confederate forces drove the federal troops back to Boca Chica Bay. News of Lee's surrender on April 9 didn't reach Brownsville until May 18, 1865.

22. BONHAM STATE PARK

LOCATION

Fannin County. 28 miles east of Sherman on U.S. 82 to Bonham, 1 mile south on TX 78, 2 miles east on FM 271. Mailing address: 1363 State Park 24, Bonham TX 75418-9285. Phone: 903-583-5022. For all state park reservations, call the centralized reservations system, 512-389-8900, or www.ReserveAmerica.com online. Call the state park information number, 800-792-1112, for information and fee updates.

FACILITIES

Fees: entrance, facility, activity use; subject to change.

Camping: 14 back-in RV/tent sites with electricity and water, 14 tent sites, group tent site, group barracks for 94 people with kitchen and dining hall, modern restrooms with showers, trailer dump station. Fee charged.

Recreation: picnic area, playgrounds, lake swimming, lighted fishing pier, boat dock and ramp (5-mph speed limit on lake), pavilion, 11-mile trail for mountain biking and hiking.

WEATHER

July high averages 95 degrees, January low 31 degrees.

MAIN ATTRACTIONS

This 261-acre park, with its gently rolling hills, is located on the edge of the blackland prairies and the post oak savanna vegetation regions of Texas. The rocky slopes are dominated by eastern red cedars and oaks. Grasslands of little bluestem and bushy bluestem are interspersed throughout the woodlands. The shore of the 65-acre lake and the creek drainages are covered with black willow, hackberry, cottonwood, osage orange, and shagbark hickory trees.

Wildlife in the park is mainly centered around the small lake. Beavers were once so numerous that they undermined the earthen dam with their excavations and controlled the level of the lake. Raccoons, skunks, and opossums are often seen, especially in the evening hours.

Nearby attractions include the Sam Rayburn Library and Home in Bonham and the Eisenhower Birthplace State Historic Site in Denison.

23. BORGER: HUBER PARK

Hutchinson County. Located in city at 104 Pine St. Mailing address: Box 5250, Borger, TX 79008. Phone 806-273-0957. Camping 10 back-in RV sites with water, electricity; chemical toilets, trailer dump station. This 17-acre city park has picnic areas, playgrounds, swimming pool, tennis. No fees, no reservations. Open all year, 3-day limit.

24. BOWIE CITY PARKS

Montague County. Mailing address: City of Bowie, 304 Lindsay, Bowie, TX 76230. Phone: 940-872-1114.

Pelham Park: Within city on Pelham St. Facilities: 40 acres with 10 back-in RV/tent sites with water and electricity, swimming pool, picnic tables, sports fields. Fee charged.

Selma Park: Southwest from Bowie 3.5 miles on TX 59, south 3.6 miles on FM 2583. *Facilities:* 40 acres on Lake Amon G. Carter with 15 back-in RV/tent sites with water and electricity, 21 sites with electricity, 5 screened shelters, modern restrooms, cold showers, no drinking water. Picnicking, lake swimming, boat ramp. Fees charged.

25. BRADY: LAKE BRADY PARK

McCulloch County. 4 miles west of Brady on FM 2028, 1 mile north on FM 3022. Concessionaire. Mailing address: 724 Fife St., Brady, TX

78825. Phone 866-623-9401, 325-597-1073. Internet: www.bradylake
.org. Camping 25 RV/tent pull-through sites with full hookups, 45 with
water and electricity, 10 with water or electricity, 10 tent sites with water, 22 tent sites with electricity, 200 acres primitive RV/tent camping,
4 rental RVs, 1 cabin, 20 cabanas, modern restrooms, showers, trailer
dump station. Recreation: picnic shelters, pavilion, playgrounds, lake
swimming, bathhouse, fishing, boat ramp, store. Fees charged.

26. BRADY: RICHARDS PARK

McCulloch County. Located west of town off U.S. 87 on Memory Lane.
Mailing Address: Box 351, Brady, TX 76825. Phone: 325-597-2152.
Camping: 65 pull-through RV/tent sites with electricity, 47 with water,
15-acre camping area, flush toilets, trailer dump station. Fees charged.
Recreation: picnicking, group pavilion, playgrounds; fishing, swimming,
and boating on Brady Creek. Fees charged, reservations accepted. Open
all year.

27. BRAZOS BEND STATE PARK

LOCATION

Fort Bend County. 30 miles south of Houston on TX 288 to
Rosharon, 11 miles west on FM 1462, 1 mile north on FM 762.
Mailing address: 21901 FM 762, Needville, Texas 77461. Phone:
979-533-5101. For all state park reservations, call the centralized
reservations system, 512-389-8900, or www.ReserveAmerica.com
online. Call the state park information number, 800-792-1112, for
information and fee updates.

FACILITIES

Fees: entrance, facility, activity use; subject to change.

Camping: 77 pull-through RV/tent sites with water and electricity, 14
screened shelters, modern restrooms, showers, trailer dump station,
three primitive youth group camping areas, primitive equestrian camping. Fees charged. Fees charged.

Recreation: picnic areas, playgrounds, 2 group picnic pavilions (capacity
75 each), dining hall (capacity 150), 21.6-mile hiking trail with 7.2 miles
for bikes, .5-mile accessible interpretive trail, boardwalk and observation
deck for wildlife viewing, fishing on 6 lakes, 2 lighted piers, fish-cleaning
tables, observatory with stargazing, weekend programs (fees charged),
Texas State Park Store.

WEATHER

July high averages 94 degrees, January low 41 degrees.

MAIN ATTRACTIONS

The overnight and day-use facilities, the extensive hiking trails, six lakes offering fishing and wildlife observation, and the abundant wildlife make Brazos Bend one of the most exciting state parks in Texas. The eastern park boundary is the Brazos River, accessible only by trails. Other trails lead around the lakes, which host a large population of alligators, waterfowl, and wading birds. There are six observation platforms on Elm Lake and an observation tower overlooking Forty-Acre and Pilant lakes. The observation stations provide good spots for bird-watching and photography.

Fishing in the small lakes is excellent for bass, crappie, and perch. George Observatory, operated by the Houston Museum of Natural Science, offers public programs Saturdays 3 p.m. to 10 p.m. For information on stargazing with the three telescopes, call the Observatory at 979-553-3400 or the Museum at 281-242-3055.

HIKING

The 15 miles of hike and bike trails circle the six lakes, parallel Big Creek, and lead visitors along the Brazos River. The trails are surfaced with small pebbles and are easy to follow. There are approximately 20 miles of other trails that were once cow paths or roads. They are not regularly maintained and may or may not lead to anywhere in particular. However, they do offer opportunities for exploring. The ½-mile Creek-

Alligators are abundant at Brazos Bend State Park.

field Lake Nature Trail loops through the wetland area. The specially designed accessible trail features a boardwalk, observation deck for wildlife viewing, shaded benches, and interpretive panels with tactile bronzes of commonly observed wildlife. The Habitats and Niches exhibit includes a hands-on alligator discovery area, a tactile model of the park, and an open-captioned video for visitors with hearing impairments. An audio-cassette with nature interpretation is available for checkout from park headquarters.

PLANTS AND ANIMALS

The 4,897-acre park is situated in the Brazos River floodplain in the Gulf Coast region of prairies and marshes. About 450 acres are upland prairies; the remainder consists of marshes and riparian woodlands. Pecans, live oaks and other oak species, hackberries, and elms form the hardwood forest. Yaupon holly, dwarf palmettos, and numerous shrubs and vines grow under the forest canopy. Weeping willow and Chinese tallow trees are common around the lakes.

Two of the small lakes are natural oxbow lakes formed from Big Creek, which meanders throughout the park. Three other oxbow lakes were formed when the creek was channelized, and Pilant Lake is a 450-acre marsh. The lakes are congested with aquatic vegetation, especially water hyacinths and cattails.

The lakes, marshes, and woodlands provide excellent habitats for a diverse wildlife population. Waterfowl winter by the thousands on the lakes. Herons, egrets, anhingas, and other wading birds and shorebirds frequent the shallow lakes; gallinules tiptoe across the lotus pads; and alligators tumble off logs into the water like turtles. More than 300 species of birds have been seen in the park—ask at the entrance for a checklist.

Hundreds of white-tailed deer live in the forest. Other common mammals in the park include armadillos, raccoons, opossums, squirrels, bobcats, gray foxes, and coyotes. Feral hogs and Russian boars are occasionally seen but should be avoided. Poisonous snakes in the park include the cottonmouth, copperhead, coral snake, and rattlesnake. Of the 21 species of reptiles and amphibians in the park, alligators are numerous in the lakes and sloughs. Observe with caution—they can lunge with lightning speed.

28. BRIDGEPORT: WISE COUNTY PARK

Wise County. 35 miles northwest of Fort Worth on U.S. 287 to Decatur, 13 miles west on FM 1810 through Chico, on Lake Bridgeport. Mailing address: Box 899, Decatur, TX 76234. Phone: 940-627-6655, reservations 940-644-1910; 8 a.m.–4:30 p.m. Tue.–Sat. Camping: on Lake Bridgeport, 88 acres with 15 back-in sites with full hookups, 20 with water and electricity, 1 modern restroom with shower. Day-use area with

38 picnic tables, 1 pavilion with kitchen, 2 open-air pavilions. Recreation: picnic, playgrounds, nature trail, bicycle trail, swimming in pool and lake, fishing, boat ramps. Fees charged.

29. BROWNFIELD: COLEMAN PARK

Terry County. Mailing address: 500 W. Main, Room 102, Brownfield, TX 79316. Phone 806-637-6421. Within city on First St. Facilities: 12 back-in RV sites with full hookups. Fees charged.

30. BROWNSVILLE: ADOLPH THOMAE JR. PARK

Cameron County. North of Brownsville on FM 1847 to Arroyo City, 6 miles east on FM 2925. Mailing address: 37844 Marshall Hutts Rd., Rio Hondo, Texas 78583. Phone: 956-748-2044. Camping: 35 campsites with water, electricity, and sewage hookups; 2 picnic/tent areas, flush toilets, showers. Recreation: 2 lighted fishing piers, boat ramp, playground, wildlife observation tower. This wooded 57-acre park is surrounded by Laguna Atascosa National Wildlife Refuge and has 1.7 miles of shoreline on Arroyo Colorado. Fishing, boating, and wildlife observations are the main attractions. Fees charged, reservations accepted. Open all year.

31. BUESCHER STATE PARK

LOCATION

Bastrop County. 10 miles southeast of Bastrop on TX 71, northeast on FM 153.
Mailing address: Box 75, Smithville, Texas 78957-0075. Phone: 512-237-2241. For all state park reservations, call the centralized reservations system, 512-389-8900, or www.ReserveAmerica.com online. Call the state park information number, 800-792-1112, for information and fee updates.

FACILITIES

Fees: entrance, facility, activity use; subject to change.

Camping: 25 campsites with water only, 40 campsites with water and electricity, 4 screened shelters, modern restrooms with showers, trailer dump station. Fees charged.

Recreation: picnic areas and playgrounds, fishing on a 30-acre lake, pavilion, recreation hall with kitchen, hiking, scenic drive, Texas Park Store.

WEATHER

July high averages 96 degrees, January low 38 degrees.

MAIN ATTRACTIONS

Buescher State Park has 1,016 acres of mixed hardwoods, brushy shrubs, and loblolly pines; the park encompasses a small lake. Visitors can explore the lake edge or hike on the 7.5-mile round-trip trail.

PLANTS AND ANIMALS

The different soil types in Bastrop County each produce a characteristic plant community. In Buescher, gummy, reddish clay soils support post oak, blackjack oak, eastern red cedar, and brush shrubs dominated by yaupon holly. Sparta sandstone weathers into a light-colored sandy soil on which grow loblolly pine, oak, and hickory. A gravelly substratum supports pine, oak, farkleberry, and American beauty-berry. The pines, which dominate most of Park Road 1 between Buescher and Bastrop, thrive in Buescher only in those few areas where porous sandy or gravelly soils allow drainage while trapping enough water to support the trees.

The diverse vegetation provides a variety of wildlife habitats. More than 200 species of birds have been recorded in the area. Ducks, geese, warblers, and hawks are a few of the migratory birds that complement the large population of resident species in the spring and fall.

Some species of animals, such as the flying squirrel, reach the western limit of their distribution in Bastrop County. The patchy vegetation results in small local populations of animals that have become separated from the main body of their species. For example, the largest remnant population of the endangered Houston toad occurs in Buescher and Bastrop state parks, with the remaining population in Houston's Memorial Park. Such correlations between animal populations and zones of vegetation provide dramatic examples of the complex environmental interactions between soils, plants, and animals.

32. BUFFALO LAKE NATIONAL WILDLIFE REFUGE

LOCATION

Randall County. 10 miles west of Canyon on U.S. 60 to Umbarger, 3 miles south on FM 168.

Mailing address: Box 179, Umbarger, Texas 79091. Phone: 806-499-3382.

FACILITIES

Camping: 25 campsites with water only, group camping area, flush and chemical toilets. Group reservations accepted. Fees charged.

Recreation: picnicking, auto tour, wildlife photography, nature trail, bird-watching. Refuge hours: 8 a.m. to 8 p.m. April–September 30; 8 a.m. to 6 p.m. October–March 31.

MAIN ATTRACTIONS

This refuge in the Texas Panhandle covers 7,667 acres of shortgrass prairie, managed marshes, riparian woodlands, and croplands. A 5-mile wildlife drive winds through the refuge and passes a Windmill for Wildlife exhibit, a working windmill with an observation deck and photo blind to view birds and animals attracted to the water. Plan your drive in the early morning or evening when wildlife is most active. Many migrating songbirds, waterfowl and wading birds, and eagles and other raptors stop over in the refuge during spring and fall migrations. The refuge bird checklist documents 344 species of resident, migrant, and overwintering birds that frequent the marsh, prairies, and woodlands. In addition, you may catch a glimpse of coyotes, deer, bobcats, and prairie dogs. An interpretive trail leads to a 100-acre prairie dog town off TX 168 on the east side of the refuge. Hikers and birders will enjoy the half-mile trail into Cottonwood Canyon, a tree-lined corridor. Restrooms are located at the end of the trail.

In the mid-sixties, 800,000 migrating ducks and 40,000 Canada geese from the Central Flyway overwintered on Buffalo Lake. Then as irrigation lowered the water table, the springs and Tierra Blanca Creek which fed the lake disappeared. Now, the dry lake bed is managed as a patchwork of cropland and native vegetation. Farmers harvest two-thirds of the corps and leave the rest for wildlife. The refuge floods Stewart Marsh in the spring and fall to provide a temporary rest stop for migrant songbirds and shelter and aquatic plant food for waterfowl. The management practice for the shortgrass prairie simulates the historic migrating bison herds. Cattle intensely graze pastures for a short time, then each pasture is rested for a year.

33. CADDO LAKE STATE PARK

LOCATION

Harrison County. 15 miles northeast of Marshall on TX 43, 1 mile east on FM 2198.

Mailing address: 245 Park Road 2, Karnack, Texas 75661. Phone: 903-679-3351. For all state park reservations, call the centralized reservations system, 512-389-8900, or www.ReserveAmerica.com online. Call the state park information number, 800-792-1112, for information and fee updates.

FACILITIES

Fees: entrance, facility, activity use; subject to change.

Camping: 20 campsites with water only, 20 campsites with water and electricity, 8 campsites with water, electricity, and sewage hookups; 8 screened shelters, 9 cabins, modern restrooms with showers, trailer dump station. Fees charged.

Recreation: picnic areas, playgrounds, interpretive center, boat ramp, canoe rentals and pontoon boat tours daily except Wednesday, 1.5-mile hiking trail, ¾-mile nature trail.

WEATHER

July high averages 88 degrees, January low 48 degrees.

MAIN ATTRACTIONS

The park is situated on Big Cypress Bayou near its confluence with Caddo Lake. Though not on the lake proper, the park offers access to its maze of winding waterways. Bald cypress trees draped with Spanish moss line the shore and grow into the shallow portions of the lake. They create a ghostly atmosphere, especially in early-morning fog or against the darkening sky at dusk. Boating and fishing for bass, crappie, bream, and catfish are popular activities.

HIKING

A nature trail and several miles of hiking trails lead the visitor through the dense vegetation, with birds and other creatures calling in the distance. A guide to the trees along the three-quarter-mile interpretive trail is available at the entrance to the park.

PLANTS AND ANIMALS

Its 32,500 acres make Caddo Lake the largest naturally formed lake in the South. Originally, it was created by a massive logjam, which caused a widening of Big Cypress Bayou near its confluence with the Red River. In 1874, the Army Corps of Engineers cleared the jam, and in 1914 it constructed a dam, which maintains the present lake.

Beavers build their lodges in Caddo Lake.

The soil in this area is composed of poorly draining clays with outcroppings of sandy deposits. Pine trees, post oaks, and blackjack oaks occur on the sandy, faster-draining soils; the moist bottomlands are filled with various species of oaks, hickory, flowering dogwood, basswood, sweetgum, American hornbeam, prickly ash, honey locust, walnut, and many other hardwoods. The swampy lake is surrounded and invaded by bald cypress trees, their knees protruding up through the shallow, placid water.

Each spring, the woods come alive with flowering trees. Tiny crimson blossoms cover the leafless limbs of the redbuds, and the snowy flowers of the dogwoods decorate the forest. The white fringe tree, with its delicate flowers, blooms beneath the towering oaks and pines. Many wildflowers, common and rare, as well as ferns, vines, and mushrooms can be seen along the trails.

Wildlife is abundant in the woodlands and along the lakeshore. Deer, raccoons, opossums, squirrels, foxes, and skunks live in the forest. Alligators, turtles, and waterfowl may be seen if one explores the picturesque channels of the lake. Many birds, both resident and migratory, occur in the differing habitats of the park.

HISTORY

Caddo Lake, named after the Indians who once inhabited East Texas, played a significant role in the early history of the state. Before railroads, Port Caddo—second only to Galveston in the amount of cargo shipped—was the port of entry for Northeast Texas. Sidewheeler steamships carried cotton and other freight from Jefferson via Big Cypress Bayou, the Red River, and the Mississippi to New Orleans.

The first locomotive in Texas was used to transport freight 14 miles inland from Swanson's Landing to Jonesville. After the locomotive was melted down during the Civil War, mules were used to pull the railroad cars. Freshwater pearls were discovered in mussels in the lake around the turn of the century, attracting many people to the area for the next decade.

Jefferson, 15 miles northwest on FM 134, was once the most prosperous city in Northeast Texas. Until the 1870s, it was the major river port and manufacturing center in the area—in 1867, Jefferson was the first Texas town to use gas to light its streets, and it boasted the first commercially manufactured ice in 1868. Jefferson had a population over 30,000 before its decline after the railroad was established in nearby Marshall. Much of the splendor of those early years is still preserved, with more than thirty buildings designated as state historic structures. The Jefferson Historic Pilgrimage, held on the first weekend in May, relives the Old South traditions with costumes and festivities.

34. CADDO NATIONAL GRASSLANDS

LOCATION

Fannin County. 43 miles east of Sherman on U.S. 82 to Honey Grove, 11 miles north on FM 100.
Mailing address: 1400 US Hwy 81/287, P.O. Box 507, Decatur, Texas 76234. Phone: 940-627-5475. Internet: www.fs.fed.us/r8/texas.

FACILITIES

Lake Davy Crockett: From Honey Grove north on FM 100 12 miles to FM 409, left ½ mile. Primitive camping sites, picnicking, drinking water, chemical toilets on 388-acre lake, picnic tables and boat ramp on east shore. Fees charged.

Lake Coffee Mill: From Honey Grove, north on FM 100 12 miles, left (west) on FM 409 4.4 miles, south at sign ¼ mile to entrance. Tent camping, chemical toilets, drinking water. Boat ramp, boating, skiing, and fishing on 750-acre lake.

Bois D'Arc equestrian trailhead: From Honey Grove west on U.S. 82 for 1.9 miles to FM 1396, north 11.2 miles to Carson, north 3.9 miles on FM 2029, then east 2.5 miles on FM 409 to trailhead. 18 primitive camping sites, drinking water nearby, chemical toilets. 25-mile equestrian/hiking trail maintained by the Caddo Trailriders Association.

Lake Fannin: From Bonham north 2.7 miles on TX 78 to FM 273/808, north 6 miles on FM 273/808 to FM 273 junction, north 4.6 miles to FM 2554 junction, north on FM 2554 1.3 miles, then turn west into park. 45-acre lake with primitive camping on north shore, drinking water, hike-bike trail around lake, boat launch. Concessionaire rents CCC lodge and cabins (call for status). Fees charged.

MAIN ATTRACTIONS

The Caddo National Grasslands cover 17,830 acres of post oak and blackjack oak savannas and grasslands. The grasslands, scattered throughout Fannin County, are managed for fishing and hunting and leased for cattle grazing. Bobwhite quail, mourning doves, and deer are hunted, and the lakes are stocked with bass, bream, and catfish. Boats on the lakes are restricted to less than 10 horsepower motors.

PLANTS AND ANIMALS

These oak savannas and grasslands are located in the Cross Timbers vegetation zone. Severely eroded by poor agricultural practices in the late 1800s and early 1900s, they were purchased by the federal government in the 1930s. To prevent further erosion, the cattle that are now grazed here are periodically rotated between native grasslands and areas planted in Bermuda grass.

The bison and the prairie dog are two native mammals that once called this part of Texas home. The bison were systematically slaughtered in the late 1800s in an attempt to eliminate a major food source for the Indians. Later, in the 1930s, because they competed with ranchers for range vegetation, millions of prairie dogs were poisoned with strychnine-treated grain.

35. CAMP WOOD: WES COOKSEY PARK

Uvalde County. 35 miles northwest of Uvalde on TX 55, on Lake Nueces. Mailing address: P.O. Box 313, Camp Wood, TX 78833. Phone: 830-597-3223. Internet: www.campwood/cookseypark. Camping: 30 RV/tent sites with water and electricity, some with sewer. Modern restrooms, showers, trailer dump station. Fees charged. Recreation: picnic areas, swimming, fishing, boat ramp. Open all year.

36. CANYON LAKE

LOCATION

U.S. Army Corps of Engineers. Comal County. Project office: 16 miles north of New Braunfels on FM 306. Mailing address: 601 Coe

Campground	water	fee area	flush toilets	season	dump station	warm-water showers	electricity
Canyon Park	•	•		Apr. 1–Sept. 30			
Cranes Mill	•	•		all year		•	
Potters Creek	•	•	•	all year	•	•	•
North Park	•	•		Mar. 1–Oct. 31			

Rd., Canyon Lake, Texas 78133. Phone 830-964-3341. Camping reservations: 877-444-6777, www.recreation.gov. Internet: www.swf-wc.usace.army.mil/canyon/. Click: Recreation.

FACILITIES

Day-use only: Comal Park, open March 1–September 30 from 7 a.m. to sunset, boat ramps, 65 shady picnic sites, swim beach, playground. Canyon Beach Park, swimming beach adjacent to Canyon Park. Overlook Park, on south end of dam site with restrooms and access to the 1-mile Dam Crest Trail, closes at sunset. Guadalupe Park, along river below dam, premier trout fishing location, ADA accessible fishing pier, no restrooms.

CANYON LAKE

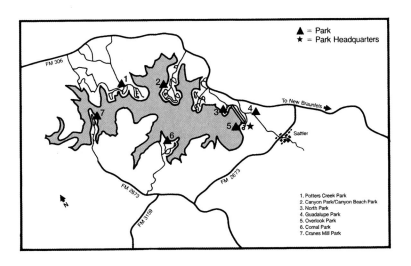

▲ = Park
★ = Park Headquarters

1. Potters Creek Park
2. Canyon Park/Canyon Beach Park
3. North Park
4. Guadalupe Park
5. Overlook Park
6. Comal Park
7. Cranes Mill Park

Potter's Creek: 119 RV/tent sites with water and electricity, group shelter, 10 designated tent sites, 5 group campsites for 2–3 RVs, 7 screened shelters with cold running water, electrical outlets, ceiling fan and picnic table; modern restrooms with showers, two dump stations, two boat ramps, beach swimming area. Fees charged. Reservations through www.recreation.gov.

Canyon Park: 150 campsites (no RV hookups), vault toilets (no showers), boat ramp, swim beach, 3 group pavilions (2 overnight, 1 day use), marina with restaurant and boat rental. Fee charged. Open April 1–September 30.

Crane's Mill Park: 46 campsites (no RV hookups), vault toilets, showers, boat ramp, 24-hour fishing dock, marina with boat rentals. Fees charged. Open year-round 7 a.m. to 10 p.m. with limited camping Oct. 1–Feb. 29.

North Park: 19 campsites (no RV hookups), vault toilets (no showers), no boat ramp; Popular area for SCUBA diving. Fees charged. Open March 1 – Oct. 31.

MAIN ATTRACTIONS

Built for flood control and water storage on the Guadalupe River, Canyon Lake covers 8,231 surface acres at its normal level and has 80 miles of shoreline. It is one of the deepest reservoirs in Texas, with an average depth of 47 feet. Walleye, hybrid striped bass, and small-mouth bass are stocked in the lake, and there is a trout fishery below the dam. There is no hunting on the property. Natural Bridge Caverns, one of the largest and most interesting caves in Texas, is west of New Braunfels off TX 46 on FM 1863. Tubing and white water recreation are popular on the Guadalupe River between the dam and New Braunfels.

Besides the typical water-related activities, Canyon Lake offers a system of trails for hikers, bikers, and horses. Hikers can enjoy scenic views along the 1-mile Dam Crest Trail and the one-fourth mile Guadalupe South Trail along the bald cypress-lined banks of the Guadalupe River. The Madrone Trail, an 8.2-mile hike/bike trail is an intermediate to advanced level single track with several technical sections. The Old Hancock Trail, a 3.5 mile trail along the north shoreline, is open to hikers, bikers, and horse riding.

37. CAPROCK CANYONS STATE PARK AND TRAILWAY

LOCATION

Briscoe County. 50 miles south of Amarillo on IH-27, 45 miles east on TX 86 to Quitaque, 3 miles north on FM 1065.

Mailing address: Box 204, Quitaque, Texas 79255. Phone: 806-455-1492. For all state park reservations, call the centralized reservations system, 512-389-8900, or www.ReserveAmerica.com online. Call the state park information number, 800-792-1112, for information and fee updates.

FACILITIES

Fees: entrance, facility, activity use; subject to change.

Camping: Honea Flat Camping Area, 35 RV/tent sites with water, electricity, modern restrooms, playgrounds, trailer dump station. South Prong Tent Camping Area, 20 primitive sites, chemical toilets. South Prong Primitive Camping Area, walk-in sites, chemical toilets. Little Red Tent Camping Area, 10 primitive sites, chemical toilets. North Prong Primitive Camping Area, 1-mile walk in, chemical toilets. Wild Horse Equestrian Camping Area, 12 sites, 2 10 × 20 foot corrals, no restrooms, no water; 1-mile hike/ride to primitive area for 20 people with 2 corrals, no restrooms, no water.

Recreation: group pavilion in equestrian area, picnic areas; boating, fishing, and swimming in Lake Theo (water levels vary); bison and wildlife viewing, scenic driving tour with free cassette or CD guide ($5 deposit), historic sites, interpretive programs, seasonal horse rentals by concessionaire; 90 miles of hike/bike/equestrian trails that vary from the very difficult in rugged terrain with cliffs and dropoffs, steep climbs, and descents, to trails with less than 3% grade. Texas State Store.

WEATHER

July high averages 91 degrees, January low 19 degrees.

MAIN ATTRACTIONS

The official State Bison Herd and a part of the State Longhorn Herd, as well as wild pronghorns and imported aoudad sheep, graze the extensive grasslands of the 15,314-acre park. The park preserves an area of rugged beauty in the deeply dissected canyons that border the Caprock Escarpment in the Panhandle. Erosion has sculpted picturesque formations and carved scenic canyons in the brick-red sediments. Wildlife is often seen along the trails and roads. Though one of the state's most beautiful parks, the remote location keeps the wilderness setting from being overrun with visitors.

Hiking, mountain biking, and horseback riding are the prime ways to experience the rugged beauty of the canyons leading off the Caprock Escarpment. The Caprock Canyons Trailway connects through the park and offers 64.25 miles for hiking, backpacking, mountain biking, and equestrian use.

Lake Theo covers 120 acres when filled to capacity. During the summer the lake is quite low, and the fishing pier may be well out of the water. The lake is stocked, and catches of channel catfish, largemouth bass, sunfish, and crappie are common. There is also a shaded picnic area and a swimming beach.

HIKING AND HORSEBACK RIDING

Hiking trails ideal for day hikes or backpacking lead through the picturesque canyons, along streambeds at the foot of castlelike formations, and atop ridges overlooking the maze of canyons and the colorful badlands extending eastward. The Upper and Lower Canyon trails form a figure 8, and each has a campground with a composting toilet. The 2-mile Eagles Point Trail connects two day-use areas. The equestrian camping area, three-quarter mile from the equestrian trailhead, has a composting toilet and connects with a 10-mile loop trail and a 1.5-mile trail to a county road. In a "rails to trails" acquisition, a three-county network of old railroad beds has been converted to the 65-mile Caprock Canyons State Park Trailway. The trails, easy grades of 1 percent or less, take hikers and horseback and bicycle riders through a cross section of West Texas ecology from mesquite and sand sage, over the caprock escarpment, and on to the High Plains.

Trailheads about every 10 miles provide parking, camping, water and/ or chemical toilets, depending on the site. Obtain day-use and camping permits and information at the trail headquarters in Quitaque on FM 1065, 806-455-1492.

PLANTS AND ANIMALS

The park is located at the juncture of the High Plains, which extend west into New Mexico, and the Rolling Plains lying to the east. Over eons of time, streams cut deep, convoluted canyons into the escarpment, or cliff, that separates the two plains. Weathering exposed a caprock of erosion-resistant caliche and gravel of the Ogallala formation deposited 3 to 11 million years ago. The Ogallala overlays softer red sandstones and shales approximately 200 million years old and older Permian siltstones laced with crumbling white veins of gypsum. When the protective cap wears away, erosion carves magical formations into the softer layers below. Caprock Canyon and Palo Duro Canyon State Parks illustrate the power of small seasonal streams to sculpt the landscape.

Plants characteristic of both the Rolling Plains and the High Plains grow in the park. In the moist North and South Prong canyons, Rocky Mountain junipers are common, while Mohr shinnery oaks grow on the drier slopes. Cottonwoods grow along wet drainages. The prairies consist of buffalo, grama, and beard grasses as well as yucca and prickly pear and tasajillo cacti. Many of the prairies were overgrazed and have been invaded by mesquite and red-berry juniper trees.

The park is rich in wildlife. An evening drive or hike will often reveal scaled and bobwhite quail, jackrabbits, mule deer, and the impressive aoudad sheep. Introduced in 1957, the sheep increased so rapidly that the park allowed some hunting in the past to reduce the population to a number compatible with the available food supply. Coyotes can be heard serenading the moon, while raccoons, badgers, and the secretive ringtail prowl through the night. Bison, once kings of the prairies, were exterminated in the late 1800s, but once again roam the prairies of the park, along with pronghorn antelopes.

In 1997, Texas Parks and Wildlife relocated almost two dozen Southern Plains Bison from the nearby JA Ranch, originally the 100,000-acre spread founded by Charles Goodnight in 1877. Goodnight, who became one of the state's most renowned ranchers, realized the bison was doomed and established a herd of 200 on an isolated pasture. The genetic purity of that herd has been preserved and used to repopulate Yellowstone and other national parks. Texas Parks and Wildlife hopes the herd will grow to several hundred within several decades.

One of Texas' largest colonies of free-tailed bats resides in 742-foot-long Clarity Tunnel along Caprock Canyons Trailway during their summer breeding season. Every year from mid-August to mid-September the park conducts evening tours to view the bats.

More than 175 species of birds have been seen in the park. Golden eagles nest in the canyons, and such rare birds as the red-necked grebe and the red-throated loon have used the lake during migrations. The steep red cliffs are the home of a ledge-nesting bird familiar to us all but unexpected in this rugged setting: the domestic pigeon. A bird checklist is available.

HISTORY

The north plains of Texas are rich in historic lore of the Comanches, frontier forts, and early cattle barons. After the Comanches were finally driven onto reservations in Oklahoma and the bison were eliminated, ranchers moved onto the plains, herded the longhorns, and later introduced improved breeds of cattle. George Baker established the Quitaque Ranch in what is now the park with 2,000 heads of cattle in 1878.

The famous Panhandle rancher Charles Goodnight, whose two million-acre spread included Palo Duro Canyon, bought Baker's ranch for 22 cents an acre in 1880. The parkland passed through many hands until 1936, when it was purchased by Theo Geisler, who lived there in a dugout house until 1940. The state acquired the land in 1973.

38. CASTROVILLE REGIONAL PARK

Medina County. 20 miles west of San Antonio in Castroville, 6 blocks south of U.S. 90. Mailing address: 816 Alsace Street, Castroville, TX 78009. Phone: 830-931-0033, castrovilleregionalpark@castroville.us. WiFi available (user fee).

This 126 wooded acres on the Medina River originally was part of the McMullen Grant, a parcel of land granted by the Governor of Spain in 1766 to the Indians of Mission San Jose and later deeded to Henri Castro and the Society of the Colonization of Texas. Camping: 40 pull-through RV sites with full hookups, tent camping in designated area, modern restroom with showers, on-site laundry, trailer dump station. Recreation: swimming pool, playground, picnic tables, group pavilions, volleyball and tennis courts, fishing, 11 hiking trails and loops. Fees charged. Open all year.

39. CEDAR HILL STATE PARK

LOCATION

Dallas County. West of Dallas on IH-20, exit FM 1382, 4 miles south. Mailing address: 1570 FM 1382, Cedar Hill, Texas 75104. Phone: 972-291-3900. For all state park reservations, call the centralized reservations system, 512-389-8900, or www. ReserveAmerica.com online. Call the state park information number, 800-792-1112, for information and fee updates.

FACILITIES

Fees: entrance, facility, activity use; subject to change. WiFi available (user fee).

Camping: 355 sites with water, electricity, shaded tables, 30 primitive walk-in sites, modern restrooms, showers, trailer dump station. Campsites vary in size of parking pads and some are multi-level with steps, so specify any special requirements when making reservations. Fees charged. Open 8 a.m. to 10 p.m. for day use, overnight for fishing and camping.

Recreation: 200 picnic tables, 4 playgrounds, 4.5 miles of hiking/backpacking trails, 15 miles of mountain bike trails, stocked perch pond for youngsters, gravel swimming beach, 2 boat ramps (ten lanes), 2 group picnic pavilions (capacities 50 and 100); Joe Pool Marina with ski boat, bass boat, jet ski, and pontoon boat rental, indoor/outdoor fishing barge, convenience store; historic Penn Farm with period buildings.

WEATHER

July high averages 95 degrees, January low 36 degrees.

MAIN ATTRACTIONS

This 1,826-acre wooded park lies on the southwestern shore of Joe Pool Lake and serves the recreational needs of the Dallas-Fort Worth metroplex. The rugged hills, wooded canyons, and prairie grasslands provide a refuge from the asphalt avenues and urban sprawl of the surrounding metroplex. The park sits at the juncture of the limestone hills typical of central Texas and the blackland prairies that once dominated the north Texas landscape.

The rocky hills of the Cedar Mountain Escarpment that rise over Joe Pool Lake drop steeply into the bottomlands of Mountain Creek. Early pioneers farmed the rich blackland soils, grazed livestock on the slopes, and cut the prairie grasses for hay. The 1,100-acre homestead farm of John Anderson Penn exists within the park boundaries. The Penn family lived on the farm, built in 1860, and ranched the area until 1970. The hand-hewn structures and period artifacts provide a glimpse into the daily lifestyle of the first settlers. Many of the original stacked rail fences have survived the years. The reconstructed and historic buildings from the mid-1800s through the mid-1900s serve as an example of the family farms that once typified rural Texas. The farm is open 7 days a week for self-guided tours. Call 972-291-5940 for program information.

Besides 4.5 miles of hiking trails, Cedar Hill State Park is home to the premier North Texas mountain bike trail. The DORBA trail, named for the volunteers of the Dallas Off Road Biking Association, was built by mountain bikers for mountain bikers. More than 1,200 acres are crisscrossed with 15 miles of single-track trails that challenge the technical skills of all riders. The trail is closed after heavy rains. Call 972-291-3900 for trail conditions.

With two lighted fishing jetties and a stocked perch pond for youngsters, fishing is a popular park activity. Lake fishing brings in catches of largemouth black bass, crappie, and catfish. Boating, water and jet skiing, and swimming are major summer activities on the lake. The park provides 2 concrete, 4-lane boat ramps and lighted boat trailer parking.

PLANTS AND ANIMALS

Prairies, such as the one that gave the nearby town Grand Prairie its name, once dominated the landscape from north Texas to Canada. Farming destroyed this important plant and animal association that was unique to North America. Cedar Hill preserves 5 small remnants of native tall grass prairie, which are the most important natural resource in the park. The tall grass prairies association includes Indian grass, little bluestem, big bluestem, sideoats gama, switch grass, and many species of wildflowers.

The combination of rugged hills, remnant prairies, wooded canyons, and the impounded lake creates a variety of wildlife habitats. Upland forests of cedar elm, honey locust, mesquite, and juniper trees provide shelter for bobcats, coyotes, foxes, squirrels, armadillos, and raccoons. Nearly 200 species of birds occur in the park through the year, including the flamboyant painted bunting.

The rocky hills may look tough, but as an example of the delicate balance between plants and animals and human land use, several birds that once thrived in the tallgrass prairie and juniper-oak woodlands of the park are extinct, threatened, or no longer present in the diminished habitats of the region. The tallgrass prairie, now urbanized, was essential migratory habitat for the Eskimo Curlew now considered extinct. The endangered golden-cheeked warbler, which nests only in old-growth juniper-oak forests of central Texas, was spotted in the park in 2004 after an absence of 35 years. The endangered black-capped vireo, another songbird suffering from habitat destruction by ranchers and urban sprawl, nests in the brushy transition zone between prairie and forest. Without periodic fires, the woodlands overgrow the brushy habitat. The vireo disappeared from the park in 1993.

NEARBY ATTRACTIONS

The City of Grand Prairie operates two parks on Joe Pool Lake (see separate listing). Loyd Park (open year round) has full camping and recreational facilities. Lynn Creek Park (open March through October) offers lake swimming and picnic facilities. The 633-acre Cedar Ridge Preserve, formerly the Dallas Nature Center, offers 10 miles of hiking trails, a native plant nursery, butterfly gardens, and picnic areas. Operated by the Audubon Dallas, the preserve is 20 minutes outside of Dallas at 7171 Mountain Creek Parkway, 972-709-7784. Closed Mondays.

40. CHILDRESS: BAYLOR/CHILDRESS LAKES

Childress County. From Childress, north 2 miles on U.S. 287, west on Rt. 238 to FM 2466, 2.5 miles to Lake Childress, 2 miles farther west to Lake Baylor. Mailing address: 231 Bluebonnet Lane, Childress, TX 79201. Phone: 940-937-2102. Facilities: Lake Baylor, South Ramp, 15 hookups with water, electricity, modern restrooms, showers, trailer dump station; North Ramp, primitive camping, no facilities. Lake Childress, primitive camping, no facilities. Call ahead for water conditions. As of 2008, the lakes had received no appreciable runoff in over a decade and the boat ramps were high and dry.

41. CHINATI MOUNTAINS STATE NATURAL AREA

LOCATION

Presidio County. 22 miles west of Presidio on FM 170.
Mailing address: c/o Big Bend Ranch State Park, Box 2319, Presidio, Texas 79845. Phone: 432-229-3416.

FACILITIES

Until a management plan outlining appropriate use of the Chinati tract is created, the site is closed to the public.

MAIN ATTRACTION

Formerly known as the Mesquite Ranch, the 37,885-acre property lies near the Rio Grande in the Chinati Mountains, the fourth highest mountain range in Texas. It is just west of Big Bend Ranch State Park. The Richard King Mellon Foundation donated the property in 1996 as part of its American Land Conservation Program, which secures nationally significant sites across the U.S. through the Conservation Fund.

PLANTS AND ANIMALS

Located in the Chihuahuan Desert, the park has plant and wildlife species similar to the nearby Big Bend National Park and Big Bend Ranch State Park. The site supports 16 species of bats, making it one of the most diverse concentrations of bat species in the U.S. The highly diverse terrain includes dramatic granite bluffs, spring-filled woodland canyons, and grass and wooded plateaus. The elevation varies from 3,200 feet at Mesquite Headquarters to 7,728 feet atop Chinati Peak. Average rainfall is 14.8 inches, with a January average low temperature of 32°F and July average high of 89°F.

42. CHOKE CANYON STATE PARK

LOCATION

McMullen and Live Oak counties.
South Shore Unit: 4 miles west of Three Rivers on TX 72.
Calliham Unit: 11 miles west of Three Rivers on TX 72. Mailing address: Box 2, Calliham, Texas 78007. Phone: 361-786-3868. For all state park reservations, call the centralized reservations system, 512-389-8900, or www.ReserveAmerica.com online. Call the state park information number, 800-792-1112, for information and fee updates.

FACILITIES

Fees: entrance, facility, activity use; subject to change.

Note: Campers arriving after 10 p.m. must call the park before 5 p.m. to get the gate combination. Park gates open 5 a.m. to 10 p.m.

South Shore Unit: day-use only, boat launch, 3 picnic shelters, 1 group picnic shelter, modern restrooms, fish cleaning station, open 6 a.m.–10 p.m.

Calliham Unit

Camping: 40 back-in RV/tent sites with water and electricity, 16 walk-in lakefront tent sites with water and tables, group camping area, restrooms with showers, trailer dump station. Fees charged.

Recreation: boat ramp, picnic area, and 20 screened shelters; group dining hall (capacity 100) with outdoor grills and restrooms; group recreation hall (capacity 40) with kitchen, barbecue pit; sports complex with gymnasium (with stage, folding chairs, and air-conditioning and heating-capacity 300); shuffleboard, tennis, volleyball, and full basketball courts; man-made, 75-acre lake; 2-mile hiking trail and 1-mile birding trail; wildlife educational center with programs.

North Shore Equestrian Area: 1,200 acres of gently rolling brush land and rugged and rocky terrain with 18 miles of trails. Available for use only Saturdays and Sundays from 8:00 a.m. to 5:00 p.m. Permits and reservations required from Calliham Headquarters.

WEATHER

July high averages 95 degrees, January minimum 41 degrees.

MAIN ATTRACTIONS

Water sports, wildlife, and a day away from the city attract visitors to this park. Fishermen troll the waters for largemouth, striped, and white bass, crappie, sunfish, and flathead, channel, and blue catfish. Swimmers, boaters, and skiers play in the lake while picnickers enjoy the shoreline and game courts. Bird-watchers look for crested caracaras, or Mexican eagles, turkeys, herons, egrets, ducks, and other wading and water birds and migrants attracted to the reservoir. A wooded camping and picnicking area exists along the river below the dam in the South Unit. Brushy scrub growth typical of South Texas covers the shoreline and most of the park.

Choke Canyon was named for the "choking" of floodwaters by the steep banks of the Frio River. An earthen dam impounds the river just upstream from Three Rivers, where the Frio, Atascosa, and Nueces rivers join. The 26,000-acre lake supplies water for Corpus Christi. In addition to the 1,485 acres set aside for the two state park units, the James Daugherty Wildlife Management Area preserves 8,700 acres for hunting.

PLANTS AND ANIMALS

Choke Canyon lies in the northern portion of the Rio Grande Plains vegetational region of Texas. Thorny chaparral and mesquite-grassland savannas characterize this area. Huisache, black brush, guajillo, prickly pear, mesquite, and other shrubby, thorny plants cover the rocky, rolling hills and alluvial plains. As early as February, bluebonnets, paintbrushes, huisache daisies, and firewheels blanket the countryside with myriad colors.

This area has been ranching country since the first longhorn was roped and branded. Though overgrazing has allowed mesquite and chaparral to invade the grasslands, most of the area retains its wild character. As a result, wildlife abounds. White-tailed deer, Rio Grande turkeys, javelinas, and coyotes claim the brushlands as their home and often roam through the state park, and alligators live in the reservoir.

HISTORY

This area of Texas gave birth to the legend of the cowboy and the cattle drive. After the Civil War, the state of Texas was bankrupt, many of the men had been killed in action, and millions of wild longhorns roamed the chaparral thickets of South Texas. But the only profit from the ornery cows came from skinning them and shipping their hides to New Orleans. When the railroads brought the eastern markets as close as Kansas, Texans saw a fortune in the wild cattle and began the longest and largest human-influenced migration ever. Within twenty years, railroads reached Texas and a colorful era of American history ended, but the indomitable spirit of the cowboy had forever burned its brand into the American psyche. Folk historian and author J. Frank Dobie grew up in nearby Tilden. His numerous books on the ranching, wildlife, and folklore of South Texas bring that rich era alive for modern generations.

43. CLEBURNE STATE PARK

LOCATION

Johnson County. 7 miles west of Cleburne on U.S. 67, 6 miles south on PR 21.
Mailing address: 5800 Park Rd. 21, Cleburne, Texas 76031. Phone: 817-645-4215. For all state park reservations, call the centralized reservations system, 512-389-8900, or www.ReserveAmerica.com online. Call the state park information number, 800-792-1112, for information and fee updates.

FACILITIES

Camping: 58 back-in RV/tent sites with water and electricity, some with sewage, 6 screened shelters, group facilities (2 bunkhouses, kitchen, dining hall, capacity 48 people). Modern restrooms, trailer dump station. Fees charged.

Recreation: picnic areas and playgrounds, hiking/nature trail, swimming in Cedar Lake, fishing, boating (5-mph speed limit), boat rentals, store (summer only).

WEATHER

July high averages 97.4 degrees, January low 34 degrees.

MAIN ATTRACTIONS

Fishing, canoeing, and sailing on the spring-fed lake are the primary attractions in this 528-acre park. The crystal springs, now under Cedar Lake, have attracted many to their clear waters. The springs were well known to Indians, and Comanches are said to have made frequent encampments nearby. Over a hundred years ago, wild horses are thought to have been corralled in the area—look for the barbed wire still embedded in the trees. In more recent times, bootleggers used the springwater for their brew.

PLANTS AND ANIMALS

The dominant tree in the park is the Ashe juniper, which forms dense cedar brakes on the thin soil overlying the Edwards and Comanche Peak limestones. Around and below the lake grow Texas and bur oaks, hackberry, elm, and Texas ash. Smaller trees and shrubs include flame-leaf sumac, catclaw acacia, redbud, and Mexican buckeye.

The spring-fed lake attracts many species of birds, including the endangered golden-cheeked warbler. Large numbers of black and turkey vultures roost in the trees surrounding the lake. In the early-morning hours, white-tailed deer are commonly seen grazing in the open mead-

Early morning fog blankets the small lake at Cleburne State Park.

ows. Dawn and dusk are the best times to look for raccoons, opossums, and skunks, and occasionally a mountain lion may be sighted.

The still of the evening may be accented by the serenade of coyotes or the hooting of owls. In the fall, an early-morning fog sometimes hangs over the lake, creating an eerie mood, while in the spring bluebonnets and other wildflowers bloom profusely.

44. COLORADO BEND STATE PARK

LOCATION

San Saba County. West of Lampasas on FM 580 to Bend, south on gravel road at sign for state park for 4 miles. Mailing address: Box 118, Bend, Texas 76824. Phone: 325-628-3240.

FACILITIES

Fees: entrance, facility, activity use; subject to change.

Camping: 22 drive-up tent sites and 14 riverbank sites with picnic tables, water nearby, 2 group camp areas, 2 backpacking areas, composting toilets. Fees charged.

Recreation: picnicking, swimming in river, fishing, boat ramp, mountain biking, hiking, backpacking. Weekend tours of Gorman Falls and the wild caves are offered; fee charged. Call the park to reserve tours. Visitation limited to capacity of the parking lot, about 300 cars, which is rarely reached.

WEATHER

July high averages 98 degrees, January low 33 degrees.

MAIN ATTRACTIONS

This 5,328-acre park preserves a section of the Colorado River long known for good fishing and splendid scenery. The cypress-lined river winds past high cut banks, a 60-foot waterfall, and floodplains forested with giant pecan, sycamore, and oak trees. The park has 15.8 miles of hiking trails and 14 miles of mountain bike trails that explore the rugged hills, springs and creeks, and riverbank woodlands.

Two of the most scenic attractions in the park, Gorman Falls and the undeveloped wild caves, can be visited only on a weekend guided tour. Gorman Creek, a spring-fed stream, flows through the park and plummets over a high cliff to the river below. Travertine formations border the rim and decorate the cliffside of this spectacular waterfall, and fern and mosses thrive in the splash zones. Such delicate formations and plant life could easily be destroyed by overuse by park visitors. Visitors on the cave tour can expect crawling through small and sometimes difficult passages. Hard hats are supplied, but you must bring flashlights.

The wooded hills and riparian woodlands along the river provide habitat for some 155 species of birds. Of the Hill country specialties in the area, the endangered golden-cheeked warbler and black-capped vireo nest in the park. In the winter, bald eagles sometimes venture up the river from Lake Buchanan, 10 miles downstream.

45. COOPER LAKE STATE PARK

LOCATION

Hopkins County. Doctors Creek Unit, Delta County. East of Commerce on TX 24 to Cooper, east for 1 mile on TX 154, south for 2 miles on FM 1529 to the park entrance; or north from Interstate 30 at Exit 122 on the west side of Sulphur Springs for 14 miles on TX 19, then west on County Road 4795 for 2 miles to the Corps of Engineers office, cross the lake dam and drive ½ mile farther to the park entrance.

South Sulphur Unit, Hopkins County. Take I-30, Exit 122 (west of Sulphur Springs) north for 10 miles on TX 19, west on TX 71 for 4 miles, north for 1 mile on FM 3505 to the park entrance; or east from Commerce on TX 71 for 16 miles, north for 1 mile on FM 3505 to the park entrance.

Mailing address: Cooper Lake State Park, Doctors Creek Unit, 1664 FM 1529 South, Cooper, Texas 75432. Phone: 903-395-3100. South Sulphur Unit, 1690 FM 3505, Sulphur Springs TX 75482. Phone: 903-945-5256. For all state park reservations, call the centralized reservations system, 512-389-8900, or www. ReserveAmerica.com online. Call the state park information number, 800-792-1112, for information and fee updates.

FACILITIES

Fees: entrance, facility, activity use; subject to change.

Camping: Doctors Creek Unit—42 back-in RV/tent sites with water and electricity, 5 screened shelters, 2 cottages with A/C, modern restrooms, showers, trailer dump station. Fees charged. South Sulphur Unit: 87 back-in RV/tent sites with water and electricity, 15 walk-in tent sites, 15 equestrian sites, 14 furnished lakeside cabins, 18 screened shelters, 4 with A/C, beds (no linens), microwave and fridge; modern restrooms, showers, trailer dump station. Fees charged.

Recreation: Doctor's Creek—picnic area, 2 playgrounds, sandy swimming beach, 3-lane boat ramp, fish cleaning table, volleyball court, amphitheater, picnic pavilion (capacity 50), 1-mile nature trail, 2–3-mile hike/bike trail. South Sulphur Unit—3 picnic areas, playgrounds, 2 lighted fishing piers, 2 boat ramps, pavilion (capacity 100), 5-mile hike/bike trail, 10.5-mile equestrian trail, amphitheater, volleyball court, sandy swimming beach, Texas State Park Store.

WEATHER

July high averages 94 degrees, January low 30 degrees.

MAIN ATTRACTIONS

The 3,026-acre Cooper Lake State Park consists of two units, Doctors Creek Unit, 715.5 acres and South Sulphur Unit, 2,310 acres. In addition to the normal shoreline and water sports activities of impounded lakes, both units offer hiking and nature trails accessible to backpacking, mountain biking, and horses. Both weekend anglers and professional guides consider the 19,000-acre Cooper Lake to be one of the best all-around fishing lakes in the region. Species commonly caught include blue and channel catfish, blue gill, Florida largemouth bass, crappie, and hybrid striped bass.

PLANTS AND ANIMALS

Construction on the South Sulphur River to form Cooper Lake, 19,300 acres, began in 1986 and was completed in 1991. Doctors Creek Unit opened January 3, 1996; South Sulphur Unit opened April 27, 1996. Both park units are leased from the U.S. Army Corps of Engineers for 25 years.

The vegetation of Cooper Lake State Park is dominated by post oak and various native grass species. Other tree species include winged elm, bois d'arc, Texas sugarberry, eastern red cedar, roughleaf dogwood, eastern persimmon, American elm, honey locust, and mesquite. Wildlife includes swamp rabbits, eastern cottontails, nine-banded armadillos, white-tailed deer, coyotes, bobcats, various waterfowl, bald eagles, beavers, raccoons, and wild hogs.

46. COPPER BREAKS STATE PARK

LOCATION

Hardeman County. 30 miles east of Childress on U.S. 287 to Quanah, 12 miles south on TX 6.

Mailing address: 777 Park Road 62, Quanah, Texas 79252-7679. Phone: 940-839-4331. For all state park reservations, call the centralized reservations system, 512-389-8900, or www.ReserveAmerica.com online. Call the state park information number, 800-792-1112, for information and fee updates.

FACILITIES

Fees: entrance, facility, activity use; subject to change.

Camping: 11 campsites with water only, 25 campsites with water and electricity, 10 campsites with water only for equestrian use, group campground with water only, modern restrooms with showers, trailer dump station. Fees charged.

Recreation: picnic areas and playgrounds; half-mile nature trail with trailguide pamphlet; 9.5-mile trail for backpacking, mountain biking, and equestrian use; excellent interpretive exhibits; swimming beach, boat ramp, dock, fishing pier, and 2 lakes with summer paddleboat rentals; state longhorn herd; amphitheater with theatrical production in June, Texas State Park Store.

WEATHER

July high averages 97 degrees, January low 24 degrees.

MAIN ATTRACTIONS

Fishing and swimming are popular activities at Lake Copper Breaks, a 60-acre impoundment of Devils Creek. The lake is stocked with catfish, bass, and perch. A self-guided nature trail identifies many of the plants and explains the ecology of the area. An excellent museum, located in the headquarters building, explains the history of the Indians in the region, ranching, and early pioneer life. Also featured are taxidermy and paintings of the wildlife and exhibits of the plants of the North Texas plains. Part of the state longhorn herd is kept in the park.

PLANTS AND ANIMALS

The terrain of the parks consists of 2,000 acres of rolling plains broken by hills and canyons. The red shales and clays forming the colorful hills were deposited 230 million years ago during the Permian age. Low-grade copper deposits give a greenish tint to strata scattered through the area. Mining was once attempted but proved unsuccessful.

This part of North Texas was once covered with grasslands of grama, bluestem, Indiangrass, cottontop, and other species. Large herds of bison grazed the rolling hills, and pronghorn antelope bounded across the prairies unimpeded by fences. After the bison were eliminated by buf-

Fishing is popular in Copper Breaks State Park.

falo hunters, cattle were introduced and allowed to severely overgraze the land.

Without the grasses to protect the fragile land, erosion stripped away much of the topsoil, and brushy plants became established. Today, mesquite trees and red-berry junipers dominate. Originally, grasslands covered 60 to 70 percent of the land; now they occupy less than 30 percent.

The park is home to an abundance of wildlife adapted to the mesquite and juniper woodlands. Mule deer, rabbits, raccoons, armadillos, opossums, bobcats, porcupines, coyotes, songbirds, raptors, and lizards frequent the rugged canyons. Ducks, herons, and aquatic life live in the lakes. Each winter, Lake Copper Breaks is stocked with rainbow trout. Wildlife and bird checklists are available at the park headquarters.

HISTORY

The history of the park, and of all of North Texas, is deeply involved with the Comanche and Kiowa Indians, the efforts to drive the Indians onto Oklahoma reservations, and the development of ranching.

Of particular historical interest is the capture of Cynthia Ann Parker in 1860 by Texas Ranger Captain Sul Ross on the Pease River, three miles from the park. The Comanches originally captured Cynthia Ann in 1836 when she was nine years old on a raid of Fort Parker near present day Mexia. (See Old Fort Parker.) Cynthia married the chief and had three children. Her son, Quanah, became the last of the Comanche war chiefs and was finally forced to surrender after losing a battle in Palo Duro Canyon. He moved to the reservation in Oklahoma and became an Indian leader and confidant of President Teddy Roosevelt. After her recapture, Cynthia Ann never adjusted to the ways of the whites and soon died of a broken heart.

Brown pelicans often rest on the fishing pier at Padre Balli Park.

47. CORPUS CHRISTI: PADRE BALLI PARK

Nueces County. On the north end of Padre Island, from Corpus Christi, southeast on PR 22. Mailing address: 15820 Park Road 22, Corpus Christi, TX 78418. Phone: 361-949-8121. Camping: 54 RV sites with water, electricity, bathhouse and laundry, trailer dump station; 12 paved tent pads with water and electricity, primitive beach camping; restrooms, cold-water rinse showers for tent campers and public. Fees charged. Recreation: swimming in the Gulf of Mexico, 1,240-foot lighted fishing pier, boating, concessions. Open all year.

48. DAINGERFIELD STATE PARK

LOCATION

Morris County. 40 miles north of Longview on U.S. 259 to Daingerfield, 2 miles east on TX 49.
Mailing address: 455 Park Road 17, Daingerfield, Texas 75638.
Phone: 903-645-2921. For all state park reservations, call the centralized reservations system, 512-389-8900, or www.ReserveAmerica.com online. Call the state park information number, 800-792-1112, for information and fee updates.

FACILITIES

Fees: entrance, facility, activity use; subject to change.

Camping: 10 pull-through RV/tent sites with full hookups, 40 back-in sites with water and electricity, 12 tent sites, group lodge (20 people, five bedrooms, two baths, weekend reservation required), modern restrooms, showers, overflow camping. Fees charged.

Recreation: picnic areas, playgrounds, swimming in Lake Daingerfield, boating (5 mph speed limit), boat ramp and dock, fishing pier with fish-cleaning facility, 2.5-mile hiking trail, seasonal pedal boat and canoe rentals (March–October), amphitheater, Texas State Park Store.

WEATHER

July high averages 94 degrees, January low 42 degrees.

MAIN ATTRACTIONS

The park preserves 551 acres of beautiful mixed pine-hardwood forest and includes a picturesque 80-acre lake. A scenic hiking trail circles the lake, which is stocked for fishing. Swimming, canoeing, and paddleboating are popular. In early April, the park roads, campgrounds, and picnic areas are covered with a canopy of snow-white dogwood blossoms, and in the fall, brilliant colors decorate the park.

PLANTS AND ANIMALS

The forest surrounding the small reservoir is an excellent example of East Texas woodland dominated by loblolly pines and a variety of oak species. Seepages along the porous hillsides support a rich growth of woodland herbs, including luxuriant cinnamon ferns.

Lake Daingerfield is the home of domesticated ducks eager to accept food from park visitors. More interesting to bird-watchers are the rare red-cockaded woodpeckers and the large, red-crested pileated woodpeckers that can be heard drumming against dead pine trees in the forest; a checklist of birds is available at the park headquarters. Squirrels, rabbits, deer, and armadillos are commonly seen in the park.

HISTORY

The first iron plant in Texas was built near the park in 1855. Other plants were soon constructed in the area, including one operated by the Confederate government to manufacture gun barrels. Production had virtually ceased by 1910 but was renewed during World War II, when the government built the plant now owned by the Lone Star Steel Company.

Today, Daingerfield State Park is located in the center of the iron-smelting industry in East Texas. Morris and the three surrounding counties have the only iron ore deposits that presently can be mined economically in Texas. The deposits of brown ore occur as nodules or thin strata near the tops of the sand-covered hills.

49. DAVIS HILL STATE PARK

LOCATION

Liberty County. 1 mile north of SH 105, approximately 16 miles east of Cleveland.
Mailing address: c/o Park Region 4 Headquarters, 105 San Jacinto, La Porte, Texas 77571. Phone: 281-471-3200. For all state park reservations, call the centralized reservations system, 512-389-8900, or www.ReserveAmerica.com online. Call the state park information number, 800-792-1112, for information and fee updates.

FACILITIES

The park is closed to the public pending development with access only by special request. Before a master plan can be established, a baseline inventory of the number and species of plants and animals and the historical and archaeological resources must be conducted.

MAIN ATTRACTIONS

Davis Hill is a salt dome mound 1.5 miles in diameter rising 265 feet high in elevation. Salt domes form when underground pressures force a column of salt toward the surface and create a mound. The park occupies 1,734 acres on the west bank of the Trinity River with one mile of frontage along Davis Bayou. Vegetation is similar to the Big Thicket National Preserve with pine-oak woodlands, meandering streams, and prairies.

Davis Hill was named after General James K. Davis, an influential political and military figure throughout the 1800s. Davis served as Adjutant General of the Texas Army in 1842 and a member of the 1848 Constitutional Convention. He and his family moved to Texas from Alabama in 1834 and established the Lake Creek Plantation in 1843. The plantation occupied 300 acres on the flanks of Davis Hill near Davis Bayou. Historical documentation indicates Davis raised cotton and owned about 35 slaves. Hopefully, research will yield clues to the land-use history of Davis Hill in order to better manage the park's cultural and natural resources.

50. DAVIS MOUNTAINS STATE PARK

LOCATION

Jeff Davis County. 30 miles northwest of Alpine on TX 118 through Fort Davis.

Mailing address: Box 1458, Fort Davis, Texas 79734. Phone: headquarters 915-426-3337, Indian Lodge 432-426-3254. For all state park reservations, call the centralized reservations system, 512-389-8900, or www.ReserveAmerica.com online. Call the state park information number, 800-792-1112, for information and fee updates.

FACILITIES

Fees: entrance, facility, activity use; subject to change.

Camping: 27 pull-through RV/tent sites with full hookups and cable TV, 34 sites with water and electricity, 33 tent sites, primitive camping area. Modern restrooms, showers, trailer dump station. Indian Lodge hotel with 39 rooms. Fees charged.

Limpia Canyon Primitive Area: this special use area of the park north of Hwy 118 includes 10 miles of backcountry hiking trails with primitive tent campsites, primitive equestrian campsites. Access is through gated entry with secure parking. Fees charged.

Recreation: picnic areas and playgrounds, hiking trails, interpretive exhibits (summer only), swimming pool for Indian Lodge guests, amphitheater with summer programs, restaurant, Texas State Park Store.

MAIN ATTRACTIONS

Davis Mountains State Park, 1,869 acres of rolling foothills, includes the most scenic portions of Keesey Creek and Keesey Canyon. The area is renowned for its scenic vistas, its expansive ranches, McDonald Observatory, and the reconstructed Fort Davis. This is one of the most beautiful state parks in Texas.

The park's interpretive center provides information about the geology, plants, and animals of the Davis Mountains. The center overlooks a wildlife watering station that attracts many birds, squirrels, and other animals. Interpretive programs are scheduled throughout the summer.

The 74-mile Davis Mountains Skyline Drive is one of the most impressive and highest roads in the state. The drive passes through wooded canyons, past the state park and observatory, and along beautiful Limpia Creek; the loop returns through the town of Fort Davis.

The scenic loop passes the University of Texas' McDonald Observatory, which crowns the top of the 6,809-foot Mount Locke. The Visitors Center offers daily tours of the research facilities and solar viewing programs. On Tuesday, Friday, and Saturday evenings, public Star Parties allow visitors to view the heavens through a 22-inch and a 16-inch fully computerized telescope, both housed in domes. The telescope park also includes a 22-inch Newtonian telescope, an 8-inch, fixed-eyepiece scope, a 14-inch Celestron telescope, and a pair of 14 3 100-mm Parks Optics binoculars. The Visitors Center includes exhibits and a gift shop. For more information, call 432-426-3640 or see http://mcdonaldobservatory.org/visitors.

A windmill and tank provide water for wildlife at Davis Mountains State Park.

HIKING

Nine miles of hiking trails wander through the developed southern section of the park. A 2-mile loop circles habitat for the rare Montezuma quail and connects with a 1.5-mile spur to Indian Lodge. Another .5-mile spur connects to park headquarters. A 4.5-mile one-way trail traverses a mountain ridge with scenic panoramas of the plains below. The trail leaves the park and descends to historic Fort Davis National Historic Site. A shorter hike is possible by intersecting the trail at the scenic overlook on the park's Skyline Drive, which parallels the trail.

PLANTS AND ANIMALS

The park encompasses both the desert plains grasslands, which surround the mountains, and the oak-pinyon-juniper woodlands common to the intermediate elevations. Emory and gray oaks and one-seed juniper are the dominant trees in the park. Conspicuous shrubs include the yellow trumpet flower, evergreen sumac, little-leaf leadtree, Apache plume, little walnut, and catclaw acacia. In the spring and summer, the grasslands and slopes abound with evening primrose, red penstemon, scarlet gilia, and blue flax. Bluebonnets cover the slopes at the lower elevations and provide breathtaking scenes.

Birds representative of both the desert grasslands and the mountain woodlands are found in the park. More than 140 species have been recorded, including the rare Montezuma quail, which has been eliminated from most of its original range. Scrub jays are common camp visitors, and barn swallows can be seen in the spring nesting under the eaves of Indian Lodge. A checklist is available.

The Davis Mountains, the most extensive mountain complex in the state, are a series of large, irregularly shaped peaks capped with flat layers of volcanic rock. Within the park, reddish brown and gray lava flows and crumbling, soft to glassy volcanic material called tuff are prevalent.

The rocks exposed in Keesey Canyon, in the heart of the park, and behind the parade grounds of Fort Davis are a type of lava called rhyolite. The volcanic rocks of the Davis Mountains are believed to have oozed up to the surface through multiple fractures in the earth's crust. More recent faulting in the area has split the volcanic rock layers, with as much as 200 feet of vertical displacement in some sections. Prominent faulting is evident near the Barrel Springs State Route sign on the scenic loop.

Outside the park, several peaks formed by intrusive igneous material are found. Mount Livermore and Sawtooth Mountain were formed by pluglike intrusions of molten rock that pushed upward through the earth, cooled before reaching the surface, and were later exposed by erosion. Mount Livermore, 8,381 feet high, is the dominant feature of the range. Blue Mountain, at 7,331 feet, rises southwest of Indian Lodge; Sawtooth Mountain is visible from the scenic loop drive; and Mount Locke, at 6,809 feet and topped by McDonald Observatory, is northwest of the park.

The boulders at the Rock Pile Roadside Park, along the scenic loop drive, came from small intrusions forming a rock called syenite. The famous polished boulders are believed to have been used by the Indians for defleshing animal skins.

HISTORY

The Davis Mountains are rich in historic lore. In the mid-1800s, Mescalero Apaches lived in the mountains and had a farming village near the present site of Fort Davis. They irrigated their fields with water diverted from Limpia Creek. The Comanches camped in the area on their migrations from Oklahoma to Mexico.

In 1849, an overland route for the stage from San Antonio to San Diego was surveyed through the Davis Mountains. Henry Skillman established three stage stations in the mountains to allow drivers to change horses and to provide accommodation for the passengers.

The Indians resisted the encroachment of the Anglos with repeated attacks on the mail coaches and wagon trains. In 1854, Fort Davis, named after Jefferson Davis, the U.S. secretary of war and later president of the Confederacy, was established to combat the hostile Indians.

McDonald Observatory with its visitor center and programs is a short distance from Davis Mountains State Park.

The fort was abandoned during the Civil War and reoccupied in 1867. By 1885, the Indians had been driven from the area, and the fort was decommissioned in 1891.

Partially rebuilt by concerned citizens in the 1940s, Fort Davis was purchased by the U.S. Congress in 1963 and became a national historic site. The remaining adobe and stone buildings were reconstructed. The eighteen residences on Officers' Row, two troop barracks, a warehouse, and the hospital now stand as they did originally; there is also a museum. The fort, which broadcasts a recorded military parade and mounted review across the parade grounds, provides a vivid perspective on a bygone era. Fort Davis is the most impressive example in the nation of the frontier forts that once stretched across the West to protect early settlers.

51. DAVY CROCKETT NATIONAL FOREST

LOCATION

Off Hwy 7, 28 miles west of Lufkin and 15 miles east of Crockett. Mailing address: 18551 State Highway 7 East, Kennard, TX 75847. Phone: 936-655-2299. Internet: www.fs.fed.us/r8/texas/

FACILITIES

Camping: Camping is permitted throughout the forest except during fall deer hunting season when it's restricted to 20 designated hunter campsites. You can camp anywhere and along the 20-mile Four C National Recreation Trail which begins at Radcliff Lake. Midway, the Walnut Creek campsite has five tent pads, a shelter, and pit toilet. Neches Bluff Overlook, located at the north end of the trail in the Neches River bottomland pine-hardwood forests, has picnicking and primitive camping facilities. The 54-mile Piney Creek Horse Tail has 2 designated campsites. Water and pit toilets are available at the Piney Creek Trailhead.

The USFS advises that beginning in May the heat, ticks, mosquitoes, and chiggers combine to make hiking, backpacking, and horseback riding "an ordeal." The best seasons for using the trails are spring and autumn. Always take insect repellent.

Ratcliff Lake Recreation Area: 76 RV/tent sites (26 with electrical hookups), hot and/or cold water showers. Recreation: picnicking, swimming, bathhouse, boating (no gas motors), barrier-free fishing pier, 1.5-mile "Tall Pines" hiking trail, ¾-mile "Trail Tamers" ADA accessible trail. Fees charged.

MAIN ATTRACTIONS

Davy Crockett National Forest, covering 161,497 acres in Houston and Trinity counties, is bordered on the northeast by the Neches River. The forest includes Ratcliff Lake, a 45-acre lake offering fishing, swimming, and boating—electric motors, paddleboats, and canoes only. Concessions, a bathhouse, and two day-use picnic pavilions are available. In the summer months, park rangers present programs at the amphitheater and conduct guided walks on a 1.5-mile forest trail.

In early March, dogwood trees fill the forest with splashes of white blossoms amid barren limbs of the deciduous trees. The forest roads offer numerous scenic drives. Tour signs direct drivers along the most beautiful routes. The Dogwood Trail Tour follows Forest Service Road 509 in the Alabama Creek Wildlife Management Area southeast of the Apple Springs Work Center. The USFS provides maps and audio tour tapes of the forest and the Ratcliff Lake Recreation Area in English and Spanish.

Piney Creek Horse Trail meanders 54 miles through the Davy Crockett National Forest. The primitive trail follows Forest Service roads, tram roads, pipeline right-of-ways, game trails, highways, and cleared forest trails. Trailhead parking area is available at the main access points, and triangular markers indicate the route. Camping is permitted anywhere along the trail and at the two horse camps. One camp has potable water.

HIKING AND CANOEING

A 1½-mile "Tall Pines" trail leads through the park. The Four C National Recreation Trail begins at Ratcliff Lake and travels through 20 miles of forest to the Neches Overlook. Primitive campgrounds are available along the trail, but there is no potable water. The hiking trail passes through the 4,000-acre Big Slough Wilderness Area. The Big Slough Canoe Trail, within the wilderness, is not maintained and is difficult to traverse. For maps and other information, contact the district headquarters.

52. DEVILS RIVER STATE NATURAL AREA

LOCATION

Val Verde County. North from Del Rio on TX 277 for 45 miles, turn left on Dolan Creek Rd. (gravel) and go 18.6 miles to the park boundary.
Mailing address: HC 01, Box 513, Del Rio, Texas 78840. Phone: 830-395-2133. For all state park reservations, call the centralized reservations system, 512-389-8900, or www.ReserveAmerica.com online. Call the state park information number, 800-792-1112, for information and fee updates.

FACILITIES

Fees: entrance, facility, activity use; subject to change.

Camping: 7 primitive campsites accessible by vehicle but with no potable water—bring your own. A group dining hall with well-equipped kitchen and a large conference room are available. A bunkhouse contains 5 rooms with 2 single bunk beds per room. Mattresses are provided, but not linens and pillows. The facilities include two restrooms with showers and lavatories. Rooms can be rented separately.

Recreation: 12-mile loop hike/bike trail. River access (1.5 miles) by hiking, biking, or park tour only. The park has a put-in point, but no take out, for canoes and kayaks. Nearest take out is 10 miles downriver on private land only available to commercial outfitters. Take out on Lake Amistad is 32 miles downriver at no cost. Catch and release fishing only, no live bait, no motorized boats allowed. Visiting archaeological pictograph sites allowed only on tours or pre-approved basis. Fees charged.

WEATHER

July high averages maximum 98 degrees, January low 38 degrees.

MAIN ACTIVITIES

The park preserves many archaeological and pictograph sites, some more than 8,000 years old. All areas of the park are off-limits except developed trails to prevent vandalism of rock art and disturbance of the endangered black-capped vireo. The black-capped vireo nests in the park from March to August. A 12-mile loop trail takes hikers through the broken canyon country with half the length traversing the rim and half in the canyons.

HISTORY

Deep canyons with rock shelters dissect this area of Texas. As the last Ice Age receded, leaving a cooler, moister climate, humans lived in the rock shelters and hunted bison and other big game now extinct. Nearby Seminole Canyon State Park, with similar topography, has beautiful exhibits and daily tours of some of the most outstanding rock art in the state.

53. DEVIL'S SINKHOLE STATE NATURAL AREA

LOCATION

Edwards County. 6 miles north of Rocksprings on U.S. 377. Mailing address: Devils Sinkhole State Natural Area, PO Box 678, Rocksprings, TX 78880. Phone: 830-683-3762. Devils Sinkhole Visitors Center is in Rocksprings at 101 N Sweeten St. Access only with special, pre-arranged tours. All tours meet at the visitors center. To arrange tours, call the Devils Sinkhole Society, 830-683-BATS (2287).

FACILITIES

With only minimal development, the park provides picnic sites, a chemical toilet, and trail development for wheelchair accessibility up to 50 feet of the sinkhole to allow viewing of the freetail bat emergence. Access to the park can be obtained only by contacting Kickapoo Cavern State Park for a prearranged tour. Access into the sinkhole cavern is prohibited. A fee is charged for tours. Call Kickapoo Cavern for information on tour dates and fees.

WEATHER

July high averages maximum 95 degrees, January low 35 degrees.

MAIN ATTRACTION

Formerly part of the Whitworth Ranch, the 1,860-acre natural area preserves Devil's Sinkhole, first discovered by Anglo settlers in 1867. The sinkhole has a 40×60-foot opening with a vertical drop to the main

In the summer, bats emerge from sinkholes and caves on the Edwards Plateau to forage for insects.

cavern of 140 feet. The main cavern is circular and reaches a depth of 350 to 400 feet.

PLANTS AND ANIMALS

The most obvious life form found in the Sinkhole is the large population of Brazilian freetail bats, present from February through November. Most are females that migrate to Texas to rear their young. The bat population often doubles by June when the females give birth to their single offspring. Each evening at dusk, millions of bats emerge en masse from the cave to forage for moths, producing an unforgettable wildlife phenomena.

A population of 3,000–4,000 cave swallows also inhabits the cave. The birds form a sweeping vortex as they circle the sinkhole and drop into the chamber. Just as they disappear, the bats begin to emerge, first like wisps of smoke, then like a great conflagration. Often red-tailed hawks wait overhead to pick off an easy meal as the wave of bats flows out of the cave and disappears toward the darkening horizon.

Standing water within the cave, which reaches below the water table, supports two unique crustaceans: an endemic amphipod and a rare aquatic isopod. A Mexican fern species occurring in few other locations in the United States grows on the vertical shaft of the cave.

The vegetation and topography of the park is typical of the Edwards Plateau, with deeply cut canyons on the southern end of the site. The canyons support escarpment black cherry, Buckley oak, Lacey oak, and pinyon pine. Plateau live oak dominates on the more arid uplands. The endangered Tobusch fishhook cactus also grows within the park.

54. DINOSAUR VALLEY STATE PARK

LOCATION

Somervell County. 24 miles west of Cleburne on U.S. 67 through Glen Rose, 3 miles north on FM 205.Mailing address: Box 396, Glen Rose, Texas 76043. Phone: 254-897-4588. For all state park reservations, call the centralized reservations system, 512-389-8900, or www.ReserveAmerica.com online. Call the state park information number, 800-792-1112, for information and fee updates.

FACILITIES

Fees: entrance, facility, activity use; subject to change.

Camping: 46 back-in RV/tent sites with water and electricity, North Primitive Area with backpack campsites (1 to 5.5 miles). Modern restrooms, showers, trailer dump station. Fees charged.

Recreation: picnic areas, playgrounds, 7 miles of hiking and backpacking trails, day-use horseback riding trails in the South Equestrian Area, 5.5 miles of mountain bike trails, group picnic pavilion, 2 life-size dinosaur models, Texas State Park Store.

WEATHER

July high averages 97 degrees, January low 34 degrees.

MAIN ATTRACTIONS

More than a hundred dinosaur tracks are visible in the flat limestone bed of the scenic Paluxy River. Life-size dinosaur models and summer interpretive programs explain the significance of the tracks and how they were discovered. Be sure to view the exhibits in the visitor center. The Paluxy River, whose meanderings helped uncover the dinosaur tracks hidden in the rock, winds through the wooded hills and offers campers swimming and fishing. A portion of the official Texas longhorn herd, in an enclosure above the river, can be viewed from a trail. Fossil Rim Wildlife Center, a non-profit drive-through wildlife park with 1,000 animals, is 3 miles west of Glen Rose (see page 113).

HIKING, BIKING, AND HORSES

A system of hiking and mountain biking trails leads through the hills, picturesque tributaries, and along wooded ridges with scenic views. Primitive camping is allowed in the North Primitive Area, and horseback riding in the South Primitive Area. Obtain a trail map and permits at park headquarters.

PLANTS AND ANIMALS

The park preserves evidence of plant and animal life that existed more than 100 million years ago. At the time of the dinosaurs, Texas was moist and warm, with vast swamps, mud flats, and shallow bays. For more than 100 million years, dinosaurs, the "terrible lizards," were the dominant creatures. Some were as small as a dog, while the 40-ton, 70-foot-long Brontosaurus was a giant.

Dinosaur tracks more than 100 million years old are visible in the bedrock of the Paluxy River.

The dinosaurs waded through the shallow water and across mud flats, leaving deep imprints in the soft mud. The impressions were gradually covered with hundreds of feet of sediment, which preserved the tracks. By modern times, the river had cut through to the original layer containing the tracks, exposing more than a hundred prints of the large plant-eating Pleurocelus and the smaller meat-eating Acrocanthosaurus.

Besides the dinosaur tracks, the park includes a beautiful section of the Paluxy River. The camping and picnic grounds are located in the wooded river bottomland. Elms and a variety of oaks grow along the river, and juniper trees dominate the rocky, dry uplands. Alongside the dinosaur tracks, more recent footprints of deer, raccoons, opossums, skunks, and foxes can be seen in the sand. Of the many species of resident and migrant birds, the endangered golden-cheek warbler nests in the mature cedar (juniper) woodlands. The endangered black-capped vireo nests in scrubby areas, and wild turkeys forage through the riparian woodlands. Nearly 200 species of birds, including waterfowl along the river, occur in the park through the year.

55. DUMAS: TEXOMA PARK

Moore County. Western edge of Dumas on U.S. 87. Mailing address: City Park Dept., Box 438, Dumas, Texas 79029. Phone: 806-935-4101. Internet: www.ci.dumas.tx.us/texhoma.htm. Camping: 24 free RV sites with water nearby and electricity, flush toilets, trailer dump station; 24-hour parking limit. Recreation: picnic areas and playgrounds. Closed in winter. Minimal facilities but okay for an overnight stay.

56. E.V. SPENCE RESERVOIR

Coke County. Colorado River Municipal Warer District. Mailing address: Box 869, Big Spring, TX 79721-0869. Phone: 432-267-6341. Internet: www.crmwd.org. Click: Natural Resources: Recreation.

Lake View Park: north from Robert Lee .6 mile on TX 208, west 1.5 miles on FM 1904. Facilities: primitive camping on 100 acres, no water, pit toilets, picnic tables, boat ramp. Fee charged.

Paint Creek Park: west from Robert Lee 7.8 miles on TX 158, north .5 mile to park. Primitive camping with picnic table and grill, no water, pit toilets. Marina closed due to low lake levels.

Wildcat Park: west from Robert Lee 4.5 miles on TX 158, north .6 mile to park. Phone: 325-453-2801. Concessionaire operated: motel, mobile home rental, 28 RV sites with full hookups, primitive camping on 150 lakefront acres with tables and grill but no water, restrooms, showers;

store, bait shop, café, swimming, fishing, boat ramp. Open all year, fees charged.

57. EAGLE MOUNTAIN LAKE STATE PARK

LOCATION

Tarrant County. Northeast of Fort Worth off TX 199.
Mailing address: c/o Park Region 8 Headquarters, 1638 Park Rd.
16, Tyler, Texas 75706-9143. Phone: 903-595-2938.

FACILITIES

Eagle Mountain State Park is a 400-acre undeveloped park in suburban Fort Worth. The park was acquired in 1980 and pending development is accessible only by special request.

MAIN ATTRACTION

The 9,000-acre lake on the East Fork of the Trinity River provides drinking water for Fort Worth. When developed, the park will offer the typical water-oriented and lakeshore activities. Lakes in the Dallas-Fort Worth area accommodate millions of visitors annually, so this suburban addition to the state park system is destined to be a popular recreation site.

58. EISENHOWER STATE PARK

LOCATION

Grayson County. 3.5 miles north of Denison on TX 75A to FM
1310, 2 miles west to PR 20.
Mailing address: 50 Park Road 20, Denison, Texas 75020-4878.
Phone: 903-465-1956. For all state park reservations, call the
centralized reservations system, 512-389-8900, or
www.ReserveAmerica.com online. Call the state park information
number, 800-792-1112, for information and fee updates. E-mail:
espc@texoma.net

FACILITIES

Fees: entrance, facility, activity use; subject to change.

Camping: 50 pull-through RV/tent sites with full hookups, 35 sites with water and electricity, 48 tent sites, paved group RV site with 37 sites with water and electricity, 35 screened shelters, campground pavilion, overflow camping area. Modern restrooms, showers, trailer dump station. Fees charged.

Recreation: picnic areas, recreation hall (day or overnight use, ac/heat, kitchen), lighted fishing pier, fish-cleaning facility, boat ramp and dock, lake swimming, private marina, hiking and mountain biking trails, ATV biking area, Texas State Park Store.

WEATHER

July high averages 90 degrees, January low 32 degrees.

MAIN ATTRACTIONS

Eisenhower State Park is on the 40-mile-long Lake Texoma, formed in 1944 by damming the Red River in Texas below its confluence with the Washita River in Oklahoma. Lake Texoma, with white, striped, and black bass as well as other game fish, has long been a favorite among fishermen. Water sports of all types are popular on the lake. Some camping and fishing supplies may be purchased at the marina. A boat launch, boat shelters, and facilities for boat repairs are available.

Nearby attractions include the Eisenhower Birthplace State Historic Site in Denison. Hagerman National Wildlife Refuge, with 11,300 acres, is 15 miles west of Denison on Lake Texoma.

Shoreline cliffs border much of Lake Texoma in Eisenhower State Park.

HIKING AND BIKING

A hiking trail extends the length of the park. Visitors can drive to all campsites, but backpackers may choose to use the trail to reach their campgrounds and explore the park. Also, the Army Corps of Engineers maintains the 14-mile-long Cross Timbers Hiking Trail on Lake Texoma, west of the state park. Obtain a map from the Corps headquarters at the dam site. The Corps operates various parks on Lake Texoma and offers tours of the dam and hydroelectric facilities.

The first half mile of the hiking trail has interpretive signs and is restricted to foot traffic. The remaining 4 miles (8 miles round-trip) is open to hikers and non-motorized biking. The first 2 miles are for beginning bikers while the last 2, with steep grades and loose rock, require intermediate skills. A 10-acre area is set aside for all terrain vehicles.

PLANTS AND ANIMALS

The Red River cuts through an area of rolling hills dissected by deep canyons. Woodlands of cedar elm, oaks, osage orange, and Texas ash thrive in the canyon drainages. In the spring, the shrubby rough-leaf dogwood, with its clusters of tiny, fragrant white flowers, and beautiful redbud trees add color to the woods. Prairie grasses and a wide variety of wildflowers dominate the uplands.

The 457-acre park is on a part of the lake typified by steep cliffs rising abruptly out of the water. The cliffs are formed by a limestone cap covering a thick layer of clay and sandstone. The weathering of the exposed clay under the limestone ledges causes large sections of the cliffs to cave into the lake. Many unfortunate homeowners with houses perched on the scenic cliffs across from the park are fighting a losing battle trying to stabilize the crumbling cliff edges.

Waterfowl, shorebirds, and many migrants, including the osprey, are attracted to the large lake. Deer, raccoons, squirrels, and gray foxes frequent the park. Fossils, the remains of a rich marine life of 100 million years ago, are abundant in the limestone outcrops. The rounded imprints of large ammonites and fossilized oysters can be found along the limestone ledges overlooking the lake.

59. ENCHANTED ROCK STATE NATURAL AREA

LOCATION

Gillespie County. 18 miles north of Fredericksburg on FM 965. Mailing address: 16710 Ranch Rd. 965, Fredericksburg, Texas 78624. Phone: 830-685-3636. For all state park reservations, call the centralized reservations system, 512-389-8900, or

Wildflowers decorate the cracks at Enchanted Rock.

www.ReserveAmerica.com online. Call the state park information number, 800-792-1112, for information and fee updates.

Note: The park closes when it reaches parking capacity, which occurs frequently on spring and summer weekends, sometimes as early as 11 a.m. The park usually reopens at 5 p.m. Call ahead or have alternate plans. Nearby parks include Pedernales Falls, Kerrville-Schreiner, Inks Lake, and Longhorn Cavern State Parks; Lyndon B. Johnson State and National Historical Parks; LCRA parks on Lake Buchanan.

FACILITIES

Fees: entrance, facility, activity use; subject to change.

Camping: 60 primitive campsites with composting toilets, 46 walk-in tent campsites with water only, modern restrooms with showers. No vehicle camping or overnight parking of RVs allowed. Fees charged.

Recreation: picnicking, hiking trails, rock climbing throughout the park and at 48 sites rated according to difficulty, pavilion with 10 tables, Texas State Park Store.

MAIN ATTRACTIONS

Enchanted Rock is in the heart of the Texas Hill Country. Its 1,643 acres encompass a massive granite dome rising 325 feet above the surrounding terrain. The dome, the tip of an extensive underground block called a batholith, is surpassed in size only by the famous Stone Mountain in Georgia. Enchanted Rock was purchased by the Texas Parks and Wildlife Department with the assistance of the Nature Conservancy in 1978. This unique site has been designated a state natural area. The designation indicates that to preserve its natural beauty, much of the area will be protected from overuse by visitors. Enchanted Rock is one of my favorite parks.

The awe-inspiring dome has long been the source of superstitions and legends. The Indians believed it to be inhabited by spirits because of the strange creaking noises often heard on cool nights. The surface of the rock contracts as the temperature drops after a hot day, causing the eerie sounds. Tales and superstitions involving the dome grew among early settlers, who considered the rock enchanted or bewitched.

South of Enchanted Rock, the picturesque German settlement of Fredericksburg is famous for its period architecture, German restaurants, and bakeries. Also in Fredericksburg is the Admiral Nimitz Museum and Historical Center, with many mementos of World War II.

HIKING

A trail from the campgrounds leads to the top of the dome and down again. The hike is fairly strenuous and slippery in wet weather, but it is well worth the effort to gain a true appreciation of the size and beauty of the dome. The park is a favorite for rock climbers. A small rock crevice cave is near the top on the far side of the dome.

PLANTS AND ANIMALS

Enchanted Rock is part of the Llano uplift, or the Central Texas mineral region, an area with granite bedrock surrounded by the limestone of the Edwards Plateau. Nearly a billion years ago, during the Precambrian era, a massive plug of molten lava was forced toward the earth's surface. As the lava cooled beneath the earth, it hardened into a dome of granite. The granite remained unexposed for millions of years while oceans deposited thousands of feet of limestone above it. Uplifts during the late Paleozoic era, approximately 275 million years ago, caused erosion of this overlying limestone, eventually exposing the granite dome to the surface.

The surface of the granite dome weathers by a process called exfoliation. Joints and fractures develop, which cause the surface of the rock to peel away in layers like the skin of an onion, leaving a smooth, rounded dome. Wind, rain, and frost weather the granite into sand, which is washed into creeks and rivers. The sandy banks and shores of the rivers that flow across the Hill Country to the Gulf are formed from the eroded granite of the Llano uplift.

Many of the plants found in the sandy soil around the granite dome do not occur on the adjacent alkaline soil formed from the Edwards Plateau limestone. Texas hickory, blackjack oak, and post oak are abundant in the park, where the dominant tree of the Edwards Plateau, Ashe juniper, is rare. The red sandy soil and the composition of the woodlands give Enchanted Rock a decidedly different appearance from the white chalky soil and vegetation typical of the Edwards Plateau.

Enchanted Rock is a textbook example of the changes bare rock undergoes during the process of soil building. The development of the plant community as soil accumulates is very evident. Beautiful multi-colored lichens cover the red granite like splattered paint. Lichens are composed of fungi and algae growing together in a symbiotic relationship: a fungus cannot produce its own food but provides the substrate, or house, for the alga, which manufactures enough food to support both of them. Over time, lichens and the effects of weather slowly break down the rock to form soil.

Ferns and mosses are the next plants to get a toehold in the scant soil hidden in the cracks and depressions of the rock. Like miniature forests, rock ferns thrive around the sheltered bases of dislodged boulders. As more soil accumulates, the seeds of annuals find a home and decorate the depressions and irregularities with a colorful display of blooms. In deeper soil, perennials set their roots and become firmly established.

The deeper depressions, or soil islands, support a healthy growth of grasses, prickly pear cacti, and rain lilies, which magically appear soon after a thunderstorm. Surprisingly, oaks, buckeyes, and other trees flourish in the deep cracks and crevasses on top of Enchanted Rock. The mountain is far from being a bare, lifeless dome of exposed granite—it beckons those with the spirit of discovery to explore its every crack and crevice.

After a rain, the surface of the dome takes on an ephemeral appearance. Shallow depressions fill with water and, like mirages, seem to dance in the reflected sunlight. Ghost shrimp, hatching from long-dormant eggs, scurry through the temporary ponds to hurriedly mate and lay drought-resistant eggs before the sun can reclaim the water of their transitory homes.

The animals seen at Enchanted Rock are typical of the Hill Country. White-tailed deer are common, as are rock squirrels, jackrabbits, raccoons, and skunks. Lizards scamper across the sun-baked rocks and dive into shaded crevices for shelter. Vultures and an occasional migrating eagle circle on the columns of warm air rising from the massive dome. In the spring, vermilion flycatchers flit through the trees along the creeks like tiny balls of fire. Chickadees and titmice noisily forage for insects, and by night diminutive screech owls patrol the open savannas at the base of the rock.

HISTORY

Enchanted Rock is rich in Indian artifacts up to 8,000 years old. Projectile points indicate that prehistoric groups hunted deer, birds, and fish and gathered plants in the area. Bedrock metates, round holes in the rock used to grind nuts and seeds, can be seen in the park, and archaeological sites are scattered along the spring-fed creeks flowing around the dome.

When Europeans arrived in the 1700s, Tonkawa and other Indians inhabited the region. By the 1800s, Comanches and Apaches had been forced out of the Great Plains and into Texas. In 1841, Texas Ranger Captain John Hays, who had been separated from his company, repulsed a band of Comanches from a vantage point near the summit of the dome. A plaque commemorates the location of the battle.

60. FAIRFIELD LAKE STATE PARK

LOCATION

Freestone County. 6 miles northeast of Fairfield via FM 488 to FM 2570 to PR 64.
Mailing address: 123 State Park Rd. 64, Fairfield, Texas 75840.
Phone: 903-389-4514. For all state park reservations, call the centralized reservations system, 512-389-8900, or www.ReserveAmerica.com online. Call the state park information number, 800-792-1112, for information and fee updates.

White-tailed deer graze in the fields around Fairfield Lake.

FACILITIES

Fees: entrance, facility, activity use; subject to change.

Camping: 99 pull-through RV/tent sites with water and electricity, 36 sites with water, hike-in primitive camping at the end of a 2.1-mile, one-way hike/bike/equestrian trail, modern restrooms, showers, trailer dump station. Fees charged.

Recreation: picnic areas, playgrounds, hiking and mountain biking, lake swimming, fish cleaning station, lighted fishing pier, group dining hall, amphitheater, Texas State Park Store.

WEATHER

July high averages 95 degrees, January low 35 degrees.

MAIN ATTRACTIONS

The state park is located on the 2,400-acre Fairfield Reservoir, an impoundment of Big Brown Creek. The reservoir—formed to provide cooling water for a lignite-fueled power plant, visible on the shore opposite the park—is one of the top three bass-producing lakes in the state. A survey in 1979 showed that the lake supported 112 pounds of largemouth bass per acre, with the record bass weighing over 10 pounds. Channel catfish, redfish, and hybrid striped bass are also year-round favorites for fishermen.

HIKING, BIKING, AND HORSE RIDING

The 3-mile primitive camping trail connects to the 9-mile Dockery Trail around the perimeter of the park to combine for 12 miles of hike/bike and day-use equestrian trails. The park also has a 2-mile nature trail and 1-mile bird-watching trail. The trails lead along the lakeshore and through native grasslands and oak woodlands. Wildlife seen along the trails include osprey (year-round), bald eagles (November through February), white-tailed deer, raccoons, foxes, beavers, squirrels, and armadillos, as well as resident and migrating songbirds and water birds on the lake.

PLANTS AND ANIMALS

The 1,460-acre park is in the post oak savanna vegetation zone of Texas. The heavy forest is composed of a wide variety of oaks, interspersed with hickory and eastern red cedar. Yaupon holly and other small bushes make up the understory or shrub layer of the forest. Scattered through the woodlands are open grasslands with tallgrass prairie species, including Indian grass, switchgrass, little bluestem, and eastern gama grass. In the spring, flowering dogwoods and redbuds decorate the woods, and wildflowers cover the prairies with a blanket of colors.

Wildlife thrive throughout the park but are most numerous at the edges of prairies and woodlands, where the grassland and forest habitats overlap. Acorns from the many oaks provide an excellent food source for white-tailed deer, squirrels, and other animals.

Many habitats for birds occur within the park. Woodpeckers, crows, and other woodland species live in the forest; juncos, sparrows, and prairie species inhabit the grasslands. Bald eagles, geese, ducks, terns, kingfishers, cormorants, and wading birds are attracted to the reservoir.

A massive strip-mining operation west of the reservoir supplies the power plant with lignite, a low-grade fuel with a carbon content less than that of true coal. The decimated land is a painful reminder of the cost we must pay for our increasing demand for energy.

61. FALCON STATE PARK

LOCATION

Zapata and Starr counties. 80 miles southeast of Laredo on U.S. 83 past Falcon, 2.5 miles southwest on FM 2098, north on PR 46. Mailing address: Box 2, Falcon Heights, Texas 78545. Phone: 956-848-5327. For all state park reservations, call the centralized reservations system, 512-389-8900, or www.ReserveAmerica.com online. Call the state park information number, 800-792-1112, for information and fee updates.

FACILITIES

Fees: entrance, facility, activity use; subject to change.

Camping: 30 pull-through RV/tent sites with full hookups, 30 with water and electricity, 24 screened shelter some with a/c, 55 tent sites with water, modern restrooms, showers, trailer dump station. Fees charged.

Recreation: picnic areas, playgrounds, lake swimming, fishing, water sports, boat ramp, group recreation hall with kitchen for day-use or overnight-use, 3 miles of hiking/mountain biking trails, bird-watching, 1-mile self-guided nature trail, Texas State Park Store.

Note: A three-lane boat ramp accesses the lake to an level of 269 feet and a single lane to an level of 259 feet. When the lake is below 261 feet, a temporary ramp on improved lake shore is provided, 4-wheel drive recommended. Changing lake conditions may cause the temporary ramps to be unusable.

WEATHER

July high averages 99 degrees, January low 44 degrees.

MAIN ATTRACTIONS

Falcon State Park is located on the eastern shore of Falcon Reservoir. In 1953, the Rio Grande was dammed to form the 60-mile-long, 87,000-acre lake. The dam is owned by the United States and Mexico. A hydroelectric power plant at the dam can produce 30 megawatts of electricity on the U.S. side. The state park, opened in 1965, has become a paradise for fishermen, bird-watchers, and snowbirds—retirees spending the winter in the warm climate of South Texas. Travelers may cross the bridge over Falcon Dam into Mexico and visit the towns of Nuevo Guerrero, Mier, and Miguel Alemán.

PLANTS AND ANIMALS

The park consists of rolling brushlands, lakeshore woodlands, and the large reservoir, an unusual habitat in semiarid South Texas. The upland

In the spring, wildflowers cover the shoreline around Falcon State Park.

brush country, or chaparral, is characterized by desertlike vegetation. Head-high thorny shrubs, mesquite, blackbrush, catclaw acacia, guayacan, and allthorn form an impenetrable thicket. Prickly pear and yucca are common.

When there has been ample spring rain, the desertlike environment abounds with a medley of wildflowers. Desert mallows surround the cacti, and fleabanes cover the clearings. Indian blankets decorate the roadsides with white, yellow, and red and prickly poppies crowding the fence lines. The thickets resound with the buzz of bees attracted to the dense yellow flowers of the thorny shrubs, which seem to set the brushland ablaze with their bright flashes of color.

Many subtropical species of birds frequent the park and the woodlands below Falcon Dam; ask for a checklist at the park entrance. Birds seen in the park that are near the northern limit of their distribution include the plain chachalaca, white-tipped dove, red-billed pigeon, great kiskadee, tropical kingbird, groove-billed ani, green jay, common pauraque, Audubon's and Altamira orioles, and olive sparrow.

Large and boisterous ringed kingfishers and brown jays, as well as the gray hawk, can be found in the undisturbed woodlands along the river below the dam. Other subtropical birds seen in the United States primarily in South Texas include the clay-colored robin, yellow-throated vireo, long-billed thrasher, common black hawk, bronzed cowbird, and varied bunting.

The large body of water, an anomaly in South Texas, attracts many water birds and shorebirds and, occasionally, rare seabirds. The least grebe, olivaceous cormorant, least tern, and black-bellied whistling duck are commonly seen, as well as loons, herons, egrets, and many species of gulls, terns, ducks, and wading birds.

HISTORY

Many significant historical events have occurred along the lower Rio Grande. The Spanish, who first explored the area in 1638, established missions and settlements in the 1700s. After Texas won its independence, border disputes and invasions by Mexican troops were frequent until Texas joined the United States. Forts were established in Brownsville (Fort Brown), Rio Grande City (Fort Ringgold), and Laredo (Fort McIntosh). Fort Ringgold, 30 miles south of Falcon State Park, is one of Texas' best-preserved forts; it includes the house occupied by Robert E. Lee, who was stationed in Texas before he assumed command of the Confederate forces.

The Mexican towns of Guerrero and Mier, just across Falcon Dam, were sites of a historic confrontation between Texas forces and the Mexican army. In 1842, six years after Texas gained independence from Mexico, General Adrian Woll attacked and captured San Antonio, the second time the city had been occupied by Mexican troops within one year. Many Texans, outraged by the invasion, marched to join forces with Colonel Matthew Caldwell. A group of 54 volunteers from La

Grange was intercepted by Mexican forces and forced to surrender. All but 15, three of whom escaped, were massacred.

General Woll retreated to Mexico, pursued by Texans intent on revenge. General Alexander Somervell led the Texas forces against the town of Guerrero, now under the reservoir, but found it deserted. He elected to turn back, but 308 men pressed on—determined to plunder the town of Mier, where the Mexican army was bivouacked. After heavy fighting, the Texans were tricked into surrendering. The men were marched to Mexico City and, after an attempted escape en route, received the order that one in ten be executed: they were forced to select the victims themselves by drawing from a jar containing 159 white beans and 17 black beans, the black beans signifying death. The survivors were imprisoned until after the Mexican War. A statue honoring the men of Mier was erected in 1936 in La Grange.

62. FORT BOGGY STATE PARK

LOCATION

Leon County. 7 miles south of Centerville on TX 75.
Mailing address: 4994 Hwy. 75 South, Centerville, Texas 75833.
Phone: 903-344-1116.

FACILITIES

This undeveloped park is open Wednesday–Sunday for day use (8 a.m.–sunset) and overnight at 10 primitive hike-in (up to 2 miles) tent sites. Activities available include swimming and fishing in a 15-acre lake and use of small boats. The park has picnic tables, a reservable open air group pavilion, restrooms without showers, and a boat ramp. A hiking trail around the lake is under construction. A 2-mile hiking/mountain bike/nature trail loops through the rolling woodlands and a 1.5-mile hiking trail circles the lake.

WEATHER

July high averages 96 degrees, January low 35 degrees.

HISTORY

Eileen Crain Sullivan donated the 1,847-acre park to the Texas Parks and Wildlife Department in 1985. In 1840, the families of John Byrns and Christopher C. Staley of Tennessee established the first settlement north of the Old San Antonio Rd. between the Navasota and Trinity rivers. John and James Erwin and their families from Mississippi, along with several other pioneer families, joined them. When raiding Indians killed Staley in February 1840, the settlers built a palisade fort for protection.

The 75-square-yard fort enclosed 2 blockhouses and 11 dwellings that housed 75 people. To protect the settlers, Republic of Texas President Mirabeau B. Lamar authorized a military company for the fort under the leadership of Captain Thomas Greer. Indians killed Greer in 1841, who was on an excursion to scout Keechi Creek. Plagued by sickness, the Byrns and Erwin families eventually left the fort and returned to their respective homes. When the Indian attacks decreased a few years later, the fort fell into disrepair.

PLANTS AND ANIMALS

Farmers tilled the land within the park for almost a century until the 1930s when the Sullivan family took the property out of cultivation. After 60 years of lying fallow, the land along Boggy Creek has reclaimed much of the pristine beauty that dominated the region 150 years ago.

The wooded, rolling hills, meadows, and wetlands support abundant wildlife. White-tailed deer, raccoons, squirrels, foxes, and beavers thrive in the rich habitat. A large portion of the park floods during wet periods and provides excellent habitat for waterfowl and aquatic wildlife. Post oak, hickory, elm, sweetgum, and pecan, with understory of American beautyberry, dogwood, sassafras, yaupon, and hawthorn grow in the riparian woodlands. Little bluestem, Indiangrass, purpletop, switchgrass, and stands of the highly endangered Centerville Brazos mint grow in the savannah grasslands.

63. FORT GRIFFIN STATE HISTORIC SITE

LOCATION

Shackelford County. 35 miles northeast of Abilene on TX 351 and U.S. 180 to Albany, 15 miles north on U.S. 283.
Mailing address: 1701 North US Hwy 283, Albany, Texas 76430.
Phone: 325-762-3592. Internet: ft-griffin@ths.state.tx.us;
www.thc.state.tx.us/hsites/hs_fort_griffin.shtml. On January 1, 2008, Texas Parks & Wildlife transferred this park to the Texas Historical Commission.

FACILITIES

Camping: 3 back-in RV/tent sites with full hookups, 20 with water and electricity, 5 walk-in tent sites with water, group equestrian campground with water for horses only (capacity 35 rigs). Modern restrooms, showers, trailer dump station. Fees charged.

Recreation: picnic areas and playgrounds, interpretive exhibits, historic buildings, state longhorn herd, amphitheater with weekend programs in the summer, group shelter, historic reenactments, 3-mile historic hiking trail, 1.5-mile nature trail, fishing in Brazos River, Texas State Park Store.

WEATHER

July high averages 94 degrees, January low 34 degrees.

MAIN ATTRACTIONS

The park preserves the ruins of Fort Griffin, one of the frontier forts established after the Civil War to rid North Texas of the Indians. The stone walls of several of the structures remain, along with two small rebuilt wooden barracks and mess hall and the original stone bakery. An added attraction is the official state longhorn herd, which can be seen grazing in pastures in the park. The visitors center has displays on the old fort, the Indians, and the longhorns.

The 506-acre park is situated on a hill overlooking the Clear Fork of the Brazos River. Mesquite trees, live oaks, prickly pear cacti, and grasses dominate the rocky higher grounds, while elm, hackberry, and pecan trees grow along the river bottom and shade the picnic and camping area.

HISTORY

Fort Griffin, established in 1867, played a major role in driving the Kiowa and Comanche Indians from North Texas. The Indians, who courageously defended their homeland from the advancing wave of white

Fort Griffin was one of the frontier forts built to protect settlers from Indian attacks.

settlers, often sought refuge in Indian Territory, Oklahoma, an area that was supposedly off limits for the army. In 1871, a raiding party nearly captured General William Sherman, the commander who ravaged the South during the Civil War; the Indians succeeded in stealing all of the general's horses. Sherman immediately ordered his troops to follow the Indians into Oklahoma and subdue them.

By 1874, more than half of the Comanches had died from war, smallpox, and cholera. Buffalo hunters had nearly eliminated the bison, a chief source of food for the Indians. Finally, in 1874, Colonel Ranald Mackenzie defeated the Comanches in Palo Duro Canyon and slaughtered 1,500 of their horses in Tule Canyon, south of Palo Duro Canyon State Park. Without horses, the Indians were unable to acquire food for the approaching winter and were forced to remain on the reservations in Oklahoma. The following year, under the leadership of the great war chief Quanah Parker, the Comanches surrendered.

With the Indian hostilities over, buffalo hunters completed the extermination of the bison from the Texas plains, and the era of the cowboy began. Millions of longhorn cattle—the descendants of Spanish cattle introduced into Texas in the 1600s—freely roamed the rich grasslands of South Texas. Two hundred years of surviving in a harsh environment had created a breed of rugged cattle that would become a symbol of the Old West.

The 1870s saw the birth of the trail drive, and during the next two decades some 10 million longhorns were driven to northern markets. When railroads reached Texas in the 1880s, the laborious and financially risky drives were no longer necessary. Soon barbed-wire fences dominated the range, and selective breeding was producing cattle with more beef and less brawn than the longhorns. The very traits that had guaranteed its survival on the open range almost doomed the longhorn to extinction.

The western author J. Frank Dobie gathered a small herd of longhorns in the 1920s, which eventually became the state herd. Today the herd of about 125 animals is selectively bred for all the longhorn characteristics, not just impressive horns. The breeding herd is maintained at Fort Griffin, while the steers, which have the longest horns, are also displayed in several other state parks.

64. FORT PARKER STATE PARK

LOCATION

Limestone County. From Mexia, 6.6 miles south on TX 14 to Park Rd 28. Mailing address, state park: 194 Park Road 28, Mexia, Texas 76667. Phone: 254-562-5751. E-mail: fortparker@glade.net. For all state park reservations, call the centralized reservations system, 512-389-8900, or www.ReserveAmerica.com online. Call the state park information number, 800-792-1112, for information and fee updates.

FACILITIES

Fees: entrance, facility, activity use; subject to change.

Camping: 25 campsites with water and electricity, 10 sites with water, 10 screened shelters, group primitive camping area for organized youth groups only, group barracks for 96 people with kitchen and dining hall, modern restrooms with showers, trailer dump station. Fees charged.

Recreation: picnic areas, playgrounds, group picnic pavilion, group recreation hall (ac/heat, stove, fridge, capacity 50), boat ramp and dock, 1-mile hike/mountain biking trail, fishing pier, fish-cleaning station, lake swimming, sports fields, canoe and paddleboat rentals, Texas State Park Store.

WEATHER

July high averages 95 degrees, January low 34 degrees.

MAIN ATTRACTIONS

The state park is situated on a 750-acre impoundment of the Navasota River. Fishing is popular; catches of sunfish, catfish, crappie, and largemouth bass are typical. The heavily wooded shoreline is a good place for nature study, bird-watching, and photography.

The park's Nature Center explains the history of the Civilian Conservation Corp's construction of the park, the ecology of the forest, grassland, and lake, and has a children's interactive room. Hiking trails include a .5-mile nature loop with a walking guide, a 1.5-mile hike/bike loop and a 1.5-mile, one-way trail around the western shoreline.

Old Fort Parker, operated by the City of Groesbeck, one mile south of the state park, is a reconstructed stockade fort built in 1834 to protect pioneer families. (See listing, page 247.) Raiding Comanches abducted 9-year-old Cynthia Ann Parker, who married the chief and became mother of Quanah Parker, the last Comanche chief. The site is open 9 a.m.–5 p.m. Wednesday through Sunday, closed Christmas, New Year's Day. The Confederate Reunion Grounds State Historic Site, operated by the Texas Historical Commission, is 6 miles south of Mexia on TX 14, then 2.5 miles west on FM 2705. The historic gathering place was dedicated 1889 "to perpetuate the memories of fallen comrades, aid disabled survivors and indigent widows and orphans of deceased Confederate soldiers, and to preserve the fraternity that grew out of the war." The day-use park has historic buildings, picnicking, nature trails, and fishing in the Navasoto River.

PLANTS AND ANIMALS

The 1,485-acre state park is located in the gently rolling deciduous woodlands of the post oak savanna of Texas. The dense forest surrounding

Gray foxes live in the woodlands in Fort Parker State Park.

the lake consists of post oak, cedar elm, eastern red cedar, pecan, hickory, and yaupon. The undisturbed woods and the lake provide a variety of wildlife habitats.

Great blue herons and great egrets wade in the shallows of the numerous inlets, while kingfishers perch poised on overhanging limbs, ready to dive for small fish. Ducks, geese, and cormorants overwinter on the lake, and many species of warblers migrate through the park each spring and fall. Ask for a bird checklist at the park headquarters.

Raccoons, opossums, and gray foxes leave their tracks in the moist soil along the shore. Cottontail rabbits, gray squirrels, and white-tailed deer are commonly seen in the early morning and evening.

65. FORT RICHARDSON STATE PARK AND HISTORIC SITE AND LOST CREEK RESERVOIR STATE TRAILWAY

LOCATION

Jack County. 60 miles northwest of Fort Worth on TX 199, in Jacksboro.

Mailing address: 228 State Park Road 61, Jacksboro, Texas 76458. Phone: 940-567-3506.
For all state park reservations, call the centralized reservations system, 512-389-8900, or www.ReserveAmerica.com online. Call the state park information number, 800-792-1112, for information and fee updates.

FACILITIES

Fees: entrance, facility, activity use; subject to change.

Camping: 41 back-in or pull-through RV/tent sites with water and electricity, 11 screened shelters with water and electricity, walk-in primitive camping, modern restrooms with showers, trailer dump station. Fees charged.

Recreation: picnic areas, nature and hiking trails, interpretive exhibits, reconstructed fort buildings, military reenactments, living history presentations, swimming in reservoir, fishing in Quarry Lake (stocked with catfish and rainbow trout).

WEATHER

July average high 97 degrees, January low 32 degrees.

MAIN ATTRACTIONS

The 389-acre park preserves seven original buildings and two reconstructed barracks. The fort protected settlers from raiding Comanches, Kiowas, and Kiowa-Apaches between 1867 and 1878. The large stone building housing the hospital and morgue, refurnished to a frontier hospital, dominates one end of the parade ground. On either side of the parade ground are the original officers' quarters, which were built with cottonwood timber, and the barracks. A reconstructed officers' barrack serves as an interpretive center. The bakery, which produced 600 loaves of bread daily, the commissary, the guardhouse, and the magazine are clustered near the hospital.

The Lost Creek Reservoir State Trailway connects Lost Creek Reservoir and Fort Richardson. The 10-foot-wide, 10-mile-long trail runs through the park, along Lost Creek, and along the shores of Lake Jacksboro and Lost Creek Reservoir. The trail provides access to scenic areas for viewing wildflowers and wildlife and to the creek and lakes for fishing and swimming. Four inches of base material create a smooth, stable surface. Trailheads begin at each end in the park and reservoir. The multi-use trail accommodates hiking, biking, and horseback riding. The 2-mile Prickly Pear hiking trail passes through open prairie and the 1/4-mile nature walk follows Lost Creek.

PLANTS AND ANIMALS

The fort was situated on the south bank of the small but beautiful Lost Creek. The creek drainage is heavily wooded with elm, hackberry, and oak trees. Large expanses of prairie surround the creek. Prickly pear cacti and mesquite trees have invaded portions of the prairie, especially around the old hospital. A short nature trail, beginning at the campgrounds, leads through a wooded area along the creek.

The wooded stream attracts many birds, while grassland species such as bobwhite quail and meadowlarks inhabit the meadows. Waterfowl are occasionally seen on the small quarry lake near the entrance. Buffalo were once common to the area, and buffalo wallows can be seen south of the parade ground.

HISTORY

With no protection from the U.S. Army during the Civil War, the white settlements in North Texas were under continual threat of Indian attack. After the war, a series of frontier forts was reestablished to rout the Indians.

Fort Richardson, named in honor of General Israel B. Richardson, was strategically located only 70 miles from Indian Territory in Oklahoma. The Indian raiding parties would swoop down from Oklahoma, attack a settlement or supply train, and hastily retreat to the protection of their own territory.

In 1874, an expedition from Fort Richardson led by Colonel Ranald Mackenzie, of the famed Mackenzie's Raiders, destroyed a large Comanche village in Palo Duro Canyon and defeated the famous war chief Quanah Parker. With no provisions, shelter, or horses, the Indians were unable to continue their raids and were at last forced out of Texas.

66. FORT TRAVIS SEASHORE PARK

LOCATION

Galveston County. Galveston County Parks Department. On TX 87 at western end of Bolivar Peninsula close to the ferry landing. Mailing address: 900 SH 87, PO Box B, Port Bolivar, TX 77650. Phone: 409-684-1333, reservations 409-934-8100. Internet: www.galvestonparks-seniors.org/locations/ls_overview.asp; info.parks.seniors@co.galveston.tx.us.

FACILITIES

Camping: 70 acres, primitive tent camping only, 6 cabanas with electricity, water; restroom with showers. Fees charged, open all year. Note: In

September 2008, Hurricane Ike caused considerable damage. Check for condition of park facilities.

Recreation: picnic tables with grills, fishing from jetty, bird-watching, historical bunkers and batteries of Fort Travis, originally built in 1836 and rebuilt several times until decommissioned in 1949.

67. FOSSIL RIM RANCH WILDLIFE CENTER

LOCATION

Somervell County. From Glen Rose 3 miles west on U.S. 67, 1 mile south on CR 2008. Mailing address: PO Box 2189 (2155 CR 2008), Glen Rose, TX 76043. Phone: 254-897-2960, 888-775-6742. Internet: www.fossilrim.com.

FACILITIES

Foothills Safari Camp: 7 tented cabins with ac/heat, twin beds, bath, meals incl. at glass-walled pavilion overlooking wildlife watering hole. Lodge: 3-story remodeled hunting lodge with 5 rooms with Jacuzzis, fireplaces, balconies overlooking wildlife pastures, rated AAA "Gem." (No on-property camping or RV facilities. Dinosaur Valley State Park is 3 miles north of Glen Rose.)

MAIN ATTRACTIONS

Unlike many drive-through wildlife parks, Fossil Rim is non-profit organization and an accredited member of the Association of Zoo and Aquariums. The 1,800-acre conservation facility participates with the Species Survival Plan (SSP), which keeps a genetic database on all captive endangered species in North America and selects approved facilities to breed animals matched for genetic diversity. A behind-the-scenes guided tour of the Intensive Management Area offers close views of the endangered species. Large naturalistic enclosures house breeding cheetahs, rhinos, scimitar-horned oryx, Mexican gray wolves, and Atwater prairie chickens, and other rare species in the SSP.

The 9.5-mile wildlife driving loop passes through natural pastures and rolling hills stocked with more than 1,000 free-roaming animals. Giraffes bend down to feed from outstretched cups of animal chow, zebras peer into car windows, ostriches block the roads as if demanding a toll of food, herds of addax graze beside the road, and regal sable antelopes seem to pose for photos. The Overlook Café provides a break stop halfway along the loop with fast food, gift shop, and Children's Animal Center. Guided wildlife tours are available in open Jeep safari vehicles, which the animals really cue on for the generous food handouts.

68. FRANKLIN MOUNTAINS STATE PARK

LOCATION

Mailing address: 1331 McKelligon Canyon Road, El Paso, TX 79930. Phone: 915-566-6441. For all state park reservations, call the centralized reservations system, 512-389-8900, or www. ReserveAmerica.com online. Call the state park information number, 800-792-1112, for information and fee updates.

FACILITIES

Camping: 5 RV sites with no hookups; primitive, walk-in tent sites; composting toilets; no water available. Fees charged.

Recreation: 44 picnic sites with shade shelters, 118 miles of multi-use trails for hiking, biking, horse riding. No motorized vehicles (including ATVs) are allowed on any dirt road or trail. The Wyler Aerial Tramway leads to the top of Ranger Peak from the south end of the park. (See separate listing.)

WEATHER

July high averages 95 degrees, January low 30 degrees.

MAIN ATTRACTIONS

When the state legislature established the Franklin Mountains State Park in 1979, it created the largest urban park in the nation, though one of the most rugged and desolate. The entire 24,247.56 acres, covering 37 square miles, lies within the city limits of El Paso. Through the decades, the park is slowly being developed with picnicking, hike/bike trails, and camping facilities.

The pass in the Franklin Mountains which gives El Paso its name was used for thousands of years as a route between what is now Mexico and the United States. Native American groups lived in the mountains for 12,000 years. They left pictographs on boulders and in rock shelters and mortar pits used to grind seeds in rock. The park preserves from urban sprawl and development the history and delicate ecology of the desert mountains.

The hills and canyons of the mountains offer outdoor recreationists hiking, mountain biking, horse riding, and rock climbing. Many trails loop through the picnic area and others lead off of Loop 375/Trans-Mountain Road. The trail system will eventually be developed into a 118-mile network. All trails are open for hiking, 51 miles for mountain biking, and 22 miles for multi-use including horse riding. Rock climbing, especially in winter when northern sites are snowed in, is also popular.

PLANTS AND ANIMALS

The plants and animals of the Franklin Mountains typify the Chihuahuan Desert with a predominance of lechuguilla, sotol, ocotillo, and numerous species of yuccas and cacti. Several endemic species, especially cacti, grow nowhere else on the planet. Much of the wildlife in the desert has developed a nocturnal lifestyle to escape the heat and predators. Golden eagles nest in the mountains, bats roost in secretive caves, and cougars prowl the slopes searching for mule deer and other prey. Foxes, rodents, and other small mammals and numerous species of snakes and lizards thrive in the harsh environment.

69. FREDERICKSBURG: LADY BIRD JOHNSON MUNICIPAL PARK

Gillespie County. 3 miles southwest of Fredericksburg on TX 16. Mailing address: 432 Lady Bird Drive, Fredericksburg, TX 78624. Phone: 830-997-4202. Internet: www.fbgtx.org/other/rvpark.htm. Camping: 113 RV/tent sites with full hookups and cable TV, high-speed WiFi, undeveloped tent sites, modern restrooms, showers, trailer dump station. Reservations accepted by phone only. Fees charged, monthly rates available in winter. Recreation: picnic areas and playgrounds, swimming in pool and small lake, fishing, boat ramp (no motorboats), golf course, tennis courts, volleyball, recreation hall. Open all year. This park has excellent and diverse facilities; it may be crowded in the summer.

70. FREEPORT: QUINTANA BEACH COUNTY PARK

LOCATION

Brazoria County. 5 miles south of Freeport on FM 1495 across the Intracoastal Canal, 3 miles north on County Rd. 723 to Quintana, east on Fifth St.
Mailing address: 330 5th Street, Quintana, TX 77541. Phone: 979-233-1461 or 800-872-7578. Internet: www.brazoriacountyparks. com/. Note: In September 2008, Hurricane Ike caused considerable damage. Check for condition of park facilities.

FACILITIES

Camping: 19 pull-through RV sites with full hookups, 37 back-in RV/tent sites with full hookups, 6 cabins (a/c-heat, TV, microwave, coffee pot, fridge, range, showers; bring bed linens, towels, cooking/eating utensils), primitive camping, no water, bathhouse, laundry, modern restrooms, showers. Reservations accepted, fees charged. Open all year. Facilities 200 yards from beach.

Recreation: picnicking on and off the beach, half mile of beach, swimming; jetty, surf, and pier fishing; 2 historic houses with nature exhibits; shelling, hiking trails, playgrounds. Open daily dawn to dusk.

MAIN ATTRACTIONS

The beautiful beaches and rolling surf of the Gulf of Mexico attract visitors to this park for a day, or longer, of fun in the sun. Two historic houses from the 1880s have been moved to the park and restored. One has displays of seashells, beach ecology, area history, and a touch-and-feel table for the youngsters. Fishermen catch speckled trout and redfish, and beachcombers collect interesting shells washed ashore. Hiking trails lead to a World War II gun emplacement and through wetlands and dunes bordering the beach.

FREEPORT: SAN LUIS COUNTY PARK

LOCATION

Brazoria County. Take FM 332 southeast of Lake Jackson to Surfside beach, then 13 miles northeast on County Rd. 257, before the San Luis Pass toll bridge. Also referred to as Brazoria County Access Point.
Mailing address: 14001 CR 257 (Blue Water Highway), Freeport, TX 77541. Phone: 979-233-6026, 800-372-7578. Internet: www. brazoriacountyparks.com/. Note: In September, 2008 Hurricane Ike caused considerable damage. Check for condition of park facilities.

FACILITIES

Camping: 69 back-in RV sites with full hookups, 4 cabins (a/c-heat, TV, microwave, coffee pot, fridge, range, showers; bring bed linens, towels, cooking/eating utensils), bathhouse, laundry, modern restrooms, showers.

Recreation: quarter-mile bay front for fishing and sailing; picnicking area, park store, group pavilion, playground, recreation hall, boat ramp.

MAIN ATTRACTIONS

At the northern end of Follets Island at San Luis Pass, this 17-acre park is an ideal spot for fishing and sailing in the bay. The colorful sails of windsurfers dot the water, and shell collectors stroll the beach. Bird-watchers enjoy the many shorebirds and wading birds attracted to the surf and wetlands, and photographers find a picturesque setting for sunset and sunrise pictures.

71. GALVESTON ISLAND STATE PARK

LOCATION

Galveston County. 6 miles southwest of the Galveston City Seawall on FM 3005.
Mailing address: 14901 FM 3005, Galveston, Texas 77554. Phone: 409-737-1222. For all state park reservations, call the centralized reservations system, 512-389-8900, or www.ReserveAmerica.com online. Call the state park information number, 800-792-1112, for information and fee updates.

FACILITIES

Fees: entrance, facility, activity use; subject to change. WiFi available (user fee). Note: Hurricane Ike in September 2008 did considerable damage. Check for condition of park facilities.

Camping: 150 campsites with water and electricity on beachside; bayside group trailer area with 20 sites with water and electricity, 10 screened shelters, modern restrooms with showers, trailer dump station. Fees charged.

Recreation: picnic areas, playgrounds, swimming beach, surf fishing, fish-cleaning station, interpretive center, self-guiding nature trail, 4 miles of hiking/mountain bike trails, wildlife observation platform and bird blind, ¼-mile nature trail, boat ramp adjacent to the park, Texas State Park Store.

WEATHER

July high averages 86 degrees, January low 46 degrees.

MAIN ATTRACTIONS

Spanning the width of Galveston Island from rolling surf to protected bayfront, the park encompasses 2,013 acres of sand dunes, marshes, bay-ous, mud flats, and coastal prairies. More than 1,000 acres of ecologically important wetlands are preserved on an island rapidly being developed into resort property.

Crabs scurry for cover on the beach when disturbed.

The wide, 1.6-mile-long beach attracts swimmers, surfers, sunbathers, and beachcombers. Bayou fishing and wade fishing in the marshes are popular activities, as is surf fishing for flounder, drum, and trout. Four miles of nature trails wind through the salt marshes, with observation platforms, bird-viewing blinds, and boardwalks over bayous.

The Mary Moody Northern Amphitheater features outdoor dramas every evening except Mondays throughout the summer. Past performances include *The Sound of Music* and *Showboat*. Call 409-737-1744 for the summer play schedule.

PLANTS AND ANIMALS

The vegetation of the park is characteristic of a barrier island continually swept by the wind, pounded by the surf, and periodically stricken by tropical storms and hurricanes. The soil is sand and silt deposited by the Gulf currents and washed onto the island. The marshes vary in salinity from 3 parts salt per thousand parts water, nearly fresh, to salty, with 33 parts salt per thousand parts water. The vegetation must adapt to the varying salinity, as well as to the salty soil and the wind.

Dominant grasses are marshhay cordgrass, smooth cordgrass, and seashore saltgrass. In high areas with deeper soil, vines and shrubby plants produce thick tangles. Wildflowers grace the park almost year-round. Evening primroses and composites decorate the dunes, and gaillardias, asters, and goldenrods, among others, bloom on higher ground.

The wetlands are rich in wildlife. Hundreds of species of waterfowl and wading birds winter here in the marshes. In the early spring, the thousands of birds that have migrated across the Gulf of Mexico reach land on or near Galveston Island, and as spring progresses, the marshes are alive with breeding activity of the resident species. Throughout most of the year, the wet areas abound with hordes of mosquitoes that covet the blood of warm-blooded creatures, especially humans.

HISTORY

When discovered by Europeans, Galveston Island was the home of the Karankawa Indians, and there are several archaeological sites on the island today. The first European settlement came in 1817, when the colorful Jean Lafitte established a center for his smuggling and pirating activities on the island.

Galveston grew into a thriving shipping port during the 19th century but major storms in 1867, 1871, 1875, and 1886 kept it from surpassing nearby Houston as a center of commerce. The great storm of 1900 devastated the island and killed 5,000 to 10,000 people. It prompted the construction of the seawall that protects the northern half of the island.

The city of Galveston is famous for its resort facilities and its many historic buildings. The Bishop's Palace, open daily except Tuesdays, is the city's most celebrated landmark. The Galveston Historic Foundation is restoring to period specifications many buildings, especially those along the historic Strand Street. Galveston is resplendent with parks, museums, festivals, and fine seafood restaurants.

72. GARNER STATE PARK

LOCATION

Uvalde County. 31 miles north of Uvalde on U.S. 83.
Mailing address: 234 RR 1050, Concan, TX 78838. Phone: 830-232-6132. For all state park reservations, call the centralized reservations system, 512-389-8900, or www.ReserveAmerica.com online. Call the state park information number, 800-792-1112, for information and fee updates.

FACILITIES

Fees: entrance, facility, activity use; subject to change.

Camping: 213 back-in RV/tent sites with water and electricity, 132 back-in RV/tent sites with water, 37 screened shelters, 17 cabins, group camp with 5 screened shelters with bunk beds and dining hall, modern restrooms with showers, trailer dump stations, group day-use screened shelter for 75 people with equipped kitchen. Fees charged.

Recreation: picnic areas, playgrounds, picnic shelter with a dining hall (capacity 75), .6-mile surfaced hike/bike trail, 5.5-mile unpaved hiking trail, swimming and tubing in Frio River. Summer only: miniature golf, paddleboat rental, nightly jukebox dance, concession snacks, Cowboy Sunset Serenade (cowboy songs and poetry, fee charged).

Note: The park closes when maximum parking capacity is reached, often on summer and holiday weekends by 11:00 a.m. The park reopens when sufficient parking is available. The summer nightly dance frequently reaches parking capacity with access closed as early as 8:30 p.m. Have alternate plans if the park is closed. Closures do not affect those with reservations.

WEATHER

July high averages 97 degrees, January low 37 degrees.

MAIN ATTRACTIONS

Recreation in the park is centered around the broad, wooded bottomlands and the spring-fed Frio River. The variety of summer activities and the large number of camping and day-use facilities make Garner one of the most popular parks in the state. There are short trails along the river and a paved trail along portions of the road. This park is suitable for a quiet outdoor experience only during the fall and winter months.

The 1,420-acre park is named after John Nance Garner, who was vice president under Franklin Roosevelt. The Garner home and museum in Uvalde is open daily.

The park is situated along open grasslands and wooded bottomlands bordering the scenic Frio River. The flat meadows end abruptly with steep, rocky hillsides and sheer cliffs typical of the rough terrain of Central Texas. The bottomlands are shaded with numerous pecan trees, and live oak and mesquite trees grow in the grassland savannas. Much of the grassland has been invaded by brush and trees, which provide good habitat for the deer, turkeys, and rabbits common to the park. The hills are covered with juniper, live oak, mountain laurel, and evergreen sumac.

73. GOLIAD STATE PARK

LOCATION

Goliad County. 25 miles southwest of Victoria on U.S. 59 to Goliad, 1 mile south on U.S. 183.

Mailing address: 108 Park Rd. 6, Goliad, Texas 77963. Phone: 361-645-3405. For all state park reservations, call the centralized reservations system, 512-389-8900, or www.ReserveAmerica.com online. Call the state park information number, 800-792-1112, for information and fee updates.

FACILITIES

Camping: 20 pull-through RV/tent sites with full hookups, 24 back-in RV sites with water and electricity, 14 primitive tent sides with water nearby, 5 screened shelters, trailer dump station, modern restrooms with showers. Fees charged.

Recreation: picnic areas and playgrounds, nature trail with trail guide booklet, interpretive exhibits, swimming pool (summer only), fishing and boating on the San Antonio River, historical buildings and museum, dining hall with kitchen.

WEATHER

July high averages 96 degrees, January low 43 degrees.

MAIN ATTRACTIONS

The Spanish mission Nuestra Señora del Espíritu Santo de Zuñiga is the dominant feature in the park. The mission, built in 1749 for the purpose of converting the Aranama and Tamique Indians to Christianity, operated for 110 years—longer than any other Spanish mission in Texas. The church has been restored, as have the adjoining granary and workshop. The granary now serves as a museum of Indian and Spanish colonial exhibits and artifacts. The original foundation and floors of the priests' quarters and the ruins of the living quarters are immediately behind the granary.

Ruins of the mission Nuestra Señora del Rosario, founded in 1754 by Franciscan missionaries, are 6 miles southwest of Goliad on U.S. 59. The mission, which attempted to convert the Karankawa, Cujane, and Coapite Indians, was abandoned and reoccupied periodically; it achieved only limited success.

The park also includes General Ignacio Zaragosa's birthplace. Zaragosa is one of Mexico's most famous military heroes. He commanded the Mexican army that defeated the invading French at the Battle of Puebla on May 5, 1862. That victory is celebrated as a national holiday in Mexico, Cinco de Mayo, and is observed throughout South Texas.

The Presidio La Bahía is just south of the park on U.S. 183; it has been restored to its original condition. The presidio—built near Mission Espíritu Santo to protect it from hostile Indians—grew into one of the most important Spanish frontier forts. Today it is the finest example in Texas of a Spanish fort.

The Spanish mission in Goliad SP was built in 1749.

In March 1836, Colonel James Fannin and his men were forced to surrender to the Mexican army at the Battle of Coleto Creek. They were marched to the Presidio La Bahía at Goliad. By order of Santa Anna, 342 of the prisoners were executed on March 27. The graves and a memorial to those heroic Texans are located near the presidio. Fannin Battleground State Historic Site, 9 miles east of Goliad on U.S. 59, marks the location of the battle of Coleto Creek.

HIKING

The self-guided Aranama Nature Trail, only one-third of a mile long, provides an excellent introduction to the plant and animal communities of the area. A guidebook to the trail, explaining the plants and the ways the Indians used them, is available from the park headquarters, along with a comprehensive bird list.

PLANTS AND ANIMALS

Goliad State Park contains 184 acres of gently rolling plains at the crossroads of three major ecological regions in Texas. The plant and animal life is characteristic of the Gulf Coast prairies and marshes, South Texas plains, and post oak savannas. Much of the park lies along the San Antonio River; Goliad's dense riparian woodland is composed of live oak, cedar elm, hackberry, and anaqua trees.

A majority of the original grassland of the South Texas plains, which spawned the great Texas cattle empire, is now covered with impenetrable thorny brush. After a hundred years of overgrazing, the land has been irreparably altered. Prairie that once stretched from horizon to horizon is now a tangle of brushy, thorny plants. Snakewood, lotebush, blackbrush, bluewood, and mesquite have invaded the grassland that was once common around Goliad.

Located at the juncture of three biotic zones, the park contains a rich diversity of plants and animals. The natural area is an important landfall for migratory birds. More than 300 species have been recorded in the park, including the subtropical groove-billed ani, olivaceous cormorant, brown-crested flycatcher, long-billed thrasher, and olive sparrow.

74. GONZALES: INDEPENDENCE PARK

Gonzales County. In Gonzales where U.S. 183 crosses the Guadalupe River. Mailing address: P.O. Box 547, Gonzales, Texas 78629. Phone: 830-672-3192. Internet: parks&recreation@cityofgonzales.org, www .cityofgonzales.org. Camping: 21 sites (4 pull-through and 17 back-in) with full hookups, primitive tent area, trailer dump station. With swimming pool, golf course, rodeo arena, softball and volleyball fields, and picnic pavilions, expect this 169 acres city park to be heavily used by locals, but it would be suitable for an en route overnight stay. Fees charged, reservations accepted, open all year.

Nearby attraction: The Gonzales Pioneer Village, with 10 reconstructed log houses from the 1800s, is one-half mile north of town on U.S. 183. Open weekends only.

GONZALES: J. B. WELLS PARK

South of Gonzales at intersection of U.S. 183 and TX 183. Mailing address: P. O. Box 547, Gonzales, TX 78629. Phone: 830-672-3192. Internet: parks&recreation@cityofgonzales.org, www.cityofgonzales.org. 169-acre park. *Camping:* 151 RV sites with full hookups (100 more planned).

1-mile hike/bike trail, covered pavilion, Gonzales Arena (rodeo) and show barn. Fees charged. More of a stop-over than a long-term place to stay.

GONZALES: LAKE WOOD RECREATION AREA

Gonzales County. On Lake Wood and Guadalupe River; 48 acres. 3 miles west of Gonzales on U.S. 90A, 3 miles south on FM 2091. Mailing address; 167 CR 254, Gonzales, TX 78629. Phone: 830-672-2779. Camping: 16 back-in RV/tent sites with full hookups, 3 pull-through sites with water and electricity, tent sites with water and electricity, primitive tent sites, modern restrooms, hot showers. Fees charged. Reservations accepted. Recreation: picnic area, park store, swimming in lake, boat ramp, fishing. Open all year.

75. GOOSE ISLAND STATE PARK

LOCATION

Aransas County. 8 miles north of Rockport on TX 35 to PR 13, at the north side of Copano Bay.
Mailing address: 202 S. Palmetto St., Rockport, Texas 78382-7965. Phone: 361-729-2858. For all state park reservations, call the centralized reservations system, 512-389-8900, or www.ReserveAmerica.com online. Call the state park information number, 800-792-1112, for information and fee updates.

FACILITIES

Fees: entrance, facility, activity use; subject to change.

Camping: 102 pull-through RV/tent sites with water and electricity, 25 walk-in (150 yards) tent sites with water nearby, modern restrooms, showers. Some camp sites are bay-front cabana style shade shelters and some in wooded areas. Fees charged.

Recreation: picnic areas, playground, 1,620-foot lighted fishing pier, boating in Copano Bay, boat ramp, guided bird tours during spring migration February–April, 2 fish-cleaning tables, group recreation hall (no kitchen, capacity 50), Texas State Park Store.

WEATHER

July high averages 92 degrees, January low 45 degrees, humid.

MAIN ATTRACTIONS

Goose Island State Park—at the confluence of Aransas, Saint Charles, and Copano bays—offers the visitor excellent fishing and bird-watching. The shallow bay teems with fish and attracts a large variety of birds. Saltwater fishermen catch trout, flounder, sheepshead, and redfish from the shore, pier, and boats.

Aransas National Wildlife Refuge, 30 miles north by car, has a number of nature trails, a loop drive, an observation tower, and an excellent interpretive center with displays, media presentations, and literature. Whooping cranes live in the refuge from October through April and occasionally can be seen from the tower.

The best way to see the whoopers is to take a commercial tour boat that operates from Fulton and Rockport. For a list of tour boats, call the

Rockport Chamber of Commerce, 800-242-0071, www.rockport-fulton
.org. Most tours leave daily November through April 1 and cost about
$30 for adults.

Nearby Rockport has a ski basin, a beach, the Texas Maritime Museum, and fine seafood restaurants. Fulton Mansion State Historic Structure is on Fulton Beach Road. It was built in 1872 and has been restored
by the Parks and Wildlife Department.

PLANTS AND ANIMALS

The 314 acres of Goose Island State Park encompass two distinct
ecosystems: the bay and the uplands. Gulls, pelicans, oystercatchers,
egrets, herons, shorebirds, and many species of ducks feast on fish and
other small creatures in the bays and marshes.

Millions of migrating shorebirds and waterfowl winter along the
Texas coast, making Goose Island a favorite for bird-watchers. Situated
on the Central Flyway, the park attracts many birds on their way to and
from the tropics. More species of birds have been sighted in the Rockport area during the annual Audubon Christmas Bird Count than in any
other place in the country.

Live oaks, red bay trees, and yaupon hollies form dense thickets in the
sandy coastal uplands. The thickets are an excellent habitat for raccoons,
skunks, squirrels, and opossums.

One of the national champion coastal live oaks, *Quercus virginiana*, is
near the park. The tree measures 35 feet in circumference, is 44 feet
high, and has a crown spread of 89 feet. This ancient tree, at least a
thousand years old, is located north of the main park entrance and
overlooks the bay.

76. GOVERNMENT CANYON STATE
NATURAL AREA

LOCATION

Bexar County. San Antonio, from Loop 1604 and Culebra Road
(FM 471), go west 3.5 miles to Galm Road, turn north (right)
on Galm and go 1.6 miles to gate with signs on the left. Mailing
address: 12861 Galm Rd., San Antonio, TX 78254. Phone: 210-
688-9055.

FACILITIES

Fees: entrance, facility, activity use; subject to change. WiFi available
(user fee).

This natural-area park is still under development with trail and
primitive campsite construction ongoing. Currently day-use only with

no camping. Open Friday–Monday 8 a.m.–6 p.m., closed Tuesday–Thursday. Access to Backcountry trails closes at 4 p.m. and access to Frontcountry trails at 5 p.m. Protected Habitat Area trails open September through February only.

Recreation: picnic pavilion with 10 tables, restrooms, modern restrooms, Texas State Store. Trails: By 2008, more than 30 miles of trails were completed and open in the three designated areas of the park. Frontcountry, hike/bike with future equestrian use planned: Lytle's Loop 4.8 miles and Savannah Loop 2.3 miles. Backcountry, hiking only: Bluff Spur 1.8 miles and Overlook Trail 1 mile; hike/bike: Caroline's Loop 2.5 miles, Far Reaches 3 miles, Joe Johnston route 4 miles, Little Windmill .6 mile, Recharge Trail 1.2 miles, Twin Oaks 2 miles, Wildcat Canyon 1.7 miles. Protected Habitat Area (September–February), hiking only: Black Hill Loop 5.1 miles, Cave Creek 1.7 miles, La Subida .8 miles, Sendero Travesero .5 mile.

MAIN ATTRACTIONS

In 1993, Parks and Wildlife acquired 8,642 acres almost within the city limits of San Antonio. The former ranch contains the historic Government Springs, a rich archaeological site from prehistoric and historic times. A stone house, believed to be from the Civil War era, still stands near the springs, which were a stop-over on the old San Antonio to Fredericksburg road and an outpost for an Indian fort.

The park includes portions of blackland prairie, but 88 percent lies within the recharge zone of the Edwards Plateau. Rugged limestone hills dissected by deep canyons typify the park. The oak-juniper forest provides habitat for the endangered golden-cheeked warbler, which breeds only in old-growth juniper woodlands of central Texas. The primary recreational focus will be hiking, wildlife viewing, and picnicking, with minimal camping and development due to the ecologically sensitive nature of the recharge zone and endangered species.

77. GUADALUPE MOUNTAINS NATIONAL PARK

LOCATION

Culberson and Hudspeth counties. Headquarters Visitors Center and Pine Springs Campground: 110 miles east of El Paso or 55 miles southwest of Carlsbad, New Mexico, on U.S. 62/180. Dog Canyon Ranger Station: 12 miles north of Carlsbad on U.S. 285, 57 miles south on NM Highway 137, or 5 miles south of Carlsbad on U.S. 62/180, then take County Road 408 for 60 miles to NM 137. Mailing address: 400 Pine Canyon Road, Salt Flat, Texas 79847. Phone: Headquarters Visitor Center 915-828-3251, Dog Canyon Ranger Station 505-981-2418. Internet: www.nps.gov/gumo.

FACILITIES

Camping: 10 backpacking campgrounds require a free permit from the Headquarters Visitor Center or Dog Canyon Ranger Station; 19 RV sites and 21 tent sites with no hookups at Pine Springs, 4 RV sites and 9 tent sites with no hookups at Dog Canyon; modern restrooms without showers at Pine Springs and Dog Canyon. Fees charged.

Recreation: picnicking, more than 80 miles of hiking and nature trails, interpretive exhibits with trail guide pamphlets and animal checklists.

MAIN ATTRACTIONS

Towering 5,000 feet above the desert basin, the sheer cliffs of the Guadalupe Mountains can be seen from a distance of 50 miles. The park encompasses the southern edge of the range, deep canyons that cut into the rugged mountains, and the surrounding desert. A crystal clear stream flows through the heavily wooded McKittrick Canyon, described as the most beautiful spot in Texas. Each fall, the bigtooth maple trees turn breathtaking hues of crimson, burgundy, and orange. We have trouble

White gypsum dunes on the west side of the Guadalupe Mountains.

deciding between Big Bend and the Guadalupe Mountains as our favorite Texas vacation spot.

Nearby attractions include Carlsbad Caverns National Park, 45 miles northeast of the Headquarters Visitors Center. Camping and lodging are available in commercial facilities at Whites City. The Living Desert Zoological and Botanical State Park is in Carlsbad. Plant and animal life of the Chihuahuan Desert is displayed in natural settings. There is no camping in the park.

HIKING

Major access to the park is by hiking. There are more than 80 miles of improved trails, leading to the top of Guadalupe Peak, the highest spot in Texas, into picturesque McKittrick Canyon, and into the pine- and fir-covered high country. There are short day hikes and many opportunities for backpacking. A topographic map is essential for mountain hiking. Maps and backcountry camping permits are available at the Headquarters Visitors Center.

The trails in the park vary from paths on relatively level terrain to rugged, steep trails only for well-conditioned, experienced hikers. Water is available only at the trailheads in Pine Springs Campground and in McKittrick Canyon, at the Visitors Center and at the Dog Canyon Ranger Station and trailhead. During the summer, a gallon of water per day per person is required for overnight camping, half a gallon for day hikes. Park regulations prohibit the use of surface water for drinking or washing.

Smith Spring and Manzanita Spring are reached by a one-mile hike from the Frijole Ranch Museum. Smith Spring is in a luxuriant small canyon tucked away between the mountain ridges. Manzanita Spring magically appears below the dry mountain slopes and forms a circular pond attracting much wildlife. From the trail, the mirror surface of the water reflects the blue West Texas sky and an unusual nipple-shaped peak in the distance.

From the Pine Springs trailhead, trails lead atop Guadalupe Peak, 8,749 feet above sea level, and to a series of loop trails in the high country. The well-maintained Guadalupe Peak Trail climbs over 3,000 feet in 4.5 miles. The view from the top of Texas encompasses vast salt basins and gypsum sand dunes to the west and the Delaware Mountains to the south. The Guadalupe Mountains and Lincoln National Forest stretch to the north in New Mexico.

The Tejas Trail climbs to the ridge along the southern escarpment of the mountains. The Bear Canyon Trail to the summit is steep and badly eroded, causing hazardous footing. The Bush Mountain, Bowl, and Juniper trails intersect a short distance from the summit of the Tejas Trail and connect with others to form a variety of mountain loops. There are three designated campsites along the trails.

Two trails lead from the McKittrick Canyon Visitors' Center. The Permian Reef Geology Trail climbs the steep ridge out of the park into

Lincoln National Forest. It passes through the heart of the gigantic fossilized sponge and algae reef that forms the Guadalupe Mountains. Some of the best examples of more than 500 fossil species found in the park are exposed along the trail.

The trail into McKittrick Canyon provides a walk along the fairly flat terrain of the shaded streambed. The Pratt Lodge Historic Site, 2.4 miles into the canyon, is an ideal picnic spot with tables and restrooms in the summer. The trail continues another mile to the Grotto picnic area. The canopy of trees beneath the towering mountain peaks and the gently babbling stream produce a cathedral-like atmosphere along the trail.

McKittrick Trail ascends McKittrick Ridge and connects with the Tejas and other mountain trails. A primitive campsite is located half a mile below the ridgetop or 7.6 miles from the visitors center.

The Dog Canyon Campground and trailhead are in a remote section of the park, reached by a 2-hour drive from Carlsbad. The Tejas and Marcus trails traverse Dog Canyon and West Dog Canyon and connect with the high-country trail system. The trails, not as steep as the trail from Pine Springs, lead to spectacular views of the park.

PLANTS AND ANIMALS

Because the Guadalupe Mountains are at the southern tip of the Rockies, the northern edge of the Chihuahuan Desert, and the western extension of the Central Plains, the park contains a diverse mixture of plants and animals. The northern range of many Mexican species merges with the southern limit of Rocky Mountain species.

The park includes plants adapted to the Chihuahuan Desert, the sheltered canyons cut into the mountain slopes, and the high country. Creosote bush, lechuguilla, white-thorn acacia, and snakeweed dominate the desert basin surrounding the southern end of the mountain range. Yucca, sotol, agave, prickly pear cactus, and one-seed juniper grow on the lower mountain slopes.

The heads of the canyons are wooded with pinyon pine, alligator juniper, gray oak, Texas madrone, agarita, and sumac. Farther up the watersheds, deciduous trees, maples and oaks, dominate. A coniferous forest of ponderosa and limber pines and Douglas firs grows on the upper slopes and mountaintops. The Bowl, a protected depression north of Hunter Peak, is heavily wooded with conifers and is a favorite destination for hikers.

Millions of years of erosion have dissected the slopes with deep canyons which harbor delicate ecosystems in their protected interiors. McKittrick Canyon is the most spectacular and accessible of such canyons. Bigtooth maples, Texas madrones, pines, and a variety of oaks and other hardwoods shade the perennial stream as it cascades through the scenic canyon. Quiet pools bordered with sawgrass reflect the rugged mountains and blue sky above. The sawgrass, with its long serrated blades, is as much at home in this mountain setting as it is on the Gulf Coast, where it is common.

Animals such as the pronghorn antelope, kit fox, peccary, and kangaroo rat live in the desert and on the drier lower slopes. Mule deer, elk, mountain lions, coyotes, and gray foxes range from the lower slopes into the protected canyons and wooded high country. Mountain species include the rare black bear, gray-footed chipmunk, and an introduced species of elk. The mountain bighorn sheep and Meriam's elk, which used to roam the high country, have been extirpated by human activities.

More than 270 species of birds have been recorded in the park. The endangered peregrine falcon nests in the park, and golden eagles may be seen soaring along the escarpment edge. Seven species of owls occur in the various habitats of the park, and six species of hummingbirds have been sighted among the many cacti and wildflowers that bloom from the desert floor to the mountain ridges.

From 230 million to 280 million years ago, a shallow sea covered West Texas. A massive reef, formed mainly by lime-secreting algae, developed along its southern shore. The horseshoe-shaped reef, the largest known, stretched for 350 miles and was more than a mile wide and several hundred feet high. Eventually, the outlet to the sea was closed off, and the briny water evaporated, forming thick deposits of salt and gypsum. Then the area was covered with thousands of feet of stream-deposited sediments. Each of those complex processes occurred over millions of years.

Uplifts, tilting, and block faulting began 10 million to 12 million years ago and gradually elevated the area far above sea level. Erosion began the slow process of removing the overlying rock, finally exposing portions of the fossilized reef and carving the rugged canyons we see today. The Guadalupe Mountains, rich in fossil marine organisms, have many caverns created as groundwater dissolved the limestone bedrock.

The weather in the Guadalupe Mountains is known for two characteristics: changeability and high winds. Thunderstorms can build over the mountains in hours, and windstorms can sweep the ridges and down the canyons with hurricane velocity. Semitrailers have been blown off the highway through Guadalupe Pass, and the trailer once serving as the ranger station in McKittrick Canyon was blown down the canyon like a tumbleweed.

In the lower elevations, temperatures average in the eighties in the summer and in the low thirties during the winter. Mountain temperatures will be 10 to 15 degrees lower, and wind can reduce effective temperatures even more.

The area averages about 20 inches of precipitation a year, with the high country being wetter. In contrast, the surrounding desert averages 8 to 10 inches per year. The rainy months extend from June to September, but campers should be prepared for rain during any season. Wool clothing, which retains body heat even when wet, is advisable for winter hiking and backpacking.

HISTORY

Pictographs (rock paintings in red, yellow, and black) and petroglyphs (designs carved into the rock) have been discovered in and around the national park. The abstract and naturalistic human and animal forms are difficult to date but are thought to be several hundred to possibly over a thousand years old. The sites are not accessible to the public.

The Guadalupe Mountains were the last stronghold for the Mescalero Apaches. A marker at Manzanita Springs describes the last battle where the Indians were routed in 1869. The Indian settlement at that location was attacked, the village and winter stores destroyed, and the survivors driven into the mountains. With no hope of living through the winter, the Apaches surrendered and were placed on a reservation near Fort Stanton, New Mexico.

Poor conditions on the reservation led to a final revolt in 1880. That revolt resulted in a slaughter of the Mescaleros on a plateau near El Capitan. By the late 1880s, all the Mescaleros in the United States were on reservations.

The Butterfield Overland Stage was routed through Guadalupe Pass in 1858. A more southerly route with a dependable water supply and army protection was chosen after 11 months of operation. The ruins of the stage station, the Pinery, are located at the entrance to Pine Springs Campground.

The remnants of several ranching operations are evident in the park. Pipes that carried water from Smith Spring up the mountain slope to a stock tank in the Bowl are still visible. The remains of the Williams Ranch can be seen in the desert grassland west of the mountains. Much of the parkland was a working ranch until 1972, when the national park was established.

78. GUADALUPE RIVER STATE PARK AND HONEY CREEK STATE NATURAL AREA

LOCATION

Comal and Kendall counties. 29 miles north of San Antonio on U.S. 281, 8 miles west on TX 46, 3 miles north on PR 31. Mailing address: 3350 Park Road 31, Spring Branch, Texas 78070. Phone: 830-438-2656. For all state park reservations, call the centralized reservations system, 512-389-8900, or www.ReserveAmerica.com online. Call the state park information number, 800-792-1112, for information and fee updates. Note: The portion of the park across the river from the facilities is closed pending development.

FACILITIES

Fees: entrance, facility, activity use; subject to change.

Camping: 48 back-in RV/tent sites with water and electricity, 37 sites with water hookups, 9 walk-in tent sites with water. Modern restrooms, showers, trailer dump station. Fees charged.

Scenic Honey Creek flows into the Guadalupe River.

Recreation: picnic areas, playgrounds, canoeing, fishing, swimming, tubing, 3-mile hiking trail, 5.3-mile equestrian/mountain biking trail (no equestrian camping), guided tours of Honey Creek State Natural Area, Texas State Park Store. The park offers a guided hike along Honey Creek Canyon Saturdays 9–11 a.m. and weekly programs in the natural area throughout the year.

WEATHER

July high averages 94 degrees, January low 34 degrees.

MAIN ATTRACTIONS

The Guadalupe is one of the most beautiful rivers in the state. Large bald cypress trees shade its winding, picturesque banks and make it ideal for swimming, canoeing, and fishing. The river, which makes three U-shaped curves through the park, separates the northern portion of the park from the developed southern section. The Guadalupe, with both tranquil portions and white-water rapids, is a favorite of canoeists. There are four sections of rapids in the park. Canoes may be carried through the picnic grounds and launched in the day-use area, but most people prefer to launch their canoes at the low-water crossings outside the park.

The 2,294-acre Honey Creek State Natural Area is adjacent to Guadalupe River State Park and is accessible only by guided tours. A two-hour interpretive tour emphasizes history, geology, flora, and fauna and runs on Saturdays at 9:00 a.m. Reservations are not required, but call Guadalupe River State Park to confirm. The natural area has no facilities other than the two-mile nature trail.

The diverse landscape of Honey Creek supports Ashe juniper, live oak, agarita, and Texas persimmon in the rocky uplands. An eradication program to remove invasive juniper and Baccharis from the prairies is bringing back stands of native Indiangrass, little bluestem, and switchgrass. Hardwoods shade the creek as it deepens into a shallow canyon until sycamore and bald cypress and other flood plain species dominate. Texas palmetto, columbine, and maidenhair fern grow along the rock banks and spatter dock floats on the surface of the crystalline water.

The diversity of habitats provides a home for a variety of wildlife. Wild turkeys, armadillos, ringtails, white-tailed deer, and many types of frogs and fishes inhabit the preserve. Several species of endemics with limited ranges can also be found. Look for Cagle's map turtle, Guadalupe bass, four-lined skink, green kingfisher, Texas salamander, and the Honey Creek Cave salamander. Also, the endangered golden-cheeked warbler nests within the park.

In the mid-1800s, many German immigrants settled in Central Texas. Today, many of the towns in this area still reflect a distinctively German heritage. New Braunfels, 30 miles east on TX 46, is known for its German food. Landa Park, on the crystal springs that form the Comal River, is the site of Wurstfest in early November. The festival celebrates sausage, or wurst, and beer with traditional German singing, dancing, and music. Several outfitters along the Guadalupe River rent canoes and inner tubes.

Natural Bridge Caverns, one of the most scenic caves in Texas, is 16 miles west of New Braunfels on FM 1863.

PLANTS AND ANIMALS

The park preserves 1,900 acres of Central Texas Hill Country and a scenic section of the Guadalupe River. Sycamore, pecan, bald cypress, and hackberry trees shade the bottomlands and terraces along the river. Many of the large trees in the day-use area have been destroyed by flooding. Others lean in a downstream direction, attesting to the fury of the flooding common to Central Texas.

The river winds its sinuous course through limestone hills and plateaus, which themselves were carved by millions of years of erosion. Ashe juniper and oak trees dominate the dry uplands and provide the necessary habitat for the rare and beautiful golden-cheeked warbler. After rearing its young in the live oak-juniper woodlands of Central Texas, this colorful bird returns to the forests of Central America. About 260 species of birds, including many migrants, have been seen in the park. Other wildlife in the park are white-tailed deer, coyotes, gray foxes, bobcats, and raccoons. Armadillos are numerous, especially near the river, where they can easily burrow into the sandy banks.

The park is on the drainage zone for the Edwards Aquifer. Water seeps into the porous limestone hills and flows underground along an impervious layer of rock, emerging as springs wherever the rock is exposed to the surface. The springs form the San Antonio River in San

Antonio, the Comal River in New Braunfels, the San Marcos River in San Marcos, and Barton Springs in Austin.

79. HASKELL CITY PARK

LOCATION

Haskell County. From U.S. 277, east on South 7th for 2 blocks; from U.S. 380, south on Ave. C for 6 blocks. Mailing address: Box 1003, Haskell, Texas 79521. Phone: 940-864-2333.

FACILITIES

30 pull-through RV/tent sites with full hookups, modern restrooms, hot showers, trailer dump station, picnic tables, playgrounds, swimming pool, sports courts, .6-mile hiking path by creek. First night free, open all year, minimal facilities and upkeep suitable for en route overnight.

80. HILL COUNTRY STATE NATURAL AREA

LOCATION

Bandera County. 1 mile south of Bandera on TX 173, 10 miles west on FM 1077.
Mailing address: 10600 Bandera Creek Rd., Bandera, Texas 78003. Phone: 830-796-4413. For all state park reservations, call the centralized reservations system, 512-389-8900, or www. ReserveAmerica.com online. Call the state park information number, 800-792-1112, for information and fee updates.

FACILITIES

Fees: entrance, facility, activity use; subject to change.

Open: February through November: 7 days a week. December through January: Friday noon through Sunday 10:30 p.m. Open Christmas and New Year's week. Call the park for information.

Camping: 3 walk-in tent areas (capacity 75) with chemical toilets, walk-in tent areas; 2-acre (capacity 20 rigs) shaded equestrian area, large barn with a concrete floor and electricity, water for horses, fire rings, picnic tables, a chemical toilet, 12 horse stalls and 3 picket lines; group lodge for equestrian or non-equestrian use (capacity 12) with bathroom, kitchen (stove/refrigerator), ac/heat, horse stalls/corrals; 6 equestrian sites with water for horses; 3 primitive backpack areas (1.5 to 3.5 miles) with total capacity for 88, late arrival camping area.

Note: Campers must pack out all trash for disposal, including hay and animal by-products. Potable water is not available, all water must be treated. All horses brought to the park must have proof of negative Coggins disease test.

Recreation: 36 miles of trails for hiking, biking, horse riding; 3 designated swimming areas in creek.

WEATHER

July high averages 94 degrees, January low 31 degrees.

MAIN ATTRACTIONS

The rugged beauty of the 5,370 acres of this natural area attracts those who like the outdoors. This is not a park for party picnickers or RV campers. Thirty-four trails lead through the park, allowing adventurers to explore and make their own discoveries. But take care not to get lost. Campers must backpack 1.5 to 3.5 miles to three primitive camping areas with no water or other facilities. This is really getting away from city life. Since ground fires are prohibited, backpackers must use portable stoves and pack out all their garbage.

A majority of the park's visitors come to ride their horses. Riding clubs from all over Texas and surrounding states converge on the natural area for outings. All 36 miles of the trail system are jointly used by backpackers, day hikers, and horseback riders, with 32 miles available for mountain biking.

PLANTS AND ANIMALS

Visitors to this park will discover what the Texas Hill Country is really like. The rocky hills covered with scrubby junipers and oaks may look unimpressive, but closer investigation reveals a captivating beauty. Steep canyons harbor large trees, lush vegetation, and fern-lined springs. Sunfish dart under rocks in the spring-fed West Verde Creek. The picturesque, shallow creek provides a permanent oasis for wildlife. It winds through the hills providing water even when other, intermittent streams dry up.

A diversity of plants and animals live in the rugged terrain of the park. Visitors are likely to see white-tailed deer, armadillos, raccoons, skunks, and opossums, as well as a few snakes, lizards, and abundant birdlife. Turkeys, roadrunners, and quail scurry through the brush, and numerous sparrows, vireos, warblers, and other songbirds occur in the park, including the golden-cheeked warbler, which nests nowhere else but the juniper-covered hills of Central Texas.

The previous owner, Louise Lindsey Merrick, donated the ranch with the provision that it be "kept untouched by modern civilization, with everything preserved intact." We are fortunate to have access to such a large tract of unspoiled land in a part of Texas generally privately owned and inaccessible to the public.

81. HUECO TANKS STATE HISTORIC SITE

LOCATION

El Paso County. 32 miles east of El Paso on U.S. 180, 6 miles north on FM 2775.
Mailing address: 6900 Hueco Tanks Rd. #1, El Paso, Texas 79938-8793. Phone: 915-857-1135. For all state park reservations, call the centralized reservations system, 512-389-8900, or www.ReserveAmerica.com online. Call the state park information number, 800-792-1112, for information and fee updates.

FACILITIES

For the protection of cultural and natural resources, visitation is limited with special reservation and entry restrictions. Call for information.

Fees: entrance, facility, activity use; subject to change. WiFi available (user fee).

Camping: 17 campsites with water and electricity, 3 without electricity, modern restrooms with showers, trailer dump station. Fees charged.

Recreation: picnic areas, hiking trails through the rocks, rock climbing, guided tours on weekends, amphitheater with summer programs.

Note: Reservations are highly recommended. For day-use reservations for the next day only or for camping or tour reservations, call the site at 915-849-6684, 8 a.m. to 5 p.m. Mon.–Fri. For all other day-use reservations, call the Central Reservation Center at 512-389-8900. Park Hours: Winter (October 1 through April 30) 8 a.m. to 6 p.m. Summer (May 1 through September 30) 7 a.m.–7 p.m. Fri.–Sun.; 8 a.m.–6 p.m. Mon.–Thurs.

WEATHER

July high averages 95 degrees, January low 30 degrees.

MAIN ATTRACTIONS

The park preserves more than 3,500 Indian pictographs painted in an outcropping of intrusive igneous rock in the Chihuahuan Desert. The paintings vary from crude figures to intricate masks and detailed

Indians painted masks and other figures on the rocks at
Hueco Tanks.

drawings of animals, people, and mythological figures. The colors of the
drawings were made with combinations of mineral-based pigments. For
example, masks are painted in red, black, gray, white, or a combination
of colors. A.T. Jackson's Picture Writing of Texas Indians and Forrest
Kirkland and W.W. Newcomb's Rock Art of Texas Indians discuss the
drawings. Archaeological research completed since the latter book was
published has assisted in dating the paintings.

HIKING

A series of unmarked trails leading through the large boulders enables
the visitor to view many of the beautiful pictographs. Guided tours
through the area are available on weekends. Some of the shorter trails are
easily accessible, and longer, more rigorous hikes traverse the ridgetops.

PLANTS AND ANIMALS

About 34 million years ago, molten rock welled up within the earth
and cooled before reaching the surface. Erosion over the intervening
millennia stripped away the overlying limestone, revealing the hardened

igneous rock to the elements. Today, the rocks stand as an island in the midst of the Chihuahuan Desert.

The igneous hills, composed of syenite porphyry, rise 300 to 450 feet above the desert floor and provide dramatic relief to the flat terrain. Weathering and other, undetermined factors have created large potlike depressions in the hills that collect rainwater. These basins, or huecos, have attracted humans for possibly 10,000 years. Animals tend to congregate at the water holes, especially migrating birds and large wandering mammals such as bobcats, coyotes, foxes, and mountain lions. A checklist of the birds in the park is available at the headquarters.

The temporary ponds support an interesting community of fairy shrimp, tadpole shrimp, and clam shrimp. The shrimp eggs survive the dry periods and hatch with the next rain. Many animals feed on the crustaceans, especially when the water level is low.

The mountains to the east channel water into the area of the tanks, and the soil, rich in material weathered from the igneous rocks, holds the moisture better than the surrounding desert soils. As a result, the vegetation in the area is distinctively different from the creosote bush, mesquite, yucca, agave, and thorny shrubs of the surrounding desert, which receives only eight inches of rain annually. Grasslands predominate, with galleries of Arizona oak and one-seed juniper growing in the sheltered canyons.

HISTORY

Artifacts of stone tools and projectile points indicate that the water reservoirs in the hills have attracted humans for possibly 10,000 years. The oldest paintings in the park date to the Desert Archaic period, several thousand years before the time of Christ. The first painters hunted small game and harvested edible plants.

By around A.D. 1000, a more sedentary farming culture had developed, with small villages of semisubterranean pit houses. Pictographs similar to those found in the southwestern pueblos suggest concurrent dates for some of the drawings. By 1400, the villages were abandoned. Early Spanish expeditions in 1581 and 1582 make no mention of any people living in the area.

The area of the tanks was probably not inhabited again until the Mescalero Apaches arrived in the late 1700s. They left their particular style of art, with pictures of horsemen, giant snakes, and dancing figures.

82. HUNTSVILLE STATE PARK

LOCATION

Walker County. 8 miles south of Huntsville off IH-45, Exit 109, west on PR 40, next to Sam Houston National Forest.

Mailing address: Box 508, Huntsville, Texas 77342-0508. Phone: 936-295-5644. For all state park reservations, call the centralized reservations system, 512-389-8900, or www.ReserveAmerica.com online. Call the state park information number, 800-792-1112, for information and fee updates.

FACILITIES

Fees: entrance, facility, activity use; subject to change.

Camping: 94 RV/tent sites with water only, 58 sites with water and electricity, 30 screened shelters, overflow camping area, modern restrooms with showers. Fees charged.

Recreation: picnic areas, playgrounds, screened group pavilion (capacity 75), group recreation hall (capacity 200), horseback riding, lake swimming, bathhouse, fishing piers, fish-cleaning tables, boat ramps and docks, boat rental (seasonal), 1.3-mile nature trail, 3.2 miles of surfaced bicycle trails, 15.5 miles of hiking trails, 11 miles of mountain bike trails, miniature golf, Texas State Park Store.

WEATHER

July high averages 90 degrees, January low 50 degrees, high humidity year-round.

MAIN ATTRACTIONS

Huntsville State Park is located on the picturesque 210-acre Lake Raven. Shore and pier fishing is popular, with catches of crappie, bass, and catfish being typical. The shaded picnic grounds under tall pines and the wide variety of recreational opportunities available make this park a favorite, but also a crowded, retreat for nearby Houston and Huntsville city dwellers. Because use is heavy all during the summer and year-round on weekends, reservations are recommended for camping.

Nearby Huntsville was the home of Sam Houston, the commander-in-chief of the Texas revolutionary army and the republic's first president. Houston was also the state's first governor, but he relinquished the office when he refused to take the oath of allegiance to the Confederacy. His home and the Sam Houston Memorial Museum are in Huntsville.

HIKING

More than 20 miles of multi-use hike/bike/horse trails, loops, and cut-offs weave through the creek bottoms, rolling hills, pine forests, and shores of Lake Raven. The 7-mile Chinquapin Trail circles through the heart of the park and around Lake Raven. The 9.5 mile Triple C Trail, named after the Civilian Conservation Corps who constructed the park in 1937, follows the boundary of the park. In the spring, blooming dogwood trees highlight the 1.9-mile Dogwood Trail. Portions of the 1.5-mile Prairie Branch Trail are closed to bikes due to erosion. The .2-mile Loblolly Trail and .8-mile Coloneh Trail offer short strolls through pine-scented woodlands. A .3-mile access trail connects with the Lone Star Trail, which meanders for 140 miles through the Sam Houston National Forest. No private horses are allowed on the equestrian trails, they must be rented from the park concessionaire.

PLANTS AND ANIMALS

The 2,083-acre park lies in the Piney Woods of East Texas and is surrounded by Sam Houston National Forest. The dominant trees in the park are the towering pines, which shade the campgrounds and picnic areas. The snowy flowers of the dogwood decorate the woods in late March, and the leaves of sweetgum and red maple lend a colorful touch each fall.

Lake Raven was created in the thirties when the Civilian Conservation Corps impounded three creeks that run through the park. Hardwoods, including black willow, river birch, green ash, oak, and elm species, grow along the creek bottomlands.

A checklist to the birds of the park lists 223 species. Many species of wood warblers are attracted to the rich forestland during spring and fall migrations. In spite of its name, ravens are not found on the lake, merely the common crow. The red-cockaded woodpecker is a rare find in the park. Deer can be seen feeding in the early morning, and raccoons often raid garbage cans and unprotected food at night.

83. INKS LAKE STATE PARK

LOCATION

Burnet County. 9 miles west of Burnet on TX 29, south on PR 4. Mailing address: 3630 Park Road 4 West, Burnet, Texas 78611. Phone: 512-793-2223. For all state park reservations, call the centralized reservations system, 512-389-8900, or www. ReserveAmerica.com online. Call the state park information number, 800-792-1112, for information and fee updates.

FACILITIES

Fees: entrance, facility, activity use; subject to change. WiFi available (user fee).

Camping: 137 RV/tent campsites with electric and water hookups, 50 sites with water hookups, 10 walk-in tent sites with electricity, 9 backpack tent areas (1.5-mile hike) with primitive toilets but no water, 22 mini-cabins (4 people) with ac/heat, water, electricity. Modern restrooms with showers, trailer dump station.

Recreation: picnic areas and playgrounds, 7.5 miles of hiking trails, swimming in lake, scuba diving, fishing with fishing piers, boating, boat rentals, 9-hole golf course, amphitheater, Texas State Park Store with year-round canoe, paddleboat, and jet ski rental.

WEATHER

July high averages 98 degrees, January low 33 degrees.

MAIN ATTRACTIONS

Inks Lake, with 803 surface acres, is one of the most beautiful lakes in Central Texas; it is popular for fishing, boating, water sports, and scuba diving. Picturesque creeks and some of the most beautiful wildflower settings in the state add to the charm of the park.

Each April, the Highland Lakes Bluebonnet Trail, which passes through the park, attracts thousands of wildflower lovers. Festivals in many of the area communities coincide with the colorful display of roadside flowers. Longhorn Cavern State Park, which offers tours of the caverns, is a short distance south on PR 4.

HIKING

The 1,200-acre park encompasses the rolling hills and wooded slopes surrounding Inks Lake. The trails meander through rugged landscapes of weathered pink granite, oak-juniper woodlands, and grassy savannas. The 7.5 miles of hiking trails include a 1.5-mile backpacking trail.

The creeks and coves at Inks Lake are perfect for summer recreation.

PLANTS AND ANIMALS

Inks Lake is in the Central Texas mineral region, one of the most geologically interesting parts of the state. The area is characterized by colorful outcroppings of granite, schist, and gneiss, rocks formed underground and exposed millions of years later by erosion. The sandy pink soil and massive dome mountains provide quite a contrast to the chalky limestone hills of most of Central Texas.

The most common rock seen in the park is Valley Spring gneiss, formed from sedimentary rocks that were recrystallized deep in the earth by heat and pressure. The pink gneiss, a metamorphic rock more than 600 million years old, is one of the oldest rock formations in the state. Near the park, outcroppings of Packsaddle schist, a gray metamorphic rock, can be seen adjacent to the gneiss. Granite, formed by molten rock that intruded into the older rocks, forms pink fingers that spread across the pink and gray metamorphic rocks.

Wildlife is abundant in the park, and white-tailed deer are commonly seen in the campgrounds toward evening. Many species of waterfowl are attracted to the lake, and numerous songbirds frequent the shoreline woods, especially during migration.

84. IRAAN: CITY PARKS

LOCATION

Pecos County. Alley Oop Park at intersection of TX 349 and U.S. 190. The Landing on TX 349 south behind the airport.
Mailing address: P.O. Box 457, Iraan, Texas 79744. Phone: 432-639-2301.

FACILITIES

Alley Oop Park: 10 RV/tent sites with full hookups, TV cable, tent area, water, restroom with shower nearby. The Landing: 12 RV sites with full hookups. The 15-acre Alley Oop Park commemorates the author of the comic strip Alley Oop, and the Yates Oil Field, with the most productive wells in North America. One 1,283-foot-deep well produced 3,036 barrels per hour. Playground has dinosaur figures, picnic area, little shade. Fees charged, reservations accepted, open all year.

85. JOE POOL LAKE, LOYD PARK

Tarrant County. Grand Prairie, IH-20, exit south on Great Southwest Parkway, west on Harwood, south on Arlington Webb Rd., west on

Ragland Rd. to park entrance. Mailing address: 3401 Ragland Rd., Mansfield, Texas 76063. Phone: 817-467-2104. Camping: 221 campsites with water and electricity, restrooms, showers, group camping, walk-in primitive camping with chemical toilets, trailer dump station. Recreation: picnic areas, playgrounds, group pavilion, boat launch, fishing, designated swimming area, 5.5 miles of hiking and mountain bike trails, ball field. Reservations accepted. Fees charged. Open year-round. Open March–October. Fees charged.

The nearby Lynn Creek Park, with swimming, picnicking, playgrounds, and boat launches, is day-use only.

86. KERRVILLE-SCHREINER PARK

LOCATION

Kerr County. Operated by City of Kerrville. 1 mile south of Kerrville on TX 16, 2 miles southeast on TX 173. Mailing address: 2385 Bandera Hwy., Kerrville, TX 78028. Phone: 830-257-2392. E-mail: kerrpark@kerrville.org. Internet: www.Kerrville.org, click Visitors.

FACILITIES

Camping: 44 pull-through RV/tent sites with full hookups; 22 pull-through sites with water and electricity; 58 tent sites; 23 mini-cabins with ac/heat, two bunk beds, showers; 1 family cabin with ac/heat, queen bed, two sets bunk beds, bathroom, shower, kitchenette with fridge, microwave, satellite TV; laundry facilities. Fees charged. Note: the gate to the south unit remains locked at all times and requires access code for entrance.

Recreation: picnic areas, covered and open, playgrounds, group recreation hall, group dining hall with full kitchen, 8 miles multi-use hike/bike trails, river swimming, lighted fishing pier, boat ramp, amphitheater.

WEATHER

July high averages 94 degrees. January low 34 degrees.

MAIN ATTRACTION

TX 173 divides the 517-acre park into two units, each with full facilities. Picnicking in the shade of the tall riparian trees and fishing in the Guadalupe River are the primary activities in the Flatrock Lake Unit. Anglers catch crappie, bass, perch, and catfish from the bank, boat, and a lighted fishing pier. One area of the riverfront is designated as an unsupervised swimming area.

Most of the 8-mile hike/bike trail system winds through the juniper-oak woodlands that cover the rolling limestone hills of the Hill Country Unit across the highway. Numerous loops and connections allow a combination of long and short hikes. Trails lead from the picnic and day-use areas, circle the wooded campgrounds, and parallel the park boundary. Another trail follows the river. Each year, the park serves as the hub of the Easter Hill Country Bicycle Tour.

PLANTS AND ANIMALS

The Flatrock Lake Unit offers picnicking and camping along the shaded banks of the Guadalupe River. Bald cypress, hackberry, sycamore, and pecan trees grow along the river; mesquite trees, live oaks, and grassy savannas dominate the uplands.

The vegetation of the Hill Country Unit is typical of the limestone hills of Central Texas. Plateau live oaks, Texas oaks, and Ashe junipers cover the ridges and the drainages that flow into the Guadalupe River.

Each spring, bluebonnets cover the grassy savannas in both units of the park. Indian blankets, Mexican hats, and a wide variety of other wildflowers add color to the rolling hills and riverbanks throughout the summer.

The park's many oaks and its shrubby vegetation provide abundant acorns and forage for a large population of deer and turkeys. At dusk, deer frequently graze along the roadsides in the Hill Country Unit. Other animals likely to be seen are armadillos, squirrels, rabbits, and many species of birds. Ask at the park entrance for a checklist of the birds.

87. KICKAPOO CAVERN STATE PARK

LOCATION

Kinney County. 22.5 miles north of Bracketville on RR 674. Mailing address: P.O. Box 705, Bracketville, Texas 78832. Phone: 830-563-2342. For all state park reservations, call the centralized reservations system, 512-389-8900, or www.ReserveAmerica.com online. Call the state park information number, 800-792-1112, for information and fee updates.

FACILITIES

Fees: entrance, facility, activity use; subject to change.

Access: The park gate is kept locked and entrance must be scheduled in advance of visiting. Call for details and tour reservations.

Camping: primitive camping with no water, restrooms or may not be available.

Recreation: Visitors can hike cross-country on old jeep trails, explore an undeveloped cave, and observe the plants, birds, and wildlife of the Edwards Plateau. You'll need to come prepared, though, with sturdy shoes for hiking the rocky hills, water, and powerful flashlights for cave exploration. The park has 18 miles of hiking trails and 14 miles of mountain bike trails.

A 2-acre picnic area with water and restrooms with showers is available for day use.

WEATHER

July high averages in mid-90s, January low in mid-30s.

PLANTS AND ANIMALS

The 6,400-acre park preserves an unusual section of the Texas Hill Country. Besides the flora and fauna associated with a deep cave system, the park preserves one of the rare populations of pinyon pine trees growing in the rocky soils of the Edwards Plateau. These pines, normally growing in mountains and high deserts of the western United States, thrive in small, isolated pockets in several central Texas counties. True to form, a porcupine was in the top of one of the trees when I visited the park. Plateau live oaks, Ashe juniper, and mesquite trees with open grassy savannas cover the rocky hills of the park.

Of the abundant bird life in the park, several rare species live in the park, including the gray vireo, varied bunting, and Montezuma quail. Also, one of the largest breeding populations of the endangered black-capped vireo on state-owned lands occurs in the park. Uncommon reptiles and amphibians in the park include the barking frog, mottled rock rattlesnake, and Texas alligator lizard.

Erosion has carved 15 caves in the limestone hills of the park. Kickapoo Cavern, 1,400 feet long, contains impressive dripstone formations. Stuart Bat Cave, 1,068 feet long, serves as a migratory stopover for large numbers of Brazilian freetail bats from mid-March through October. Staff-guided tours of Kickapoo Cavern and the evening bat flight from Stuart Bat Cave are available on a prearranged basis with fees charged. Kickapoo Cavern is undeveloped and the tour moderately strenuous. Lighting and appropriate gear and clothing are required. Reservations for the Stuart Bat Cave bat flight observations are scheduled from early April through mid-October.

88. KINGSVILLE: KAUFER-HUBERT MEMORIAL PARK AND SEAWIND RV RESORT

Kleberg County. 13 miles south of Kingsville on U.S. 77, 9 miles east on FM 628 to Baffin Bay; turn off U.S. 77 at the sign for the King's Inn. 20

acres on Baffin Bay. Mailing address: 1066 East FM 628, Riviera, Texas 78379. Phone: 361-297-5738. E-mail address: seawing@rivnet.com; Internet: http://home.granderiver.net/~seawind/index.htm. Camping: 159 pull-through RV/tent sites with full hookups and telephone, 8 tent sites, modern restrooms, showers, laundry, trailer dump station. Three-month minimum for winter extended stay. Fees charged. Recreation: picnic areas, fishing, boat ramp, recreation hall, 500-foot pier, 2-story observation tower, 1-mile exercise trail, playground, ball fields, sandy beach and skeet shooting. Open all year. The nearby King's Inn is famous for its excellent seafood.

89. LAKE ARROWHEAD STATE PARK

LOCATION

Clay County. 9 miles south of Wichita Falls on U.S. 281, 7 miles east on FM 1954.
Mailing address: 229 Park Road 63, Wichita Falls, Texas 76310-8444. Phone: 940-528-2211. E-mail: lasp@wf.net. For all state park reservations, call the centralized reservations system, 512-389-8900, or www.ReserveAmerica.com online. Call the state park information number, 800-792-1112, for information and fee updates.

FACILITIES

Fees: entrance, facility, activity use; subject to change.

Camping: 48 back-in RV/tent sites with water, electricity, 19 tent sites with water, 4 equestrian sites with water, electricity, walk-in primitive camping, modern restrooms, trailer dump station, store. Fees charged.

Recreation: picnic areas and playgrounds, horseback riding, lake swimming, lighted fishing piers, boat ramp, fuel dock, water sports, jet ski rental, hiking, 18-hole disc golf course; group dining hall with stove, fridge, microwave, central air/heat (capacity 50).

WEATHER

July highs average 99 degrees, January lows 29 degrees.

MAIN ATTRACTIONS

Lake Arrowhead, with 13,500 acres, offers fishing and other water-related activities. Relief from the blazing summer sun is found only under the shade shelters in the picnic and camping areas. Lake Arrowhead was formed in 1965 to provide water for Wichita Falls. The city deeded the park to the state in 1970.

Overgrazing of what used to be prairie has resulted in the invasion of thorny mesquite trees. The lakeshore around the picnic, camping, and playground areas is bulwarked with concrete and rocks to discourage erosion. The lake itself is a flooded oil field with many large offshore derricks. Black-tailed prairie dogs can be seen in the park and waterfowl and wading birds frequent the lake. Anglers catch crappie, perch, catfish, and bass.

90. LAKE B.A. STEINHAGEN, "DAM B"

LOCATION

U.S. Army Corps of Engineers. Jasper and Tyler counties. Project office: 47 miles east of Livingston on U.S. 190, south on FM 92 on west side of reservoir.
Mailing address: 890 FM 92, Woodville, Texas 75979-9631. Phone: 409-429-3491. For camping reservations, call toll-free 877-444-6777 or www.recreation.gov. On the Internet, see www.swf-wc .usace.army.mil/townbluff/.

FACILITIES

Magnolia Ridge Park: East from Woodville 11 miles on U.S. 190, north 1.5 miles on FM 92 to the park entrance road. *Facilities*: 32 back-in RV/tent sites with electricity and water, 8 sites without water or electricity, and 1 screened shelter with electricity and water, restroom, showers, trailer dump station. Group picnic shelter, playground, fishing dock, nature trail, children's fishing pond, no swim beach. Gatehouse (409-283-5493) open 6 a.m.–10 p.m. Reservations through ReserveUSA, 877-444-6777 or online www.reserveusa.com. Fees charged. Open all year.

Campground	water	fee area	flush toilets	season	dump station	electricity
Magnolia Ridge	•	•	•	all	•	•
Sandy Creek	•	•	•	all	•	•

LAKE B.A. STEINHAGEN

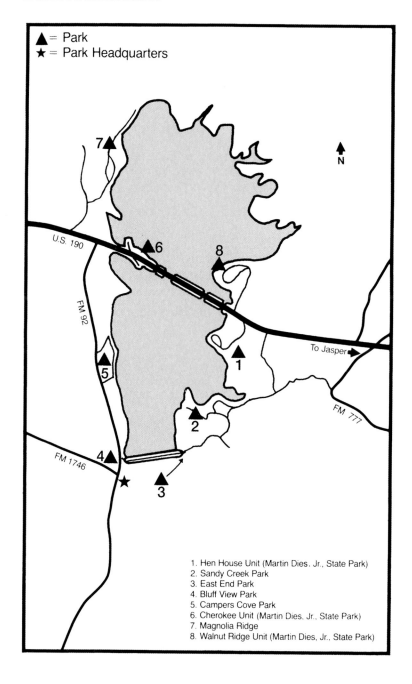

▲ = Park
★ = Park Headquarters

N

7▲

U.S. 190

6▲

8▲

FM 92

To Jasper ➡

5▲

1▲

FM 777

2▲

4▲

FM 1746

★

3▲

1. Hen House Unit (Martin Dies, Jr., State Park)
2. Sandy Creek Park
3. East End Park
4. Bluff View Park
5. Campers Cove Park
6. Cherokee Unit (Martin Dies, Jr., State Park)
7. Magnolia Ridge
8. Walnut Ridge Unit (Martin Dies, Jr., State Park)

Sandy Creek Park: West from Jasper 10 miles on U.S. 190, south 1.3 miles on FM 777, west 2.5 miles on CR 155 to park entrance. 72 RV/tent sites water and electricity, 6 with water, 2 screened shelter sites with electricity and water, restrooms, showers, trailer dump station. Fishing piers, boat ramps and docks. No swim beach. Gatehouse (409-384-6166) open 6 a.m.–10 p.m. Reservations through ReserveUSA, 877-444-6777 or online www.reserveusa.com. Fees charged. Open all year.

Campers Cove Park: East from Woodville 11 miles on U.S. 190, south 2.4 miles on FM 92, east .6 mile on CR 4130 to entrance. *Facilities:* no camping or facilities until park is renovated. Only the boat ramp and picnic tables are available. No fees. Open April 1–Sept. 30.

MAIN ATTRACTIONS

Town Bluff Dam impounds approximately 10,950 acres; the lake has 160 miles of shoreline but averages only 7 feet in depth. Fishing is popular on the lake, with white bass, spotted bass, largemouth bass, and catfish being the common catches. The Neches River, which forms the lake, flows through the East Texas pine forests and swamps. Martin Dies, Jr., State Park is also located on the lake, and the Big Thicket National Preserve headquarters is south of Woodville off U.S. 69 on FM 420.

PLANTS AND ANIMALS

Shortleaf and loblolly pines and southern magnolias grow on the white-and-red sands around the lake, while dwarf palmettos and bald cypress and tupelo trees line the swampy inlets. The open water of the lake, its shallow inlets, and the rich woodlands provide food and shelter for numerous species of waterfowl, wading birds, and forest birds. Deer, squirrels, and other wildlife are also abundant.

Great blue herons nest on many of the lakes in east Texas.

A section of the property is operated by the Parks and Wildlife Department for wildlife management. Wild orchids and insectivorous plants have been found in a 4,000-acre section set aside for research.

91. LAKE BARDWELL

LOCATION

Mailing address: 4000 Observation Drive, Ennis, TX 75119. Phone: 972-875-5711. E-mail: CESWF-OD-BR@swf.usace.army. mil. Internet: www.swf-wc.usace.army.mil/bardwell/main.htm. For reservations through the National Recreation Reservation System, call 877-444-6777, or online at www.recreation.gov.

FACILITIES

Mott Park: 270 acres with 33 back-in RV/tent sites with water and electric hookups, 7 sites with no hookups, trailer dump station, flush toilets, showers, boat ramp and dock, group shelter (capacity 4 RVs, 100 people), fishing, swim beach. No picnic sites. Fees charged. Open April 1–September 30. Gatehouse open 6 a.m.–10 p.m.

High View Park: 155 acres with 39 pull-through RV/tent sites with water and electricity, sanitary dump station, flush toilets, showers. Picnic area, swim beach, boat ramp and dock, full-service marina. Fees charged. Open all year. Gatehouse open 6 a.m.–10 p.m.

Waxahachie Creek Park: 205 acres with 65 pull-through RV/tent sites with water and electricity, 7 sites with no hookups, flush toilets, showers, trailer dump station, group shelter (capacity 8 RVs, 200 people), picnic area, boat ramps, nature trail. Fees charged. Open all year. Gatehouse open 6 a.m.–10 p.m.

Campground	water	fee area	flush toilets	season	dump station	showers	electricity
High View	•	•	•	all	•	•	•
Mott Park	•	•	•	Apr. 1–Sept. 30	•	•	•
Waxahachie Creek	•	•	•	all	•	•	•

LAKE BARDWELL

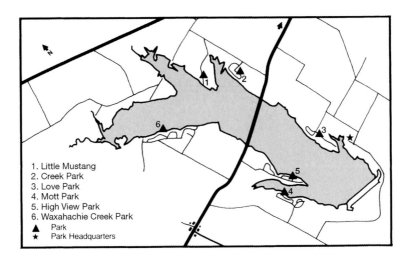

1. Little Mustang
2. Creek Park
3. Love Park
4. Mott Park
5. High View Park
6. Waxahachie Creek Park
▲   Park
★   Park Headquarters

Little Mustang Creek Park: 163 acres with boat ramp and dock. Fees charged. Day use, open all year.

Love Park: 439 acres with picnic area, boat ramp, pit toilet, drinking water, swim beach, group shelter. Fees charged. Day use, open April 1–September 30.

MAIN ATTRACTIONS

Built for flood control of Waxahachie Creek and for local water supply, the reservoir covers 3,570 acres at a normal level with 25 miles of shoreline. Numerous species of waterfowl, ducks, herons, egrets, and cormorants frequent the lake, which is surrounded by rich blackland prairie farmland. Bluebonnets, Indian paintbrushes, and other wildflowers carpet the rolling shoreline each spring. Hunting is permitted in the ten wildlife management areas around the lake.

92. LAKE BASTROP RECREATION AREA

LOCATION

Bastrop County. Lower Colorado River Authority.
Mailing address: Box 220, M221, Austin, TX 78767. Office: 3700 Lake Austin Blvd., Austin, TX. Phone: 800-776-5272 ext. 1922. Internet: www.lcra.org/parks/results.html#developed-parks. For

reservations, call the Texas Parks and Wildlife Reservation Center, 512-389-8900 more than 48 hours in advance. TPWD charges $5 for LCRA reservations.

FACILITIES

North Shore Park: From Bastrop north on TX 95 to FM 1441, east 2.5 miles to the park entrance. *Camping*: 6 pull-through RV/tent sites with full hookups, 11 back-in sites with water and electricity, modern restrooms, showers, trailer dump station. Fees charged.

Recreation: located on 900-acre Lake Bastrop with picnic areas, playgrounds, pavilion, boat ramp and dock, lake swimming, fishing, volleyball, trails.

South Shore Park: From Bastrop north on TX 95 for .5 mile, east on TX 21 for 2 miles, left onto South Shore Road (CR 352). *Camping*: 38 back-in RV/tent sites with water and electricity, 16 mini-cabins with two sets of bunk beds, electricity, outside water, ac/heat, picnic table, grill. Fees charged. *Recreation*: located on 900-acre Lake Bastrop with picnic areas, playgrounds, pavilion, boat ramp and dock, lake swimming, fishing, volleyball, trails.

93. LAKE BELTON

LOCATION

U.S. Army Corps of Engineers. Bell and Coryell counties. Project office: 4 miles north of Belton on TX 317 to Belton Dam. Mailing address: 3740 FM 1670, Belton, Texas 76513. Phone: 254-939-2461. Internet: www.swf-wc.usace.army.mil/belton/. For camping reservation, call 877-444-6777 or online at www.recreation.gov.

FACILITIES

Live Oak Ridge Park: 48 back-in RV/tent sites with water and electricity, modern restrooms, showers, trailer dump station. Lake swimming, boat ramp. Free WiFi available on trial basis at the camper activity building. Fees charged. Open all year. Gatehouse open 6 a.m.–10 p.m.

Cedar Ridge Park: 68 back-in RV/tent sites, 8 screened shelters, modern restrooms, showers, trailer dump station. Picnic area, playground, laundry, boat ramps, fishing dock, swim beach, basketball. Fees charged. Open all year. Gatehouse open 6 a.m.–10 p.m.

LAKE BELTON

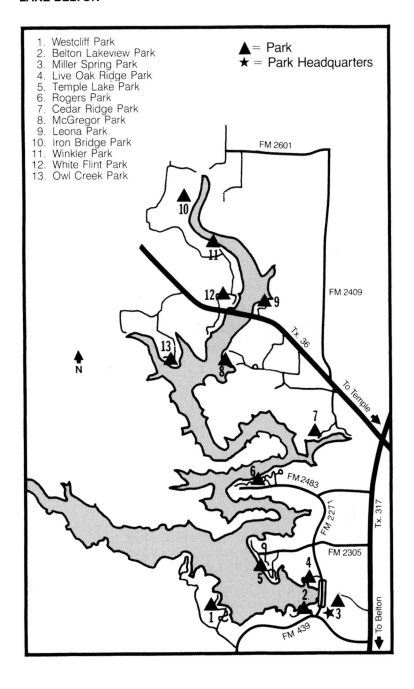

1. Westcliff Park
2. Belton Lakeview Park
3. Miller Spring Park
4. Live Oak Ridge Park
5. Temple Lake Park
6. Rogers Park
7. Cedar Ridge Park
8. McGregor Park
9. Leona Park
10. Iron Bridge Park
11. Winkler Park
12. White Flint Park
13. Owl Creek Park

▲ = Park
★ = Park Headquarters

Yellow coreopsis wildflowers cover the fields around Lake Bastrop.

Turkey Roost Group Camp Area: Located within Cedar Ridge Park, 6 single and 2 double RV/tent sites with water and electricity, modern restroom with showers, group pavilion. Site will accommodate 10 RVs and/or 20 tents. Fees charged. Open all year.

Westcliff Park: 27 RV/tent sites, 27 with water and electricity, 4 primitive sites, modern restrooms, showers, trailer dump station. Picnic shelters, playground, swim beach, boat ramp. Fees charged. Open all year. Gatehouse open 6 a.m.–10 p.m.

Winkler Park: 14 back-in RV/tent sites with water only, modern restrooms, showers. Picnic area, lake swimming, fishing. Fees charged. Open all year. Gatehouse open 6 a.m.–10 p.m.

White Flint Park: 13 back-in RV/tent sites with water and electricity and covered table, 12 screen shelters, boat ramp, modern restroom, trailer dump station.

MAIN ATTRACTIONS

Built on the Leon River, Lake Belton covers 12,300 surface acres and has 136 miles of shoreline. White bass, largemouth bass, walleye pike, and channel catfish are common catches in the lake. In the fall, the leaves of Texas oak and sumac color the shoreline with brilliant shades of red. Scenic cliffs rise above the lake, offering excellent panoramic views of the area.

Numerous species of ducks and other water birds overwinter on the reservoir. There are 3,900 acres of wildlife management areas for hunting. This is a metropolitan lake with more than 2.5 million visitors yearly.

94. LAKE BENBROOK

LOCATION

U.S. Army Corps of Engineers. Tarrant County. Project office: 12 miles southwest of Fort Worth on U.S. 377 to Benbrook. Lake access points on U.S. 377 at 1.2, 2.4, and 5.7 miles south of IH 20/820.
Mailing address: Box 26619, Fort Worth, Texas 76126-0619. Phone: 817-292-2400. E-mail: ceswf-od-bb@usace.army.mil. Internet: www.swf-wc.usace.army.mil/benbrook/. For reservations call 877-444-6777 or online at www.recreation.gov.

FACILITIES

Holiday Park, South Holiday Campground: 79 back-in RV/tent sites with water and electricity (5 with screened shelters and 1 equestrian site), 26 sites with no hookups, modern restrooms with showers, boat ramp, fishing pier. Park offers access to 14 miles of equestrian, nature, and hiking trails. Fees charged. Open all year.

Mustang Point Park, Bear Creek Campground: 2 back-in RV/tent sites with full hookups, 38 back-in sites with water and electricity, group camping pavilion with 6 water and electricity hookups, modern restrooms, showers,

Campground	water	fee area	flush toilets	season	dump station	cold-water showers	electricity
Holiday Park	•	•	•	all	•	•	•
Mustang Point Park	•	•	•	all			
Rocky Creek	•	•	•	all			
Bear Creek	•	•	•	all	•	•	•

LAKE BENBROOK

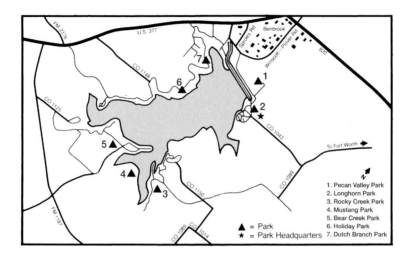

1. Pecan Valley Park
2. Longhorn Park
3. Rocky Creek Park
4. Mustang Park
5. Bear Creek Park
6. Holiday Park
7. Dutch Branch Park

▲ = Park
★ = Park Headquarters

trailer dump station. *West Creek Circle Area*: Equestrian and primitive camping, vault toilet, no water. Mustang Point Park offers access to 14 miles of equestrian and hiking trails. Fees charged. Open all year.

Mustang Point Park Campground and Swimming Beach: undesignated camping at 9 picnic tables and anywhere along lakeshore (vehicles allowed off pavement), group camping pavilion with 6 water and electricity hookups, water faucets, boat ramp, swim beach. Fees charged. Open all year.

Rocky Creek Park: 11 RV/tent sites with covered table and water nearby, one restroom (no shower). Camping and facilities also within park at Rocky Point Marina, 817-346-2199.

MAIN ATTRACTIONS

Lake Benbrook, on the Clear Fork of the Trinity River, covers 3,770 surface acres with 40 miles of shoreline. Cottonwood and willow trees shade the shores, and oaks and other hardwoods forest the creek drainages. The trees provide good habitats for migrating songbirds, making the park attractive to bird-watchers. Fourteen hundred acres are managed for hunting.

Because of its proximity to Fort Worth, the lake is heavily used by city dwellers, especially on weekends. Fishing and water sports are the most popular activities.

HIKING, NATURE, EQUESTRIAN TRAILS

The Corps of Engineers maintains 14 miles of hiking and equestrian trails around the lake. Trailheads lead from Dutch Branch Park, South

Holiday Park, and Westcreek Circle (in Mustang Point Park). An additional 10 miles of trails lead Rocky Creek Park. At Holiday Park, a nature trail begins behind campsite #1 and leads to a photo blind where views of herons, migrant shorebirds, pelicans, wintering waterfowl, and osprey are possible. The blind is a ¾-mile roundtrip and the entire trail a 1.7-mile roundtrip. The 1.5 mile Crest of Benbrook Dam trail follows the top of the dam and is popular with joggers and bikers. Biking is not permitted on any Benbrook trail. Pecan Valley Park (day use) offers access to the paved hike/bike Fort Worth Trinity Trail, which follows the Trinity River and its tributaries for 25 miles.

95. LAKE BOB SANDLIN STATE PARK

LOCATION

Titus County. 10 miles southwest of Mount Pleasant on FM 127, south on FM 21.
Mailing address: 341 State Park Road 2117, Pittsburg, TX 75686.
Phone: 903-572-5531. For all state park reservations, call the centralized reservations system, 512-389-8900, or www.ReserveAmerica.com online. Call the state park information number, 800-792-1112, for information and fee updates.

FACILITIES

Fees: entrance, facility, activity use; subject to change.

Camping: 75 back-in RV/tent sites with water and electricity, 2 primitive hike-in camping areas, 12 screened shelters, 8 limited use cabins (ac/heat and 2 sets of bunk beds, no linens, no bathrooms), modern restrooms, showers, trailer dump station. Fees charged.

Recreation: picnic areas, playgrounds, group picnic pavilion, lake swimming, lighted fishing pier, fish-cleaning facility, boat ramp, 5 miles of hiking and mountain biking trails.

WEATHER

July high averages 94 degrees, January low 32 degrees.

MAIN ATTRACTIONS

The 9,460-acre Lake Bob Sandlin and adjoining Lake Monticello and Lake Cypress Springs offer numerous recreational opportunities for fishermen, water sports enthusiasts, and those who just want a few days away from the city. Largemouth bass are the main attraction for fishermen, who also report good catches of crappie, channel catfish, white bass, and sunfish. Hikers enjoy the 1.5-mile loop hiking trail through deep woods and naturalized pastures within the park.

PLANTS AND ANIMALS

This park is within the Post Oak Savanna vegetation region of Texas, characterized by oaks, hickories, and other deciduous trees and grasslands. Because of its proximity to the Piney Woods, loblolly pine and sweetgum trees also grow abundantly within the park. Ferns, mosses, and other shade and moisture-loving plants thrive in the dense forests bordering the lake. Old home sites and pastures in the park have become naturalized with a combination of invading native plants and escaped ornamentals, such as Japanese honeysuckle and chinaberry trees.

The moist woods, streams, and shoreline provide excellent habitat for small mammals, frogs, turtles, and snakes. Visitors often see whitetailed deer grazing at dusk, armadillos rooting through the leaf-covered forest floor, and nutrias, South American beaverlike rodents, swimming along the shoreline. Birdlife is abundant, with both resident species and migrants in the spring and fall. The lake attracts herons, egrets, and numerous species of waterfowl.

96. LAKE BROWNWOOD STATE PARK

LOCATION

Brown County. 16 miles northwest of Brownwood on TX 279, 6 miles east on PR 15.
Mailing address: 200 State Highway Park Road 15, Lake Brownwood, TX 76801. Phone: 325-784-5223. For all state park reservations, call the centralized reservations system, 512-389-8900, or www.ReserveAmerica.com online. Call the state park information number, 800-792-1112, for information and fee updates.

FACILITIES

Fees: entrance, facility, activity use; subject to change.

Camping: 20 back-in RV/tent sites with full hookups, 46 sites with water and electricity, 9 tent-only sites with water and electricity, 12 sites with water nearby, 10 screened shelters with water and electricity (tent only), 9 2-person cabins and 7 4-person cabins (cabins have double beds, ac/heat, fridge, stove, restroom, showers, no camping allowed at cabins), 4 group lodges for 4, 8, 10, 26 people (freezer, microwave, oven, coffee pot, fireplace, outside grill and tables), 1 group camp bunkhouse/dining hall for 32 people. Modern rest rooms, showers, trailer dump station. Fees charged.

Recreation: picnic areas, hiking and nature trails with trail-guide booklet, swimming in lake, fishing, lighted pier, boating, paddleboat rentals.

WEATHER

July high averages 94 degrees, January low 34 degrees.

MAIN ATTRACTIONS

The park is on Lake Brownwood, which covers 7,300 acres and has 95 miles of shoreline. The sandy, shaded shores are ideal for picnicking, camping, and swimming. Water sports and fishing are major activities on the lake. Catches include black and white bass, largemouth bass, catfish, crappie, and bream.

The town of Brownwood received its name from Captain Henry S. Brown, a revolutionary soldier and the first white man to travel through the region. The first home in the area was built in 1854, but frequent Indian raids discouraged settlement by whites. After Chief Bigfoot and Chief Jape were defeated in 1874, the Anglo population increased rapidly.

HIKING

The park has two short trails: a hiking trail approximately one mile long and a three-quarter-mile nature trail. Ask for a trail-guide pamphlet at the entrance.

PLANTS AND ANIMALS

The 538-acre park is in the Cross Timbers and prairies region of Texas in an area of rolling hills separated by narrow valleys. The ridgetops are composed of erosion-resistant limestone, the slopes and valleys of softer shale and sandstone. The dam forming Lake Brownwood was constructed across a deep, narrow gap cut through one of the limestone ridges by Pecan Bayou.

Live oak trees cover the limestone ridges, while grasslands with invasions of mesquite and prickly pear cover the valleys, where the bedrock is shale. Cedar elms, post oaks, and hackberries are also numerous in the park.

The limestone beds exposed in and around the park are rich in fossils more than 310 million years old. More than 500 types have been found in the alternating layers of limestone and shale. Fossils are particularly abundant in the strata at the spillway. Ross Maxwell's Geologic and Historic Guide to the State Parks of Texas describes the geology of the area in detail.

97. LAKE BUCHANAN: BLACK ROCK PARK

LOCATION

Lower Colorado River Authority. Llano County. 12 miles west of Burnet on TX 29, 4 miles north on TX 261. 10 acres on Lake Buchanan. Mailing address: Box 220, M221, Austin, TX 78767. Office: 3700 Lake Austin Blvd., Austin, TX 78703. Phone: 800-776-5272 ext. 1922. Internet: www.lcra.org/parks/results. html#developed-parks. For reservations, call the Texas Parks and Wildlife Reservation Center, 512-389-8900 more than 48 hours in advance. TPWD charges $5 for LCRA reservations.

FACILITIES

Camping: 10-acre park with 3 pull-through RV/tent sites with full hook-ups; 15 with water and electricity, 12 cabins (ac/heat, 2 sets bunk beds, electricity, outside water, table, grill), 25 tent sites, primitive camping area, modern restrooms, cold showers, trailer dump station.

Twin Falls flows into Lake Buchanan.

Recreation: picnic sites and playground, swimming, fishing, boat ramp. Open all year. Fee charged. Lake Buchanan is a picturesque lake for boating and bird-watching. Bald eagles winter on the lake.

LAKE BUCHANAN: CANYON OF THE EAGLES LODGE AND NATURE PARK

LOCATION

Lower Colorado River Authority. Llano County: 3.5 miles west from Burnet on TX 29, south 1.5 miles on RM 2341. Mailing address: 16942 Ranch Rd. 2341, Burnet, TX 78611. Phone: 512-715-0290, 800-977-0081. Internet: www.canyonoftheeagles.com/. For campsite reservations, call the Texas Parks and Wildlife Reservation Center, 512-389-8900 more than 48 hours in advance. TPWD charges $5 for LCRA reservations.

FACILITIES

Lodge with 64 duplex-cabin rooms, pool, restaurant.

Camping: 24 back-in RV sites with full hookops, 23 tent sites with water and vault toilets, 10 primitive tent sites with vault toilets, no water, group camping area for 100 people. Modern restrooms showers.

Recreation: 940 acres on Lake Buchanan, 14 miles of nature trails, picnicking, swim beach, bathhouse, pier, store, birdwatching, canoe and kayak rental, nature programs, stargazing with 16-inch Ealing Cassegrain telescope.

With 840 undeveloped acres, the park provides hiking trails and nesting habitat for the endangered black-capped vireo and golden-cheeked warbler, which nests nowhere else except in the cedar-covered hills of central Texas. The lodge is home of the Vanishing Texas River Cruises which offers vineyard cruises March–May, wildflower cruises April–May, bald eagle cruises November–March, and dinner cruises May–October.

98. LAKE CASA BLANCA INTERNATIONAL STATE PARK

LOCATION

Webb County. 5 miles east of Laredo on U.S. 59, east on Loop 20 (Bob Bullock Loop) to State Senator Judith Zaffirini Road. Mailing address: 5102 Bob Bullock Loop, Laredo, TX 78044.

Phone: 956-725-3826. For all state park reservations, call the centralized reservations system, 512-389-8900, or www.ReserveAmerica.com online. Call the state park information number, 800-792-1112, for information and fee updates.

FACILITIES

Fees: entrance, facility, activity use; subject to change.

Camping: 66 back-in RV/tent sites with water and electricity, 10 walk-in tent sites with water, modern restrooms, showers, trailer dump station. Fees charged.

Recreation: picnic areas, playgrounds, 6 day-use group facilities with recreation and dining pavilions, sports courts, ADA-accessible fishing pier, lake swimming, boat ramp, 2 miles of mountain bike trails, bird-watching, Texas State Park Store.

WEATHER

July high averages 99 degrees, January low 45 degrees.

MAIN ATTRACTIONS

Recreation in this 370-acre park centers on the picnic and group-use areas and the 1,100-acre Lake Casa Blanca. Anglers in the 30-foot-deep lake catch crappie, largemouth bass, hybrid stripers, and yellow, blue, and flathead catfish. The lake, the largest body of water for 50 miles, provides a winter home for gulls, terns, herons, and other waterfowl and shorebirds. The brushy chaparral of blackbrush, mesquite, huisache, prickly pear, and other thorny shrubs typical of south Texas attracts numerous birds, including rare Mexican species such as the white-collared seedeater. A golf course operated by Webb County is nearby.

99. LAKE COLORADO CITY STATE PARK

LOCATION

Mitchell County. 30 miles east of Big Spring on IH-20, 5 miles south on FM 2836.
Mailing address: 4582 FM 2836, Colorado City, Texas 79512.
Phone: 325-728-3931. For all state park reservations, call the centralized reservations system, 512-389-8900, or www. ReserveAmerica.com online. Call the state park information number, 800-792-1112, for information and fee updates.

FACILITIES

Fees: entrance, facility, activity use; subject to change.

Camping: 9 pull-through RV/tent sites with water and electricity, 69 back-in sites with water and electricity, 34 sites with water; 11 stone mini-cabins, fridge, microwave, ac/heat, maximum 8 people. Modern restrooms, showers, trailer dump station. Fees charged.

Recreation: picnic areas, playgrounds, hiking trails, Texas State Longhorn herd, lake swimming, lighted fishing pier, boat ramp, water sports, jet ski rental, recreation hall (capacity 75) with kitchen, group picnic pavilion (capacity 40), Texas State Park Store.

WEATHER

July highs average 95 degrees, January lows 46 degrees.

MAIN ATTRACTIONS

The park is on the shore of a 1,618-acre lake, a reservoir that provides cooling water for a power plant adjacent to the park. The lakeshore has little shade for picnicking or camping, but there are nice sandy beaches for swimming and 2 fishing piers. In the summer, the lake is heavily used by motorboaters and does not offer a quiet retreat from the city.

PLANTS AND ANIMALS

Scrubby mesquite trees, prickly pear cacti, agarita bushes, and a few junipers cover the rolling terrain surrounding the lake. In the spring, an assortment of wildflowers are sprinkled among the grasses. A portion of the State Longhorn herd grazes along the shoreline and white-tailed deer, raccoon, and armadillo frequent the park. A variety of waterfowl use the lake. Anglers catch crappie, perch, catfish, bass, and red drum.

100. LAKE CORPUS CHRISTI STATE PARK

LOCATION

San Patricio County. 35 miles northwest of Corpus Christi on IH-37, 4 miles south on TX 359, north on FM 1068.
Mailing address: Box 1167, Mathis, Texas 78368. Phone: 361-547-2635. For all state park reservations, call the centralized reservations system, 512-389-8900, or www.ReserveAmerica.com online. Call

Sunrise over Lake Corpus Christi.

the state park information number, 800-792-1112, for information and fee updates.

FACILITIES

Fees: entrance, facility, activity use; subject to change.

Camping: 25 pull-through RV/tent sites with full hookups, 23 pull-through sites with water and electricity, 60 tent sites with water, 25 screened shelters with water, electricity, inside table, outside grill, modern restrooms, showers, trailer dump station. Fees charged.

Recreation: picnic areas and playgrounds, bird-watching, swimming in lake, fishing, 1 lighted pier, boating, pavilion. Paddleboats, canoes, pontoon boats, and ski boats can be rented.

WEATHER

July high averages 94 degrees, January low 44 degrees.

MAIN ATTRACTIONS

Lake Corpus Christi, with 21,000 acres and 200 miles of shoreline, is the outstanding feature of the park. The lake was formed when the Nueces River was impounded in the thirties by the Civilian Conservation Corps to provide water for Corpus Christi, 35 miles southeast. The lake is noted for its abundance of big blue, yellow, and channel catfish, perch, bass, and crappie. Swimming, boating, and water-skiing are popular.

The rolling terrain of the 365-acre park is covered with thorny shrubs characteristic of the South Texas brush country and the lower Rio Grande Valley. Blackbrush acacia, lotebush, bluewood, mesquite, and lime prickly ash form a dense woodland around the shoreline.

The mild climate and diverse vegetation support more than 300 species of birds, making the area favored for bird-watching; a checklist is available at the entrance. Many species of shorebirds, wading birds, and waterfowl are attracted to the lake, and the woodlands provide habitat for a wide variety of migrating birds arriving from their trans-Gulf flight in the spring. Mammals common to the park include the spotted skunk, raccoons, and opossums.

The coastal region of Texas was once inhabited by Karankawa and Lipan Apache Indians, who resisted conversion to Christianity by the Spanish. The Nueces River, which forms the reservoir, was the disputed boundary between Texas and Mexico until the Mexican War established the Rio Grande as the official boundary.

101. LAKE CYPRESS SPRINGS

LOCATION

Franklin County. 6 parks administered by the water district. Mailing address: Franklin County Water District, PO Box 559, Mount Vernon, TX 75457. Phone: 903-537-4536, reservations 903-860-7799. Internet: www.fcwd.com. Reservations accepted with three-day minimum. Fees charged.

FACILITIES

W. D. Jack Guthrie Park: east of Mount Pleasant on IH-30 to Mount Vernon, south on FM 115, southeast on FM 21, south on FM 3007. *Camping*: 39 campsites with water and electricity, flush toilets, showers, trailer dump station, primitive camping. *Recreation*: playgound, boat ramp, designated swimming area, tennis, basketball, softball. Closed November 1–February 28.

Mary King Park: east of Mount Pleasant on IH-30 to Mount Vernon, south on FM 115, southeast on FM 21, south on FM 3007, south side of lake. Day-use only, no facilities. Closed November 1–February 28.

Walleye Park: south from Mount Vernon on FM 115, southeast on FM 21, south on FM 3122. *Camping:* 66 back-in RV/tent sites with water and electricity, primitive camping area, 5 screened shelters, flush toilets, showers, trailer dump station. *Recreation:* playground, group pavilion, boat ramp. Open all year.

Overlook Park: south from Mount Vernon on FM 115, southeast on FM 21, south on FM 2723. *Camping:* primitive camping with tables, water, flush toilets, trailer dump station. *Recreation:* boat ramp. Closed November 1–February 28.

Twin Oaks Park: group camping only, 3-day minimum, 15 RV sites with full hookups, restrooms, showers. Closed November 1–February 28.

Dogwood Park: from Mount Vernon, TX 37, south 1 mile, south on FM 3007 for 2.5 miles. On south side of dam with 10-acre undeveloped tent camping area, flush toilets, boat ramp, lake swimming. Closed November 1–February 28.

102. LAKE FAYETTE

LOCATION

Lower Colorado River Authority. Fayette County. East from La Grange 10.2 miles on TX 159 to Lake Fayette. Mailing address: Box 220, M221, Austin, TX 78767. LCRA Office: 3700 Lake Austin Blvd., Austin, TX 78703. Phone: 800-776-5272; at park 979-249-3504. Internet: www.lcra.org/parks/results.html#developed-parks. For reservations, call the Texas Parks and Wildlife Reservation Center, 512-389-8900 more than 48 hours in advance. TPWD charges $5 for LCRA reservation.

FACILITIES

Oak Thicket Park: Camping: 85-acre park on 2,000-acre lake with 20 back-in RV/tent sites with water and electricity; 8 screened shelters with electricity, water, picnic table, grill; 8 cabins (4, 6, 14 people) with ac/heat, kitchenette, bathroom, satellite TV, picnic table, grill; modern restrooms, showers, trailer dump station. *Recreation:* picnic areas, playgrounds, sandy swim beach, boat ramp, fishing pier. Fees charged. A short nature and bird-watching trail with benches along the way loops through the campground. A 3-mile multi-use hike/bike trail follows the lake shore and overland to connect with Park Prairie Park.

Park Prairie Park: Camping: 20-acre park with 12 primitive tent sites, group camp area with 3 tent sites and 1 screened shelter, flush toilet. *Recreation:* boat ramp, dock, fishing pier, lake swimming. Fees charged.

103. LAKE GEORGETOWN

LOCATION

U.S. Army Corps of Engineers. Williamson County. Project office: 30 miles north of Austin on IH-35 to Georgetown, 4 miles west on FM 2338.
Mailing address: 500 Lake Overlook Drive, Georgetown, TX 78628-4901. Phone: 512-930-5253. Internet: www.swf-wc.usace .army.mil/georgetown/. For reservations call 877-444-6777, or online at www.recreation.gov.

FACILITIES

Jim Hogg Park: 143 back-in RV/tent sites with water and electricity, 5 screened shelters, restrooms, showers, dump station, fishing dock. Open year round 6 a.m. to 10 p.m. with 24-hour exit.

Cedar Breaks Park: 64 sites with water and electricity, restrooms, showers, dump station, 2 fishing docks. Open all year 6 a.m. to 10 p.m.

LAKE GEORGETOWN

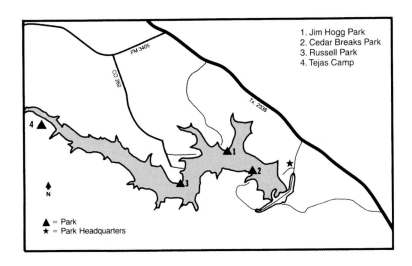

1. Jim Hogg Park
2. Cedar Breaks Park
3. Russell Park
4. Tejas Camp

▲ = Park
★ = Park Headquarters

Russell Park: group camp area, group picnic shelter, swim beach, hike/bike trail, boat ramp, restrooms. Open April 1 to September 30. Fees charged for all parks.

Tejas Camp: 12 tent sites with tables and water. Open all year.

The 16-mile Good Water Trail connects Russell and Cedar Breaks parks via Tejas Camp.

MAIN ATTRACTIONS

Lake Georgetown, formerly called North Fork Lake, covers 1,310 acres at its normal level. The dam, completed in 1980, impounds the North Fork of the San Gabriel River.

104. LAKE GRANGER

LOCATION

U.S. Army Corps of Engineers. Williamson County. Project office: 32 miles north of Austin on IH-35 past Georgetown, 23 miles east on FM 971 through Granger. Mailing address: 3100 Granger Dam Road, Granger, Texas 76530. Phone: 512-859-2668. Internet: http://swf67.swf-wc.usace.army.mil/granger/. For reservations call 877-444-6777, or online at www.recreation.gov.

FACILITIES

Wilson H. Fox Park: Camping: 58 back-in RV/tent sites with water and electricity, 5 screened shelters, modern restrooms, showers, trailer dump station. *Recreation:* picnic, group shelter, playground, swim beach, boat

Campground	water	fee area	flush toilets	season	dump station	showers	electricity
Wilson H. Fox	•	•	•	all	•	•	•
Taylor	•	•	•	all	•	•	•
Willis Creek	•	•	•	all	•	•	•

LAKE GRANGER

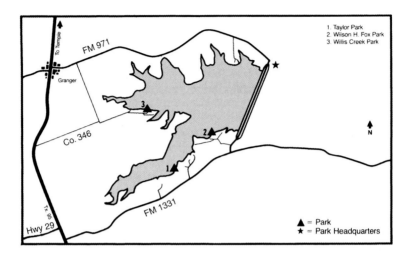

launch, fishing dock, fish-cleaning station. Fees charged. Open year-round 6 a.m.–10 p.m.

Taylor Park: Camping: 48 back-in RV/tent sites with water and electricity, primitive camping area, modern restrooms, showers, trailer dump station. *Recreation:* picnic, playground, swim beach, boat launch, Comanche Bluff Hiking Trail. Fees charged. Open March 1–September 30, 6 a.m.–10 p.m.

Willis Creek Park: Camping: 27 back-in RV/tent sites with water and electricity, 10 primitive sites, modern restrooms, showers, trailer dump station. *Recreation:* picnic, group shelter, boat launch, equestrian trail. Fees charged. Open year-round 6 a.m.–10 p.m.

MAIN ATTRACTIONS

Lake Granger, an impoundment of the San Gabriel River, covers 4,400 acres at its normal level. The Texas Parks and Wildlife Department manages 10,600 acres on the lake for wildlife and hunting.

The lake, in the Blackland Prairies region of Texas, is characterized by rolling hills and wooded creek drainages. In the fall, kettles of broad-winged hawks can be seen circling slowly overhead; in the winter, waterfowl frequent the lake, and ospreys often fly overhead. Chestnut-collared longspurs and a variety of sparrow species live in the fields. In the spring, migrating birds forage among the treetops, and wildflowers bloom abundantly, covering the hillsides overlooking the lake with bluebonnets, Indian paintbrushes, winecups, and other colorful species.

105. LAKE GRAPEVINE

LOCATION

U.S. Army Corps of Engineers. Denton and Tarrant counties.
Project office: 23 miles northeast of Fort Worth on TX 121, past
Grapevine to dam.
Mailing address: 110 Fairway Dr., Grapevine, Texas 76051. Phone:
817-865-2600. Internet: www.swf-wc.usace.army.mil/grapevine/. For
reservations call 877-444-6777, or online at www.recreation.gov.

FACILITIES

Camping: Silver Lake and Twin Coves have individual and group sites,
tent and RV camping, and accept reservations. Both parks have gate
attendants and close to day users at 10 p.m. Camping and day-use fees
are charged at all parks. Murrell Park has primitive camping, water, restrooms, boat ramp, hike/bike trail. Parks not listed are day use.

Cattle egrets are common visitors at Lake Grapevine.

Campground	water	fee area	flush toilets	season	dump station	cold-water showers	electricity
Murrell	•	•		Mar.–Oct.			
Silver Lake	•	•	•	all	•	•	•
Twin Coves	•	•	•	Apr. 1–Oct. 31	•	•	•

Recreation: picnicking, equestrian trail in Walnut Grove Park, nature trail in Twin Coves Park, swimming area in Meadowmere Park, water sports, fishing, boat ramps, marinas at Silver Lake, Oak Grove, and Murrell parks, golf course below dam, hunting with permit. The nine-mile Northshore hike and bike trail connects Rockledge Park and Twin Coves Park. Another six-mile portion is on the west end of the lake.

MAIN ATTRACTIONS

Lake Grapevine, just north of the Dallas–Fort Worth airport, covers 7,380 acres and has 60 miles of shoreline. The lake is popular with powerboat operators. Fishing for white bass is a favorite activity, especially in the spring. Hunting is permitted in the 800-acre wildlife management area. The recreational facilities of the lake are heavily used by residents

LAKE GRAPEVINE

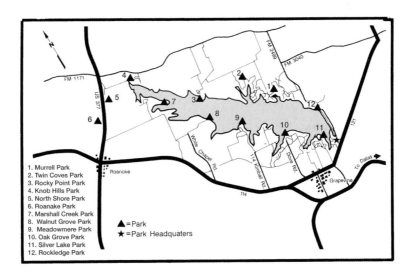

1. Murrell Park
2. Twin Coves Park
3. Rocky Point Park
4. Knob Hills Park
5. North Shore Park
6. Roanake Park
7. Marshall Creek Park
8. Walnut Grove Park
9. Meadowmere Park
10. Oak Grove Park
11. Silver Lake Park
12. Rockledge Park

▲ = Park
★ = Park Headquaters

of the Dallas-Fort Worth metroplex, especially on weekends. More than 5 million people visit the lake each year.

106. LAKE HORDS CREEK

LOCATION

U.S. Army Corps of Engineers. Coleman County. 30 miles west of Brownwood on U.S. 84 to Coleman, 8 miles west on FM 53. Mailing address: 230 Friendship Park Road, Coleman, Texas 76834-8741. Phone: 325-625-2322. Internet: www.swf-wc.usace.army .mil/hords/. For reservations call 877-444-6777, or online at www.recreation.gov.

FACILITIES

Camping: Flatrock Park has 5 back-in RV/tent sites with full hookups, 51 sites with water and electricity, modern restrooms, trailer dump station. Lakeside Park has 16 back-in RV/tent sites with full hookups, 52 sites with water and electricity, 6 campsites with screened shelters, modern restrooms, trailer dump station. Fees charged. Open all year.

Recreation: both parks have picnic, lake swimming, fishing pier, fish cleaning stations, nature trails.

MAIN ATTRACTIONS

Lake Hords Creek is one of the smallest Corps of Engineers lakes, with only 500 surface acres at a normal level and an average depth of 17 feet. The reservoir provides water for the town of Coleman. Before the completion of the dam in 1948, the West Texas town had to supplement its water supply by importing water in railroad cars.

Largemouth bass and red-ear sunfish are caught in the lake. Hunting is allowed by permit on 800 acres of the property.

Campground	water	fee area	flush toilets	season	dump station	screened shelters	electricity
Flatrock Park	•	•	•	all	•		•
Lakeside	•	•	•	all	•	•	•

LAKE HORDS CREEK

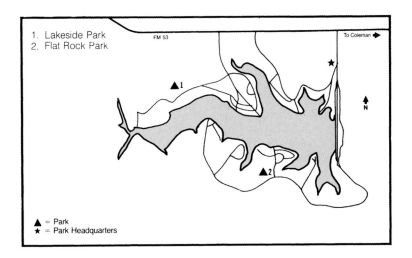

1. Lakeside Park
2. Flat Rock Park

FM 53

To Coleman ➤

★

N

▲ = Park
★ = Park Headquarters

107. LAKE HOUSTON PARK

LOCATION

City of Houston. Montgomery County. Forty-seven miles north
of Houston on U.S. 59 to New Caney, 2 miles east FM 1485 to
Encampment Road, then south to park headquarters.
Mailing address: 22031 Baptist Encampment Rd., New Caney,
Texas 77357. Phone: 281-354-6881. Fax: 281-354-7824. Internet:
www.houstontx.gov/parks/lakehoustonpark.html. For reservations
call either the park directly or the Texas Parks and Wildlife
Reservation Center, 512-389-8900. Note: In September 2008,
Hurricane Ike caused considerable damage. Check for condition of
park facilities.

FACILITIES

Camping: 24 walk-in tent sites, 6 walk-in group sites, 2 overflow camp
sites, 1 equestrian site, 2 primitive hike-in (2 miles) sites, modern restrooms with showers across creek; 1 ac/heated group cabin for 26 with
full kitchen, 1 ADA accessible group lodge for 12 people. No linens or
cooking/dining utensils supplied. Fees charged, open all year.

Recreation: picnic areas, playgrounds, 12-mile wooded hike/bike trail, 8 miles
of equestrian trails, group dining hall with kitchen (capacity 100), fishing
and swimming in Peach Creek and the East Fork of the San Jacinto River.

WEATHER

July high averages 93 degrees, January low 46 degrees.

MAIN ATTRACTIONS

First of all, Lake Houston State Park is not on or near Lake Houston, so don't plan a weekend of water skiing in the park. But the park does offer 12 miles of hiking and biking on wooded trails, 8 miles of equestrian trails, and 10 miles of riverfront along the meandering Peach Creek and San Jacinto River. The trail system leads through pine-hardwood forest and offers excellent hiking, biking, bird-watching, creek wading, and swimming. Anglers fish the San Jacinto River for catfish and bass. During periods of low water, the creeks run shin deep, perfect for wading but impossible to canoe. Located just thirty minutes from the chaos of rush-hour Houston, the 4,913-acre park offers a calm respite for those seeking the solitude of nature.

The Lake Houston Nature Center opened in 2007 with four rooms of ecosystem displays for forest and wetland habitats, amphibians, reptiles, and invertebrates, and a mural depicting the life cycle of butterflies. Call or check the website for a schedule of naturalist-led programs and hikes throughout the year.

PLANTS AND ANIMALS

Situated at the confluence of scenic Peach Creek and the East Fork of the San Jacinto River, the park includes loblolly-oak woodlands, cypress bogs, open grasslands, a small lake, and shallow, tree-lined creeks. The variety of habitats, from pine needle carpeted woodlands to swampy wetlands, sustains white-tailed deer, gray squirrels, raccoons, and a large number of birds. In an area fragmented by freeways and subdivisions, the unbroken woodlands provide an important refuge for the dwindling number of neotropical songbirds that require extensive tracts of contiguous forests to reproduce. The trail system allows visitors to discover delicate mushrooms in the spring and fall, the aroma of sunbaked pine needles, a cooling splash in a shaded creek in the summer, and the crimson leaves of sweetgum trees in the autumn.

108. LAKE JACKSONVILLE PARK

LOCATION

Cherokee County. 3 miles southwest of Jacksonville off U.S. 79 (College Ave.). Mailing address: Box 1390, Jacksonville, Texas 75766. Phone: 903-586-4160; City Parks Department, 903-586-6274.

FACILITIES

Camping: 10 back-in RV pads with water and electricity, 4 back-in RV pads with screened shelter, water, and electricity, 7 tent sites, 6 screened shelters, modern restrooms, showers, trailer dump station. Fees charged.

Recreation: picnic area, boat ramp, designated swimming area, fishing, hiking. Open all year.

109. LAKE LAVON

LOCATION

U.S. Army Corps of Engineers. Collin County. Project office: northeast of Dallas on TX 78, 5 miles past Wylie, 2 miles north on FM 386.
Mailing address: 3375 Skyview Dr., Wylie, Texas 75098-5798.
Phone: 972-442-3141. Internet: www.swf-wc.usace.army.mil/lavon/.
For camping reservations, call 877-444-6777 or online at www.recreation.gov.

FACILITIES

Collin Park Marina (concessionaire 972-442-5755, www. collinpark.com): 2200 St. Paul Rd., Wylie, TX 75098. 5 miles north of Wylie on FM 2514. 45 pull-through or back-in RV sites with full hookups, 12 tent campsites with water, picnic area, swim beach, restrooms, showers, boat launch, boat rental. Fees charged, open all year. Campground gate locked at sunset.

Campground	water	fee area	flush toilets	season	dump station	cold-water showers	electricity
Collin Park Marina	•	•	•	all	•	•	•
East Fork	•	•	•	all	•	•	•
Lavonia	•	•	•	Apr. 1–Sept.30	•	•	•
Clear Lake	•	•	•	Apr. 1–Sept.30	•	•	•
Lakeland Park	•	•	•	Apr. 1–Sept.30			

LAKE LAVON

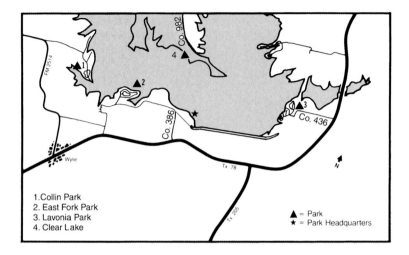

1. Collin Park
2. East Fork Park
3. Lavonia Park
4. Clear Lake

▲ = Park
★ = Park Headquarters

East Fork Park: 3 miles northeast of Wylie on TX 78, 2 miles west on Skyview Dr. 50 back-in RV/tent sites with water and electricity, 12 tent sites, group camp area with shelter, modern restrooms, showers, dump station, boat ramp. Open year round. Gatehouse open 6 a.m.–10 p.m. East Fork Harbor Marina 972-442-1143 is located in the concession area.

Lavonia Park: 5 miles northeast of Wylie on TX 78, 2 miles west on County Road 486. 38 back-in RV/tent sites with water and electricity, 15 tent sites, modern restrooms, showers, trailer dump station, boat ramp. Open year-round. Gatehouse open 6 a.m.–10 p.m.

Clear Lake: 7 miles north of Wylie on FM 2514, 6 miles east on FM 3286, 5 miles south on FM 982. 23 RV/tent sites with water and electricity, modern restrooms with showers, group shelter, boat ramp. Open April 1–September 30. Gatehouse open 6 a.m.–10 p.m.

Lakeland Park (not shown on map): 13 miles northeast of Wylie on TX 78, 2 miles west on County Road 550. 32 primitive tent sites, group picnic shelter, restrooms, water, boat ramp, swim beach. Open April 1–September 30. Gatehouse open 6 a.m.–10 p.m.

Tickey Creek Park: south of Princeton on FM 982, east on CR 448, south on FM 3364. 17 primitive tent camp/picnic sites, pit toilet, drinking fountain, boat ramp. Open all year. Gatehouse open 6 a.m.–10 p.m.

Recreation: picnic areas, horse trail, hiking (no trails), motorcycle trails near Lavonia Park, swimming at Collin Park, fishing, water sports, boat ramps, boat rentals at Collin Park, hunting. Tickey Creek, Little Ridge, Avalon, Caddo, Mallard, and Pebble Beach parks are day-use only with picnicking, swimming, restrooms, and boat launch facilities. Day-use areas include parks.

MAIN ATTRACTIONS

Lake Lavon, averaging 14 feet deep, has 121 miles of shoreline and covers 21,400 surface acres at a normal level. The lake is surrounded by rolling prairie with scattered trees. Fishing is good for largemouth and hybrid striped bass, white crappie, and channel catfish. Wildlife management areas totaling 6,500 acres provide room for hunting and hiking. This is a metropolitan lake receiving heavy day use from the Dallas-Fort Worth area. Each year about 3 million people visit the park.

110. LAKE LEWISVILLE

LOCATION

Denton County. Parks operated by Corps of Engineers and various municipalities. See map and descriptions for directions and facilities. Day-use parks not described. As of 2008, Oakland Park is closed for renovations.

FACILITIES

Hidden Cove Park: from I-35E, TX 121 east 6.6 miles, north on FM 423 5.3 miles, west 2.1 miles m south .2 mile to park. City of The Colony (concessionaire). Mailing address: 20400 Hackberry Creek Park Rd., The Colony, Texas 75034. Phone: 972-294-1443. Camping: 5 back-in RV/tent sites with full hookups, 38 screened shelters with electricity and water, 15 tent sites, cabins, and primitive backpacking areas. Group camping area with screened shelters and dining hall. Fees charged. Reservations accepted.

Campground	water	fee area	flush toilets	season	dump station	showers	electricity
Hidden Cove Park	•	•	•	all	•	•	•
Lake Park	•	•	•	all	•	•	•
Pilot Knoll	•	•		all	•	•	•
Hickory Creek (C. of E.)	•	•	•	all	•	•	•
Stewart Creek Park	•	•	•	all	•		

LAKE LEWISVILLE

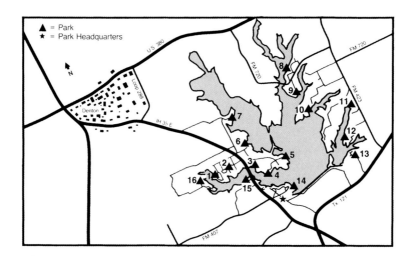

Lake Park: from I-35E exit FM 407 E/ Lake Park Rd., east 1 mile to park. City of Lewisville. Mailing address: 1197 W. Main Street, Lewisville, TX 75067. Phone: 972-219-3742. Camping: 6 pull-through RV/tent sites and 94 back-in sites with water and electricity, 19 tent sites, modern restrooms, showers, laundry room, trailer dump station. Playground, swim beach, fishing barge, courtesy docks, 18-hole golf course (972-219-5661), 9 Hole Executive Golf Course.

Stewart Creek Park: from The Colony take TX 423 north to North Colony Blvd. to Sparks Road into park. City of the Colony. Mailing address: 6800 Main Street, The Colony, TX 75056. Phone: 972-624-2329. Camping: 5 RV/tent sites with water and electricity, 30 tent sites with water, modern restrooms, trailer dump station, picnic shelters, playground, sports courts, boat ramp, lake swimming.

Hickory Creek Park: from Lewisville north on I-35E to FM 2181/Swisher Rd exit (Exit 458), west on Turbeville Road for .2 mile, south on Point Vista Road to park. Corps of Engineers. Mailing address: 1801 N. Mill Street, Lewisville, Texas 75057. Phone: 469-645-9100. For reservations, call 877-444-6777, or online at www.recreation.gov. Camping: 124 back-in RV/tent sites with water and electricity, 10 primitive tent sites with water faucets and pit toilet, restrooms with showers, trailer dump station, picnic area, swim beach, boat launch, playground. Fees charged, open all year. Park gate open 6 a.m. to 10 p.m.

Pilot Knoll Park: from I-35E in Lewisville, FM 407 west to Chinn Road then north to Chapel Road, turn north, then turn east on Orchard Hill Lane to park. Highland Village. Mailing Address: 218A Orchid Hill Road, Argyle, TX 76226. Phone: 940-455-2228. *Camping*: 54 back-in RV/tent sites with full hookups, 10 tent sites, 3 screened shelters, modern restrooms, showers, trailer dump station, playground, lake swimming, boat launch, hike/bike nature trails, cable TV, WiFi. Fees charged, open all year.

MAIN ATTRACTIONS

Lake Lewisville, on the Elm Fork of the Trinity River, covers 25,596 acres and has 200 miles of shoreline. The former Lake Dallas became part of the reservoir when a new dam impounded the river in 1955. Receiving more than 5 million visitors annually, the various parks on the lake are heavily used by residents of the Dallas-Fort Worth area. Hunting and hiking are allowed on the 9,000 acres set aside for wildlife management.

An archaeological survey conducted in the area uncovered evidence including a Clovis point, of human occupation 10,000 to 11,000 years ago. Laws requiring surveys of areas targeted for federal and state construction have enabled archaeologists to piece together more information on the ways of life and migrations of the earliest Americans.

HIKING, BIKING EQUESTRIAN TRAILS

The Corps of Engineers, Texas Parks and Wildlife, and various municipal agencies, maintain a system of multi-use trails around Lake Lewisville. The 8-mile Pilot Knoll Hiking and Equestrian Trail begins near Pilot Knoll Park with trailer parking available at the Bishop Lane trailhead. The 6-mile Elm Fork Hiking and Equestrian Trail has 2 miles open to horses. The trail will eventually connect Pilot Knoll Park to Sycamore Bend Park. Hikers can access the trail at the Old Alton Bridge and horse riders from the existing Pilot Knoll trail.

Summer tanagers nest along the shoreline of Lake Lewisville.

The 20-mile Ray Roberts Lake/Lake Lewisville Greenbelt Corridor begins at the Ray Roberts Dam and ends at the headwaters of Lake Lewisville. 12 miles of trails are designated for equestrian and 10 for hike/bike use. Trailheads at FM 455, FM 428, and Hwy. 380 access the multi-use trail system (see Ray Roberts Lake State Park).

111. LAKE LIVINGSTON STATE PARK

LOCATION

Polk County. 2 miles south of Livingston on U.S. 59, 4 miles west on FM 1988, northwest on FM 3126, on the east shore of Lake Livingston.
Mailing address: 300 Park Road 65, Livingston, TX 77351. Phone: 936-365-2201. For all state park reservations, call the centralized reservations system, 512-389-8900, or www.ReserveAmerica.com online. Call the state park information number, 800-792-1112, for information and fee updates.

FACILITIES

Fees: entrance, facility, activity use; subject to change.

Camping: 66 back-in RV/tent sites with full hookups, 69 sites with water and electricity, 26 with water hookups, 10 screened shelters, group campground and pavilion (capacity 50) with water and electricity, modern restrooms, showers, trailer dump station. Fees charged.

Recreation: picnic areas, playgrounds, group picnic pavilion, activity center (capacity 100), 4.4-mile hiking trail, 5-mile mountain biking trail, 2.7-mile nature trail, 2.5-mile equestrian trail, seasonal Texas Park Store and Marina (bait, gas, dock facilities, March–October), swimming pool, bathhouse, boat ramps, fish-cleaning shelters.

WEATHER

July high averages 94 degrees, January low 37 degrees.

MAIN ATTRACTIONS

Water-oriented activities centered around Lake Livingston are the major attraction of the park. The lake has 84,800 surface acres and 452 miles of shoreline; it is 52 miles long. An interpretive trail and several miles of hiking trails wind through the park. The park livery stable rents horses and offers breakfast and dinner tours. Scheduled rides leave four to six times daily. No private horses allowed. Call the stables, 936-967-5032, for information.

PLANTS AND ANIMALS

The 635-acre park is located in the pine-oak woodlands of East Texas. In the past, this area was managed exclusively for pine production, and most of the hardwoods were eliminated. Since the establishment of the park, the natural diversity of tree species is being allowed to develop. That diversity will support a greater variety of wildlife.

Both loblolly and shortleaf pines grow in the dense woods of the park, and the bottomlands are forested with willow, oak, elm, and hickory trees. Remnants of a tallgrass blackland prairie also occur, which provide habitat for grassland birds.

Waterfowl and open-water species such as gulls, terns, and loons are commonly seen on the lake. The endangered bald eagle and the osprey are occasionally sighted hunting for fish over the water. Warblers, seven species of woodpeckers, and many other woodland birds inhabit the forests. Ask for a checklist of the birds.

LAKE LIVINGSTON: WOLF CREEK PARK

San Jacinto County. Located on west shore of Lake Livingston. From Livingston west on U.S. 190 across lake, south on TX 156, east 3 miles on FM 224. Mailing address: Box 309, Coldspring, Texas 77331. Phone: 936-653-4312. Camping: 110 acres on Lake Livingston with 103 back-in RV/tent sites with water, 54 with water and electricity, 30 with full hook-ups, 19 primitive sites, modern restrooms, showers, trailer dump station. Fees charged. Recreation: picnic areas, playgrounds, swimming in lake, fishing, water-skiing, boat ramp, flat-boat rentals, miniature golf course, pavilion, store, 18-hole golf course nearby. Open March 1 to November 31. Excellent facilities.

112. LAKE MEREDITH NATIONAL RECREATION AREA AND ALIBATES FLINT QUARRIES NATIONAL MONUMENT

LOCATION

Hutchinson, Moore, Potter counties. Headquarters: 38 miles northeast of Amarillo on TX 136, in Fritch.
Mailing address: Box 1460, Fritch, Texas 79036. Phone: 806-857-3151. Internet: www.nps.gov/lamr.

FACILITIES

Camping: Sanford-Yake, on Sanford-Yake Road near the marina, designated campsites with covered tables, flush toilets (Memorial Day–Labor Day), trailer dump station nearby. No fees. Primitive designated sites at Fitch Fortress with flush toilets (Memorial Day–Labor Day), trailer dump station nearby. Primitive undesignated camping with chemical toilets and no water at Blue Creek Bridge, Blue Water, Bugbee, Harbor Bay, McBride Canyon, Rosita; Mullinaw and Plum Creek have horse corrals available. Blue Creek Bridge and Rosita campgrounds are designed off-road vehicle and equestrian use areas. Plum Creek has corrals and access to the Devil's Canyon hike/bike/horse trail. No campground use fees, open year round.

Recreation: picnicking, swimming at Spring Canyon below the dam, fishing, boating, marinas, docks, hunting.

MAIN ATTRACTIONS

Fishing, boating, and water sports bring visitors to this 21,600-acre reservoir. Fishing is good for walleye, catfish, bass, and crappie, and sailors enjoy the brisk breezes that sweep across the lake. Because the lake level fluctuates, the fishing and boat-launching areas on the western end of the lake are often mud flats. Boats are advised to listen for the wind warning siren, since violent thunderstorms can develop unexpectedly.

The campgrounds, equipped with tables and shade shelters, are on barren, rocky, windswept hilltops overlooking the lake. The lake has no swimming beaches, and swimming is not recommended. The dangerously steep shores are littered with loose rocks and covered, both below and above the fluctuating water level, with thorny mesquite bushes. The only swimming beach is located below the dam at Spring Canyon. Motorcycles and dune buggies often gather for events in the areas designated for off-road vehicles at Rosita and Big Blue Creek parks. A marina with a dump station is located at Sanford.

NEARBY ATTRACTIONS

Alibates Flint Quarries National Monument is on the west end of Lake Meredith at Bates Canyon off TX 136. Prehistoric peoples throughout the Southwest used the rainbow-colored agatized dolomite for tools and weapons. Mining of the flint dates back 10,000 to 12,000 years. Guided tours are offered at 10 a.m. and 2 p.m. between Memorial and Labor days and by request at other times. Wear good walking shoes and take a canteen for the one-mile, steep loop trail to the quarries. Call the National Park Service office for reservations.

113. LAKE MINERAL WELLS STATE PARK AND TRAILWAY

LOCATION

Parker County. 45 miles west of Fort Worth on U.S. 180, 2 miles east of Mineral Wells.
Mailing address: 100 Park Road 71, Mineral Wells, Texas 76067. Phone: 940-328-1171. For all state park reservations, call the centralized reservations system, 512-389-8900, or www.ReserveAmerica.com online. Call the state park information number, 800-792-1112, for information and fee updates.

FACILITIES

Fees: entrance, facility, activity use; subject to change.

Camping: 64 back-in RV/tent sites with water and electricity, 11 sites with water, 20 primitive hike-in sites (2.5 miles), 20 equestrian sites with water, 15 screened shelters, overflow camping area, modern restrooms, showers, trailer dump station. Fees charged.

Recreation: picnicking, lake swimming, fishing piers, boat launch, 9-mile hike/bike/horse trail, 5-mile hiking trail, 2.5-mile backpack trail, private store with pedal boat, canoe, and kayak rental (940-325-7152).

WEATHER

July high averages 98 degrees, January low 32 degrees.

Green herons nest along the shoreline of Lake Mineral Wells.

MAIN ATTRACTIONS

The 646-acre Lake Mineral Wells offers fishing, swimming, and boating. Separate hiking and horseback-riding trails traverse the deep canyons and wooded hills of the park.

In the early 1900s, Mineral Wells was a nationally famous health spa. The mineral water was first discovered in 1885 in the Crazy Well, at what is now the intersection of U.S. 281 and 180. The waters, containing sodium sulfate, chlorides, magnesium, and calcium, were believed to cure a long list of illnesses. In 1934, there were 150 commercial wells in operation in Mineral Wells. The large Baker Resort Hotel, now abandoned, is an example of the affluence that once graced the town.

HIKING, MOUNTAIN BIKING, AND HORSEBACK RIDING

The hiking, biking, and equestrian trails begin at the end of the paved road in the Cross Timbers camping area. The equestrian compound is located at the trailhead for the 9-mile horseback-riding loop and the backpack campsites at the end of a 2.5-mile trail. No horses or bikes allowed on the backpack trail or the 5-mile Lake Trail.

The 20-mile Lake Mineral Wells State Trailway connects Lake Mineral Wells State Park to Weatherford and Mineral Wells. Trailheads with parking, drinking water, restrooms, and trail information are located near Weatherford, Garner, the state park, and downtown Mineral Wells. Fees are charged at self-pay stations at trailheads.

Acquired as part of the Rails to Trails program, the trailway follows the 1899 roadbed of the Texas & Pacific Railway Company. The first 2 miles from Mineral Wells are paved and the remainder packed with crushed stone. The 10-foot-wide trail crosses 16 trestles including a 500-foot bridge adorned with 104 Lone Stars. The scenic path passes through rolling hills, pastures, and farmland. In the spring, wildflowers fill the picturesque landscape with a blanket of colors.

PLANTS AND ANIMALS

The 2,853-acre park features steep hills overlooking the scenic lake, deep ravines, and open savannas. Post oaks and blackjack oaks are scattered through the savannas, and the ravines are heavily wooded with pecans, cedar elms, cottonwoods, and red oaks. Ashe juniper, Texas oak, plateau live oak, mesquite, and hackberry trees are also abundant in the park.

Sand, clay, and gravel deposited more than 300 million years ago form the red, brown, and yellow sandstones, the conglomerate rocks, and the sandy soil of the park. An aquifer, or water-bearing stratum of rock, with mineral-rich water underlies the area.

114. LAKE O' THE PINES

LOCATION

U.S. Army Corps of Engineers. Marion, Upshur, Harrison, Camp, and Morris counties. Project office: 16 miles north of Marshall on U.S. 59 to Jefferson, 2.5 miles west on TX 49, 4.4 miles west on FM 729, 2.5 miles south on FM 726.
Mailing address: 2669 FM 726, Jefferson, Texas 75657.
Phone: Project Office, 903-665-3911. Camping Reservations: 877-444-6777, www.recreation.gov. Internet: www.swf-wc.usace .army.mil/lakeopines.

FACILITIES

The COE operates four parks on the lake with developed campgrounds. Alley Creek and Johnson Creek parks have group campgrounds that can be reserved at www.recreation.gov. Parks not listed in the matrix are either day use or closed. Refer to the map for locations. Three concessionaire-operated marinas also offer RV hookups: Big Cypress Marina, 1500 Big Cypress Marina Rd., Jefferson, TX 75657, 903-665-8582; Johnson Creek Marina, 440 Johnson Creek Marina Rd. (Dishman's), Jefferson, TX 75657, 903-755-2530; Bullfrog Marina, Box 502, Jefferson, TX 75657, 903-755-2712.

Alley Creek Campground: 49 back-in RV sites with water and electricity, 30 tent sites with water nearby, group pavilion with 12 campsites with parking pad, water, electricity; modern restrooms with showers, trailer dump station. Day-use picnic area, playground, swim beach, boat ramp, courtesy dock, fishing dock. Fees charged, open March 1–September 30.

Brushy Creek Campground: 62 back-in RV sites with water and electricity, 37 tent sites with water nearby (12 with electricity), modern restrooms

Campground	water	fee area	flush toilets	season	dump station	showers	electricity
Alley Creek	•	•	•	Mar.–Sept.	•	•	•
Brushy Creek	•	•	•	all	•	•	•
Buckhorn Creek	•	•	•	Mar.–Sept.	•	•	•
Johnson Creek	•	•	•	all	•	•	•

LAKE O' THE PINES

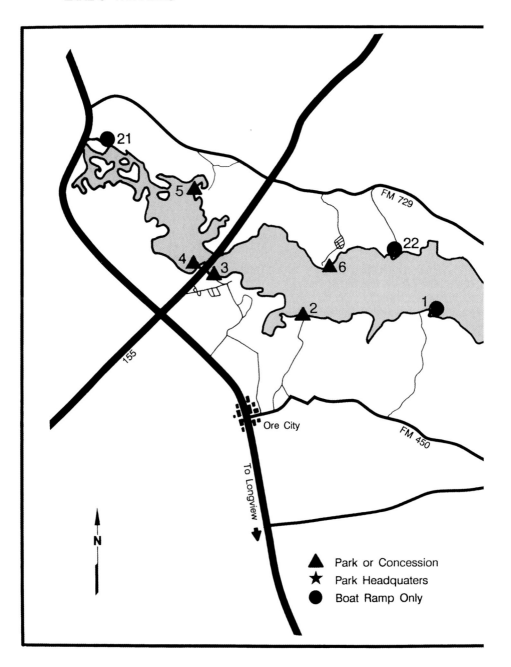

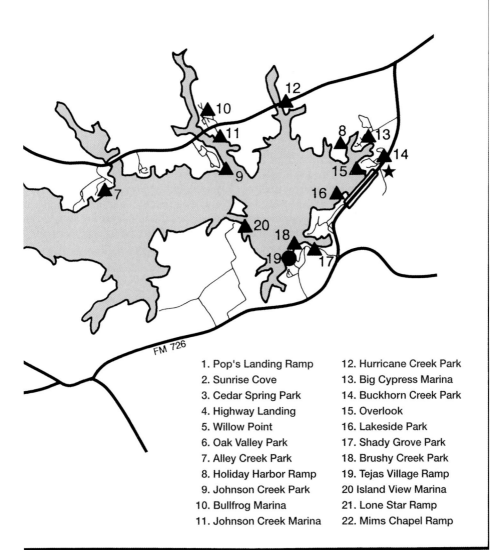

1. Pop's Landing Ramp	12. Hurricane Creek Park
2. Sunrise Cove	13. Big Cypress Marina
3. Cedar Spring Park	14. Buckhorn Creek Park
4. Highway Landing	15. Overlook
5. Willow Point	16. Lakeside Park
6. Oak Valley Park	17. Shady Grove Park
7. Alley Creek Park	18. Brushy Creek Park
8. Holiday Harbor Ramp	19. Tejas Village Ramp
9. Johnson Creek Park	20 Island View Marina
10. Bullfrog Marina	21. Lone Star Ramp
11. Johnson Creek Marina	22. Mims Chapel Ramp

with showers, trailer dump station. Day-use park with playground, swim beach, boat ramp, courtesy dock, fishing dock. Fees charged, open all year.

Buckhorn Creek Campground: 58 back-in RV sites with water and electricity, 38 tent sites with water nearby, modern restrooms with showers, trailer dump station, playground, lake swimming, boat ramp, courtesy dock, fishing dock. Fees charged, open March 1–September 30.

Johnson Creek Campground: 63 back-in RV sites with water and electricity, 22 tent sites with water nearby (5 walk-in), group camp area with 12 campsites with water and electricity, modern restrooms with showers, trailer dump station. Day-use park with playground, swim beach, boat ramp. Fees charged, open year-round.

MAIN ATTRACTIONS

Built on Cypress Creek for flood control and water storage, the lake covers 18,700 surface acres at a normal level; it has 144 miles of shoreline. White crappie, largemouth bass, spotted bass, and bluegill sunfish are common catches. Hunting is allowed on part of the property.

Lake O' the Pines is in the Piney Woods of East Texas. The shore is heavily forested with loblolly pines and a variety of oaks and other hardwoods. The diverse vegetation, varying from the well-draining uplands to creek bottoms and the open lake, supports an abundant population of wildlife, especially birds. Located on the Central Flyway, the area attracts many migrating songbirds in the spring and fall as well as waterfowl in the winter. A checklist of the birds is available at the project office.

HISTORY

Archaeological surveys conducted in the reservoir area have uncovered numerous artifacts from the various tribes collectively known as the Caddo Indians. In 1541, the first Europeans explored what is now East Texas and found the Caddos, a culturally advanced confederation of tribes. They were originally very cordial to Europeans but later rebelled against the depredations inflicted upon them by the Spanish.

In 1835, the Caddos were forced to sign a treaty in which they ceded all their lands, which had been included in the Louisiana Purchase in 1803, to the U.S. government. They were forced to move at their own expense beyond the borders of the United States to Texas. The Caddos found no peace in Texas, and after Texas gained its independence from Mexico they were driven into Oklahoma. East Texas is rich in the archaeological heritage of those inhabitants of the Piney Woods.

Jefferson, 10 miles east of the lake, has many beautifully reconstructed buildings from the mid-1800s. Before railroads crossed the state, the town was the main port of entry for East Texas. Steamboats carried goods down Big Cypress Bayou to the Red River, which connected with the Mississippi and New Orleans. Restored buildings and museums in Jefferson depict the rich history of the area.

115. LAKE PAT MAYSE

LOCATION

U.S. Army Corps of Engineers. Lamar County. Project office: From Paris, 15 miles north on U.S. 271, 3 miles west on FM 906. Mailing address: 1679 Farm Road 906 West, Powderly, TX 75473-3337. Phone: 930-732-3020. For camping reservations, 877-444-6777, www. recreation.gov. Internet: http://corpslakes.usace.army.mil/ visitors/states.cfm?state=TX.

FACILITIES

Camping: Lake Pat Mayse offers camping in four parks. Lamar Point has back-in RV/tend sites with no hookups, Pat Mayse East and West and Sanders Cove have back-in sites with water and electric hookups, tent camping, and flush or pit toilets. Overlook and Clay Bluff are day use. All parks but Overlook have boat ramps. Lamar Point, Pat Mayse East, and Sanders Cove provide designated lake swimming areas. Fees charged, open all year.

Recreation: picnicking, nature trails, swimming, water sports, fishing, boat ramps, hunting.

MAIN ATTRACTIONS

Lake Pat Mayse covers 5,990 acres and has 67 miles of shoreline. The park includes gently rolling grasslands and forests of oak, pine, elm, and

Campground	water	fee area	flush toilets	season	dump station	electricity
Lamar Point	•			all		
Pat Mayse East	•	•		all		•
Pat Mayse West	•	•	•	all	•	•
Sanders Cove	•	•	•	all	•	•

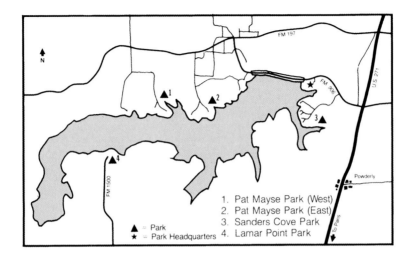

1. Pat Mayse Park (West)
2. Pat Mayse Park (East)
3. Sanders Cove Park
4. Lamar Point Park

▲ = Park
★ = Park Headquarters

hickory. The lake was formed by impounding Sanders Creek, a tributary of the Red River. Fishing is excellent in the lake, especially for large-mouth and sand bass, white crappie, and channel and flathead catfish. Public hunting and hiking are permitted on the 14,925-acre wildlife management area. Game species include white-tailed deer, squirrels, quail, and doves.

Visitors to this area should look for historic homes in Paris. Also, Gambill Wildlife Refuge, northwest of Paris on FM 79, then west on FM 2820, is a good bird-watching area.

116. LAKE PROCTOR

LOCATION

U.S. Army Corps of Engineers. Comanche County. Project office: 5.5 miles northeast of Comanche on U.S. 377, 2 miles north on FM 2861.
Mailing address: 2180 FM 2861, Comanche, Texas 76442-7248.
Phone: 254-879-2424. Internet: www.swf-wc.usace.army.mil/proctor/.
For camping reservations, 877-444-6777, www.recreation.gov.
Internet: http://corpslakes.usace.army.mil/visitors/states.cfm?state=TX.

FACILITIES

Camping: All three parks provide pull-through RV/tent sites with water and electric hookups, group camping, modern restrooms, trailer dump

Campground	water	fee area	flush toilets	season	dump station	electricity
Copperas Creek	•	•	•	all	•	•
Promontory	•	•	•	all	•	•
Sowell Creek	•	•	•	all	•	•

station, swimming area, fishing docks, boat ramps. Fees charged, open all year. High Point Park is closed (2009) due to flood damage, but the hiking/equestrian trailhead at the park entrance remains open.

MAIN ATTRACTIONS

Built for flood control and water storage on the Leon River, the reservoir covers 4,610 acres and has 38 miles of shoreline. The lake is a prime spot for largemouth bass, as well as crappie and catfish. Early spring through June is the best time for fishing. Located on the Central Flyway, the lake is popular for waterfowl hunting. As many as 100,000 ducks may be seen on the lake during migration. Ask at the entrance facility or the project office for a brochure on fishing and hunting in the area.

LAKE PROCTOR

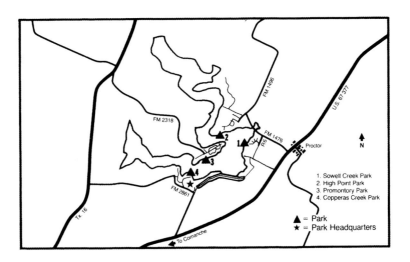

1. Sowell Creek Park
2. High Point Park
3. Promontory Park
4. Copperas Creek Park

▲ = Park
★ = Park Headquarters

The open meadows bordering the campgrounds are blanketed with colorful wildflowers in the spring. Ground squirrels and quail scurry through the bluebonnets and Indian paintbrushes, and meadowlarks crouch beside their dome nests of grass.

117. LAKE RITA BLANCA CITY PARK

LOCATION

Hartley County. Operated by the City of Dalhart. 2 miles south of Dalhart on U.S. 385/87 to FM 281, 1.5 miles west to park. Mailing address: Box 2005, Dalhart, TX 79022. Phone: 806-244-5511 (City Hall).

FACILITIES

Camping: 24 back-in RV/tent sites with water and electricity, pit toilets, trailer dump station. Fees charged, no reservations, open all year. Recreation: The 1,668-acre park, once a state park, is a stop on the Panhandle Plains Wildlife Trail of the Great Texas Wildlife Trails system. The park has picnic tables and pavilion, playgrounds, 2 rock-climbing walls, and a hike/bike trail around the lake.

HISTORY

The park traces its legacy back to the cattle days of the XIT Ranch, the 3 million-acre spread that stretched from Lubbock to the Oklahoma border. The irregular ranch averaged only 30 miles wide but was the largest fenced ranch in the world.

PLANTS AND ANIMALS

Lake Rita Blanca, a dammed reservoir on Rita Blanca Creek, is located on the High Plains of the Texas Panhandle. Historically, the blue grama-buffalo grass vegetation supported vast herds of bison. During the trail-drive era, some of the largest ranches in Texas thrived in the area. Today, the lake is one of the largest wintering grounds for waterfowl in the central flyway. The lake attracts from 40,000 to 100,000 geese and large numbers of ducks throughout the winter. During spring and fall migration, neotropical song birds find the lake an important stopover. Wildlife occurring year-round in the park include bald eagles, mule deer, scaled quail, and swift, gray and red foxes.

118. LAKE SAM RAYBURN

LOCATION

U.S. Army Corps of Engineers. Jasper, San Augustine, Nacogdoches, Sabine, and Angelina counties. East of Lufkin. Project office: southeast of Lufkin on TX 63, east on FM 255 to dam. Mailing address: Route 3, Box 486, Jasper, Texas 75951. Phone: 409-384-5716. Internet: www.swf-wc.usace.army.mil/samray/. For camping reservations, call 877-444-6777 or online at www. recreation.gov.

FACILITIES

Angelina National Forest (see listing page 21): San Augustine County (936-275-2762), and private marinas operate day-use parks and campgrounds on the lake. The COE operates six parks with camping.

Campground	water	fee area	flush toilets	season	dump station	showers	electricity
Cassells-Boykin (Angelina County)	•	•	•	all	•		•
Ebenezer Park	•	•		all	•		•
Jackson Hill	•	•		Mar.–Sept.	•		
Mill Creek	•	•	•	all	•	•	•
Rayburn	•	•	•	all	•	•	
San Augustine	•	•	•	all	•	•	•
Shirley Creek	•	•	•	all	•	•	•
Twin Dikes	•	•	•	all	•	•	•
Sandy Creek (USFS)	•	•	•	all		•	
Caney Creek (USFS)	•	•	•	all	•	•	
Harvey Creek (San Augustine County)		•		all			
Hanks Creek Park	•	•	•	all	•	•	•
Townsend Park (San Augustine County)		•		all			

LAKE SAM RAYBURN

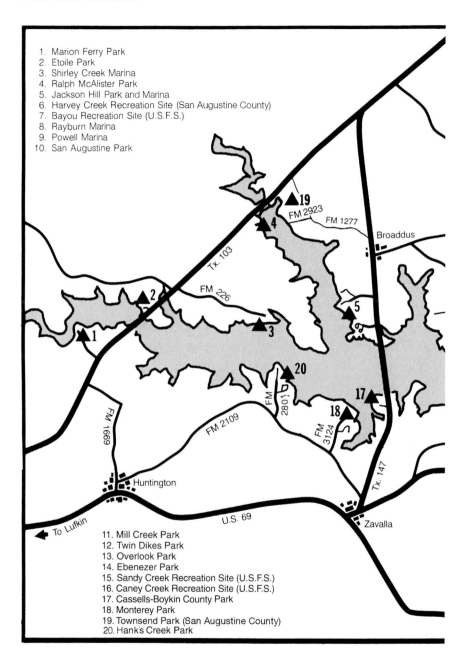

1. Marion Ferry Park
2. Etoile Park
3. Shirley Creek Marina
4. Ralph McAlister Park
5. Jackson Hill Park and Marina
6. Harvey Creek Recreation Site (San Augustine County)
7. Bayou Recreation Site (U.S.F.S.)
8. Rayburn Marina
9. Powell Marina
10. San Augustine Park

11. Mill Creek Park
12. Twin Dikes Park
13. Overlook Park
14. Ebenezer Park
15. Sandy Creek Recreation Site (U.S.F.S.)
16. Caney Creek Recreation Site (U.S.F.S.)
17. Cassells-Boykin County Park
18. Monterey Park
19. Townsend Park (San Augustine County)
20. Hank's Creek Park

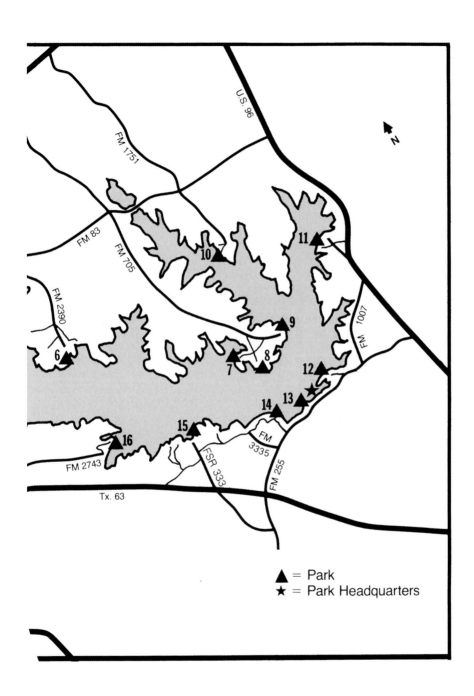

US. 96

FM 1751

FM 83

FM 705

FM 2390

11

10

9

6

8

7

12

FM 1007

13

14

15

16

FM 3335

FSR 333

FM 255

FM 2743

Tx. 63

N

▲ = Park
★ = Park Headquarters

Ebenezer: from Jasper 23 miles NW to Recreational Road 255 on south shore. 20 back-in RV sites with water and electricity, 10 back-in RV equestrian-only sites with water and electricity and corral, 20 tent sites, modern restrooms with showers, trailer dump station. Swim beach, picnic tables, group hall, 1.3-mile equestrian trail. Ebenezer is the only park on the lake that allows horses. Fees charged, open year-round.

Twin Dikes: from Jasper 23 miles NW to Recreational Road 255, on south shore. 46 back-in RV/tent sites with water and electricity (6 with sewer), 27 sites with no hookups, 3 sites with screened shelters, electric, water and sewer, 1 group shelter modern, restrooms with showers, trailer dump station; boat ramps (no swim beach). Fees charged, open year round. The adjacent Sam Rayburn Marina Resort, www.samrayburnmarinaresort.com, 409-698-2696, has cabins, motel, RV Park, and swim beach

Mill Creek Park: from Brookeland Loop 149 north 1 mile to Spur 165, west .6 mile to park. 110 back-in RV/tent sites with water and electricity, group shelter, modern restrooms with showers, designated swim beach, playgrounds, trailer dump station, boat ramp. Fees charged, open all year.

San Augustine Park: from Pineland 5.6 miles west on FM 83, 3.8 miles south on FM 1751. 100 back-in RV/tent sites with water electricity (5 tent only), group shelter, modern restrooms with showers, trailer dump station, playground, designated swim area, dock, boat ramp. Fees charged, open all year.

Rayburn Park: from Pineland 23 miles SW on FM 3127 on the north shore. 8 pull-through RV/tent sites and 16 back-in sites with water and electricity, 21 sites without hookups, modern restrooms with showers, trailer dump station; picnic area, playground, boat launch (no swim beach). Fees charged, open all year.

Hanks Creek Park: from Huntington 12 miles SW on FM 2801, on NW shore. 44 RV/tent sites and 8 screened shelters with water and electricity, group camp area with hookups, modern restrooms with showers, trailer dump station; day-use area scheduled for 2008 with playground, boat launch, docks, fishing pier. Fees charged, open all year.

Day-use parks: Monterey Park, Marion Ferry, Etoile, Ralph McAlister Park: boat launch only, no fees.

Cassells-Boykin County Park (Angelina County park, 409-384-5231): from Lufkin 22 miles south on U.S. 69 to Zavala, 4 miles east on TX 147 to FM 3123, turn north before reaching bridge. 10 back-in RV/tent sites and 17 tent sites (17 have water and electricity), modern restroom, trailer dump station; lake swimming, ADA accessible fishing pier, pavilion, boat launch. Fees charged, open all year.

Four private marinas offer cabins, RV/tent camping with full hookups, boat rentals, tackle stores, and swim beaches: Shirley Creek Marina and Campground (936-854-2233, marina@shirleycreek.com, www.shirleycreek.com), Powell Marina (409-584-2624, www.powellpark.com, powellpark@jas.net), Sam Rayburn Marina Resort (409-698-2696, www.

samrayburnmarinaresort.com), Jackson Hill Park and Marina, (936-872-9266, terry@jacksonhill.us, www.jacksonhill.us).

MAIN ATTRACTIONS

The lake, formed on the Angelina River, is the largest reservoir entirely within the state. It covers 114,500 surface acres and has 560 miles of shoreline; its average depth is 25 feet. Originally called McGee Bend, the reservoir was renamed in 1963 to honor the late House Speaker, Sam Rayburn, from Bonham. In addition to flood control and water storage, the dam serves as a source of hydroelectric power.

Fishermen can expect excellent catches, including largemouth bass, both black and white bass, walleye pike, striped bass, Florida bass, and bream. Squirrel and waterfowl hunting is popular in the area.

The lake, located in the midst of Angelina National Forest, has a red-and-white-sand shoreline heavily wooded with pines and oaks. The open water of the lake attracts many waterfowl in the winter, and the numerous wooded inlets provide ideal habitats for wading birds and shorebirds. Gulls, terns, and occasionally a bald eagle or an osprey can be seen flying over the lake. During the spring and fall, the forest is a stopover for many species of migrating songbirds.

Archaeological surveys of the area have uncovered dozens of ancient campsites and at least one large village site. It is believed that the region was occupied over the past thousand years by at least five distinct cultural groups, including some Caddoan groups. There is evidence that numerous tribes lived in the area around 1650, and the Cherokees occupied the land from about 1828 to 1839.

119. LAKE SOMERVILLE (CORPS OF ENGINEERS PARKS)

LOCATION

U.S. Army Corps of Engineers. Burleson, Lee, and Washington counties. Project office: 14 miles northwest of Brenham on TX 36, half mile west of Somerville.
Mailing address: 1560 Thornberry Dr., Somerville, Texas 77879.
Phone: 979-596-1622. Internet: www.swf-wc.usace.army.mil/somerville/. For reservations, call toll free 1-877-444-6777 or online at www.recreation.gov.

FACILITIES

Lake Somerville State Park (see listing), Welsh Park (City of Somerville, 979-596-2286), Overlook Park and Marina (979-289-2321), and Big

Campground	water	fee area	flush toilets	season	dump station	showers	electricity
Yegua Creek	•	•	•	all	•	•	•
Rocky Creek	•	•	•	all	•	•	•
Welch Park	•	•	•	all		•	

Creek Park and Marina (979-596-1616), and Lake Somerville Marina and Campground (979-289-2321, 800-264-7804, www.lakesomerville-marina.com) offer camping on Lake Somerville. The COE has two parks with camping facilities.

Rocky Creek Park (COE): from Somerville 4 miles south on TX 36 to FM 1948, west 5 miles to park road, north .5 mile to park. 74 back-in RV/ tent sites with water and electricity, 75 sites with water hookup, 46 tent sites with water nearby, modern restrooms, showers, trailer dump station; picnic area, group shelter, playgrounds, boat launch, nature trail. Fees charged, open all year. Gatehouse hours 6 a.m.–10 p.m.

Yegua Creek Park (COE): from Somerville 4 miles south on TX 36 to FM 1948, west for 2.5 miles to park. 47 back-in RV/tent sites with water and electricity, 35 tent sites with water nearby, restrooms, showers, trailer dump station; playground, boat launch, nature trail, (off-road vehicle area closed due to vandalism). Fees charged, open all year. Gatehouse hours 6 a.m.–10 p.m.

Welsh Park (City of Somerville, 979-596-2286): from Somerville 4 miles south on TX 36 to FM 1948, turn west across railroad tracks, turn north and go 4 miles across dam to park. Approximately 20 RV/tents sites with water nearby, modern restrooms, showers, boat ramp. Fees charged, open all year.

MAIN ATTRACTIONS

The lake, built on Yegua Creek, a tributary of the Brazos River, provides flood control and water storage for the area. At nonflood levels, the lake covers 11,460 acres and has 85 miles of sandy shoreline. Fishing is good for largemouth bass, white bass, channel catfish, and white crappie. Hunting is allowed on 3,500 acres leased by the Texas Parks and Wildlife Department.

Yegua Creek and Big Creek parks have short nature trails leading through post oak, live oak, mesquite, and eastern red cedar. In the summer, the fields are carpeted with colorful wildflowers, such as coreopsis,

LAKE SOMERVILLE

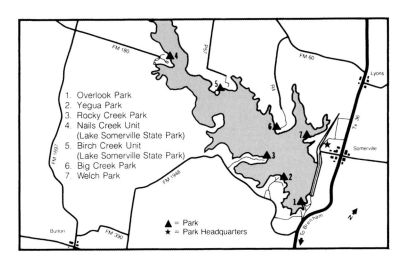

1. Overlook Park
2. Yegua Park
3. Rocky Creek Park
4. Nails Creek Unit
   (Lake Somerville State Park)
5. Birch Creek Unit
   (Lake Somerville State Park)
6. Big Creek Park
7. Welch Park

▲ = Park
★ = Park Headquarters

Indian blankets, and winecups. Quail, meadowlarks, and ground squirrels going to and from their nests dart through the fragrant flowers.

LAKE SOMERVILLE STATE PARK

LOCATION

Refer to map with Lake Somerville, Corps of Engineers parks.
Birch Creek Unit: 25 miles southwest of Bryan on FM 60, 8 miles
southwest of Lyons on FM 60, south on PR 57. Mailing address:
Mailing address: 14222 Park Road 57, Somerville, TX 77879-9713.
Phone: 979-535-7763. E-mail: Birch.Creek@tpwd.state.tx.us.
Nails Creek and Trailway, Wildlife Management Area: 29 miles
west of Brenham on U.S. 290, 13 miles north on FM 180. Mailing
address: 6280 FM 180, Ledbetter, Texas 78946-7036. Phone: 979-
289-2392. E-mail: Nails.Creek@tpwd.state.tx.us. For all state park
reservations, call the centralized reservations system, 512-389-8900,
or www.ReserveAmerica.com online. Call the state park information
number, 800-792-1112, for information and fee updates.

FACILITIES

Fees: entrance, facility, activity use; subject to change.

Nails Creek: 20 back-in RV/tent sites with water and electricity, 20 back-in
RV/equestrian sites with water and electricity and horse pens, 7 equestrian

sites with water and horse pens, 10 primitive walk-in tent sites, modern restrooms, showers, trailer dump station, group picnic area. Fees charged.

Birch Creek: 103 back-in RV/tent sites with water and electricity, 20 walk-in tent sites with water, equestrian campsites, group RV area for 14 with water, electricity, and dining hall. Modern restrooms, showers, trailer dump station. Fees charged.

Recreation: picnic areas, playgrounds, group picnic pavilions, sports courts, lake swimming, water activities, boat ramps, fish-cleaning stations, hiking, mountain biking, birding, Texas State Park Store.

Trailway: 4 primitive campgrounds on hike/bike/horse trail with 50 sites total, only non-potable water available.

WEATHER

July high averages 95 degrees, January low 48 degrees.

MAIN ATTRACTIONS

Lake Somerville, with 11,460 acres, is popular for boating, water sports, swimming, and fishing. Catches of largemouth bass, white bass, channel catfish, and crappie are common. The tall oaks and gently sloping lakeshore provide a scenic setting for picnicking and camping, and the sandy beaches are good for swimming. The lake was formed in 1967 by impounding Yegua Creek 20 miles upstream from its confluence with the Brazos River. The 5,200-acre park was acquired in 1969 from the Army Corps of Engineers.

Nearby attractions include the University of Texas Winedale Museum, at Round Top on TX 237, which features early Texas architecture and furnishings. Washington-on-the-Brazos State Historical Park, a day-use area, is 21 miles northeast of Brenham on TX 105.

HIKING

In addition to the 640-acre Birch Creek Unit and the 300-acre Nails Creek Unit, the park includes 4,260 acres of woodlands connecting the two units. The area contains 29 miles of trails for hiking, mountain biking, horseback riding, and backpacking. The Lake Somerville Trailway System, located around the west end of the reservoir, connects Birch Creek State Park with Nails Creek State Park with 13 miles of multi-use trails. The trail passes through gently rolling terrain of oak-hickory forests, marshlands, and meadows. The park has one of the best spring wildflower displays in the Texas State Park System.

Waterfowl hunting (October to mid-February) is allowed at the 350-acre Flag Pond, located along the trailway 4 miles from the Nails Creek Unit and 9 miles from the Birch Creek Unit, and in the adjacent wildlife management area. For nonhunters, the lake has interpretive trails and a wildlife viewing platform. Campgrounds for equestrians and backpackers and chemical toilets are located along the trailway. Well water for horses only is available at Newman Bottom and Wolf Pond.

PLANTS AND ANIMALS

The soil of the park was formed from weathered Yegua sandstone and clays from the Caddell formation deposited more than 42 million years ago. Petrified wood that is 40 million years old may be found in the park. The sandy soil supports a luxuriant growth of post and blackjack oak trees and dense stands of yaupon holly bushes.

Wildflowers are abundant throughout the spring and summer. The yellow heads of coreopsis, with their reddish centers, and white daisy-like fleabane decorate the roadsides. Bright yellow-and-red gaillardias, the delicate pink flowers of sensitive briers, and purple winecups add to the spring display of color.

The reservoir has created a variety of wildlife habitats in addition to the naturally occurring post oak and hickory woods, scattered grasslands, and bottomland forests. Waterfowl frequent the open waters, wading shorebirds the mud flats and marshes, and prairie species the cleared pasturelands.

Wildlife in the park is abundant. White-tailed deer, armadillos, and rabbits are commonly seen, especially at dusk, while foxes, coyotes, and raccoons are more secretive. Many species of water birds are attracted to the lake. In the winter, olivaceous cormorants are common, and bald eagles and ospreys are occasionally sighted. The habitats around the lake attract more than 260 species of birds. A checklist is available at the park entrance.

120. LAKE STILLHOUSE HOLLOW

LOCATION

U.S. Army Corps of Engineers. Bell County. 9 miles southwest of Temple on IH-35 to Belton, 4 miles west on U.S. 190. Project office: 3 miles west of Belton on U.S. 190, 2 miles south on FM 1670. Mailing address: 3740 FM 1670, Belton, TX 76513. Phone: 254-939-2461. Internet: www.swf-wc.usace.army.mil/stillhouse/. For camping reservations, call 877-444-6777 or online at www. recreation.gov.

FACILITIES

Camping: NOTICE–Dana Peak Park is closed indefinitely due to complete flood destruction of all park facilities in 2007. Only the boat ramp

LAKE STILLHOUSE HOLLOW

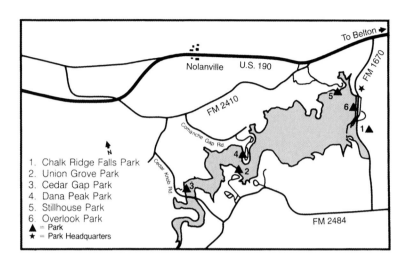

1. Chalk Ridge Falls Park
2. Union Grove Park
3. Cedar Gap Park
4. Dana Peak Park
5. Stillhouse Park
6. Overlook Park
▲ = Park
★ = Park Headquarters

Ospreys circle Lake Stillhouse Hollow hunting for fish.

and fishing dock area are open at Union Grove Park, and some trail bridges are closed in Chalk Ridge Falls. All other facilities remain open but some restrooms are temporary porta-potties.

Recreation: picnicking, nature trail at Chalk Ridge Falls Park below the dam, exercise trail at Overlook Park, swimming at Stillhouse and Dana Peak parks, fishing, water sports, boat ramps, marina at Stillhouse Park; hunting. Stillhouse Park is day-use only.

MAIN ATTRACTIONS

Lake Stillhouse Hollow, on the Lampasas River, covers 6,430 acres at its normal level and has 58 miles of shoreline. The lake has more than 1 million visitors a year, primarily boaters and swimmers. Bird-watching is also popular. A large number of waterfowl can be seen in the winter, as well as an occasional osprey. Hunting is allowed on 4,381 acres of the wildlife management area.

121. LAKE TAWAKONI STATE PARK

LOCATION

Hunt County. 50 miles east of Dallas on U.S. 80 to Wills Point, north on FM 47, north on FM 2475 to White Deer Landing Rd. Mailing address: 10822 FM 2475, Wills Point, Texas 75169. Phone: 903-560-7123.

FACILITIES

Fees: entrance, facility, activity use; subject to change.

Camping: 29 back-in and 32 pull-through RV/tent sites with water and electricity (2 ADA accessible), group youth area (capacity 35), modern restrooms, showers, trailer dump station. Fees charged.

Recreation: picnic area, swimming beach, 5.5 miles of hiking trails, boat ramp.

WEATHER

July high averages 95 degrees, January low 30 degrees.

MAIN ATTRACTIONS

Winding through Hunt, Rains, and Van Zandt counties, Lake Tawakoni and the parks along its 200 miles of shoreline provide water-oriented recreation for much of central northeast Texas. The 376-acre state park preserves 5.2 miles of shoreline along the south central shore of the lake. The park is popular for boating activities, fishing, hiking, and picnicking. The Sabine River Authority operates other parks on the 36,700-acre reservoir.

Second-growth post oak woodlands cover the rolling terrain and shoreline. Parks and Wildlife manages a small tract of tall grass prairie within the park. Only small, scattered remnants remain of this complex ecosystem that once covered much of the heartland of the continent.

LAKE TAWAKONI: WIND POINT PARK

Sabine River Authority. Hunt County. 51 miles northeast of Dallas on U.S. 67, 15 miles southeast on U.S. 69 to Lone Oak, 1 mile south on FM 513, 4 miles west on FM 1571, on Lake Tawakoni. Mailing address: 6553 State Park Road 55, Lone Oak, Texas 75453. Phone: 903-662-5134; fax: 903-662-5749. Internet: www.sratx.org/basin/recreation.asp.

FACILITIES

Camping: 90 pull-through RV/tent sites with full hookups, 69 with water and electricity, 15 screened shelters, 8 cabins with kitchens, modern restrooms, showers, trailer dump station. 2 day-use lodges with kitchens and restrooms. Reservations accepted for cabins, shelters, lodges. Fees charged.

Recreation: picnic areas and playgrounds, baseball diamonds, nature trail, swimming, 300-foot lighted fishing pier, boat ramps, marina, store. Open all year.

122. LAKE TEXANA: BRACKENRIDGE PLANTATION CAMPGROUND

Lavaca-Navidad River Authority. Jackson County. 25 miles northeast of Victoria on U.S. 59 to Edna, 6 miles east on TX 111. 250 acres on Lake Texana. Mailing address: 891 Brackenridge Pkwy., Edna, Texas 77957. Phone: 361-782-5456. Internet: www.brackenridgepark.com. Camping: 20 campsites with water and electricity, 80 campsites with water, electricity, and sewage hookups; group campsite with all hookups; flush toilets, showers, trailer dump station. Reservations accepted. Fees charged. Recreation: picnic areas, hiking trails, swimming in reservoir, fishing, water-skiing, boat ramp, marina, playground, golf course nearby, pavilion, store. Open all year. Good facilities. The park is located on the site of the old town of Texana. The Harry Hafernick Recreation Center has an auditorium, meeting rooms, and a TV area for park users.

LAKE TEXANA: MUSTANG WILDERNESS PARK

Lavaca-Navidad River Authority. Jackson County. 30 miles northeast of Victoria on U.S. 59. From U.S. 59, exit Loop 522 at Ganado, west 1 mile to FM 2982, south 2.1 miles, left on County Road 249 to park entrance. 250 acres on Lake Texana. Mailing address; Box 429, Edna, Texas 77957. Phone: 361-782-5229. Camping: 29 primitive campsites spaced along a 2-mile trail on a peninsula. Sites accessible by boat or hiking; no water, tables, or restrooms. Fees charged. Recreation: 5 miles of hiking trails, fishing, boating, boat ramp. Open all year.

LAKE TEXANA STATE PARK

LOCATION

Jackson County. 25 miles northeast of Victoria on U.S. 59 to Edna, 6 miles east on TX 111.
Mailing address: 46 Park Road 1, Edna, Texas 77957. Phone: 361-782-5718. For all state park reservations, call the centralized reservations system, 512-389-8900, or www.ReserveAmerica.com online. Call the state park information number, 800-792-1112, for information and fee updates.

FACILITIES

Fees: entrance, facility, activity use; subject to change.

Camping: 86 back-in RV/tent sites with water and electricity, 55 tent sites with water, modern restrooms with showers, trailer dump station. Entrance gate open from 7 a.m. to 10 p.m. Senior and seasonal camping fee discounts.

Recreation: picnic areas, playgrounds, group picnic area with pavilion, amphitheater, lighted fishing piers, fishing jetty, fish-cleaning facilities, boat ramp, lake swimming and water sports, 1.5-mile nature trail (.3-mile meets ADA requirements), nature center, canoe and paddleboat rental, Texas State Park Store.

WEATHER

July high averages 98 degrees, January low 40 degrees.

MAIN ATTRACTIONS

The park is located on the shores of Lake Texana, an impoundment of the Navidad River. The lake, with 11,000 surface acres and 125 miles of shoreline, is suitable for all water sports, including boating, canoeing, fishing, and swimming. There are three fishing piers, and catches of crappie, sunfish, bass, and catfish are common.

The 575-acre park is on the Gulf Coast prairie in the wooded Navidad River bottom. Large live oaks, hackberries, elms, and pecans shade the camping and picnicking areas. Numerous hawks spend the winter along the shores of the lake. Many waterfowl and shorebirds can be seen on the lake, and deer, armadillos, rabbits, and squirrels are common.

Lake Texana is named after the extinct town of Texana, which was located below the dam. This county seat was an important shipping and trading center until 1880, when its citizens refused to vote financial support to a railroad between Rosenberg and Victoria. The railroad company established Edna 8 miles west of Texana, and within three years the county seat was transferred and Texana ceased to exist.

123. LAKE TEXOMA

LOCATION

U.S. Army Corps of Engineers. Grayson and Cooke counties. Project office: 3.5 miles north of Denison on TX 75A. Mailing address: 351 Corps Rd., Denison, Texas 75020-6425. Phone: 903-465-4990. For camping reservations, call 877-444-6777 or online at www.recreation.gov.

FACILITIES

The Corps of Engineers offers 3 campgrounds in Texas and 7 in Oklahoma with more that 600 campsites. The 22 commercial marinas and campgrounds provide RV camping with full hookups, cabins, boat rental, and tackle and grocery stores. Hikers enjoy the 14-mile Cross Timbers Trail (Texas) and horse riders have 40 miles of equestrian trails on the Oklahoma side.

Camping: See the matrix for parks with camping. Many of the parks have gatehouses open from 6 a.m. to 10 p.m. There is free primitive camping on the Cross Timbers Hiking Trail. Many private marinas offer RV and tent camping and cabins.

Resorts and Marinas with RV Parks:

Lighthouse Resort and Marina: 300 Lighthouse Dr., Pottsville, TX 75076, 800-300-9300, questions@lighthouseresort.com, www.lighthouseresort.com.

Campground	water	fee area	flush toilets	vault toilets	season	dump station	showers	electricity	swimming beach	cabins
Big Mineral Marina	•	•	•	•	summer	•	•	•	•	•
Dam Site (COE)	•	•	•	•	all	•	•	•		
Flowing Wells	•	•	•	•	Apr. 1–Oct. 31					
Juniper Point (COE)	•	•	•	•	Apr. 1–Oct. 31	•	•	•		
Preston Bend Recreation Area (COE)	•	•	•	•	Apr. 1–Oct. 31	•	•	•		
Lighthouse Marina	•	•	•		all	•	•	•		•
Cedar Mills Marina	•	•	•	•	all	•	•	•	•	
Paradise Cove Marina	•	•		•	all	•	•	•		•
Rock Creek	•	•	•	•	all	•		•		•
Walnut Creek Resort	•	•	•		all	•		•		•
Cedar Bayou Marina	•	•	•	•	Jan.–Nov.		•	•	•	
Highport Marina	•	•	•		all	•		•		
Grandpappy Point Marina	•	•	•		all	•	•	•		•

Paradise Cove Resort: 503 Paradise Cove Road, Pottsville, TX 75076, 888-367-5518, www.paradisecovetexoma.com.

Big Mineral Resort and Marina: PO Box 576, Gordonville, TX 76245, 903-523-4287, www.bigmineral.com/.

Grandpappy Point Marina: 132 Grandpappy Drive, Denison, TX 75020, 888-855-1972, www.grandpappy.com.

Cedar Bayou Marina: 513 Cedar Bayou Blvd., Gordonville, TX 76245, 903-523-4222, www.cedarbayou.com.

Highport Marina and Resort: 120 Texoma Harbor Dr., Pottsville, TX 75076, 903-786-8365, 800-569-4650, www.highport.com.

Walnut Creek Resort: PO Box 346, Gordonville, TX 76245-0346 903-523-4211, www.walnutcreekresort.com.

Recreation: picnicking, hiking on the Cross Timbers Hiking Trail, swimming, water sports, fishing, boat ramps, hunting.

MAIN ATTRACTIONS

Built on the Red River, bordering Texas and Oklahoma, Lake Texoma is the tenth-largest reservoir in the United States. It serves as a flood control and water conservation facility and provides hydroelectric power to the surrounding area. Up to 70 megawatts of electricity can be generated by the power plant. Tours of the plant are offered in the afternoons.

At a normal level, the lake covers 89,000 acres and has 580 miles of shoreline. Denison Dam, a rolled earthfill dam 15,200 feet long, is the twelfth largest in volume in the United States. Eisenhower State Park, Hagerman National Wildlife Refuge, and Tishomingo National Wildlife Refuge in Oklahoma are also on the reservoir.

Lake Texoma is one of the most popular Corps of Engineers lakes in the country. Several privately operated facilities for boat storage and overnight accommodations are available. Large striped bass may be caught in the lake, along with crappie, white bass, black bass, catfish, and sunfish. Wildlife management projects provide hunting areas. Separate hunting and fishing licenses are required for Texas and Oklahoma, but a special fishing license is available for those fishing only in the lake.

HIKING

The 14-mile-long Cross Timbers Hiking Trail meanders through Juniper Point, Cedar Bayou, Paw Paw Creek, and Rock Creek parks. In addition to those sites, hikers may camp at the primitive sites along the trail. Wilderness camping permits and maps are available at the dam headquarters. The trail brochure covers some of the history and plant and animal life of the Cross Timbers vegetation zone of Texas.

124. LAKE TRAVIS PARKS

Travis County. Administered by Travis County Parks, 1010 Lavaca, 3rd Floor, Austin, Texas 78701. Phone: 512-854-7275. Internet: www.co.travis.tx.us/parks/facilities.asp.

ARKANSAS BEND PARK

Travis County. Location: from Austin 13 miles west on U.S. 183, 11 miles west on FM 1431, south on Lohman's Crossing 4.4 miles to Sylvester Rd.

Facilities: 195 acres on Lake Travis with 50 tent sites, primitive camping, pit toilets, boat ramp, lake swimming. Fees charged.

CYPRESS CREEK PARK

Travis County. Location: from Austin 15.5 miles west of FM 2222, at 13800 Bullick Hollow Rd. Facilities: 25 acres on Lake Travis with 40 tent sites, pit toilets, boat ramp, lake swimming. Fees charged.

PACE BEND PARK

Travis County. Location: 30 miles west of Austin on U.S. 71, right on FM 2322, 4 miles to park entrance. Address: 2701 FM 2322, Spicewood, Texas 78669. Phone: 512-264-1482.

Camping: 20 sites with water, electricity, restrooms, showers, dump station; 419 primitive sites with no facilities. Fees charged. Open all year. Primitive camping (tables, toilets) is also available at Arkansas Bend and Cypress Creek parks.

Recreation: the park encompasses 1,520 acres on a four-mile-long peninsula on Lake Travis. The rugged park features scenic limestone cliffs dropping straight into the water, as well as gentle sloping beaches ideal for swimming and boating. No roads cut across the mile-wide, two-mile-long central area of the peninsula. Wildlife thrives in the oak-juniper woodlands and mesquite-bluestem grass savannas of the central area of the park, while the bordering shorelines receive heavy recreational use. Archaeological sites are presently in review.

SANDY CREEK PARK

Travis County. Location: 13 miles west of Austin on U.S. 183, 2 miles west on FM 1431, 7 miles south to Lime Creek Road. Camping: camp sites with tables, water, flush toilets, dump station; picnicking, boating, fishing, and hiking. Fees charged. Open all year.

125. LAKE WACO

LOCATION

U.S. Army Corps of Engineers. McLennan County. Project office: west of Waco on FM 1637.
Mailing address: 3801 Zoo Park Dr., Waco, TX 76708. Phone: 254-756-5359. Internet: www.swf-wc.usace.army.mil/waco/. For reservations, call 877-444-6777 or online at www.recreation.gov.

LAKE WACO

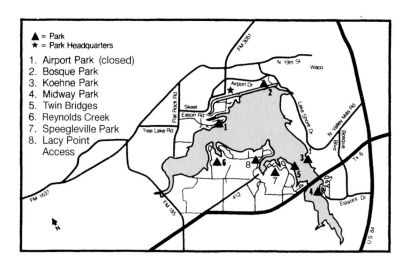

FACILITIES

Reynolds Creek Park: 51 campsites with water and electricity, 6 primitive tent sites, modern restrooms, showers, trailer dump station, playground, picnic tables, boat ramp, hike/bike trail. Fees charged.

Midway Park: 11 back-in RV/tent sites with full hookups, 22 sites with water and electricity, 4 double RV sites, 5 primitive tent sites, modern restrooms, showers, trailer dump station, playground, picnic tables, boat ramp. Fees charged.

Speegleville Park: 21 back-in RV/tent sites with water and electricity, 9 sites with electric only, 2 screened shelters, modern restrooms, showers, trailer dump station, picnic tables, boat launch. Fees charged.

Airport Park: closed.

Recreation: picnicking, swimming, lake activities, hike/bike tails. Day Use parks (6 a.m. to 10 p.m.): Bosque Park (below dam, fishing), Speegleville II Park with Lacy Point Access (boat ramp, 6-mile hike/bike/equestrian trail), Twin Bridges (2 swim beaches, 60 covered picnic sites, group shelter, boat ramp), Koehne Park (10 covered picnic tables, boat ramp, courtesy dock), Flat Rock Park (boat ramp). Anglers report excellent catches of catfish and good catches of largemouth bass, crappie, white bass, and sunfish.

MAIN ATTRACTIONS

Built for flood protection and water storage for the city of Waco and nearby areas, Lake Waco covers 7,240 acres at its normal level and has

Sail boats offer an escape on Lake Waco.

60 miles of shoreline. The lake is heavily used by residents of Waco and the surrounding area for fishing, boating, and swimming—each year, more than 3 million people visit the park. Hunting is permitted on 3,000 acres by permit only.

126. LAKE WHITNEY
(CORPS OF ENGINEERS PARKS)

LOCATION

U.S. Army Corps of Engineers. Bosque and Hill counties. Project office: 18 miles southwest of Hillsboro on TX 22, south of Whitney at dam.
Mailing address: 285 CR 3602, Clifton, Texas 76634. Phone: 254-622-3332. Internet: www.swf-wc.usace.army.mil/whitney. For camping reservations, call 877-444-6777 or online at www.recreation.gov.

FACILITIES

Camping: The COE operates 12 parks on Lake Whitney. Parks not listed on the matrix are either day use or closed. Access to Cedron Creek, Lofers Bend, Plowman Creek, Soldiers Bluff, and McCown Valley is controlled by a gatehouse and open 6 a.m.–10 p.m. Cedron Creek, Lofers Bend, and McCown Valley have some ADA-accessible facilities. McCown Valley has 5 cabins, screened shelters, and 29 equestrian

Campground	water	fee area	flush toilets	season	dump station	showers	electricity
Cedar Creek	•	•	•	all			
Cedron Creek	•	•	•	Apr. 1–Sept. 30	•	•	•
Kimball Bend	•	•	•	all	•		•
Lofers Bend (East and West)	•	•	•	Mar. 1–Sept. 30	•	•	•
Plowman Creek	•	•	•	all	•	•	•
Soldiers Bluff	•		•	all			•
Steeles Creek	•		•	all			
Walling Bend (East and West)	•		•	all			
McCown Valley	•	•	•	all	•	•	•

campsites. Plowman Creek has 10 primitive equestrian sites and access to the 12.5 mile Hopewell multi-use trail. Water to the parks may be cut off during freezing weather.

Recreation: picnicking, nature trail with trail-guide pamphlet at Lofers Bend Park, swimming, fishing, boat ramps at all but Soldiers Bluff, marina at Lofers Bend Park, hunting. Hikers, mountain bikers, and horse riders can access the 12.5 mile Hopewell Trail at Plowman Creek Park, Kimball Bend Park (north trailhead), or Lakeside Village and Powelldale Mountain (south trailhead).

MAIN ATTRACTIONS

Lake Whitney was built to control flooding on the Brazos River, to generate hydroelectric power, and to act as a reservoir for the local water supply. The lake covers 23,550 acres at a normal level and has 190 miles of shoreline; hunting is permitted on 14,000 acres. Check with project office for permits and details. More than 2 million people visit the lake each year.

PLANTS AND ANIMALS

The rolling hills around the lake consist of grasslands and scattered patches of elm, oak, and hickory woodlands. Though the area had more woodlands before the trees were cut for farms and pastureland, the

LAKE WHITNEY

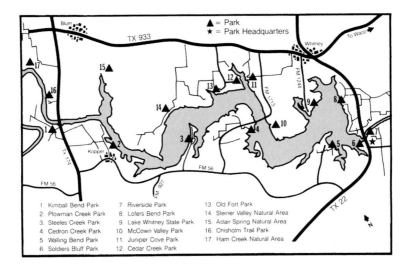

overall vegetation has not changed much in the past few hundred years. Overgrazing has resulted in the encroachment of prickly pear, broomweed, and mesquite in the pastures. On the edges of the lake, live oaks, junipers, post oaks, and cedar elms dominate, with occasional osage oranges, cottonwoods, and pecans.

Deer, raccoons, armadillos, and squirrels are common to the lake woodlands, and a wide variety of birds frequent the area. Bison, antelope, bear, javelina, and beaver were once abundant but have been eliminated since the coming of the pioneers to Texas.

HISTORY

Before the land was flooded by Lake Whitney, an archaeological survey was conducted by the Smithsonian Institution in cooperation with the University of Texas. In studies conducted between 1947 and 1950, more than 70 sites of ancient human occupation were documented. The 9 sites that were thoroughly excavated supplied evidence that this area had been occupied by various Native American groups from approximately 1000 B.C. to the nineteenth century A.D.

Pictographs in one of the rock shelters show abstract human forms in red pigment. They may have been drawn by groups living in the shelter more than a thousand years ago. In the 1770s, the Tawakonis resided on the land now covered by the lake. In the mid-1800s, at least three different tribes lived in the area; they were removed to reservations in 1869. One tribe, a Choctaw group, camped in what is now Lofers Bend Park.

LAKE WHITNEY STATE PARK

LOCATION

Hill County. 18 miles southwest of Hillsboro on TX 22 to Whitney, 4 miles west on FM 1244, on the east side of Lake Whitney. See map with Lake Whitney, Corps of Engineers Parks.
Mailing address: Box 1175, Whitney, Texas 76692. Phone: 254-694-3793. For all state park reservations, call the centralized reservations system, 512-389-8900, or www.ReserveAmerica.com online. Call the state park information number, 800-792-1112, for information and fee updates.

FACILITIES

Fees: entrance, facility, activity use; subject to change.

Camping: 20 RV/tent sites with full hookups (some pull-through), 46 back-in sites with water and electricity, 71 sites with water, 12 screened shelters, modern restrooms, showers, trailer dump station. Fees charged.

Recreation: picnic areas, playgrounds, lake swimming, boat ramp, fish-cleaning facility, group recreation hall with a kitchen and ac/heat, youth group area, 2000-foot paved runway (unlighted, 122.9 MHz), 1-mile hiking-only trail, 1-mile hike/bike trail, Texas State Park Store.

WEATHER

July high averages 86 degrees, January low averages 46 degrees.

MAIN ATTRACTIONS

The 15,760-acre Lake Whitney has more than 250 miles of scenic shoreline, ranging from steep cliffs to sandy beaches. The gradually sloping shores of the lake are pleasant for swimming. Fishing, boating, and water sports are the primary activities of park visitors.

PLANTS AND ANIMALS

The 955-acre park is on a peninsula predominantly composed of grasslands and old field vegetation. Elm-hackberry woodlands occur along the lakeshore and drainages of Whitney and Frazier creeks. The common trees are cedar elm, hackberry, pecan, live oak, post oak, cottonwood, and mesquite. The prairies in the park and around the lake come to life each spring with thousands of wildflowers—bluebonnets and Indian paintbrushes cover the rolling hills with a blanket of color that seems to merge with the sky-blue water of the lake.

Almost 200 species of birds have been sighted in the park, including many waterfowl, shorebirds, quail, hawks, swallows, warblers, orioles, and sparrows. A bird checklist is available. Deer, skunks, raccoons, cottontail rabbits, and armadillos are commonly seen, especially at dusk and dawn.

127. LAKE WRIGHT PATMAN

LOCATION

U.S. Army Corps of Engineers. Bowie and Cass counties. 8 miles southwest of Texarkana off U.S. 59. Project office: 10 miles north of Queen City off U.S. 59.
Mailing address: 64 Clear Springs Park, Texarkana, TX 75501.
Phone: 903-838-8781. For reservations, call toll-free 1-877-444-6777, or online at www.recreation.gov.

FACILITIES

Camping: The COE offers camping at 5 developed parks on the lake and primitive camping with no facilities at 8 other designated locations. Parks not listed are day use or closed. Concessionaires operate marinas at Big Creek Landing (903-585-2357) and Kelly Creek (903-585-5453). Other marinas may offer camping. Atlanta State Park is located on the south side of the reservoir and Cass County Park at Moore's Landing on the south shore (see listing page 23).

Campground	water	fee area	flush toilets	vault toilets	season	dump station	showers	electricity
Clear Springs (COE)	•	•	•	•	all	•	•	•
Jackson Creek (COE)	•			•	all			
Malden Lake (COE)	•	•	•	•	all	•	•	•
Rocky Point (COE)	•	•	•		all	•	•	•
Piney Point (COE)	•	•	•		all	•	•	•
Kelly Creek	•	•	•		all	•	•	•
Big Creek Landing	•	•		•	all			•
Cass County Park	•	•	•		all	•	•	•

WRIGHT PATMAN LAKE

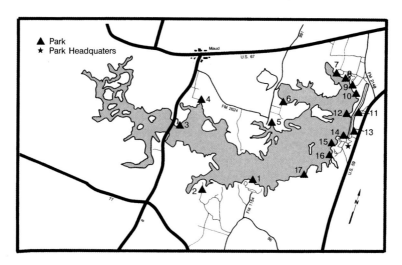

1. Atlanta State Park	8. North Shore Park	15. Piney Point Park
2. Jackson Creek Park	9. Intake Hill Park	16. Rocky Point
3. Malden Lake Park	10. Paradise Cove	17. Cass County Park
4. Herron Creek Park	11. Oak Park	
5. Kelly Creek Park	12. Elliot Blutt Park	
6. Big Creek Park	13. Sulphur Point Park	
7. Clear Springs Park	14. Spillway Park	

Recreation: swimming and fishing in lake, boat ramps, water sports, hunting. Amphitheater, playground, and nature trail at Rocky Point Park.

MAIN ATTRACTIONS

The lake, originally named Lake Texarkana, was renamed in honor of Congressman Wright Patman in 1973. Formed by impounding the Sulphur River, it covers 33,750 surface acres and has 203 miles of shoreline and an average depth of 12 feet. Visitor use has increased yearly to more than 4 million in the last decade.

PLANTS AND ANIMALS

The lake is near the Texas-Arkansas border in the East Texas Piney Woods. Pines and various oaks and other hardwoods are the dominant trees of the forested shoreline. Dogwood trees, scattered throughout the woodlands, bloom profusely in the spring.

Many wading birds and waterfowl, including loons, grebes, and ducks, overwinter on the large lake. Occasionally, a bald eagle or an osprey will be seen flying over the water hunting fish. During spring and fall migrations, warblers, swallows, and other birds find a welcome refuge in the rich woodlands.

128. LITTLEFIELD: WAYLON JENNINGS FREE RV PARK

Lamb County. In Littlefield, half mile north of U.S. 84 on U.S. 385 (Hall Ave.). Mailing address: P.O. Box 1267, Littlefield, Texas 79339. Phone: 806-385-5161. Camping: 12 back-in RV/tent sites with full hookups, 44 with water and electricity, 56 with electricity, trailer dump station, picnic shelters. Free facility offered by the city for travelers needing an overnight stay. No reservations. Open all year.

129. LLANO COUNTY COMMUNITY CENTER AND ROBINSON CITY PARK

Llano County. 2 adjacent parks, 3 miles west of Llano on FM 152. Mailing address: Chamber of Commerce, 700 Bessemer, Llano, Texas 78643. Phone: 325-247-5354. Camping: 100 campsites with water, electricity, and sewage hookups; no tables, flush toilets nearby, primitive camping with tables and water nearby. No reservations. Fees charged for RV sites. Recreation: picnicking, playground, swimming pool, golf course, exercise trail, community center.

A Llano River sunset.

LLANO: BADU PARK (LLANO RIVER PARK)

Llano County. In Llano, take TX 16 south to Legion Dr., west for .8 mile to Llano River. Mailing address: 301 W. Main, Llano, TX 78643. Phone: 325-247-4158. Facilities: 11 pull-through RV/tent sites with full hook-ups, modern restrooms, trailer dump station, hike/bike trails, swimming. Fees charged, no reservations, open all year.

130. LLANO RIVER GOLF AND RV RESORT

Llano County. 3 miles west of Llano on RR 152, adjacent to Robinson City Park. Mailing address: 301 West Main St., Llano, TX 78643. Phone: 325-247-5100. Internet: www.llanorivergolfcourse.com/. *Camping:* 25 RV sites with full hookups (6 pull-through), primitive tent area on riverbank, restrooms, showers. Fees charged.

131. LOCKHART STATE PARK

LOCATION

Caldwell County. 2 miles southwest of Lockhart on FM 20. Mailing address: 4179 State Park Road, Lockhart, Texas 78644-9716. Phone: 512-398-3479. For all state park reservations, call the centralized reservations system, 512-389-8900, or www.ReserveAmerica.com online. Call the state park information number, 800-792-1112, for information and fee updates.

FACILITIES

Fees: entrance, facility, activity use; subject to change.

Camping: 10 campsites with water and electricity, 10 campsites with water, electricity, and sewage hookups; modern restrooms with showers. Fees charged.

Recreation: picnic areas and playgrounds, short trails, swimming pool (summer only), fishing in Clear Fork Creek, 9-hole golf course, court for basketball and volleyball, recreation hall, Texas State Park Store.

WEATHER

July high averages 93 degrees, January low 44 degrees.

MAIN ATTRACTIONS

This park has the distinction of having the only state-operated golf course—those in other parks are operated by concessionaires. The 9-hole, 3,000-yard, par-35 course was constructed in the thirties by the Civilian Conservation Corps. The course crosses Clear Fork Creek several times and borders rich bottomland forests near the creek and post oak woodlands along the hillsides.

The Battle of Plum Creek was fought near the park on August 11, 1840. A group of Texas rangers and volunteers attacked a band of Comanche warriors and their families. The Indians, who had repeatedly raided settlements during the summer months, were driven westward by their defeat.

PLANTS AND ANIMALS

The 263-acre park encompasses riparian woods, paralleling the Clear Fork of Plum Creek, and post oak woodlands, covering the rocky hillsides. The deeper soil deposited along the banks of the creek supports pecans, hackberries, and sycamores. Cardinals and white-throated sparrows dart through the brush bordering the creek, and the drill of woodpeckers resounds through the early-morning air.

In the fall, hundreds of cedar waxwings are attracted to the sweet berries of the hackberry trees. Robins flock to the yaupon hollies growing under the oaks and elms on the hills and devour the shiny red berries. In the spring, wildflowers blanket the streamside, and sunfish build their nests in the clear pools below several picturesque rock dams along the creek.

132. LOST MAPLES STATE NATURAL AREA

LOCATION

Bandera County. 48 miles west of Kerrville on TX 39, south on FM 187.5 miles north of Vanderpool.
Mailing address: 37221 FM 187, Vanderpool, Texas 78885. Phone: 830-966-3413. For all state park reservations, call the centralized reservations system, 512-389-8900, or www.ReserveAmerica.com online. Call the state park information number, 800-792-1112, for information and fee updates.

FACILITIES

Fees: entrance, facility, activity use; subject to change.

Camping: 8 primitive camping areas with composting toilets on hiking trails, 30 campsites with water and electricity; modern restrooms with showers, trailer dump station. Fees charged.

Recreation: picnic areas and playgrounds, 10 miles of hiking trails, half-mile developed nature trail along the Sabinal River, interpretive exhibits, wading and limited swimming in river, fishing, Texas State Park Store.

WEATHER

July high averages 94 degrees, January low 31 degrees.

MAIN ATTRACTIONS

Lost Maples State Natural Area is famous for the bigtooth maple trees that grow in the protected Sabinal River Canyon and along tributary creeks. During late October and early November when climatic conditions have been favorable, the maples turn spectacular colors of scarlet, burgundy, and orange; up to 6,000 people may visit the park each weekend. If possible in the fall, plan weekday visits to avoid the crowds. The entrance facility houses excellent graphic exhibits on the maples and other aspects of the park's ecology. This beautiful and unique park is well worth a visit.

Prehistoric humans inhabited the Sabinal River Canyon more than 10,000 years ago, hunting the now extinct giant bison and mammoths. Later groups occupying the canyon left middens of heat-fractured stones, charcoal, and animal bones. Lipan and Mescalero Apaches, who displaced the earlier Tonkawas, raided Anglo settlers from bases within the canyon until the mid-1800s.

HIKING

Ten miles of hiking trails, marked for easy orientation, lead through the scenic Sabinal River Canyon and down fern-lined, spring-fed streams. There is no water on the trails; obtain information and trail maps from the ranger station. The designated primitive camping areas are located along the trails, some on high ridges, others on the shaded banks of winding streams. Some of the primitive camping areas are within 1 mile of the trailhead, and some are several miles farther. Lost Maples offers one of the most interesting hiking and backpacking opportunities in the state park system.

PLANTS AND ANIMALS

Nestled deep in the Central Texas Hill Country, Lost Maples consists of 2,174 acres of plateau grasslands, steep limestone canyons, and wooded slopes and bottomlands. The Sabinal River and other shallow, spring-fed streams cut canyons up to 300 feet deep through the rugged terrain. Numerous springs and seeps along the drainages support a rich diversity of plant and animal life.

The bigtooth maple trees, *Acer grandidentatum*, that grow in the park occur in isolated populations widely distributed throughout the western United States and northern Mexico. They require a fairly protected habitat of moderate temperature, humidity, and moisture. The Sabinal River Canyon in the park is the southeastern limit of the trees.

There is a noticeable diversity of plant life in the park, from the evergreen woodlands of the upper canyon slopes to the deciduous woods in the canyon bottoms. Grassy openings dominate the upland plateaus, with Ashe junipers and plateau live oaks occurring on the dry limestone slopes. Bigtooth maples, Texas and Lacey oaks, walnuts, and other deciduous trees and shrubs grow in the damper lower canyons.

The diverse conditions support more than 350 species of plants, many of which are unusual. Rare plants in the park include the spice-bush, sycamore-leaf snowbell, Texas barberry, canyon mock-orange, crossvine, witch hazel, and Texas madrone.

A rich avian and mammal community adds to the natural splendor of the park. More than 200 species of birds have been recorded, including the golden-cheeked warbler, which nests only in Central Texas, black-capped vireo, green kingfisher, zone-tailed hawk, and golden and bald eagles; ask for a checklist at the park headquarters. The most often seen mammals are white-tailed deer, rock squirrels, and armadillos. Gray foxes, ringtails, bobcats and javelinas are common but seldom encountered. Occasionally, a porcupine or mountain lion is seen in the park.

The unusual variety of plant and animal life at Lost Maples is of such significance that the park was the first to be designated a state natural area. To merit that designation, an area must contain "prime examples of ecological systems, biological features, or geological formations of exceptional educational and scientific value." The designation allows for low-density use to protect the park's scenic beauty and natural features. Because of the shallow root system of the maples, compaction of the soil by hikers could damage these beautiful trees. That is one of the ecological factors that led to the decision to develop only about 4 percent of the total acreage of the park.

133. LUBBOCK: BUFFALO SPRINGS LAKE PARK

Lubbock County Water Control and Improvement District. Lubbock County. 5 miles southeast of Lubbock on FM 835. Mailing address: 9999 High Meadow Road, Lubbock, TX 79404. Phone: 806-747-3353. E-mail: buffalogeneralinfo@yahoo.com. Internet: www.buffalospringslake.net. Free WiFi in campgrounds.

Camping: back-in RV sites with water and electricity and paved and unpaved pads, tent camp area with water nearby, 4 covered shelters, modern restrooms, showers, trailer dump stations. Recreation: picnic areas, playgrounds, fishing, boat ramps, marina, canoe rental, 9-hole pitch and putt gold course, ATV trails, 1.7-mile Audubon Society nature trail, 6 miles of hike/bike trails. Admission and facility fees charged.

134. LYNDON B. JOHNSON NATIONAL GRASSLAND

LOCATION

Wise County. Mailing address: 1400 North U.S. Highway 81/287, P.O. Box 507, Decatur, TX, 76234. Phone: 940-627-5475. Internet: www.fs.fed.us/r8/texas/recreation.

FACILITIES

Black Creek: From Decatur, northwest on U.S. 81/287 for 4.5 miles, right on CR 2175 at the rest area, cross over RR tracks, go 1 mile and turn left on Old Decatur Road. Go 4 miles, turn right on CR 2372 then go 2 miles and turn left on CR 2461 for ½ mile. After crossing steel bridge, turn left (west) on Forest Service Road 902 to the recreation area. Tent camping, picnicking, pit toilets, no drinking water. Boat ramp, boating and fishing on 30-acre lake. Hiking: trailhead for 4-mile trail to Cottonwood Lake. The 60-foot fishing bridge, restroom, some campsites, and paths are ADA accessible. Fees charged.

Cottonwood Lake: From Decatur, north on FM 730 for 10 miles, left on CR 2461, right at the fork on CR 2560 for 3 miles, left on FS Road 900. Boat ramp, boating and fishing on 40-acre lake, no drinking water; trailhead for 4-mile trail to Black Creek Lake. No camping facilities.

TADRA Point Trailhead Camp: From Decatur, north on FM 730 for 10 miles, west on CR 2461, right at fork on CR 2650 for 3 miles, left on FSR 900, 3 miles to entrance. Camping: 6 pull-through RV/tent sites, 10 horse tethers, vault toilets, no drinking water. The 5 loops of the 75-mile LBJ Multi-Use Trail system converge at the campgrounds. Fees charged.

Valley View Group Use Campground: From Decatur, north on U.S. 81/287 for 11 miles, east on FM 1655 for 8 miles, right on Roberts Rd. ½ mile to entrance. Camping: reservation only, 15 back-in RV/tent sites, primitive camping area, pit toilets, group pavilion, stock water, no drinking water, trailhead for LBJ Trail. Fees charged.

LBJ Multi-Use Trail: The 75-mile-long Lyndon B. Johnson Multi-Use Trail is open to horseback riding, mountain bikes and hiking. Trailheads are located at the TADRA Point Campsite, Valley View Group Use Campsite, and various campsites. The five loops begin and end at TADRA

Point. Open areas of the Grasslands are popular for cross-country horseback riding.

MAIN ATTRACTIONS

The LBJ National Grassland covers 20,315 acres of oak savanna and grassland in Wise and Montague counties in numerous unconnected parcels. Tenant farmers and poor farming practices had turned this prairie land into exhausted farmland by the thirties. During the Dust Bowl era, the federal government bought up the wasted farms to demonstrate soil conservation principles and to show how the land could be used for grazing and recreational purposes. The grasslands are managed for cattle grazing, oil and gas production, watershed improvement, fishing, hunting, and other recreational pursuits. Game species include white-tailed deer, turkey, quail, squirrel, and rabbit. The lakes are stocked with bass, catfish, and bream. Horseback riding and hunting are the most popular activities in the grasslands.

135. MARLIN: FALLS ON THE BRAZOS

Falls County. 28 miles southeast of Waco on TX 6 to Marlin, 4 miles southeast to FM 712, southwest to the Brazos River. Mailing address: 644 FM 712, Marlin, Texas 76661. Phone: 254-883-3203. Camping: 6 campsites with water and electricity, 7 tent sites, flush toilets, trailer dump station. Reservations accepted. Fees charged. Recreation: picnic areas and playgrounds, fishing, boat ramp, pavilion, store. Open all year.

136. MARTIN CREEK LAKE STATE PARK

LOCATION

Rusk County. 25 miles south of Marshall on TX 43, south on FM 1716.
Mailing address: 9515 County Road 2181D, Tatum, TX 75691-3425. Phone: 903-836-4336. For all state park reservations, call the centralized reservations system, 512-389-8900, or www.ReserveAmerica.com online. Call the state park information number, 800-792-1112, for information and fee updates.

FACILITIES

Fees: entrance, facility, activity use; subject to change.

Camping: 60 back-in RV/tent sites with water and electricity, primitive camping on island, 19 screened shelters, 2 cabins with ac/heat and kitchen (capacity 4), 2 screened shelters with ac/heat (capacity 5). Modern restrooms, showers, trailer dump station. Fees charged.

Recreation: picnic areas, playgrounds, group picnic pavilion, 1.5-mile hiking trail, 6-mile mountain bike trail, boat ramp, lighted fishing pier, lake swimming, Texas State Park Store with boat rentals.

WEATHER

July high averages 94 degrees, January low 35 degrees.

MAIN ATTRACTIONS

This park preserves 286 acres of pine-hardwood forest along the shores of a lake impounded to cool a lignite-fired electric power plant. The beautiful woodlands are forested with a variety of oaks, sweetgum, elms, river birch, eastern red cedar, yaupon, and farkleberry. Nature trails lead through the dense woods, along a historic roadway, through creek bottoms, and around an island reached by a footbridge. Those who want to get away from the crowds can use the primitive camping and picnic area on the island. Visitors who come about the end of October have a special treat: the woods come alive with brilliant hues of red, yellow, and burgundy.

Birds and small animals abound in the park. Look for herons, egrets, and waterfowl along the shores and deer, rabbits, and squirrels in the woods. Fishermen catch largemouth bass, crappie, catfish, and sunfish in

White-tailed deer are frequently seen in Martin Creek State Park

the 6,000-acre lake. Since the lake is artificially warmed by the power plant, fishing is good year-round.

HISTORY

The Caddo Indians historically occupied this part of the state. Later, displaced Choctaws, Cherokees, Kickapoos, and remnants of other tribes moved into the area, eventually to be exterminated or driven to Oklahoma. Part of an old Indian trail, later widened for wagons and named Trammel's Trace, runs through the park. The wagon road was a major route to Arkansas. Evidence of the roadbed still remains near the fishing pier.

137. MARTIN DIES, JR. STATE PARK

LOCATION

Jasper and Tyler counties. 50 miles east of Livingston on U.S. 190, on the east side of Lake B.A. Steinhagen.
Mailing address: 634 Private Road 5025, Jasper, TX 75951. Phone: 409-384-5231. For all state park reservations, call the centralized reservations system, 512-389-8900, or www.ReserveAmerica.com online. Call the state park information number, 800-792-1112, for information and fee updates.

FACILITIES

Fees: entrance, facility, activity use, seasonal camping rates; subject to change.

Camping: Hen House Ridge Unit: 35 pull-through RV/tent sites with water and electricity, 21 back-in sites with water and electricity, 41 tent sites, 1 mini-cabin (no cooking, linens), 20 screened shelters (2 with ac/heat, no beds). Walnut ridge Unit: 70 back-in RV/tent sites with water and electricity, 11 tent sites, 1 mini-cabin (no cooking, linens), 25 screened shelters (2 with ac/heat, no beds). Both units: restrooms, showers, trailer dump station. Fees vary seasonally.

Recreation: picnic areas, playgrounds, dining hall, lake swimming, 2 lighted fishing piers, fish-cleaning stations, boat ramps, 4-mile hike/bike trail, 2-mile nature trail, Nature Center, Texas State Park Store with boat rentals.

WEATHER

July high averages 93 degrees, January low 38 degrees.

MAIN ATTRACTIONS

The 705-acre park, which preserves a prime example of deep East Texas beech woodlands, is located on the 13,000-acre Lake B. A. Steinhagen. Nature trails wind through the mixed pine-hardwood forests, around sloughs bordered by bald cypress, and along the lake. In the spring, the snowy blossoms of dogwood trees and magnolias decorate the woods; in the fall the leaves of beeches and maples thrill the visitor with their brilliant hues of gold, red, and burgundy.

The park is separated into three units: Cherokee, Walnut Ridge, and Hen House Ridge. The Cherokee Unit is on an island and is for day-use only. The campgrounds and other facilities are located in the other two units.

Fishing and boating are popular activities on the scenic lake. Catches include catfish, crappie, sunfish, and white, spotted, and largemouth bass.

Area attractions include the Big Thicket National Preserve Visitor Station, with interpretive programs and nature trails along scenic Village Creek, 25 miles south of Woodville off U.S. 69 on FM 420. Woodville is the home of the Dogwood Festival, held on the last Saturday in March.

PLANTS AND ANIMALS

Martin Dies, Jr., State Park, named after the senator who helped obtain funds for its formation, is situated in the Big Thicket area of the East Texas Piney Woods. The park is on an old river terrace in the alluvial floodplain of the Neches River. The rich bottomland soil supports a well-developed upper- and middle-story forest. Shallow sloughs leading into the lake reach through the woodlands like long fingers.

The floodplain forest hosts a wide variety of trees from towering pines, hickories, magnolias, and American hollies to the beautiful but smaller flowering dogwoods, silver bells, fringe trees, and redbuds. Bald cypress, tupelo, and moss-covered oak trees line the sloughs and shore. Approximately 60 species of trees grow in the rich environs of the park. Ask at the entrance for lists of the trees and birds found in the area.

Lake B.A. Steinhagen was formed when the Neches River was dammed just below its confluence with the Angelina River. The Neches River Corridor Unit of the Big Thicket National Preserve begins below the dam and extends all the way to Beaumont. The state park, the units of the national preserve, and private sanctuaries protect remnants representative of the complex woodlands that once formed the Big Thicket of East Texas, the biological crossroads of seven major ecological systems.

More than 350 species of birds occur in the area, and many are seen in the state park. The large pileated woodpecker, with its flaming red crest, darts noisily from tree to tree, while stately herons and egrets pace back and forth through the sloughs like ballet dancers in slow motion.

138. MASON: FORT MASON CITY PARK

Mason County. One-half mile south of Mason on U.S. 87. Mailing address: P.O. Box 68, Mason, Texas 76856. Phone: 325-347-6656. Internet: www.masontxcoc.com/fmpark.htm. Camping: 29 back-in RV/tent sites with water, electricity, sewage hookups, dump station, hot showers. This 23-acre city park includes a community building, rodeo arena, playground, and pavilion. Fees charged, reservations accepted. Open all year.

139. MATAGORDA ISLAND WILDLIFE MANAGEMENT AREA

LOCATION

Calhoun County. 7 miles offshore from Port O'Connor, accessible only by private boat. Mainland mailing address: 1700 7th St., Bay City, TX 77414. Phone: 979-244-6804, no phone on island.

FACILITIES

Camping: 13 primitive sites at the dock area with shade cover and fire rings, Gulf beach camping accessible by hike or bike (2.5 miles from dock), Sunday Beach (east end of island) accessible by boat from the Gulf or Pass Cavallo. No water or facilities, outdoor shower and toilet facility near the dock available only during public hunts or other scheduled events. All trash must be packed out. No beach camping during fall pubic deer, dove, and hog hunts. No camping fees but a Limited Public Use Permit or an Annual Public Hunting Lands Permit, available wherever hunting license are sold for $12/year, is required for each camper at the bayside picnic shelters.

Recreation: surfing, swimming, beachcombing, bird-watching, fishing, island tours, 3 boat ramps in Port O'Connor, boat dock on island, 38 miles of beach front, 32 miles of paved, shell roadway for hiking and biking. NO electricity, NO drinking water, NO telephone, NO concessions on the island.

Access: Since the state-operated public ferry burnt, shuttle service to the island was discontinued and the state park downgraded to a wildlife management area. As of 2008/09, several charter services were offering transportation to the island from Port O'Connor. Contact: Bob Hill (361-983-4325, www.fishportoconnor.com, bike rental also), Ron Arlitt (361-983-2627, www.scalesandtales.com), Kenneth Gregory (361-983-0411, www.kennethgregory.com).

WEATHER

July high averages 91 degrees, January low 46 degrees.

SPECIAL CONSIDERATIONS

Prepare for extremes of sun, heat, and humidity. Heat exhaustion is one of the most common first aid problems on the island. Drink a lot of fluids and use sunscreen year-round. Take insect repellent, mosquitoes can be a problem all year. No lifeguards are on duty. When swimming or surfing, be alert for dangerous undertows, stingrays, sharks, and stinging man-of-wars. Watch for rattlesnakes in brushy and grassy areas. In case of emergencies, TPWD advises contacting staff (usually none available) or flagging a passing boat (good luck!). Limited cell phone service exists depending on carrier and location on island.

MAIN ATTRACTIONS

The wildlife management area provides the ultimate escape from civilization. If you want the "lost on a desert island" experience, charter a boat or take the weekend ferry to this 38-mile-long, 4-mile-wide barrier island. Before you leave, consider what is really necessary for survival in a hostile environment, because all you'll have is what you take. Besides your favorite novel, take plenty of water, sunscreen, insect repellent, and comfortable clothes. Pack light, you'll have to walk the 1.5 miles from the bayside dock to the gulfside beach. And if you want shade, you'll have to take an umbrella.

The state wildlife management area preserves 56,688 acres of the offshore island. The U.S. Fish and Wildlife Service manages an additional 11,393 acres on the southwestern end of the island. Access to the Gulf beaches is prohibited during the fall public hunting season. Dove, quail, and waterfowl hunting and regulated deer hunting from fixed stands are permitted in the management area. Between October and April, whooping cranes frequent the marshy areas of the island, which is across the bay from the Aransas National Wildlife Refuge.

HISTORY

Matagorda Island formed about 5,000 years ago when offshore currents began depositing silt carried by Rio Grande and other rivers that flow into the Gulf. The deposits sustain the series of barrier islands that protect the Texas coast from waves and storms of the open sea. From Padre Island to Galveston Island, the barrier islands featured prominently in the history of Texas. Spanish and French explorers displaced the fierce Karankawa Indians and laid claim to the islands, and many of their ships wrecked in the shallow straits. An abandoned 1852 lighthouse still stands on Matagorda Island.

During wartime, the barrier islands provided the first defense against enemy warships. Confederate forces fortified Matagorda Island and traces of their trenches are still evident. An Air Force base occupied the island during most of the 20th century. Before modern weather forecasting, frequent hurricanes destroyed early towns and inhibited economic development. Ranchers turned the rich coastal grasslands and barrier islands into some of the largest ranches in the state. Cattle grazed Matagorda Island until it became a park and wildlife preserve in the 1980s.

PLANTS AND ANIMALS

With its near access to the coast, Matagorda Island has much of the same plant and animal associations of the mainland. White-tailed deer, coyotes, raccoons, badgers, and jackrabbits easily swam the distance and became established on the island. Isolation and lack of development protected many of the threatened species that inhabit the marshes and rich coastal estuaries. Nineteen threatened or endangered species occur on the island. Look for whooping cranes November through April, peregrine falcons in the winter, brown pelicans, Ridley sea turtles, and horned lizards. The island marshes serve as important nursery areas for shrimp, oyster, blue crab, and sport fish such as red drum, spotted sea trout, tarpon, shark, mackerel, and flounder.

Thirty species of reptiles live on the island, including alligators and western diamondback rattlesnakes. More than 300 species of birds frequent the island. During the fall, migrating raptors ride the updrafts along the coast, and in the spring, many songbirds flying across the Gulf make first landfall on the islands. Shorebirds and gulls use the islands as rookeries. In winter, thousands of waterfowl feed in the shallow bays and lagoons. Matagorda Island and adjacent Aransas National Wildlife Refuge are the wintering grounds for the whooping crane.

140. MCCLELLAN CREEK NATIONAL GRASSLAND/LAKE MCCLELLAN

LOCATION

Gray County. 50 miles east of Amarillo on IH-40, 5 miles north on TX 70, 8 miles east on FM 2477.
Mailing address: Route 1, Box 55B, Cheyenne, Oklahoma 73628-9725. Phone: 580-497-2143. Internet: www.fs.fed.us/r3/cibola/districts/black.shtml.

FACILITIES

A massive wildfire in 2006 swept through the grassland and destroyed thousands of trees and many structures, including the concession building at Lake McClellan, which will not be rebuilt. *Camping*: 17 RV/tent sites with water and electricity, 16 tent sites, 24 picnic sites, toilets, showers, and the dump station on the northwest side of the lake. On the southeast side is Fisherman's Point (day-use) and East Bluff #1 with 7 camp sites.

Recreation: picnicking, fishing in stocked lake, boating when lake levels permit, hiking. The OHV trails were closed after the fire, but the USFS plans to reopen them. Lake McClellan dries completely in times of drought, so call for current lake level and status of trails before making plans.

MAIN ATTRACTIONS

Fishing and boating on the 350-acre Lake McClellan are the main attractions of this park, managed by the U.S. Forest Service. Open grasslands and heavy woods provide a variety of habitats for quail, turkey, squirrels, deer, rabbits, and coyotes. Waterfowl frequent the lake, especially during spring and fall migrations, and bald eagles in the winter.

141. MCKINNEY FALLS STATE PARK

LOCATION

Travis County. 7 miles southeast of Austin on U.S. 183, 2 miles west on Scenic Loop Rd. to McKinney Falls Parkway.
Mailing address: 5808 McKinney Falls Parkway, Austin, Texas 78744. Phone: 512-243-1643. For all state park reservations, call the centralized reservations system, 512-389-8900, or www.ReserveAmerica.com online. Call the state park information number, 800-792-1112, for information and fee updates.

FACILITIES

Fees: entrance, facility, activity use; subject to change. WiFi available (user fee).

Camping: 84 pull-through or back-in RV/tent sites with water and electricity, 8 walk-in tent sites (100-200 yards) with water, 6 screened shelters (8 beds, no linens or mattress, water, electricity, table and grill outside), youth group primitive camp area (capacity 50), group dining hall (capacity 75), modern restrooms, showers, trailer dump stations. Gate open from 8 a.m. to 10 p.m.

Recreation: picnic areas and playgrounds, 3.5-mile hike and bike trail, three-quarter-mile nature trail with trail-guide booklet, interpretive exhibits, 18-hole golf course nearby, amphitheater, Texas State Park Store.

WEATHER

July high averages 95 degrees, January low 37 degrees.

MAIN ATTRACTIONS

The outstanding feature of the 949-acre park, only a 15-minute drive from Austin, is tree-lined Onion Creek and its two picturesque water-falls. Shaded picnic areas and playgrounds are scattered along the 1.7 miles of winding shoreline. Ruins of nineteenth-century stone buildings, one of the first gristmills in Central Texas, and stone fences built with slave labor can be seen. Swimming is allowed in the creek seasonally when contaminants are in low concentration. However, McKinney Falls is one of the most attractive state parks in Texas.

HIKING

A 3.5-mile hike and bike trail runs along the creek, behind the camp-grounds, and past the entrance facility. Artifacts of human occupation since A.D. 500 have been found in Smith Rockshelter, an undercut area

Ice forms on McKinney Falls in the winter.

on a bluff overlooking the creek. A three-quarter-mile nature trail begins at the visitor center and passes through Smith Rockshelter.

PLANTS AND ANIMALS

The park, at the confluence of Onion and Williamson creeks, encompasses two major ecological regions: the Blackland Prairies and the Edwards Plateau. Since humans have eliminated the wildfires that once cleared the prairies, most of the grasslands typical of that region in the park are now overgrown with shrubs and trees. Trees common to the Edwards Plateau, such as plateau live oak, Ashe juniper, Texas persimmon, and mesquite, dominate the dry rocky uplands.

Moisture-loving plants thrive along the creek corridors. Pecan, sycamore, ash, soapberry, and majestic bald cypress trees shade the quiet pools and meandering channels. A small stand of the rare Texas peach bush, Prunus minutiflora, is located in the park.

At one time, bison and pronghorn antelope roamed the prairies surrounding the park. Now, the most commonly seen animals are the earless lizards that scamper over the bare limestone rocks, pausing only to wave their striped tails as a diversionary maneuver. Early-morning risers may chance upon a raccoon, opossum, skunk, deer, or rabbit. Eastern fox squirrels live in the trees, and armadillos root in the soft soil bordering the creek. Many birds, including turkeys, quail, migratory shorebirds, and waterfowl, frequent the rich woodlands and waterways; a checklist of the birds is available.

One mile east of the park is an unimposing hill called Pilot Knob, the remains of a volcano that erupted under the sea approximately 80 million years ago. The ash sediments from the volcano were compressed under millions of years of sand and mud deposits. They form the layer of green clay visible under the limestone ledge of the lower falls. Uplifting of the earth's surface some 25 million years ago brought the area above sea level, allowing the elements to begin the slow process of erosion that formed the land as we see it today.

HISTORY

Humans have been attracted to the beauty and life-sustaining resources of Onion Creek for more than 1,500 years. Archaeologists have uncovered artifacts from a succession of prehistoric encampments in the Smith Rockshelter. Those early nomads subsisted on the abundant mammals, fish, berries, nuts, and roots of the area.

Thomas F. McKinney, one of Stephen F. Austin's original 300 colonists in Texas, settled on 2,500 acres of land around Onion Creek in the 1850s. The massive stone walls of McKinney's two-story house, which burned in the 1940s, can be seen on a hill above the lower falls.

McKinney, who made his fortune as a merchant-trader, was the principal financier of the Texas Revolution. By the end of the Civil War, however, he was near bankruptcy and was forced to sell his property. Most of the land was purchased by the grandfather of J. E. and Annie Smith, who donated 632 acres to the state in 1970.

142. MERIDIAN STATE PARK

LOCATION

Bosque County. 40 miles southwest of Hillsboro on TX 22, 4 miles southwest of Meridian.
Mailing address: 173 Park Road #7, Meridian, TX 76665. Phone: 254-435-2536. For all state park reservations, call the centralized reservations system, 512-389-8900, or www.ReserveAmerica.com online. Call the state park information number, 800-792-1112, for information and fee updates.

FACILITIES

Fees: entrance, facility, activity use; subject to change.

Camping: 15 pull-through RV/tent sites with water and electricity, 14 tent sites, 11 screened shelters, modern restrooms, showers, trailer dump station. Fees charged.

Recreation: picnic areas, playgrounds, hiking and nature trails, birdwatching, lake swimming, fishing, boat ramp and dock, 5-mile scenic drive for vehicles and biking, group dining hall with kitchen (capacity 56), youth group area, Texas State Park Store.

WEATHER

July high averages 98 degrees, January low 40 degrees.

MAIN ATTRACTIONS

The 70-acre lake, impounded in the thirties by the Civilian Conservation Corps, and the densely wooded hillsides provide a tranquil and scenic setting for the park. Fishing for largemouth bass, crappie, channel catfish, and sunfish, as well as bird-watching, nature hikes, swimming, and picnicking are popular activities here.

Area attractions include the Texas Safari Ranch, a drive-through game park with thousands of exotic grazing animals and a carnival-like headquarters. The ranch is 10 miles southeast of the park on TX 6, then west on FM 3220.

HIKING

A number of nature trails, some with interpretive signs, lead through the various habitats within the park. The Shinnery Ridge Trail, 1.6 miles round trip, passes through oak-juniper woods and grassy prairies. The 2.3-mile Bosque Trail circles the lake. For a shorter walk, try the Little Forest and Little Spring trails, .4 and .7 mile, respectively. The plants, animals, ecology, and geology of the park are explained on signs along the Shinnery Ridge, Bosque, and Little Springs nature trails.

PLANTS AND ANIMALS

Meridian State Recreation Area is located in the Lampasas cut plains region on North Central Texas. The plants on the limestone hills and bluffs overlooking the lake are similar to those of the Edwards Plateau of Central Texas, but the vegetation of the floodplain around the park's lake resembles that of East Texas riparian lowlands.

The steep hillsides are covered with Ashe juniper, post oak, blackjack oak, and Texas mountain laurel. In the fall, the crimson leaves of Texas oaks add a splash of color to the woodlands, and in the spring the cascading violet flowers of Texas mountain laurels fill the air with an aroma reminiscent of grape Kool-Aid. Bluebonnets, gaillardias, Indian paintbrushes, and mountain pinks blanket the roadsides with color.

The endangered golden-cheeked warbler finds the northern limit of its range in the juniper-oak woodlands surrounding the park. This colorful warbler breeds only in the restricted range of the Ashe junipers in Central Texas. Bird-watchers come from across the nation to see this tiny bird, which winters in Central America.

Almost 200 species of birds have been seen along the dry stony hillsides and the moist luxuriant bottomlands of the park. Black-capped vireos (also endangered), black-chinned hummingbirds, painted buntings, and many migrating warblers, hawks, and flycatchers can be seen in the spring. Wintering birds include pied-billed grebes, ducks, flickers, purple finches, rufous-sided towhees, and various sparrows. Ask for a checklist at the park headquarters.

Late evening and early morning are the best times to see the mammals in the park. White-tailed deer feed in the open areas; raccoons, skunks, and opossums forage for food; and foxes may occasionally be seen bounding across the roads.

143. MISSION TEJAS STATE PARK

LOCATION

Houston County. 20 miles northeast of Crockett on TX 21, in Weches.

Mailing address: 120 State Park Rd. 44, Grapeland, TX 75844. Phone: 936-687-2394. For all state park reservations, call the centralized reservations system, 512-389-8900, or www.ReserveAmerica.com online. Call the state park information number, 800-792-1112, for information and fee updates.

FACILITIES

Fees: entrance, facility, activity use; subject to change.

Camping: 10 RV/tent sites with full hookups (5 are pull-through), 10 sites with water and electricity, 2 sites with water only, overflow/youth group camping area, modern restrooms, showers, trailer dump station. Winter rates available.

Recreation: picnic areas and playgrounds, nature trails with trail-guide booklet, historical structures, pavilion, Texas State Park Store.

MAIN ATTRACTIONS

In 1690, the Spanish built the mission San Francisco de los Tejas, the first mission in East Texas, to bring Christianity to the Tejas Indians. After three years of Christian influence, the Indians, whose name means "friend," rebelled and drove the Spaniards away. The location of the park is based on the discovery of a cannon believed to have been buried by the fleeing Spaniards. In the 1930s, the Civilian Conservation Corps built a hewn-log structure to commemorate the original mission. A pioneer dogtrot log cabin, built nearby in 1828, was moved to the park and reconstructed in 1974. Stop at the entrance to the park for historical brochures.

HIKING

The park has two trails through the scenic, aromatic Piney Woods. An interpretive booklet for the forest trail and a bird checklist are available. The forest trail loops around a small pond bordered with dogwood, American holly, winged elm, oak, and red maple trees. A 2-mile hiking trail leads through the deep woods, enabling visitors to experience some of the beauty and uniqueness of East Texas.

PLANTS AND ANIMALS

The 118-acre park, located on the edge of Davy Crockett National Forest, is heavily wooded with pines and several species of oaks. Willow, sassafras, and mulberry trees grow in moist areas, as do beautyberry and elderberry. Rattan vines twine around the trees as they reach for the sky.

The deep woods, especially at night, are an unforgettable experience. The tall pines and oaks filter the moonlight, giving the woods an almost ghostly appearance. Owls hooting in the shadows add to the mystique of the experience. The howl of coyotes and the startled response of a frightened cottontail remind the visitor that many of nature's creatures do not sleep at night.

HISTORY

The first Spanish explorers were impressed with the friendliness and cultural advancement of the Tejas Indians of East Texas. When the de León expedition reached the area in 1690, the Indians greeted them and invited them into the chief's lodge. In the house, a 50-foot-high structure with ten beds and reed mats, the men feasted on tamales, nuts, beans, and corn prepared in various ways.

The priests constructed a chapel in four days in the Indian village and dedicated it as San Francisco de los Tejas. The mission symbolized Spain's first formal possession of the country that became Texas. The Spanish constructed another mission in the area. By 1693, smallpox and drought had caused the Tejas to become hostile, causing the missionaries to flee, burning the mission behind them. The mission was reestablished in 1716 on the Neches River and eventually moved to San Antonio in 1731.

Mission Tejas was on the Old San Antonio Road, or El Camino Real, which was blazed in 1691 to connect the East Texas missions with Mexico City. Today TX 21 follows that route from near the Louisiana border to San Marcos, where it merges with IH-35 and continues south to Mexico.

The reconstructed log house near the park entrance is an excellent example of a pioneer home from the early 1800s. The house was built by Joseph Rice in 1828 on the Old San Antonio Road about 16 miles from the park. As his family grew, Rice enlarged the house—originally a one-room cabin—to three rooms with lofts for sleeping and storage as well as broad front and back porches. The breezeway, or dogtrot, separating the rooms was used during the hot summers for dining, sitting, and sleeping.

Caddoan Mounds State Historic Site is north of Weches on TX 21. The park interprets the history of the Caddo Indians through displays of their artifacts and mounds. There is no camping at the site.

144. MONAHANS SANDHILLS STATE PARK

LOCATION

Ward County. 30 miles southwest of Odessa on IH-20 to PR 41, 5 miles east of Monahans.

Mailing address: Box 1738, Monahans, Texas 79756. Phone: 432-943-2092. For all state park reservations, call the centralized reservations system, 512-389-8900, or www.ReserveAmerica.com online. Call the state park information number, 800-792-1112, for information and fee updates.

FACILITIES

Fees: entrance, facility, activity use; subject to change.

Camping: 26 RV/tent sites with water and electricity and shade shelters, modern restrooms, showers, trailer dump station.

Recreation: picnic areas, playgrounds, sand surfing, group dining hall, equestrian day-use area (600 acres) with trailer parking and fenced corral with water, self-guided, $1/4$-mile nature trail, interpretive center, Texas State Park Store with sand toboggan rentals.

WEATHER

July high averages 96 degrees, January low 29 degrees.

MAIN ATTRACTIONS

Picnicking and frolicking down the giant dunes are the most popular activities in the park. The park store rents surfboards for sand surfing, a favorite sport. The Dunagan Visitor Center, in the park headquarters, has exhibits explaining the significant botanical, geological, and archaeological features of the park. A self-guided nature trail leads through the dunes from the museum.

Nearby attractions include the Odessa Meteor Crater, a national historic site 25 miles east just off IH-20, and the Million Barrel Museum in Monahans.

PLANTS AND ANIMALS

The 3,840-acre park is located in the sandy plains near the western edge of the Edwards Plateau. The sand is part of a vast area of dunes known locally as the Sahara of the Southwest. The wind-blown sand was formed by years of wind erosion of Quaternary sandstone formations a million years old. The dunes are composed of well-sorted grains of quartz ranging from light gray to golden in color. The reddish brown sands in the area are quartz grains stained with iron oxide.

Most of the sand is covered with vegetation, which helps brace the dunes from the force of the wind. However, the park preserves a spectacular region of unstabilized dunes. The wind creates intricate wavelike patterns across the dunes, reminding one of ripple marks at the surf's edge. Sculptured by the restless wind, the dunes arc dramatically across

The beautiful dunes at Monahans Sandhills State Park.

the sky, with contours and shadows that merge to form an ever-changing scene of inspiring beauty. West Texas is far from the roaring surf and ocean spray, but the Monahans sandhills are as picturesque as any found along the Texas coast.

The plants and animals of the sandhills country comprise one of the most ecologically interesting communities in Texas. In order to survive, an organism must be especially adapted to the shifting sand, burning sun, nutrient-poor soil, and low annual rainfall. But the dunes are far from barren or lifeless. An amazing variety of life thrives in this rugged habitat.

The colorful dunes support desert plants such as yucca and sagebrush. Annual flowers bloom and quickly set their seeds before being inundated by the advancing sand. At different seasons, the dunes may be painted with the blooms of sunflowers, wild buckwheats, bindweeds, Indian paintbrushes, and evening primroses.

One of the most unusual plants adapted to these harsh growing conditions is the Havard shin oak, *Quercus havardii*, which is only three to four feet tall at maturity. The trees produce large acorns eaten by javelinas, prairie chickens, bobwhite quail, and rodents. The miniature trees cover thousands of acres and comprise one of the largest, but shortest, oak forests in North America.

The vegetation covering much of the sand stabilizes the dunes and provides habitat for gray foxes, coyotes, skunks, jackrabbits, armadillos, bobcats, pack rats, and kangaroo rats. Dominant grasses include sand bluestem, giant sandreed, and Panicum species. The many footprints in the sand attest to rampant nocturnal activity, but the animals themselves are seldom seen. The tiny footprints of a kangaroo rat spotted beside the slithering trail of a snake end in a confused jumble. The outcome is left to your imagination.

Groundwater is close to the surface in the sand country. Depressions between the dunes are sometimes filled with water, creating ideal spots to see wildlife in the early morning. In the past, Indians, settlers, and the railroad depended on the easily obtainable water during their passage across this desolate country.

145. MOTHER NEFF STATE PARK

LOCATION

Coryell County. 15 miles northwest of Temple on TX 36, 5 miles north on TX 236.
Mailing address: 1680 Hwy 236, Moody, Texas 76557. Phone: 254-853-2389. For all state park reservations, call the centralized reservations system, 512-389-8900, or www.ReserveAmerica.com online. Call the state park information number, 800-792-1112, for information and fee updates.

FACILITIES

Fees: entrance, facility, activity use; subject to change.

Camping: 6 back-in RV/tent sites with water and electricity, 15 tent sites, primitive camping area, modern restrooms, showers, trailer dump station. Fees charged.

Recreation: picnic areas and playgrounds, hiking trail, fishing in the Leon River, tabernacle, pavilion.

Note: Due to flood damage, this park is day-use only through at least 2008 and maybe longer. Call the park for current status.

WEATHER

July high averages 97 degrees, January low 36 degrees.

MAIN ATTRACTIONS

The first state park in Texas, Mother Neff preserves a scenic section of the Leon River. Giant oaks, cottonwoods, pecans, and cedar elms shade the luxuriant bottomland around the steep banks of the river. Bird-watching is popular in the park, as are fishing and picnicking along the picturesque river. Mother Neff is one of the most pleasant small parks in Texas.

Surrounded by cultivated farmland, the 259-acre park encompasses three distinct vegetation types, including about a hundred acres of prairies, a hundred acres of rugged limestone hills, and 50 acres of rich bottomland forests with many giant trees growing along the winding Leon River. More than 130 species of birds have been sighted in the park; ask for a checklist at the headquarters. It is easy to see why the original owner, pioneer Isabella Neff, wanted to preserve this beautiful area.

In 1916, Isabella Eleanor Neff, who had come to Texas from Roanoke, Virginia, with her husband in 1854, donated 6 acres along the Leon River to the state. One of her sons, Pat Neff, who was governor from 1921 to 1925, donated another 250 acres to establish Mother Neff Park. As governor, Neff created the Texas State Parks Board in 1923, and Mother Neff Park became the hub of the still-expanding park system. During the thirties, the Civilian Conservation Corps constructed the stone headquarters, the pavilion, and the tabernacle. The tabernacle, which is often used for weddings and church services, must be reserved several months in advance.

HIKING

A short hiking trail leads along a creek in the juniper-oak uplands. The trail follows the creek to a historic water hole, called the Wash Pond, used by Indians and early settlers and to a rock shelter or shallow cave used by the Tonkawas as a campsite.

146. MULESHOE NATIONAL WILDLIFE REFUGE

LOCATION

Bailey County. 20 miles south of Muleshoe on TX 214.
Mailing address: Box 549, Muleshoe, Texas 79347. Phone: 806-946-3341. Internet: www.fws.gov/southwest/refuges/texas/muleshoe/index.html.

FACILITIES

Camping: 6 campsites with tables and water, group camp area. No reservations. No fees. Open all year.

Recreation: auto tour of refuge, picnic area, nature trail, prairie dog town, bird-watching, wildlife photography. The refuge roads are open during daylight hours.

MAIN ATTRACTIONS

Winter visitors to this refuge can witness one of the grandest wildlife spectacles in North America: between 10,000 and 20,000

Thousands of sandhill cranes overwinter at Muleshoe NWR.

sandhill cranes. The magnificent birds begin arriving about the end of September and stay until March. The birds roost at night in the three small lakes on the refuge when water is available. At dawn they rise en masse and, bugling their piercing call, circle and leave to feed in nearby grain fields. You will never forget the sight of thousands of these 3-foot-tall birds, with their 6.5-foot wingspans, clouding the sky.

The area's agricultural practices are a factor in the large number of sandhills. Pumping the aquifer for irrigation lowered the lakes, making them a protected nighttime roost for the cranes. The birds find ample grass, leftover grain, and insects in the fields surrounding the refuge. Two factors could adversely affect the cranes in the future. Government regulations allow farmers to profit by converting marginal cropland to grass, which could greatly reduce the food available. This and other complex factors have caused the cranes' population to drop from past highs of 200,000 to a winter peak of 20,000 in the refuge. Another threat lurks along the Platte River in Nebraska, where the cranes gather before migrating to the Arctic tundra to breed. A dam is proposed for the area, which would destroy much of the cranes' habitat.

In addition to the sandhills, thousands of ducks and other waterfowl winter in the refuge, depending on the amount of water in the lakes. The refuge bird list includes 283 species, with many migrants that stop over in the spring and fall. Burrowing owls perch on burrows in the prairie dog town, and golden eagles and other raptors soar in the sky. Coyotes, badgers, rabbits, and small mammals live in the shortgrass prairie that surrounds the playa lakes.

147. MUSTANG ISLAND STATE PARK

LOCATION

Nueces County. On PR 53, 14 miles south of Port Aransas or 14 miles east of Corpus Christi, on the Gulf of Mexico.
Mailing address: Box 326, Port Aransas, Texas 78373. Phone: 361-749-5246. For all state park reservations, call the centralized reservations system, 512-389-8900, or www.ReserveAmerica.com online. Call the state park information number, 800-792-1112, for information and fee updates.

FACILITIES

Fees: entrance, facility, activity use; subject to change.

Camping: primitive camping along 5 miles of beach (occasionally closed due to high tides) with widely spaced portable toilets, rinse showers, water; 48 back-in RV/tent sites with water and electricity, modern rest-rooms, showers, trailer dump station.

Recreation: picnicking, ocean swimming, bird-watching, hiking/biking and beachcombing on 5 miles of beach, bathhouse, jetty and surf fishing, cold-water showers, Texas State Park Store.

WEATHER

July high averages 94 degrees, January low 46 degrees. Prepare for extremes of sun and heat with plenty of sunblock and fluids.

MAIN ATTRACTIONS

Swimming in the rolling surf, beachcombing, and playing in the sand are the primary activities at the park. Visitors will find some of the best surfing in Texas along the jetties of the fish pass, a cut through the island to the inland bay. Fishing is popular from the jetties.

PLANTS AND ANIMALS

The barrier islands that parallel the crescent-shaped Texas coast are of extreme ecological importance. The islands provide a variety of wildlife and plant habitats and protect the bays and the mainland shoreline. Seldom are hurricanes powerful enough to breach the islands with wind-driven waves.

Mustang Island has six distinct habitats, each of which supports a characteristic community of plants and animals: beaches, primary dunes, secondary dunes, marshes, tidal flats, and the bay. The shells of many marine organisms litter the open beaches. The primary and secondary dunes support an interesting variety of salt- and wind-adapted plants. Morning glories spread across the dunes, and sea oats and other grasses grasp for a sandy foothold.

Freshwater marshes are sustained by the rains, while salt marshes are more permanent; the marshes are the nursery grounds for many species of fish. Birds are abundant both in the marshes and along the mud flats on the inner shoreline. The mud flats support many organisms that attract shorebirds and wading birds. Ducks and waterfowl frequent the protected bay and lagoon between the island and the mainland.

The dunes are very fragile. The plants fight the wind-driven sand and, if undisturbed, will stabilize the dunes and protect them from erosion. Many dunes in the park have been reconstructed and are now at their natural height of about 15 to 20 feet. Except in the primary dunes immediately adjacent to the beach, hiking through the dunes should be avoided.

The main animals seen in the park are birds, rodents, and snakes. Rattlesnakes are common in the grassy secondary dunes, where they feed on ground squirrels, pocket gophers, and cotton rats. The tracks of raccoons, opossums, black-tailed jackrabbits, striped skunks, and coyotes can be seen leading across the dunes, an indication of the active nightlife of the wild community.

148. NAVARRO MILLS LAKE

LOCATION

U.S. Army Corps of Engineers. Navarro County. Project office: 16 miles southwest of Corsicana on TX 31 to Navarro Mills, 1.5 miles northwest on FM 667.

Campground	water	fee area	flush toilets	season	dump station	showers	electricity
Liberty Hill	•	•	•	all	•	•	•
Oak Park	•	•	•	all	•	•	•
Wolf Creek	•	•	•	Apr. 1–Sept. 30	•	•	•
Brushie Prairie Park				all			
Pecan Point Park	•	•	•	Apr. 1–Sept. 30	•	•	•

NAVARRO MILLS LAKE

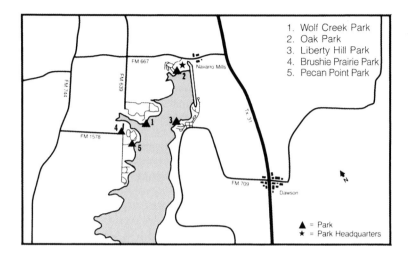

1. Wolf Creek Park
2. Oak Park
3. Liberty Hill Park
4. Brushie Prairie Park
5. Pecan Point Park

▲ = Park
★ = Park Headquarters

Mailing address: 1175 FM 667, Purdon, Texas 76679. Phone: 254-578-1431. E-mail: CESWF-OD-NM@swf.usace.army.mil. Internet: www.swf-wc.usace.army.mil/navarro/. For camping reservations, call 877-444-6777 or online at www.recreation.gov.

FACILITIES

Camping: The COE operates 4 parks with campgrounds on the lake. Parks not listed are day-use only. Liberty Hill Park has 99 RV/tent sites with water and electricity (5 with screened shelters and 6 with sewer hookups), 3 sites with no hookups. Wolf Creek Park has 50 RV/tent sites with water and electricity, 20 with no hookups. Oak Park has 48 RV/tent sites with water and electricity and a group shelter. Pecan Point Park has 5 RV/tent sites with water and electricity, 30 sites with no hookups. Brushie Prairie Park is a day-use boat launch with pit toilet, no water. Gatehouses at all campgrounds open 6 a.m. to 10 p.m.

Recreation: picnicking, hiking, swimming, fishing, boat ramps, marina at Liberty Hill Park, hunting.

MAIN ATTRACTIONS

Lake Navarro Mills, an impoundment of Richland Creek, covers 5,070 acres and has 38 miles of shoreline. Catfish and crappie are the primary game fish in the lake. Public hunting and hiking are permitted on 3,550 acres reserved for wildlife management.

149. O.H. IVIE RESERVOIR

Concho and Coleman counties. Operated by the Colorado River Municipal Water Authority. Mailing address: Box 869, Big Spring, TX 79721-0869. Phone: 432-267-6341.

CONCHO PARK

Concho County. From Ballinger, 11 miles south on U.S. 83 to FM 1929 then east 13 miles; turn north on park road 2 miles to the lake. Concessionaire operated, 325-357-4466. 30 RV/tent sites with water and electricity (3 pull-through), primitive camping, modern restrooms, showers, trailer dump station, lake swimming, fishing, boat ramp, store. Fees charged, closed Christmas week.

KENNEDY PARK

Coleman County. From Coleman, take Tex. 206 south 6 miles to U.S. 67, then west 4.6 miles to FM 503. Go south 13.8 miles to FM 1929, west 6.5 miles to the park. Concessionaire operated, 325-357-4776. 9 pull-through RV/tent sites with full hookups, 12 back-in with water and electricity, primitive camping, modern restrooms, showers, motel unit with 30 rooms with/without kitchen; lake swimming, picnic, boat ramp, store. Fees charged, open all year.

PADGITT PARK

Concho County. From Coleman 6 miles south on TX 206, 4.6 miles west on U.S. 67, 11 miles south on FM 503, 7 miles west on FM 2134 to reservoir. RV/tent sites with no hookups, primitive camping, drinking water, pit toilets, boat ramp. Fees charged.

150. OLD FORT PARKER

LOCATION

Limestone County. Operated by the City of Groesbeck. From Groesbeck four miles north on TX 14 to Park Road 35, turn west to park headquarters. Mailing address: RR 3 Box 746, Groesbeck, TX 76642. Phone: 254-729-5253, E-mail: oldfortparker@aol.com.

FACILITIES

Camping: 35 RV/tent sites with water and electricity, restrooms without showers; 2 bunkhouses with 19 rooms, community restrooms with shower, community room with couch, TV, fridge, toaster oven, microwave. Handicap accessible. Fees charged.

Recreation: replica of 1833 stockade fort, self-guided, interpretive fort tour, living history programs, monthly special events, picnicking, group meeting hall for 150 people. Hours: Open 9 a.m.–5 p.m. Wednesday through Sunday, closed Christmas, New Year's Day.

MAIN ATTRACTIONS

The 37.5-acre park preserved the replica of a stockade fort built in 1833 by early white settlers, the Parker family and other pioneers from Illinois. On May 19, 1836, a Comanche raiding party attacked the fort and kidnapped Cynthia Ann Parker, who became the mother of the famous war chief, Quanah Parker (see HISTORY). The Civilian Conservation Corps originally reconstructed the fort, which was rebuilt again in 1967. The park sponsors a monthly calendar of living history events, trail rides, rendezvous, medieval games, and pioneer reunions. Call for itineraries.

HISTORY

The settlers of the early 1800s were attracted to the rich blackland prairies of the area, the abundance of timber in the woodlands, and ample water supplies by the rivers and springs. In 1833, the Parker and several other families moved to the region form Illinois and constructed a stockade fort with blockhouses surrounded with a wall of upright split-cedar timbers.

The Indians posed no problems until 1836 when a band of Comanche and Kiowas attacked the fort and its 31 inhabitants. Five pioneers were killed and five abducted, including nine-year-old Cynthia Ann Parker and her five-year-old brother John. Four of the captives were returned to their families but Cynthia Ann remained with the Comanche and completely acclimated to their culture and lifestyle. Cynthia Ann became a legend in Texas and the West. She married Chief Peta Nocona and had three children, two sons, Quanah and Pecos, and a daughter, Topsannah, or Prairie Flower.

In 1860, Texas Ranger Captain Sul Ross captured Cynthia Ann and her two-year-old daughter, Prairie Flower, at the Battle of Pease River near the present-day Copper Breaks State Park. Cynthia Ann was returned against her will to her white family. She could not adjust to white society and was shuttled between family members. She tried to escape repeatedly but was always apprehended and forcibly returned. Pecos reportedly died of smallpox and in 1863 Prairie Flower died of the influenza. Cynthia Ann pined away and died in 1870.

Cynthia Ann's older son, Quanah, became a famous Comanche war chief who fearlessly led the battle to save his homeland from the encroaching settlers and soldiers. He refused to sign treaties that gave away his rights and freedom and never lost a battle, regardless of the odds. He fought in the battle of Adobe Wells in 1874 and used the badlands of Palo Duro Canyon as a hideout during the Red River Wars. Finally, in 1874 U. S. Army Colonel Ranald Mackenzie, surprised his tribe's encampment, captured 1,400 horses and destroyed their winter provisions. By 1875, his band of Quahada Comanche, worn down by disease and starvation, agreed to move to the reservation in Oklahoma.

A leader in times of peace as in war, Quanah helped his people adapt to the white man's ways. He settled in Fort Sill and in 1910 moved the grave of Cynthia Ann to the reservation. He learned English and became the confidant of Teddy Roosevelt, who appointed him judge of the Court of Indian Offences. He became politically active and represented the Comanche nation before Congress. Quanah Parker died on February 23, 1911, and was buried next to his mother. History recognizes him as a fearless warrior, a man of integrity, and as one of Texas' greatest heroes.

151. PADRE ISLAND NATIONAL SEASHORE

LOCATION

Kleberg County. 20 miles southeast of Corpus Christi on PR 22. Mailing address: PO Box 181300, Corpus Christi, TX 78480-1300. Phone: Malaquite Visitor Center: 361-949-8068. Internet: www.nps .gov/pais.

FACILITIES

Camping: Malaquite Beach: 26 RV/tent sites, 16 sites RV only, 8 sites tent only, water available, flush restrooms, cold showers, trailer dump station. Bird Island Basin (located on Laguna Madre side): primitive RV/ tent sites with chemical toilets. Fees charged. North Beach: primitive RV/tent camping on open beach. South Beach: primitive RV/tent camping on 60 miles of beach to Mansfield Channel, 4-wheel drive required. Yarborough Pass: primitive camping on Laguna Madre, 15.5 miles south of the visitors center, 4-wheel drive required. No camping fee but permit required.

Recreation: picnic areas, nature trail with pamphlet, interpretive programs and exhibits, ocean swimming, beachcombing, surfing, windsurfing in Laguna Madre, fishing, boat ramp, pavilion, visitor center, store.

WEATHER

July high averages 94 degrees, January low 46 degrees. Prepare for extremes of sun and heat with plenty of sunblock and fluids. Weather and tide updates, 361-949-8175.

MAIN ATTRACTIONS

Padre Island has more than 100 miles of expansive beaches with scenic dunes formed by the sea and shaped by the wind. Swimming, surfing, sunbathing, and fishing are the most popular activities. Shells and other interesting finds from the sea make beachcombing an adventure. More than 350 species of birds attract bird-watchers from across the nation, and the large, picturesque dunes thrill photographers. The variety of habitats on the island offers unparalleled opportunities for nature study. Most of the beach is accessible only by foot or with a four-wheel-drive vehicle.

HIKING

The three-quarter-mile Grasslands Nature Trail leads visitors through the rolling, grassy coastal sands that occupy a major portion of the island.

Sixty-five miles of beach and dunes stretch between Malaquite Beach and the Port Mansfield Channel. The south side of the channel to the southern tip of Padre Island covers another 35 miles. Though there are no facilities or drinking water on the beach, the entire stretch offers exciting beachcombing. Primitive camping is allowed on the beach but not in the ecologically delicate dunes.

Padre Island has the tallest dunes on the Texas coast.

Be sure to stop at the ranger station at Malaquite Beach for information about the ecology of the island, details about hiking and camping on the island, and pamphlets on the park's vegetation, birds, and other wildlife. If you are interested in undertaking a long hike, you will either have to hike back the way you came or have a friend with a four-wheel-drive vehicle pick you up. There is no ferry across the channel, so, if you are interested in hiking on the southern part of the island, you will have to drive to South Padre Island, east of Brownsville.

PLANTS AND ANIMALS

Padre Island is 113 miles long and, at most, 3 miles wide. The constant winds, salty ocean spray, sandy soil, lack of fresh water, and hot, shadeless summer days create an environment in which survival is not easy. Yet many plants and animals have successfully adapted and even thrive under the harsh conditions. Eight distinct habitats, each with its own characteristic plant and animal communities, exist within the park: beaches, foredunes, actively moving dune fields, grasslands, ponds and marshes, tidal flats, the Laguna Madre, and spoil banks, islands formed from dredging operations.

The flat beach slopes gently into the Gulf; it is generally devoid of vegetation but is the home of countless sea creatures. The shells of whelks, clams, scallops, and sand dollars litter the beach like confetti. Small fish can be seen skating across the surf and leaping above the waves. Porpoises are common offshore, and on rare occasions a whale has been stranded on the beach.

Paralleling the beach is a ridge of wind-sculptured sand dunes. These dunes are fairly well stabilized by a delicate mat of vegetation. Evening primroses with yellow flowers sparkle with early-morning dew, and the railroad vine, a morning glory, spreads its roots as far as 20 feet to help hold the shifting sand. Sea oats and other grasses silhouetted against the sky on the towering dunes help even the inexperienced photographer take professional-looking pictures. When human activity or violent weather destroys the fragile vegetation, the dunes quickly erode away.

Rolling sandhills covered by a variety of grasses and small herbaceous plants occupy most of the island behind the foredunes. Many small mammals inhabit this area, including kangaroo rats, pocket gophers, cotton rats, rice rats, ground squirrels, and jackrabbits. Coyotes prey on the small animals, as do rattlesnakes, which are numerous in the grasslands.

Low-lying marshy areas are interspersed with the grasslands. These slowly draining areas contain fresh water after rains and salt water after severe storms. Here grow cattails, marshhay cordgrass, and other plants tolerant of both fresh and salt water. Dunes constantly driven by the winds border the western side of the island. Also on the western shore are tidal flats, which attract a large number of wading birds and shorebirds.

The Laguna Madre provides a protected shelter for the many birds that nest on the spoil banks created by dredging the Intracoastal Canal.

Millions of migrating waterfowl spend their winter in this long body of shallow water.

Despite the inhospitable environment, more than 350 species of birds and 400 plant species make Padre Island their home. Shorebirds and gulls soar overhead, and colorful wildflowers and dune grasses nod gracefully in the prevailing breezes. The ceaseless roar of the surf echoes across the island with a primordial cry unchanged since first recorded by human ears. Unfortunately, garbage from ships, offshore oil rigs, and thoughtless vacationers litters almost every yard of the beautiful shoreline.

HISTORY

Padre Island, first charted in 1519, was originally named Las Islas Blancas, the White Islands. In the intervening centuries, many storm-driven ships were wrecked on the silver beaches. In 1553, a 20-ship Spanish treasure fleet caught in a hurricane lost many of its galleons to the raging sea.

In 1800, the island was granted to Padre Nicolás Balli by the Spanish government. Balli started the first ranch on the island, and cattle grazed the sandy grasslands until 1970, when the national seashore was established.

152. PALMETTO STATE PARK

LOCATION

Gonzales County. 21 miles southeast of Lockhart off U.S. 183. Mailing address: 78 Park Road 11 South, Gonzales, TX 78629-5180. Phone: 830-672-3266. E-mail: palmetto.park@tpwd.state. tx.us. For all state park reservations, call the centralized reservations system, 512-389-8900, or www.ReserveAmerica.com online. Call the state park information number, 800-792-1112, for information and fee updates.

FACILITIES

Fees: entrance, facility, activity use; subject to change.

Camping: 2 back-in RV/tent sites with full hookups, 18 sites with water and electricity, 20 sites with water, 1 oversized tent site (capacity 12), group camping area with water (capacity 100), overflow camping area, modern restrooms, showers, trailer dump station.

Recreation: picnic areas and playgrounds, nature trails with trail-guide pamphlet, bird-watching and wildflower gazing; fishing, tubing, and canoeing on the San Marcos River; recreation hall, Texas State Park Store with paddle boat rental.

WEATHER

July high averages 96 degrees, January low averages 38 degrees.

MAIN ATTRACTIONS

The botanically unique 263-acre park is located on the spring-fed San Marcos River. The most unusual features of the scenic park are the unique plant and animal communities associated with naturally occurring artesian springs and swamps. The area had numerous warm springs, mud boils, and peat deposits until the mid-1900s. However, drilling for oil and water had lowered the water table, thus eliminating those interesting hydrologic features. The park derives its name from the dwarf palmettos that grow abundantly in the swamps. Palmettos, common to East Texas marshy areas, are not usually found in dry Central Texas. The river and warm artesian wells in the park provide the right environment for lush vegetation.

There are two nature trails in the park. One leads along the steep banks of the San Marcos River, the other through the palmetto swamp. A fountain of warm sulfur-rich water flows from a natural artesian well near the start of the Palmetto Nature Trail. The spring powers one of the few operational ram-jet pumps in existence today. The pump, installed in 1936, uses no electricity; it derives its power solely from the naturally occurring water pressure of the well.

PLANTS AND ANIMALS

The ecological diversity of Palmetto State Park is the result of the various habitats created by the river, artesian springs, and swamps. The naturally flowing artesian wells maintain the water level in the swamps, enabling the dwarf palmettos and other acid-loving plants to thrive in an area far west of their natural habitat. Rich hardwood bottomlands occur along the river, while the uplands are dominated by a post oak-little bluestem community.

The distribution of many eastern and western species of plants and animals merges in this area. Approximately 240 species of birds have been sighted in the park. Many are near the western limit of their ranges, making Palmetto one of the most interesting birding spots in Central Texas. The pileated woodpecker, yellow-crowned night heron, barred owl, and the Kentucky, prothonotary, and northern parula warblers all nest in the vicinity. Ask at the park headquarters for a bird checklist.

Eastern gray squirrels and canebrake rattlesnakes are other animals in the area not usually seen farther west. The fox squirrel, pygmy mouse, eastern cottontail, raccoon, armadillo, and white-tailed deer also make their homes in the park.

The abundance and diversity of plants, particularly wildflowers, in the park area have attracted amateur and professional botanists for many years. The annual phlox cultivated worldwide is derived from a native phlox discovered in this area by Scottish botanist Thomas Drummond.

The anaqua tree, a subtropical species that reaches its northern limits in Central Texas, occurs along riverbanks in the park. The evergreen leaves have the texture of sandpaper. In the spring, the open hillsides are ablaze with bluebonnets, Indian paintbrushes, red phlox, larkspurs, and gaillardias. The fall-blooming species—goldenrod, wild hibiscus, turk's caps, and sunflowers—are no less spectacular.

HISTORY

The area was settled in 1879 by Adolph Otto and his wife, Christine. A community, named Ottine by combining their names, developed around Otto's sawmill and cotton gin. The area quickly became a popular spot for botanists from around the country and the world. Also, people were attracted to the warm sulfur springs for their alleged healing qualities. Today, the Texas Warm Springs Foundation is near the park entrance.

In 1933, the Texas State Parks Board acquired Ottine Swamp and constructed the park recreation hall with Civilian Conservation Corps labor. The historic building stands in the picnic area near the playgrounds.

153. PALO DURO CANYON STATE PARK

LOCATION

Randall County. 26 miles south of Amarillo on IH-27 to Canyon, 12 miles east on TX 217.
Mailing address: 11450 Park Road, Canyon, Texas 79015. Phone: 806-488-2227. For all state park reservations, call the centralized reservations system, 512-389-8900, or www.ReserveAmerica.com online. Call the state park information number, 800-792-1112, for information and fee updates.
Pioneer Amphitheatre Box Office: 806-655-2181, www.texas-show .com.

FACILITIES

Fees: entrance, facility, activity use; subject to change.

Camping: 79 RV/tent sites with water and electricity (some pull-through), 25 drive-up tent sites with water nearby, hike-in primitive sites (½ to

¾ mile), backpack sites (½ to 2 miles, 10 primitive equestrian sites with water and with/without pens, 3 cabins (capacity 4, linens incl.), 4 limited-service cabins (restroom nearby, no linens incl.), overflow/late arrival camping area; modern restrooms, showers, trailer dump station. Gate hours: 8 a.m. to 5 p.m. November–February, 8 a.m. to 10 p.m. March–October.

Recreation: picnic areas, playgrounds, 50 miles of hiking and mountain biking trails, interpretive exhibits (summer only), swimming in creek, miniature railroad through canyon, horse rentals, State Longhorn Herd, visitor center with museum and store, Chuckwagon snack bar (summer), amphitheater with summer drama production of the musical drama *Texas*.

WEATHER

July highs average 92 degrees, January lows 19 degrees. Flash flooding may pose a serious danger. If the water rises 6 inches on the depth gauges at any of the six water crossings, immediately seek shelter on higher ground.

MAIN ATTRACTIONS

Palo Duro Canyon, formed by the erosive action of the Prairie Dog Town Fork of the Red River and its numerous tributaries, resembles a miniature Grand Canyon. The name "Palo Duro" is Spanish for "hard wood," referring to the rot-resistant junipers growing throughout the canyon. The state park, encompassing more than 17,000 acres, is one of the largest in Texas. Part of the official state longhorn herd, a reminder of past days, can be seen grazing along the entrance road.

Erosion has carved colorful formations in the strata at Palo Duro Canyon.

The interpretive center, open in summer, explains the cultural and geologic history of the park. Each summer, in the amphitheater, the Texas Panhandle Heritage Foundation performs a drama about early pioneers in the region. Another popular attraction is the winding Sad Monkey Railroad, which provides impressive views of some of the unusual formations in the canyon.

Nearby attractions include the Panhandle-Plains Historical Museum in Canyon, one of the best museums in the state. Buffalo Lake National Wildlife Refuge is 12 miles southwest of Canyon.

HIKING AND HORSEBACK RIDING

The beauty of the canyon, evident from the scenic overlook and the loop drive, is better appreciated by hikers or horseback riders along the many trails. The park has 5 miles of marked trails and approximately 50 miles of unmarked trails. Camping is not allowed along the trails. In summer, always carry water with you.

PLANTS AND ANIMALS

Palo Duro Canyon is on the Caprock Escarpment, which divides the High Plains and the Rolling Plains of North Texas. Examples of plants and animals from each area occur in the park. The canyon, averaging 700 feet deep and a half mile to 2 miles wide in the park, provides a refuge for plants and wildlife. This protected canyon, plus the park's perennial springs, woodlands, and permanent waterways, supports a great diversity of vegetation and animal life.

Rocky Mountain, Pinchot, and one-seed junipers, mesquite trees, and other drought-resistant plants grow on the arid canyon slopes and along the canyon rim. In contrast, stately cottonwood and hackberry trees shade the streams winding through the canyon. Life-giving springs, which may flow at a rate of 15 gallons per minute, are produced where water-bearing strata are exposed; these springs form miniature oases for moisture-dependent plants.

Vast herds of bison used to roam the canyon, but they were extirpated by the buffalo hunters. Pronghorn antelope, unimpeded by the barbed wire fences, still occur in small numbers on the adjoining plains. Imported African aoudad sheep are established in the canyon.

More than 200 species of birds have been recorded in the park. In the spring and fall, kettles of circling Mississippi kites ride thermals rising from the canyon by day and roost in the tall cottonwoods bordering the streams by night. In a 1983 survey, 22 golden eagle nests were spotted in the canyon. Beavers, which make their homes in the creeks, and mule deer are best sighted in the early morning or at dusk.

To the west extends the flat unbroken prairie of the High Plains, or Llano Estacado, formed from millions of years of deposits originating in the Rocky Mountains and carried eastward by streams and rivers. The Prairie Dog Town Fork of the Red River, no more than a low-water creek most of the year, has carved through 800 feet of sediments and exposed strata hundreds of millions of years old.

The most prominent layers exposed in the park are the brick-red shale, sandy clay, and sandstone, formed by sediments from the Permian oceans of 225 million to 270 million years ago. The colorful layers are laced with veins of white crystal gypsum or satin spar. The force of erosion is evident along the creeks, as banks of red clay with alternating layers of gypsum crumble into the streambeds.

Covering the Permian sediments, which make up the canyon floor, are 300 feet of red, yellow, lavender, and gray shales and sandstones from the Triassic age, approximately 200 million years old. The harder layers of sandstone are resistant to erosion and form ridges, ledges, cliffs, and many outstanding features throughout the park. Sad Monkeys, Spanish Skirts, and Santana's Face are the imaginative names of some of the most prominent formations. The Lighthouse, the best-known landmark, is a 75-foot pillar of soft mudstone capped by a layer of erosion-resistant sandstone.

This layer cake of colorful sedimentary rock was covered during the Cretaceous by many more layers of sediments, which were eventually removed by erosion. During the Tertiary period, from 3 million to 11 million years ago, clay, sand, chalk, caliche, and gravel were deposited to create the Ogallala formation, an important aquifer, or water-bearing stratum. The Ogallala provides the irrigation water that has turned the arid Panhandle into one of the most productive farming regions in the country. A surface layer of sand, clay, and gravel, deposited during the Pleistocene epoch some 1 million years ago, underlies the grasslands so attractive to ranchers.

HISTORY

Palo Duro Canyon has been a center of human activity for more than 12,000 years. Paleo-Indian nomads hunted the mammoths and other Ice Age animals that grazed on the rich grasslands in the canyon. During the 1800s, the canyon was the domain of the Comanches, who in 1874 were defeated by the U.S. Army. A historical marker designates the site of that last major Indian battle in Texas. The Indians were led by the fierce war chief Quanah Parker.

Charles Goodnight established one of the largest ranches in Texas in Palo Duro Canyon in 1876. He began with 1,600 head of longhorn cattle and lived in a dugout house similar to the one exhibited along the park loop road. Later, Goodnight and his partner John Adair founded the J.A. Ranch; they were among the first to use controlled breeding to improve their herd, which eventually numbered 100,000.

154. PAMPA: HOBART STREET PARK

Gray County. In town on TX 70, one block north of U.S. 60. Mailing address: P.O. Box 2499, Pampa, Texas 79066-2499. Phone: 806-669-5750. Five acres with 20 sites with water, showers, electricity, primitive camp sites; dump station, flush toilets, playground, picnicking. Open year-round, free overnight, no reservations.

PAMPA: RECREATION PARK

Gray County. On U.S. 60, 2 miles east of intersection with TX 70. Mailing address: P.O. Box 2499, Pampa, Texas 79066-2499. Phone: 806-669-5750. One hundred thirty-four acres on Old City Lake; 10 RV/tent sites with water, electricity; flush toilets, dump station, group campsites, showers, free tent camping. Recreation: picnic area, playgrounds, boating, fishing, 2-mile hiking trail. Open year-round, fees charged, no reservations.

155. PEDERNALES FALLS STATE PARK

LOCATION

Blanco County. 40 miles west of Austin on U.S. 290, 7 miles north on FM 3232.
Mailing address: 2585 Park Road 6026, Johnson City, Texas 78636. Phone: 830-868-7304. For all state park reservations, call the centralized reservations system, 512-389-8900, or www. ReserveAmerica.com online. Call the state park information number, 800-792-1112, for information and fee updates.

FACILITIES

Fees: entrance, facility, activity use; subject to change.

Camping: 69 back-in RV/tent sites with water and electricity, hike/bike-in (2 miles) primitive camping, youth group site (capacity 150), modern restrooms, showers, trailer dump station.

Recreation: picnic areas, playgrounds, river swimming and fishing, canoeing, nature trail, bird viewing station with feeders and a drip bath, 19.8 miles hike/bike trails, 14 miles backpacking trails, 10 miles equestrian trails (day-use only), Texas State Store.

Note: Flash floods caused by upstream rains can turn the Pedernales River from a placid flow into a raging torrent in a matter of minutes with no warning. If the water begins to rise, leave the river area IMMEDIATELY.

WEATHER

July high averages 94 degrees, January low 32 degrees.

MAIN ATTRACTIONS

The most outstanding feature of the park is the boulder-strewn, cascading Pedernales Falls. The river, which has cut deep channels through the limestone, spills down two waterfalls into deep pools. There are two scenic overlooks and a trail to the falls. Though the bedrock is limestone, the river bottom is sandy. The sand of the Pedernales and other Central Texas rivers is carried by streams from the weathered granite formations exposed in the Llano region.

Hours can be spent scampering over the exposed rocks leading upstream from the falls. Like giant stairsteps, the strata tilt gently upward, each successive layer younger than the one below it. The river, cascading over the tilted bedrock, forms the falls that give the park its name.

Fishing is popular all along the Pedernales River, but because of hazardous water conditions, swimming, wading, and tubing are prohibited near the falls. Below the falls, the shady shoreline and the cool river provide a welcome respite from the heat of summer afternoons. The normally calm river can rise rapidly and become a torrent after thunderstorms. Access to the river is prohibited when flooding is likely.

Nearby attractions include the Lyndon B. Johnson National Historical Park, 9 miles west in Johnson City. An interpretive center describes the development of the Texas cattle industry, and a reconstructed pioneer ranch with a house, barns, and longhorn cattle illustrates the early lifestyle.

Lyndon B. Johnson State Historic Site is near Stonewall, 14 miles west of Johnson City. Tours of the LBJ Ranch, a working cattle ranch, are offered. A swimming pool and picnic areas are available in the park.

HIKING

The 7-mile Wolf Mountain Trail leads across rugged uplands and crystalline streams and down steep riverbanks into the shady riparian woodlands. Off the trail, about 2 miles from the trailhead, are areas designated for primitive camping. The camping area has no water and no facilities.

The short loop of the Hill Country Nature Trail begins in the car-camping area. The trail booklet, available at the park headquarters, describes the plants, wildlife, and ecology of this special part of Texas known as the Hill Country. The park has a total of 19.8 miles of hiking and mountain biking trails, 10 miles of equestrian trails, and 14 miles of backpacking trails.

PLANTS AND ANIMALS

Pedernales Falls State Park, formerly the 4,800-acre Circle Bar Ranch, stretches 9 miles along the Pedernales River. The park, situated on the eastern edge of the Edwards Plateau, encompasses dry rolling grasslands, rugged cedar brakes, oak-mesquite woodlands, botanically rich spring-fed canyons, and lush riverbanks lined with bald cypress.

The park provides an excellent example of the Edwards Plateau, which stretches west of Austin for more than 300 miles. The dominant plants are the Ashe juniper and the plateau live oak. Texas oak, mesquite, and small shrubs such as evergreen sumac, aromatic sumac, silktassel, and agarita are common on the dry rocky hillsides. Grama, bluestem, and muhly grasses grow in the upland clearings.

The area is dissected by many canyons rich with moisture-loving plants. Spicebush, a small shrub favored by early settlers for tea and seasoning, sycamore, Mexican plum, black cherry, and box elder trees grow in the protected environment. In contrast to the dry hillsides, lush vegetation lines the springs and seeps along the stream bottoms. Arrowhead Pool, on the Wolf Mountain Trail, is a large arrow-shaped pool at the bottom of a cascading, fern-lined waterfall.

Twin Falls Overlook, reached by the trail from the campgrounds, is at the confluence of two creeks, each with a picturesque waterfall. This ecologically sensitive area is so easily damaged by human use that hiking beyond the overlook is prohibited.

The area around the Pedernales Falls is scoured of most vegetation by periodic flooding. A few wildflowers find a temporary hold in silty patches among the rocks. Desert plants such as sotol, yucca, and prickly pear cacti grow in the fast-draining sandy soil above the flood line. Castor bean, poison hemlock, and snow-on-the-mountain are abundant on the sandy beaches below the falls. Those three plants are poisonous. The poison hemlock can easily be confused with the carrot plant, but it is extremely toxic, particularly the foliage.

Wildlife is abundant in the park. Turkey, deer, raccoons, skunks, opossums, armadillos, and more than 150 species of birds, including the bald eagle and golden-cheeked warbler, may be seen. A bird checklist is available from the entrance facility. Deer commonly graze along the roadsides and near the camping and picnicking areas. At dusk, armadillos plow noisily through the underbrush bordering the river, rooting for insects in the sandy soil.

156. PERRYTON: WOLF CREEK PARK

Ochiltree County. 12 miles south of Perryton on U.S. 83, 5 miles east, on Lake Fryer. Mailing address: Route 2, Box 20, Perryton, Texas 79070. Phone: 806-435-4559. Camping: 94 RV/tent sites with water and electricity, group site with electric hookups, primitive tent camping around lake, bathhouse with restrooms and showers, trailer dump station. Fees charged, open all year. Recreation: picnic areas, hiking trails, fishing, boat ramp, store, restaurant. Open all year.

157. PORT ARANSAS: IB MAGEE BEACH PARK

Nueces County. On the beach at Port Aransas. Mailing address: 321 North on the Beach, Port Aransas, TX 78373 Phone: 361-749-6117. Internet: http://nuecesbeachparks.com/. Camping: primitive camping on beach, 75 RV sites with water, electricity, and showers; flush toilets, trailer dump station. Fees charged. Recreation: swimming in the Gulf of Mexico, 1,240-foot lighted fishing pier, boating, concessions. Open all year. Good facilities for RVs; open beach camping.

158. PORT ARTHUR: WALTER UMPHREY STATE PARK

LOCATION

Jefferson County. From Port Arthur, southeast on TX 82 across MLK Bridge to Pleasure Island, south to Mesquite Point. Phone: 337-802-4320. Internet: http://pleasureislandtx.com/park_umph .htm. Managed by Jefferson County. Fees charged, open all year.

FACILITIES

Note: In September 2008, Hurricane Ike caused considerable damage. Check for condition of park facilities.

20 back-in RV sites with full hookups, tent area without facilities, restrooms (no showers), lighted fishing pier, boat launch, picnicking. Located at Mesquite Point on the south end of Pleasure Island, this 20-acre park is primarily for fishing and water recreation access to Sabine Lake. Pleasure Island, a narrow, 18.5-mile-long man-made island, borders the Intracoastal Canal on one side and Sabine Lake, which open into the Gulf of Mexico. Other facilities on the island include an 18-hole golf course, the Fun Depot playground, nature trails, and Pleasure Island RV Park (888-529-1775, http://pleasureislandtx.com/park_rv.htm), with full RV and water recreation facilities. *Note:* Take plenty of insect repellent, Mosquito Point got its name for a reason.

159. PORT LAVACA LIGHTHOUSE AND
BIRD SANCTUARY RV PARK

LOCATION

Nueces County. East of Port Lavaca at corner of TX 35 & TX 238 on Lavaca Bay. Operated by City of Port Lavaca. Mailing address: 700 Lighthouse Beach Road, Port Lavaca, TX 77979. Phone: 361-552-1234.

FACILITIES

Camping: 55 RV sites with water, electricity, sewer, cable, phone jacks; tent sites, 19 covered shelters with cable TV; flush toilets, showers, trailer dump station. Fishing Pier: open 24 hours, 2,000-foot, lighted, restroom without showers, fish-cleaning facility. Facilities are poor here for tents but adequate for RVs.

Recreation: picnic areas and playgrounds, swimming pool, lighted fishing pier, boat ramp, store, one-half-mile trail with bird observation tower. Fees charged, no reservations, open all year.

160. POSSUM KINGDOM STATE PARK

LOCATION

Palo Pinto County. 85 miles west of Fort Worth on U.S. 180 to Caddo, 17 miles north on PR 33.
Mailing address: Box 70, Caddo, Texas 76429. Phone: 940-549-1803. Internet: www.tpwd.state.tx.us/spdest/findadest/parks/possum_kingdom. For all state park reservations, call the centralized reservations system, 512-389-8900, or www.ReserveAmerica.com online. Call the state park information number, 800-792-1112, for information and fee updates.

FACILITIES

Fees: entrance, facility, activity use; subject to change.

Note: Due to high salt content in the water supply, Possum Kingdom does not have safe drinking water. Showers and toilets rely on non-potable water. You must bring your own supply of drinking water. For the current status, call the park or check the website, www.tpwd.state.tx.us/spdest/findadest/parks/possum_kingdom/.

Camping: 55 back-in RV/tent sites with water and electricity, 55 tent sites with water, 10 walk-in (50–150 yards) primitive tent sites, 7 cabins (6 with 1 bedroom capacity 4 and 1 with 2 bedrooms, capacity 8) with ac/heat and kitchen but no linens or utensils, overflow camping area, modern restrooms, showers, trailer dump station.

Recreation: picnic areas, playgrounds, lake swimming, fishing pier, boat ramp and dock, water sports, marina with motorized and non-motorized boat rentals, store, 2 miles of hiking/nature trails.

WEATHER

July highs average 94, January lows 34 degrees.

MAIN ATTRACTIONS

The 19,800-acre Possum Kingdom Lake, 34 miles long with 310 miles of shoreline, offers visitors swimming, fishing, water sports, and excellent scuba diving in its clear waters. Catches of black bass, striped bass, perch, and walleye pike are common. Rainbow trout are stocked in the cool waters discharged from the dam. Morris Sheppard Dam was built on the Brazos River in 1941 by the Brazos River Authority. The hydroelectric power plant at the dam can produce up to 22.5 megawatts of electricity.

PLANTS AND ANIMALS

The Brazos River, one of the major river systems in Texas, has cut through more than 200 feet of limestone and shale layers in the area of the park. The result is a meandering riverbed with steep cliffs and narrow canyons. New boating enthusiasts can explore the flooded canyons, with cliffs more than 100 feet high.

The exposed rock layers, part of the Canyon Group, were formed from sediments deposited in shallow seas around 280 million years ago. Geologists have studied the exposed strata because they are the same age as some of the limestones that hold oil reserves deep beneath the surface in West Texas.

Ashe juniper, mesquite, Texas oak, live oak, and redbud trees dominate the park, and pecans grow along the creek drainages. There is a large population of white-tailed deer, many tame enough to eat from your hands. Mountain lions, bobcats, and coyotes also find a protected home in the area. Many waterfowl frequent the reservoir, and the endangered golden eagle and ospreys are occasionally sighted. Turkeys and quail inhabit the mixed grassland savannas scattered through the rocky hills. The Possum Kingdom State Longhorn Herd is temporarily at San Angelo State Park while their home range is rested and restored.

161. PURTIS CREEK STATE PARK

LOCATION

Henderson and Van Zandt counties. 10 miles northwest of Athens on U.S. 175 to Eustace, 3 miles north on FM 316.
Mailing address: 14225 FM 316, Eustace, Texas 75124. Phone: 903-425-2332. For all state park reservations, call the centralized reservations system, 512-389-8900, or www.ReserveAmerica.com online. Call the state park information number, 800-792-1112, for information and fee updates.

FACILITIES

Fees: entrance, facility, activity use; subject to change.

Camping: 59 back-in RV/tent sites with water and electricity, 5 walk-in (10 yards) tent sites with water, 14 primitive hike-in (.65 mile) tent sites, over-flow camping area, modern restrooms, showers, trailer dump station.

Recreation: picnic area, playgrounds, group pavilion, boat ramp and dock (50 boat limit on lake), 2 lighted fishing piers, fish-cleaning station, hiking trail, Texas State Park Store.

Campers at Purtis Creek can hear great horned owls hooting in the night.

WEATHER

July high averages 96 degrees, January low 36 degrees.

MAIN ATTRACTIONS

This park, with 1,533 acres of woodlands and pastures, was designed for the fisherman. It even has its own ponds for raising fish to stock the lake. Brush and trees were left in the 355-acre impounded lake to provide habitat for fish. Though fishermen report record catches of catfish, crappie, and bluegill, it is the largemouth bass that make this park popular. The park's catch-and-release policy allows many people to catch a trophy-size bass. All bass must be released back into the lake alive, but regular limits govern the other fish. Because the lake is so small, only 50 boats are allowed on the water at a time. Boats are not allowed to create a wake, so they must travel at idle speed. People without boats can fish along the bank or from the lighted piers.

If fishing is not your forte, you can enjoy the forest of tall oaks, elms, walnuts, pecans, and eastern red cedars. Woodpeckers, warblers, vireos, and other woodland birds flit through the trees, and cormorants, herons, kingfishers, and waterfowl are attracted to the lake. The hiking trail provides a pleasant walk through a good example of the Post Oak Savanna vegetation region of Texas.

162. QUEEN CITY: CASS COUNTY PARK (MOORE'S LANDING)

Cass County. Wright Patman Lake. 1.6 miles north of Queens City on U.S. 59, north 4.4 miles on CR 3659, west/north 3 miles on CR 3558. Mailing address: 1293 County Rd. 3558, Queen City, Texas 75572. Phone: 903-796-9254. Camping: 131 pull-through and 15 back-in RV/tent sites with water and electricity, modern restrooms, showers, trailer dump station. Recreation: picnic shelters, playgrounds, boat ramp, lake swimming and water activities. Fees charged. Open all year.

163. QUITMAN: GOVERNOR HOGG SHRINE HISTORIC SITE

LOCATION

Wood County. Operated by the City of Quitman. 4 blocks south of the Wood County Courthouse on TX 37.

Mailing address: 101 Governor Hogg Pkwy., Quitman, Texas 75783. Phone: 903-763-4045. For camping reservations, call 903-763-0405.

FACILITIES

Camping: 13 back-in RV/tent sites with full hookups and cable TV, modern restrooms (no showers), trailer dump station. Fees charged.

Recreation: picnic areas, playgrounds, 2 group picnic pavilions, ½-mile nature trail with interpretive brochure, historic iron bridge, 3 museums with tours Monday through Saturday 10 a.m.–4 p.m., Sunday 1–5 p.m.

WEATHER

July high averages 86 degrees, January low 46 degrees.

HISTORY

This 27-acre park preserves three houses used by James Stephen Hogg, the first Texas-born governor of the state from 1891 to 1895. The three houses display items which belonged to the Hogg and Stinson families. The Stinson Home, where Governor Hogg's wedding was held, was built in 1869 and moved 13 miles to its present location in 1969. The Honeymoon Cottage was the first home of the Governor and Sallie Hogg (Sarah Ann Leannah Stinson). The Miss Ima Hogg Museum contains displays representative of the history of northeast Texas. The Old George Bridge, moved to the park in 1986, was built in the early 1900s.

164. RAY ROBERTS LAKE STATE PARK

LOCATION

Denton County.
Isla DuBois Unit: IH-35 north of Denton, east on FM 455 at Sanger, across dam to park entrance.
Mailing address: 100 PW 4137, Pilot Point, Texas 76258. Phone: 940-686-2148.
Johnson Branch Unit: IH-35 south of Valley View for 4 miles, east 7 miles on FM 3002.
Mailing address: 100 PW 4153, Valley View, TX 76272.
Phone: 940-637-2294. For all state park reservations, call the centralized reservations system, 512-389-8900, or www.ReserveAmerica.com online. Call the state park information number, 800-792-1112, for information and fee updates.

FACILITIES

Fees: entrance, facility, activity use; subject to change. WiFi available at Isla duBois Unit (user fee).

ISLA DUBOIS UNIT

Camping: 115 back-in RV/tent sites with water and electricity, 53 walk-in (¼–½ mile) tent sites with water, 2 walk-in (¼–½ mile) group campsites (capacity 24 each) with water nearby, 14 equestrian sites with hitching posts and water nearby, modern restrooms, showers, trailer dump station.

Recreation: picnic areas, playgrounds, group picnic pavilions, 16.5 miles of trails (12.5-mile multi-use, 4.5-mile paved ADA accessible hike/bike trail), swimming beach, lighted boat ramp, lighted fishing pier, fish-cleaning facilities, Texas State Park Store. The 8-mile Jordan Park multi-use (hike/bike/horse) trail begins in the Bluestem Grove Campground and goes to the Jordan Park Unit and beyond. The 3.5 mile Elm Fork multi-use trail connects with the 20-mile Lake Lewisville Greenbelt multi-use trail system.

JOHNSON BRANCH UNIT

Camping: 104 back-in RV/tent sites with water and electricity, 50 walk-in ¼ mile) tent sits with water nearby, group primitive area (200 acres, capacity 100, composting toilet, no water), 3 overflow camping areas, modern restrooms, showers, trailer dump station. The hike-in primitive camping area is closed until further notice.

Recreation: picnic areas, playgrounds, group picnic pavilions, fish-cleaning facilities, Texas State Park Store. Trails: 9 total miles, 5 miles for hiking and backpacking, 9 miles for hiking, 7 miles for mountain biking, 4 miles of paved trails ADA accessible, 5-mile, single-track mountain bike trail.

LODGES AND MARINAS

Lake Ray Roberts Marina at the Sanger Unit offers boat rental and storage, groceries and fishing supplies, and a restaurant (940-458-7343, www.rayrobertsmarina.com). The Lantana Lodge in the Jordan Park Unit offers dining and overnight accommodations with a ridgetop view of Ray Roberts Lake and 10 horse stalls for riders on the park's equestrian trails (940-686-0261, 866-LANTANA, www.lantanalodge.us).

WEATHER

July high averages 95 degrees, January low 30 degrees.

MAIN ATTRACTIONS

Twelve thousand acres of recreation land surround the 29,000-acre Ray Roberts Lake. The Isla DuBois Unit consists of 1,400 acres near the dam and has a 4-mile hike and bike trail and a 12-mile multi-use hike/bike/equestrian trail. The remainder of the public land around the lake is a wildlife management area with no camping. Several satellite parks on the lake have boat launches and restrooms.

Oaks and hickories of the Eastern Cross Timbers region forest the park and provide habitat for fox squirrels and other small mammals. Waterfowl and occasional bald eagles winter on the reservoir. Several archaeological sites have been recorded in the park.

The Ray Roberts Lake/Lake Lewisville Greenbelt Corridor: This 20-mile multi-use trail system (12 miles for equestrian and 10 for hike and bike use) begins at the Ray Roberts Dam and ends at the headwaters of Lake Lewisville. The trail follows the wooded banks of the Elm Fork Branch of the Trinity River with access the trail at trailheads located at FM 455, FM 428 and Hwy. 380. Canoe and kayak rentals are available by calling Greenbelt Canoe Rentals (817/228-9496). Note: the equestrian trail south of TX 428 to TX 380 is currently closed (north of HWY 428 remains open).

165. RUSK AND PALESTINE PARKS/ TEXAS STATE RAILROAD

LOCATION

Operated by American Heritage Railways. Palestine Unit: 46 miles south of Tyler on TX 155 to Palestine, 2 miles east on U.S. 84, Rusk Unit: 41 miles south of Tyler on U.S. 69 to Rusk, 3 miles west on U.S. 84.
Mailing address: PO Box 166, Rusk, TX 75785. Phone: reservations 903-683-5126, 888-987-2461. E-mail: train, reservations@ texasstaterr.com; campground, campgrounds@texasstaterr.com. Internet: www.texasstaterr.com.

FACILITIES

Rusk Unit: 55 back-in RV/tent sites with full hookups, 16 tent sites with water and electricity, group camp, modern restrooms with showers, trailer dump station. Fees charged. Picnic areas, playgrounds, group pavilion, screened group dining hall with a kitchen, 15-acre lake with fishing pier, tennis courts, .25-mile nature trail, old Rusk depot building. Depot concessions and gift shop.

Steam engines pull period cars on the 25-mile Texas State Railroad.

Palestine Unit: 12 RV/tent sites with water, restrooms (no showers), trailer dump station, picnic sites, playground, 2 group picnic pavilions, .5-mile nature trail. Fees charged. Depot concessions and gift shop.

WEATHER

July high averages 94 degrees, January low 35 degrees.

MAIN ATTRACTIONS

The Rusk and Palestine units of the state park are located at either end of the 25.5-mile-long Texas State Railroad in Cherokee and Anderson counties, respectively. Two large Victorian depots complete with antique furnishings set the mood for a ride into the past on the turn-of-the-century railroad, which features steam locomotives and period coaches.

The 4½-hour round trip takes passengers over wooden trestles and winding tracks through the heart of the East Texas Piney Woods. The railway winds past rural farmland through scenic woods, parallels sandy creeks, and crosses the Neches River. In the spring, the snow-white blossoms of the dogwoods and the colorful redbud trees add an extra dimension of beauty to the ride.

Round trips depart the Rusk and Palestine depots at 11 a.m. and return at 3:30 p.m. with a 1 ½ hour layover at the opposite depot for lunch. Normally, trains operate Friday–Sunday, but schedules may alter depending on holidays and special events. Check ahead and make advanced reservations if possible. Concessions and restrooms are available on each train and at the depots.

The Texas State Railroad was constructed in 1896 to haul wood and iron ore to a foundry near Rusk operated by the prison system. In 1906, the 5-mile line was extended another 5 miles and eventually connected Rusk and Palestine. It became a common carrier but was never profitable. From 1921 to 1969, the railroad was leased to private companies; it was transferred to the Parks and Wildlife Department in 1972.

Camping, fishing, and a short trail by the lake are available at both units. The campgrounds are adjacent to the highway, and road traffic is considerable. The lake is stocked with bass, catfish, and perch.

Jim Hogg State Historical Park, home of the first native-born Texas governor, is in Rusk. It is open for day-use only.

166. SABINE NATIONAL FOREST

LOCATION

East of Lufkin on the Texas-Louisiana border, on Toledo Bend Reservoir.
Mailing address: 5050 Hwy 21 East, Hemphill, TX 75948. Phone: 409-625-1940, 866-235-1750. Internet: www.fs.fed.us/r8/texas. Contact Sabine River Authority parks at 409-565-2273.

FACILITIES

Sabine National Forest has seven campgrounds with camping. Indian Mounds, Lakeview, Ragtown, Red Hills Lake, and Boles Field have sites with RV/tent pads. Willow Bend, with designated tent sites with water, and Haley's Ferry, with undesignated tent sites are primarily boat launching parks ramps and pit toilets. Primitive camping, at no charge, is allowed anywhere in the forest except when hunting or logging is in progress. All but Boles Field and Red Hills Lake are on Toledo Bend Reservoir. Fees charged.

RV sites are located at Indian Mounds, Lakeview, and Ragtown on Toledo Bend Reservoir, at Red Hills Lake, and at Boles Field in northern Sabine Forest. Willow Oak, with tent camping, is also on Toledo Bend Reservoir.

Primitive camping, at no charge, is allowed anywhere in the forest, except when hunting or logging is in progress. For maps and information on day-use areas, write the headquarters. Directions for reaching the parks are as follows.

Indian Mounds: Sabine River Authority, 6.6 miles east of Hemphill on FM 83, 4 miles south on FM 3382, 1 mile east on FSR 130.

Lakeview: Sabine River Authority, 9 miles south of Hemphill on TX 87, 5 miles east on FM 2928.

Campground	water	RV pads	flush toilets	chemical toilets	season	dump station	showers	boating	fishing	swimming	trails	electricity
Indian Mounds	•	•		•	Mar. 1–Oct. 15	•		•	•		•	
Lakeview	•	•		•	Mar. 1–Oct. 15			•	•		•	
Ragtown	•	•	•		all		•	•	•		•	
Red Hills Lake	•	•	•		all	•	•	•	•	•	•	•
Willow Oak	•			•	all			•	•			
Boles Field	•	•	•		all	•	•				•	•
Haley's Ferry				•	all			•	•			

Ragtown: Sabine River Authority, 13 miles southeast of Center on TX 87, 6.5 miles east on FM 139, 4 miles east on FM 3184, 1.5 miles east on FSR 132.

Red Hills Lake: Sabine National Forest, 10.5 miles north of Hemphill on TX 87, north of Milam.

Willow Oak: Sabine River Authority, 15 miles southeast of Hemphill on TX 87.

Boles Field: Sabine National Forest, 4 miles south of Center on TX 87 then 8 miles east on FM 2694.

Haley's Ferry: Sabine River Authority. From Center, TX 87 4 miles to Shelbyville, east on FM 2694 for 15 miles, south on FM 3172 for 1 mile, east onto FS 100A for 2 miles to park.

MAIN ATTRACTIONS

Sabine National Forest comprises 152,482 acres of pine-hardwood woodlands in Jasper, Sabine, San Augustine, Newton, and Shelby counties. Its eastern border is Toledo Bend Reservoir, with 186,500 surface acres and 650 miles of shoreline. The reservoir is a popular spot for fishing and boating.

All the parks in the forest, except Red Hills and Boles Field, are located on the reservoir. Red Hills is situated in the rolling hills, towering pines, and diverse hardwoods characteristic of the deep Piney Woods. There is a 17-acre lake with a sandy swimming beach, a bathhouse, and an interesting but poorly marked hiking trail. In the early spring, trilliums and other woodland flowers bloom on the rich forest floor. Only boats without motors are allowed on Red Hills Lake.

The 28-mile Trail Between the Lakes hiking trail connects Sam Rayborn Reservoir and Toledo Bend Reservoir. The trailhead for the Toledo Bend terminus is located at Lakeview Park.

167. SAM HOUSTON NATIONAL FOREST

LOCATION

40 miles north of Houston via IH-45 or U.S. 59.
Mailing address: 394 FM 1375 W, New Waverly, TX 77358. Phone:
936-344-6205, 888-361-6908. Internet: www.fs.fed.us/r8/texas.

FACILITIES

The whole forest is open for free primitive camping, except during hunting season and logging operations. Contact the headquarters for information on hunting camps.

Individual campsites cannot be reserved; group campgrounds, available at Double Lake, may be reserved. Swimming fee at Double Lake. Write the headquarters for maps and for information on day-use areas. The following parks have camping facilities. Fees charged.

Cagle Recreation Area: from New Waverly 5 miles west on FM 1375 to park on Lake Conroe.

Double Lake: 2 miles west of Coldspring on TX 150, south on FM 2025, east on FSR 210.

Kelley Pond: 11 miles west of New Waverly on FM 1375, south on FSR 204.

Stubblefield Lake: 11 miles west of New Waverly on FM 1375, 3 miles north on FSR 215.

MAIN ATTRACTIONS

Sam Houston National Forest consists of 160,401 acres in Montgomery, San Jacinto, and Walker counties. Lake Conroe, with 18,000 surface acres, offers swimming, fishing, and water sports. Within the forest, areas are designated specifically for off-road vehicles and for hiking.

Big Creek Scenic Area: west of Shepherd on TX 150, is a beautiful day-use area on the western edge of the Big Thicket. The 1,130 acres include rolling hills of mixed woodlands as well as spring-fed streams and rich bottomlands. There are several loop trails in the unit, some connecting with the Lone Star Hiking Trail and Double Lake. In contrast with the rest of the national forests in Texas, the Big Creek Scenic Area is man-

Campground	water	fee area	flush toilets	season	showers	concessions	boating	fishing	swimming	trails
Double Lake	•	•	•	all	•	•	•	•	•	•
Kelley Pond				all						•
Stubblefield Lake	•	•	•	all	•		•	•		•
Cagle	•	•	•	all	•	•	•	•	•	•

aged to preserve the wilderness setting—no logging is permitted. There are no camping or picnicking facilities, and there is no water.

Double Lake Recreation Area: located on a 20-acre lake surrounded by dense, picturesque forest. Picnicking, swimming, fishing, canoeing, and paddle-boating are available. A picnic pavilion can be reserved. A self-guided nature trail, three-quarters of a mile long, leads hikers through the towering pines and hardwoods typical of the East Texas forest, and a 5-mile trail connects Double Lake with the Big Creek Scenic Area. Throughout the summer, ranger programs and a small concession are available.

Kelley Pond Campground: provides no water; it has one chemical toilet. It is in a trail-bike area used extensively by bikers.

Stubblefield Lake Campground: on a shallow inlet of Lake Conroe, offers fishing and hiking through pine-palmetto woodlands. The 30 campsites have a pull-in area for RVs and a tent pad, picnic tables, grills, and water nearby, but no hookups. Modern restrooms have hot showers. A 1.1-mile interpretive trail loops through the woods from the trailhead north of Stubblefield Lake Campground at Forest Road 215. Interpretive signs and a brochure explain features of the forest ecosystem.

Cagle Recreation Area: on Lake Conroe provides 48 back-in RV/tent sites with full hookups, modern restrooms, hot showers, swimming, fishing, boat launch, picnic area, 85 miles of multi-use trails (hike, bike, equestrian, ORV), access to the Lone Star Hiking Trail.

MULTI-USE TRAILS

The 140-mile Lone Star Hiking Trail winds through Sam Houston National Forest. Its western trailhead is on FM 149 west of Lake Conroe. The trail passes through Kelley Pond and Stubblefield Lake campgrounds, then travels north of Huntsville State Park. It continues eastward to Double Lake and Big Creek Scenic Area; the eastern terminus is north of Cleveland on FM 1725. The trail is restricted to foot travel; however, it is much abused by trail bikers.

The five loops of the trail, along with the main trail, offer a variety of day hikes or overnight backpacking trips. Primitive campgrounds are located along the trail, but potable water is available only at Double Lake and Stubblefield Parks. For easy access, trailheads and parking areas are located throughout the trail system. Information is posted at bulletin boards at the trailheads, and maps with detailed information are available at the Coldspring and New Waverly offices.

The Multi-Use Trail system consists of 85 miles of marked trails for dirt bikes, mountain bikes, and horses. The trail, marked with 4 3 4-inch tags with red arrows, is divided into two separate loop systems, each with a trailhead and parking area. Trail maps and brochures are available at the Sam Houston District Office. Unfortunately, bikers have scarred portions of the trails with unsightly ruts and deep mud holes. The forest district has too few rangers to adequately enforce the regulations controlling the use of off-road vehicles.

168. SAN ANGELO: SPRING CREEK MARINA AND RV PARK

Tom Green County. 6 miles southwest of San Angelo on FM 584 to Fisherman's Road, then west 1.5 miles; on Lake Nasworthy. Mailing address: 45 Fisherman's Road, San Angelo, TX 76904. Phone: 325-944-3850, 800-500-7901. E-mail: springcreek@springcreekmarina-rv.com. Internet: www.springcreekmarina-rv.com. Camping: 60 pull-through RV/tent sites with full hookups, cable TV, free WiFi, primitive tent camping, 3 cabins, laundry, restrooms with showers, store. Fees charged, reservations accepted, 10:30 p.m. curfew. Recreation: lake swimming, fishing, boating (30 mph speed limit), boat rentals, nature trails.

SAN ANGELO: STATE PARK

LOCATION

Tom Green County. On Lake O.C. Fisher. From San Angelo to south entrance, take U.S. 67 west 4 miles to FM 2288, then north to entrance. To reach the north entrance from San Angelo, take U.S. 87 north to FM 2288, then west 1.4 miles.
Mailing address: 3900-2 Mercedes, San Angelo, Texas 76901-2630. Phone: gatehouse 325-949-8935, HQ 325-949-4757. E-mail: sasp@tpwd.state.tx.us. For all state park reservations, call the centralized reservations system, 512-389-8900, or

www.ReserveAmerica.com online. Call the state park information number, 800-792-1112, for information and fee updates.

FACILITIES

Fees: entrance, facility, activity use; subject to change.

Camping: 3 campgrounds on the lake's south shore and 3 north of lake. 60 back-in RV/tent sites with water and electricity, 63 sites with no hookups, 21 equestrian sites with water and electricity (10 with pens), 6 mini-cabins (capacity 6) with ac/heat and outside RV hookups, 2 group camps, primitive walk-in tent camps (400 yards). Modern restrooms, showers, trailer dump station. Some Red Concho and North Concho Equestrian Area campsites and restrooms closed seasonally. Gate hours 8 a.m. to 8–10 p.m. depending on season.

Recreation: picnic area, swimming, fishing, two group pavilions; 50 miles of multi-use trails for hiking, mountain biking, and equestrian use, 20 miles of backpacking trails, boat ramps, radio-controlled airplane area.

Tours: Park rangers offer regularly scheduled tours, and special tours for 10 or more visitors, to the 250-million-year-old Permian age animal tracks and Indian petroglyphs within the park. Other programs include nature hikes, tours to the bison and longhorn herds, equestrian tours, and stargazing.

WEATHER

July high averages 97 degrees, January low 32 degrees.

MAIN ATTRACTION

Lake O.C. Fisher, an impoundment of the North Concho River, covers 5,440 acres and has 27 miles of shoreline. The park preserves 7,700 undeveloped acres around the lake. The park is one of only three or four places in the world with well-preserved tracks of Late Permian Age animals from 280 million years ago. The tracks of 28 different animals that predate dinosaurs by 90 million years occur in the bedrock. Park rangers conduct guided tours to Little Foot Draw to see the tracks imprinted in the reddish sandstone and mudstone.

The discovery of pottery shards, spear points, and the bones of bison, antelope and deer indicate that Native Americans frequented the Concho River valley. Paleo-Indians lived throughout west Texas and hunted Ice Age mammals as long as 18,000 years ago. Spanish explorers during the 16th and 17th centuries encountered Jumano Indians who used the Concho River as a trade route to Indian groups in central and eastern Texas. Park ranger tours visit an area with Indian rock etchings that date back to A.D. 600.

PLANTS AND ANIMALS

Situated near the juncture of the Texas High Plains, Rolling Plains, Trans-Pecos, and Hill Country, the park harbors a diverse collection of plants and animals. More than 50 species of mammals and 350 species of birds, including many migrating waterfowl, can be seen during the year. The horned lizard, federally listed as threatened due to overcollecting and habitat loss, lives in rocky hills of the park. Deer and turkey are hunted in the park.

The park is also home of a portion of the official state longhorn and bison herds. The state longhorn herd, with portions in several western state parks, began as an effort by Texan historian J. Frank Dobie to preserve the rapidly disappearing icon of the trail drive era. Dobie searched the West for remaining animals with the ancestral characteristics of the longhorn and assembled a herd. The herd grew and sired the many longhorns on private ranches across the U.S. and eventually was acquired by the Texas Parks and Wildlife Department.

The department also acquired a genetically pure herd of Southern Plains Bison from the J. A. Ranch in the Panhandle to keep at Caprock Canyon and other state parks. After near extinction and 100 years of absence from their ancestral homelands, bison and longhorns once again graze the rolling grasslands of San Angelo State Park.

The Concho River derived its name from the Spanish word concho, meaning shell. The river is famous for its large blue mussels and the iridescent pearls they produce.

169. SAN ANTONIO: BRAUNIG LAKE PARK

Bexar County. Exit 130 off IH-37, south of San Antonio. San Antonio River Authority. Mailing address: 17500 Dunop Rd., San Antonio, Texas 78223. Phone: park store 210-302-4270, SARA 210-227-1373. Internet: www.sara-tx.org/site/parks/braunig.php. *Camping:* numerous primitive campsites along shaded shoreline with tables, no water, flush toilets. Recreation: fishing from bank, pier, boats, boat ramp, fish-cleaning station, bird-watching. Entrance and camping fees charged. Camping limited to 7 days per month. Built as a cooling lake for a power plant, the lake offers good fishing for largemouth and striped bass, red drum, crappie, and catfish. Numerous birds are attracted to the lake, including egrets, cormorants, pelicans, osprey, ducks, and other waterfowl. Fees charged, open all year, gates open 6 a.m. to 10 p.m.

SAN ANTONIO: CALAVERAS LAKE PARK

Bexar County. South of San Antonio on U.S. 181, 2 miles east on FM 1604. San Antonio River Authority. Mailing address: 12991 Bernhardt

Rd., San Antonio, Texas 78220. Phone: park store 210-302-4280, SARA 210-227-1373. Internet: www.sara-tx.org/site/parks/calaveras.php Camping: primitive campsites with tables and water nearby, flush toilets. Recreation: fishing for bass, catfish, and red drum; lighted pier, fish-cleaning station, boat ramp, water-skiing, fishing boat rental, concession stand. Open all year. Entrance and camping fees charged. Gates open 6 a.m. to 10 p.m.

170. SEA RIM STATE PARK

LOCATION

Jefferson County. 24 miles southwest of Port Arthur on TX 87.
Note that TX 87 is closed from Sea Rim to High Island.
Mailing address: PO Box 356, Sabine Pass, TX 77655. Phone: 409-971-2559. For state park reservations, call 512-389-8900.

FACILITIES

Fees: entrance, facility, activity use; subject to change.

Note: The park closed after severe damage from Hurricane Rita (2006), and was scheduled to reopen late 2008. Then Hurricane Ike hit in September, 2008. Repairs will probably be ongoing for some time. As of spring 2009, no opening date was scheduled. Call for the latest status.

Camping: primitive camping on beach, primitive camping on platforms in marsh accessible by boat, 20 RV sites with water and electricity, 10 tent sites with water, modern restrooms with showers, trailer dump station. Fees charged.

Recreation: picnicking, nature trail with trail-guide booklet, interpretive exhibits, observation blinds accessible by boat, swimming in the Gulf of Mexico, fishing and boating in the Gulf and marsh, hunting waterfowl in designated areas of the Marshlands Unit, interpretive air boat tours of marshes in spring, summer, and fall, Texas State Park Store.

WEATHER

July high averages 93 degrees, January low 42 degrees.

MAIN ATTRACTIONS

With 4,141 acres of marshland and 5.2 miles of Gulf beach shoreline, Sea Rim State Park provides a variety of recreational opportunities for fishermen, hunters, boaters, and nature enthusiasts. The park's gently sloping beaches are a haven for lovers of sun, sand, and surf. One of the outstanding features of the park is the 3,640-foot-long elevated boardwalk, the Gambusia Trail, which juts into the marsh. A pamphlet describes the significance of the coastal wetlands, their vital importance to wildlife, and some of the plants and animals commonly seen along the boardwalk.

The park is separated into two distinct areas by TX 87. On the coastal side is the D. Roy Harrington Beach Unit, site of the park headquarters, campgrounds, marsh boardwalk, and 5.2 miles of beaches. The Marshlands Unit, comprising the major portion of the park, is accessible only by boat. There are four camping platforms and four wildlife observation blinds along the waterways dissecting the salt marsh.

Sea Rim is located on the Greater Texas Coastal Birding Trail, a series of major bird-watching locations along the coast from Beaumont to Brownsville. The park and nearby National Wildlife Refuges (Texas Point and McFadden), as well as local woodlands, serve as important winter and spring migration points for birds in the Central Flyway. During spring migration, many species of warblers, swallows, vireos, grosbeaks, buntings, and flycatchers make first landfall in the area after flying across the Gulf from Mexico. Tens of thousands of waterfowl overwinter in the nearby marshes.

Shells line the beach in the sandy sections of Sea Rim.

PLANTS AND ANIMALS

Sea Rim State Park preserves coastal marshlands and lakes, estuaries and mud flats, and the unique sea rim marsh from which the park derives its name. Silt and mud flowing from the Sabine River are deposited by Gulf currents onto the northernmost 2.2 miles of beach in the park. Marsh grasses extend into the surf zone, forming the sea rim marsh—an excellent habitat for many types of wildlife. The shoreline is swept by the tides, creating fertile nursery grounds for marine life. This type of habitat is essential for shrimp, blue crabs, redfish, menhaden, and other crustacean and fish species. Estuarine environments such as these are of vital importance to the overall fishing economy of the Texas coast.

The abundant microscopic zooplankton and decomposing organic matter in the marsh provide food for a complex web of life. Wading birds stalk across the marsh, hunting for small fish, and probe for tiny organisms in the mud flats. Herons and egrets are common, as are clapper rails, gulls, and mottled ducks. The dense stands of marsh grass provide an important nesting habitat for many birds and mammals.

More than 289 species of birds have been recorded in the park. The Texas coastal wetlands are the wintering grounds for 45 percent of the ducks and 90 percent of the geese along the Central Flyway. The shallow lakes, mud flats, marshlands, canebrakes, scattered shrubs, and isolated trees provide migrating birds a welcome respite from their long flight across the Gulf.

Mink are infrequently seen along the boardwalk, and alligators and otters inhabit the marshlands. Nutrias, rabbits, skunks, raccoons, and opossums are year-round residents of the park, as are mosquitoes. Infestations of those pesky insects occur periodically, making repellent and a bug-proof sleeping shelter absolute necessities.

HISTORY

The coastal marshlands have been of significant importance through the ages. Shell mounds left by prehistoric Indians may represent the ancestors of the Atakapa Indians, who lived in areas from Louisiana to Galveston before they were eliminated there in the 1800s. Pirates frequented the upper Texas coast in the early 1800s, including the colorful Jean Lafitte, who founded Galveston.

171. SEMINOLE CANYON STATE PARK AND HISTORIC SITE

LOCATION

Val Verde County. 42 miles northwest of Del Rio on U.S. 90, east of the Pecos River.

Mailing address: Box 820, Comstock, Texas 78837. Phone: 432-292-4464. For state park reservations, call 512-389-8900.

FACILITIES

Fees: entrance, facility, activity use; subject to change. WiFi available (user fee).

Camping: 8 campsites with water only, 23 campsites with water and electricity, modern restrooms with showers, trailer dump station. Fees charged.

Recreation: picnic areas, playgrounds, 8 miles of multi-use trails for hiking and mountain biking, 0.6-mile interpretive trail, canyon tours of pictographs, interpretive exhibits, Texas State Park Store.

WEATHER

July high averages 89 degrees, January low 46 degrees.

MAIN ATTRACTIONS

Seminole Canyon is in an area of West Texas characterized by rugged countryside, deep canyons, and sparse vegetation. In many of the canyons, millions of years of erosion have created massive rock overhangs that were used by Indians for shelter 9,000 to 12,000 years ago. The outstanding feature of the park is the impressive pictographs, paintings thousands of years old, found on the canyon walls.

The interpretive center has informative and dramatic displays describing the cultural history of the area. Beautiful dioramas and full-size models depict the lifestyles of the inhabitants from perhaps 12,000 years ago through the ranching and railroad era of the last century. The history of the first trans-Texas railroad, which passed through the park and connected West Texas both culturally and economically with the rest of the state, is presented with period photographs and artifacts. The artwork and historical interpretation in the center are the best of any state park in Texas.

HIKING, TOURS

Some of the most spectacular pictographs in the canyon are in Fate Bell Shelter immediately below the interpretive center. Access to that historic artwork is limited to tours led Wednesday through Sunday at 10 a.m. and 3 p.m. (10 a.m. only June 1 through August 31). The trail is slightly over a mile long each way and is fairly steep. In addition to the tours, visitors can walk along a hiking trail leading to a scenic overlook 200 feet above the Rio Grande. That trail, 3.5 miles each way, is on level ground above the canyon. The park has a total of 8 miles of multi-use hike/bike trails and a .6 mile nature/interpretive trail.

PLANTS AND ANIMALS

Seminole Canyon lies close to the juncture of three major vegetation zones in Texas: the Trans-Pecos Chihuahuan Desert province, the Edwards Plateau oak-juniper association, and the South Texas brush country. In addition, the nearby 67,000-acre Amistad Reservoir creates an unusually humid habitat in an otherwise arid part of Texas. The combination of vegetation from those different regions provides a diversity of plant and animal life in the park.

Unusual birds of the Mexican borderland occur in the park, including the zone-tailed hawk, green kingfisher, black phoebe, and varied bunting. Scaled quail, verdins, pyrrhuloxias, and black-chinned sparrows are commonly seen grassland species. Sandpipers, other shorebirds, herons, and ducks frequent the backwaters of the lake in the canyons along the Rio Grande.

HISTORY

Seminole Canyon and Val Verde County are rich in history, with human artifacts dating back possibly 12,000 years. Some of the oldest pictographs in the United States are located in the park. The pictures, dating from historical times to approximately 2,000 to 8,000 years ago, were painted on the protected canyon walls using pigments mixed with animal fat. White, black, red, yellow, and orange pigments were made from complex mixtures of clay and minerals.

There are numerous shelters with pictographs in the area, some with murals up to a hundred feet long. The interpretation of the rock art can only be surmised from known meanings of similar motifs from contemporary Indians. Pictographs dating from various periods throughout the past several thousand years can be classified according to subject matter and style; Forrest Kirkland and W.W. Newcomb's *The Rock Art of Texas Indians* depicts the many types. The rock shelters also contain remnants of sandals, clothes, and baskets woven from yucca and sotol. Similar articles are still being made in Mexico today.

The canyon probably derived its name from displaced bands of Seminole Indians from Florida, who survived briefly in the arid terrain, or from the Seminole-Negroes who settled at Eagle Pass after 1870. Scouts from that group assisted in the government campaign to eradicate the Plains Indians in West Texas from 1874 to 1875.

In 1882, the Southern Pacific Railroad reached the area of the park. The route connecting San Antonio to El Paso had to cross the deep Pecos River gorge, a task that required blasting two 1,500-foot tunnels to reach the river level. The bridge was built at the confluence of the Rio Grande and the Pecos River, and the last spike completing the route was driven in 1883, three miles west of the Pecos River.

Frontier life west of the Pecos is epitomized by the Judge Roy Bean Visitor Center, 20 miles away in Langtry. The original Jersey Lilly Saloon, named for the actress Lilly Langtry, a beautiful cactus garden, and a tourist center with maps and information are open daily.

172. SILVERTON: LAKE MACKENZIE PARK

Mackenzie Municipal Water Authority. Briscoe and Swisher counties. 50 miles south of Amarillo on IH-27 to Tulia, 24 miles east on TX 86, 7 miles north on TX 207, in Tule Canyon. Mailing address: Route 1, Box 14, Silverton, Texas 79257. Phone: 806-633-4318. Internet: www.lakemackenzie.com. Camping: 25 RV/tent sites with water and electricity, 38 sites with shaded table and water nearby, restrooms, showers, trailer dump station. Mackenzie Bait & Tackle Marina rents a cabin with 3 beds, ac, mini-kitchen, outside grill, no towels provided (806-633-4335 for reservations). Fees charged. Recreation: picnic areas, hiking trails, swimming in lake, water-skiing, fishing, boat ramps, 15-mile ATV trail, pavilion, store. Open all year. Poor facilities for camping.

173. SONORA: CAVERNS OF SONORA

LOCATION

Sutton County. 10 miles west of Sonora on IH-10, 6 miles south on RR 1989.
Mailing address: Box 1196, Sonora, Texas 76950.Phone: 325-387-3105. E-mail: cavernsofsonora@cavernsofsonora.com. Internet: www.cavernsofsonora.com.

FACILITIES

Camping: 48 RV/tent sites with water and electricity, modern restrooms, showers, store, snack bar. Open all year, 24 hours. Fees charged.

Recreation: tours of commercially operated cave with spectacular formations, .5-mile nature trail, picnicking.

MAIN ATTRACTIONS

The Caverns of Sonora have some of the most beautiful formations of any cave in Texas, or in the United States. A past president of the National Speleological Society said that its beauty couldn't be exaggerated, even by Texans. The tour leads through chambers and passageways lined with soda straws, cave coral, popcorn, and cave crystals, including one

that looks like a butterfly. The signature butterfly formation was vandal-
ized in 2006 and the park is offering a $20,000 reward for information
leading to the recovery of the broken piece (see website).

Since the cave is a constant 71 degrees with 98 percent humidity (feels
like 85 degrees), no jackets are necessary. The 2-mile tour takes 1 hour
45 minutes and covers about 360 stair steps. Cameras welcomed but no
purses, packs, food, tobacco products, or pets. The cave provides a free
kennel. Tours daily except Christmas day: Tuesday after Labor Day to
February 29, 9 a.m. to 5 p.m. March 1 to Labor Day, 8 a.m. to 6 p.m.

174. SOUTH LLANO RIVER STATE PARK

LOCATION

Kimble County. 4 miles south of Junction on U.S. 377.
Mailing address: 1927 Park Road 73, Junction, Texas 76849-9502.
Phone: 325-446-3994. For all state park reservations, call the
centralized reservations system, 512-389-8900, or
www.ReserveAmerica.com online. Call the state park information
number, 800-792-1112, for information and fee updates.

FACILITIES

Fees: entrance, facility, activity use; subject to change.

Camping: 57 campsites with water and electricity, 12 walk-in tent sites
(30–70 yards), restrooms, showers, trailer dump station; primitive camping area for backpacking. Fees charged.

Recreation: picnicking, hiking, river activities, tubing, canoeing, fishing,
bird-watching, backpacking, mountain biking, Texas State Park Store.

WEATHER

July high averages 94 degrees, January low averages 32 degrees.

MAIN ATTRACTIONS

This 2,700-acre park on the south shore of the Llano River includes 2
miles of riverfront. About 440 acres of the 500-acre park are bottomland
heavily wooded with pecan trees. Hundreds of turkeys roost in the trees in
the winter and feast on the pecans. Access to the roosting area, which includes much of the park, will be limited while the turkeys are present from
October to March. The endangered black-capped vireo also nests in the
park in the spring. The park contains 18 miles of hiking and biking trails,
20 wildlife observation blinds, and an oxbow lake for fishing. Portions of

the adjacent 2,610-acre Walter Buck Wildlife Management Area are open for hiking and biking, except during hunting seasons.

During the spring and summer, be sure and visit the park's easily-accessible bird blinds. With running water and stocked with feed (2 gallons seed/day each), they make full-frame, cover-quality photography of the region's colorful specialty birds as easy as clicking your shutter. Painted buntings, vermillion flycatchers, yellow-breasted chats, summer tanagers, and golden-bellied woodpeckers are a few of the rainbow-colored residents attracted to the buffet. Also, hundreds of black-chinned hummingbirds buzz around the feeders on the porch of the park store.

175. SOUTH PADRE ISLAND PARKS: ISLA BLANCA RV PARK

Cameron County. Several blocks south of the causeway on South Padre Island. Mailing address: Box 2106, South Padre Island, Texas 78597. Phone: 956-761-5493. E-mail: JERoberts@co.cameron.tx.us. Internet: www.co.cameron.tx.us/park/blanca.htm. *Camping*: 468 RV sites with water, electricity, and sewage hookups; 71 with water and electricity; 8 cabanas with ac, kitchen, bunk beds, single bed (bring bed linens, towels); tent camping in open area, flush toilets, showers, trailer dump station. Reservations accepted by mail only. Fees charged. *Recreation*: swimming, fishing, boating, jetty pier, beach front pavilions. Open all year. Crowded RV park. The Port Isabel lighthouse, on the mainland, is open for tours.

SOUTH PADRE ISLAND: ANDY BOWIE PARK

Cameron County. From South Padre Island north on Park Road 100 to the South Padre Island Convention Center. Mailing address: Park Road 100 South Padre Island, TX 78597. Phone: 956-761-3704. Internet: www.co.cameron.tx.us/park/bowie.htm. Camping: 18 RV sites with full hookups, modern restrooms, showers, 2 beachfront picnic pavilions, playground, concessions, 20 miles beach access for driving, bayside access for fishing, windsurfing. Adjacent to the Laguna Madre Nature Trail, a World Birding Center site. Fees charged, open all year.

SOUTH PADRE ISLAND: EDWIN K. ATWOOD PARK

Cameron County. 1.4 miles north of Andy Bowie Park, day-use only, beach access for driving, a beachfront picnic pavilion, concessions. Fee charged.

176. STEPHEN F. AUSTIN STATE PARK AND SAN FELIPE STATE HISTORIC SITE

LOCATION

Austin County. 30 miles west of Houston on IH-10 to San Felipe exit, 7 miles north on FM 1458 to PR 38.
Mailing address: Box 125, San Felipe, Texas 77473. Phone: 979-885-3613. For all state park reservations, call the centralized reservations system, 512-389-8900, or www.ReserveAmerica.com online. Call the state park information number, 800-792-1112, for information and fee updates.

FACILITIES

Fees: entrance, facility, activity use; subject to change.

Camping: 40 pull-through RV/tent sites with full hookups, 38 sites with water, 20 screened shelters, group recreation hall (capacity 60) with tent camping, modern restrooms, showers, trailer dump station.

Recreation: picnic areas and playgrounds, 5-mile hiking trail and .25-mile nature/interpretive trail, historic structures, swimming pool (summer only), fishing in the Brazos River, 18-hole golf course, group dining hall (capacity 50) with ac and full kitchen, group open-air picnic pavilion (capacity 30) with water and electricity, park store.

WEATHER

July high averages 94 degrees, January low 43 degrees.

MAIN ATTRACTIONS

Stephen F. Austin State Park, named after the "Father of Texas," is located on a scenic bend of the Brazos River. The densely wooded park is ideal for a leisurely holiday, since a variety of recreational activities are available. The adjacent San Felipe State Historic Site, operated by the Texas Historical Commission, preserves the historic San Felipe de Austin. Replicas of Austin's log cabin and of a general store (now housing a museum, a statue of Austin, and other memorabilia) mark the original town site and ferry crossing.

Situated in the rich bottomland of the Brazos River, the 664-acre park provides an excellent environment for a wide variety of wildlife. Deer, raccoons, skunks, armadillos, opossums, foxes, and squirrels live in the woodlands, as do many birds. Large elms, sycamores, pecans, hackberries, and a number of oak species provide food and shelter for wildlife and a shady, tranquil setting for humans.

HISTORY

The first Anglo colonists in Texas established their headquarters at San Felipe de Austin in 1823. Stephen Austin brought several hundred families to colonize Texas on acreage granted him by the Mexican government. San Felipe was the social, economic, and political center of the colony until the Revolution in 1836. It was the location of the conventions of 1832 and 1833 and of the Consultation of 1835, which led to the Revolution.

During the Revolution, the provisional government was centered in San Felipe. The first Texas newspaper was published in the town, and the Texas Rangers were organized there. The original town, known as the Cradle of Texas Liberty, was burned by its inhabitants when they fled the advancing Mexican army.

177. STEPHENVILLE CITY PARK

Erath County. 70 miles southwest of Fort Worth on U.S. 377 to Stephenville, 2 blocks north on TX 108. Mailing address: 378 W. Long St., Stephenville, Texas 76401. Phone: 254-918-1260. Camping: 10 RV campsites with water and electricity, 50 primitive campsites, flush toilets, showers, trailer dump station. Fees charged. Recreation: picnic areas and playgrounds, nature trail, bicycle paths, swimming pool, fishing in the Bosque River, tennis courts, softball field, pavilion, recreation hall. Open all year.

178. SWEETWATER: LAKE SWEETWATER RECREATION AREA

Nolan County. 40 miles west of Abilene on IH-20 to FM 1856, 7 miles south to lake. Mailing address: 200 FM 2035, Sweetwater, TX 79556. Phone: 325-235-8816. Camping: 20 back-in or pull-through RV/tent sites with water and electricity, tent camping area (no tables, water), modern restroom, trailer dump station. Fees charged, reservations accepted, open all year. Recreation: picnic areas and playgrounds, swimming beach, fishing, boat ramp, 18-hole golf course, store.

179. TYLER STATE PARK

LOCATION

Smith County. 8 miles north of Tyler on FM 14.
Mailing address: 789 Park Rd. 16, Tyler, Texas 75706-9141. Phone: 903-597-5338. For all state park reservations, call the centralized

reservations system, 512-389-8900, or www.ReserveAmerica.com online. Call the state park information number, 800-792-1112, for information and fee updates.

FACILITIES

Fees: entrance, facility, activity use; subject to change.

Camping: 57 pull-through RV-only sites with full hookups, 20 pull-through RV/tent sites with water and electricity, 37 tent sites with water, RV rally camp with 30 sites with water and electricity, 35 screened shelters, modern restrooms, showers, trailer dump station.

Recreation: picnic areas, playgrounds, group pavilions, group dining hall, 2.5-mile hiking trail, 13-mile mountain bike trail, .75-mile nature trail, laundry tub, boat ramp and dock, and a seasonal grocery store that rents canoes, paddle boats, kayaks, and fishing boats. Texas Park Store.

WEATHER

July high averages 97 degrees, January low 32 degrees.

MAIN ATTRACTIONS

The beauty of the aromatic East Texas Piney Woods in this 985-acre park is accented by a picturesque 65-acre lake. Stocked with channel catfish and black bass, the lake is circled on one side by a hiking trail. Bicyclists will enjoy the undulating road through the park.

Nearby Tyler is famous for its beautiful roses and azaleas. The town hosts the annual Azalea and Spring Flower Trail, a route through the most colorful and historic sections of Tyler, during the last week in March. The Texas Rose Festival is scheduled in mid-October.

Another area attraction, the Governor Hogg Shrine State Historical Park, a day-use area, is in Quitman, 37 miles north of Tyler.

HIKING/BIKING

The Whispering Pines Nature Trail winds through the forest of tall pines between the park headquarters and the group camping area. A pamphlet identifies many of the plants and describes the different vegetation communities along the trail. Mountain bikers can enjoy 13 miles of forested trails.

PLANTS AND ANIMALS

Tyler State Park preserves a good example of the mixed hardwood-pine forest that once covered East Texas. The fast-draining ridgetops and the moist bottomlands are covered with a wide variety of trees, shrubs, and flowers. The drier uplands are forested with loblolly and shortleaf pines, hickories, post and blackjack oaks, and eastern red cedars, while sweetgums, elms, red oaks, and American holly trees dominate the lowlands.

A number of smaller trees and shrubs grow in the shaded forest. Sassafras with its three shapes of leaves, rusty blackhaw, sumac, farkleberry, and other shade-tolerant plants form a diverse understory of vegetation.

In the spring, dogwood and redbud trees burst into bloom, patches of mayapples cover the woodland floor and perfume the air, and delicate shield ferns grow along the creek banks. The red flowers of the trumpet honeysuckle vine dangle from pine trees, complementing the snow-white flowers of the dogwoods.

The park woods are active with gray squirrels feeding on acorns and birds singing high in the trees. After sunset, raccoons and opossums patrol the campground, investigating trash cans, and armadillos root through the leaves covering the forest floor.

180. VICTORIA: COLETO CREEK PARK AND RESERVOIR

Guadalupe-Blanco River Authority. Goliad County. 15 miles southwest of Victoria on U.S. 59. 190 acres on 3,100-acre Coleto Creek Reservoir. Mailing address: P.O. Box 68, Fannin, Texas 77960. Phone: 361-575-6366. Camping: 58 campsites with water and electricity, flush toilets, showers, trailer dump station. Four cabins with a/c, heat. Reservations accepted. Fees charged. Recreation: picnic areas, half-mile nature trail, swimming in reservoir, fishing, 200-foot lighted pier, water-skiing, boat ramp, pavilion. Open all year. Good facilities. The Fannin Battlegrounds are 5 miles southwest on U.S. 59.

VICTORIA RV PARK

City Parks Department: Victoria County. 2200 Vine Street, adjacent to Riverside Park; from U.S. 87, take Red River Street approximately 0.2 mile west to intersection of Vine Street. Mailing address: Box 1758, Victoria, Texas 77902. Phone: 361-572-2767. *Camping:* 10 acres; 18 sites with water, electricity, sewage; dump station; water available but no restrooms or tables in camping area. Fees charged, no reservations. Open all year. *Recreation:* adjacent to Riverside Park with sports field, golf, playgrounds, hike and bike trails, fishing in Guadalupe River, and the Texas Zoo, an outstanding zoo featuring animals indigenous to Texas.

181. VIDOR: CLAIBORNE WEST PARK

Orange County. 11 miles east of Beaumont on IH-10, eastern city limits of Vidor. 453 acres of woodlands, swamps, and meadows. Mailing address: 4105 North St., Vidor, Texas 77662. Phone: 409-745-2255. Camping: 10 designated campsites with water, flush toilets. Reservations accepted. Fees charged. Recreation: picnic areas and playgrounds, 5 miles of nature trails, fishing, canoeing on Cow Bayou, softball field, amphitheater for public use, group picnic shelters, 1.5-mile mountain bike trail, horseshoes, disk golf. Open all year. The combination of diverse facilities, excellent playgrounds, and a pleasant natural environment makes this one of the better county parks in Texas. The park is a wildlife and bird sanctuary and part of The Great Texas Coastal Birding Trail.

182. VILLAGE CREEK STATE PARK

LOCATION

Hardin County. In Lumberton turn east off U.S. 96 on Alma Dr. Mailing address: PO Box 8565, Lumberton, TX 77657. For all state park reservations, call the centralized reservations system, 512-389-8900, or www.ReserveAmerica.com online. Call the state park information number, 800-792-1112, for information and fee updates.

Canoers love to paddle the winding Village Creek.

FACILITIES

Fees: entrance, facility, activity use; subject to change.

Camping: 25 back-in RV/tent sites with water and electricity, 16 walk-in (50–150 yards) tent sites with water nearby, overflow walk-in (25 yards) tent sites with water nearby, group walk-in (25 yards) tent site (no water), cabin (8 people, 7 beds, ac/heat, kitchen, no linens or utensils), modern restrooms, showers, trailer dump station.

Recreation: picnicking, canoeing, hiking, swimming on sandbar, bike trails, group facility with kitchen.

WEATHER

July high averages 93 degrees, January low 38 degrees.

MAIN ATTRACTIONS

The scenic Village Creek winds through 2 miles of this 1,004-acre park. Only 44 acres are developed, leaving the remainder for exploring and nature study, bird-watching, and photography. Backpackers can camp in designated areas along a 7.2-mile trail, and hikers can also enjoy a 1.3-mile nature trail. River birch, cypress, and tupelo trees line the white sandbars of the tranquil creek, and a diversity of plant and wildlife call this portion of the Big Thicket home. See the Big Thicket National Preserve description for more information on the ecology of this area.

183. WELLINGTON: COLLINGSWORTH COUNTY PIONEER PARK

Collingsworth County. 37 miles north of Childress on U.S. 83 through Wellington. Mailing address: County Courthouse, 800 West Ave. Wellington, Texas 79095. Phone: 806-447-5408. On Salt Fork of the Red River. Camping: 32 back-in RV/tent sites with water and electricity, group camping area, flush toilets, trailer dump station. Fees charged. Recreation: picnic areas and playgrounds. Open all year.

184. WINTERS: W. LEE COLBURN PARK

Throckmorton County. City of Winters. 6 miles east of city off Texas 153 and C.R. 167. Mailing address: 310 S. Main, Winters, TX 79567. Phone: 325-723-2081, Internet: www.winters-texas.us/recreation.htm. Facilities: on Elm Creek Reservoir with 14 RV/tent sites with full hookups, flush toilets, trailer dump station, group pavilion, fishing pier, playground, swimming, hiking, sports fields.

185. WORLD BIRDING CENTER

The nine units of the World Birding Center attract birds by preserving their natural habitat, then make them visible to the public by providing feeding stations, bird blinds, boardwalks, and observation towers. Rangers lead guided birding walks, and interpretive exhibits and media explain the area's unique avian wildlife. Birdwatchers thrill at the sight of chachalacas, ring-billed pigeons, hook-billed kites, Altamira orioles, green jays, brown jays, and rare vagrant species that wander across the Mexican border. For site descriptions, bird checklists, and programmed events, see www.worldbirdingcenter.org.

1. WBC HEADQUARTERS—BENTSEN-RIO GRANDE VALLEY STATE PARK: 2800 S. Bentsen Palm Drive, Mission, TX 78572, 956-

Birdwatchers find songbirds and hawks that migrate from all over North America as well as rare Mexican species at the parks of the World Birding Center.

584-9156 ext. 221. Hours: Daily, 8 a.m. to 5 p.m. Gates locked at 10 p.m. Admission fee ($5).

2. EDINBURG SCENIC WETLANDS: 40-acre wetland and interpretive center in urban area with trails, observation platforms, interpretive center. Location: 714 S. Raul Longoria Road, Edinburg, TX 78539, 956-381-9922. Hours: Monday–Sunday, 9 a.m. to 6 p.m. Admission fee ($2).

3. ESTERO LLANO GRANDE STATE PARK: 176-acre refuge with shallow lake, riparian woodlands, thorn forest, boardwalk, observation deck, 3 miles of ADA accessible trails, guided birdwatching. Location: 3301 S. International Blvd. (FM 1015), Weslaco, TX. Mailing address: Estero Llano Grande State Park, 154A Lakeview Drive, Weslaco, TX 78596. Phone: 956-565-3919. Hours: 8:00 a.m. to 5:00 p.m. Admission fee ($4).

4. HARLINGEN ARROYO COLORADO—RAMSEY NATURE PARK: 1000 Block on South Loop 499, Harlingen, TX 78550. 55-acre park with nature center, hike/bike trails. Hours: dawn to sunset. Harlingen Parks & Recreation Office, 900 Fairpark Boulevard, Harlingen, Texas 78550. Phone: 956-427-8873. No fees.

5. OLD HIDALGO PUMPHOUSE: Museum and garden with 600 acres of floodplain woodlands in process of revegetation with native brush. Location: 902 S. Second Street, Hidalgo, TX 78557. Phone: 956-843-8686. Hours: Monday–Friday, 10 a.m. to 5 p.m., Sunday 1 p.m. to 5 p.m. Admission: adult $3, senior $2, child $1; fees subject to change.

6. QUINTA MAZATLAN: 1930s Spanish Revival mansion in the heart of McAllen with 15 acres of tropical and native landscaping, trails, feeding stations, gardens, exhibits. Location: 600 Sunset Avenue, McAllen, TX 78503. Phone: 956-688-3370. Internet: www.quintamazatlan.com. Hours: Tuesday–Saturday, 8 a.m. to 5 p.m. Thursday until dark, closed Sunday and Monday. Admission: adults $2, seniors $1, children 12 and under $1.

7. RESACA DE LA PALMA STATE PARK: 1,700 acres of native woodlands and resacas along the Rio Grande. Location: 1000 New Carmen Rd. (off Hwy. 281 or FM 1732), 4 miles west of Brownsville. Mailing address: P.O. Box 714, Olmito, TX 78575. Phone: 956-350-2920. E-mail: pablo.deyturbe@tpwd.state.tx.us. Day use only. Tram loop, 4 observation blinds, 8 miles hike/bike trails, bird walks, programs.

8. ROMA BLUFFS: 3-acre wooded bluff along the Rio Grande in historic port area of Roma with overlook, nature trails and canoeing. Riverside trails will eventually connect to 4,500 acres of nearby state and federal preserves. Location: 610 N. Portscheller St., Roma, TX. Mailing address: P.O. Box 3405, Roma, TX 78584. Phone: 956-849-4930. Hours: Monday–Friday, 8 a.m. to 4:30 p.m. Admission free.

9. SOUTH PADRE ISLAND BIRDING AND NATURE CENTER: 50 acres near the convention center with dune meadows, salt marsh, in-

tertidal flats, and wooded thickets that attract migrating birds. Laguna Madre Nature Trail with boardwalks and viewing areas open 24/7, visitor center (in progress) with exhibits. Location: 7355 Padre Blvd., South Padre Island, TX 78597. Phone: 800-SOPADRE. Admission free.

186. YOAKUM COUNTY PARK

Yoakum County. 7 miles north of Denver City on TX 214. Mailing address: P.O. Box 438, Denver City, Texas 79323. Phone 806-592-3166. Facilities: 12 back in RV-only sites with water and electricity, modern restrooms, trailer dump station, picnic, playgrounds, softball field. Open all year, 4-night limit, no reservations. Fees waived with sales receipt from any in-county purchase.

YOAKUM HUB CITY RV PARK

Dewitt/Lavaca Counties. In City Park. Mailing address: 1307 FM 3475 (Carl Ramert Drive), Yoakum, TX 77995. Phone: 361-293-5682. Internet: www.yoakumusa.com/Virtual_Tour/RV_Park/rv_park.html. *Facilities:* 150-acre park with 17 pull-through and 13 back-in RV/tent sites with full hookups, cable TV, modern restrooms, showers, 9-hole golf course, fishing pond, jogging trail, playgrounds, sports courts. Fees charged, open all year.

STATE AND NATIONAL HISTORIC SITES AND DAY-USE PARKS WITHOUT CAMPING

THE ALAMO

San Antonio. Alamo Plaza, downtown. Mailing address: 300 Alamo Plaza, San Antonio, Texas 78205. Phone: 210-225-1391. Internet: www.thealamo.org.

The Alamo

This famous Texas shrine to freedom was established in 1718 and known as Mission San Antonio de Valero. In 1836, 187 Texas volunteers held off thousands of Mexican soldiers for 13 days. They all were killed, but the cry, "Remember the Alamo," became the motto for the revolution. Sam Houston defeated the Mexican forces a month later and gained independence for Texas. The Alamo and adjacent museum are open 9 a.m. to 5:30 p.m. weekdays and Saturday, 10 a.m. to 5:30 p.m. on Sundays. Closed Christmas Eve and Christmas Day. Admission free.

THE BATTLESHIP TEXAS STATE HISTORIC SITE

Harris County. From Houston, east on La Porte Freeway, TX 225, north on Battleground Rd., TX 134. Mailing address: 3523 Battleground Rd. (Highway 134), La Porte, Texas 77571. Phone: 281-479-2431.

Once the most powerful weapon in the world, this battleship, or dreadnought as it was known, is now moored adjacent to the San Jacinto Battleground and Monument. Commissioned in 1914, it saw action for 32 years and is the only remaining ship that served in both world wars. It is longer than five football fields, had a crew of 1,800 men, and had a main battery of ten 45-caliber guns with a range of 12 miles. The ship is open for tours daily 10 a.m.–5 p.m., closed on Thanksgiving, Christmas Eve, Christmas day. Admission charged. The San Jacinto Battleground, Monument, and Museum, open 9 a.m.–6 p.m., are adjacent.

BEAUMONT: CATTAIL MARSH

Jefferson County. Operated by City of Beaumont. From Beaumont, west on IH-10 to Walden Street exit, 1 mile to Tyrell Park, follow signs to marsh unit. Mailing address: 3503 Tyrell Park Road, Beaumont, Texas 77705. Phone: 409-866-0023. Note: Hurricane Ike in September 2008 did considerable damage. Check for condition of park facilities.

Located in Tyrell Park, this 900-acre water reclamation facility has been developed into a rich marshland with 8 miles of levee trails for hiking, jogging, and horseback riding. Bird-watchers and photographers find for the more than 350 species of birds that live in the managed wetlands of cattail, pickerelweed, arrowhead, and iris. The adjacent Tyrell Park features a 1-mile nature trail, 1.8-mile equestrian trail and stables, restrooms, picnic tables and shelters, 18-hole municipal golf course, disk golf, Garden Center, sport fields. Open daily 7 a.m. to 5 p.m.

BIG SPRING STATE PARK

LOCATION

City of Big Spring, Howard County. On FM 700 near the VA Hospital. Mailing address: #1 Scenic Drive, Big Spring, Texas 79720. Phone: 432-263-4931. E-mail: bigsprsp@sbcglobal.net. To reserve the group picnic pavilion, call 512-389-8900. For all park reservations, call 512-389-8900.

FACILITIES

Fees: entrance, facility, activity use; subject to change.

Day-use only. Restrooms (no showers), lighted, group picnic pavilion for 50 people, playground, Texas State Park Store. A 2.4-mile scenic drive and walking trail leads to a viewpoint atop a 200-foot bluff, and a 2/3 mile nature trail explores the surrounding desert terrain. A seasonal interpretive center displays area Indian artifacts and fossils. Open: 8 a.m. to 8 p.m. from first day of Standard Time (end of October) through April. Open 8 a.m. to 10 p.m. from first day of Daylight Savings Time (April) through the last day of Daylight Savings Time (end of October). Fees charged.

WEATHER

July high averages 82 degrees, January low 40 degrees.

MAIN ATTRACTIONS

The 382-acre Big Spring State Park is located within the city limits of Big Spring. The city was named for a natural spring, long ago replaced by an artificial one, that served as the only watering place for bison, antelope, and humans for a 60-mile radius. The park is popular for hiking, biking, picnicking, and nature viewing. A small prairie dog town lies in a valley on the south side of the park.

The Civilian Conservation Corps constructed the park facilities in 1934. Using limestone quarried on the site, the CCC built the pavilion, headquarters, residence, pumphouse, and restroom. The 2.4-mile drive loops around the mountain following the ledge of limestone rimrock capping the bluff. The CCC built retaining walls for the drive using large blocks of limestone, some weighing as much as two tons, and used mortarless masonry techniques.

PLANTS AND ANIMALS

Big Spring sits at the northern limit of the Edwards Plateau, a limestone escarpment stretching from San Antonio westward to Sanderson.

The park caps a series of 200-foot-high bluffs at the northern edge of the plateau. Three ecological regions merge in the area of Big Spring: the Rolling Plains to the north and east; the Edwards Plateau to the south; and High Plains, or Llano Estacado, to the west. Plants and animals representing all three semiarid regions occur within the area. Mesquite, shin oak, skunkbush sumac, redberry juniper, prickly pear, and other cacti are common. Cottontails, jackrabbits, ground squirrels, and roadrunners are often seen, especially near the ponds. Burrowing owls frequent a small airport nearby.

BRIGHT LEAF PARK

City of Austin. West on FM 2222, left on Creek Mountain Road (before Mt. Bonnell Rd.), when road curves right, continue left to park. Mailing address: P.O. Box 27921, Austin, Texas 78755-7921. Phone: 512-459-7269. E-mail: FriendsOfBrightLeaf@gmail.org. Internet: www.brightleaf.org/. Operated by the Austin Community Foundation.

This peaceful 217-acre wooded park surrounded by Austin's bustling metropolitan area was donated with the stipulation that all hikes be guided. The Austin Community Foundation operates the park and offers public hikes at 9 a.m. on the second Saturday and Sunday of each month except holidays. The Sierra Club, Audubon Society, Scout groups, school classes, and hiking clubs use the area for outings. Volunteers keep the trails in excellent condition. Some trails climb over 200 feet and offer beautiful Hill Country vistas, others loop 4 miles through the park, or follow relatively level ground along scenic Dry Creek.

Miss Georgia Lucas acquired the property and named it Bright Leaf. When she died in 1994 at age 76, she bequeathed it to the Texas Parks and Wildlife Department, who transferred it to the Austin Community Foundation in 2006. The park consists of a series of canyons and ridges rising 400 feet above Lake Austin. Second-growth oak and juniper woodland are dense and harbor rare plants and animals that occur nowhere else in the world except the Texas Hill Country. The endangered golden-cheeked warbler nests in the woodlands. Other possible rare species include endangered cave-dwelling invertebrates, the bracted twistflower, canyon mock orange, and Texas amorpha plants. The interpretive hikes explain the unique ecology of this urban treasure.

CADDOAN MOUNDS STATE HISTORIC SITE

Houston County. 6 miles southwest of Alto on TX 21. 1649 State Hwy 21W, Alto, TX 75925. Phone: 936-858-3218. E-mail: caddoan-mounds@thc.state.tx.us.

A reconstructed thatched hut demonstrates how the Caddoan Indians lived.

Park hours: Tuesday–Sunday, 8:30 a.m.–4:30 p.m. for self-guided tours. Closed Tuesday, Wednesday. Day-use only, no picnicking. Facilities: Interpretive center, archaeological experiment exhibit, .7-mile interpretive trail. Fees charged. Operated by the Texas Historical Commission.

From 1000 B.C. to A.D. 1500, for 2,500 years, the Great Mound Builder culture thrived throughout the eastern woodlands of the United States. The Caddos were the westernmost group of Mound Builders. They had a complex cultural-economical-political system and for 500 years dominated East Texas and portions of Louisiana, Arkansas, and Oklahoma. The Caddos occupied this particular village site from A.D. 500 until the thirteenth century. The park includes a small museum with dioramas and artifacts and reconstructed Indian dwellings.

CASA NAVARRO STATE HISTORIC SITE

Bexar County. Downtown San Antonio at 228 S. Laredo St. Mailing address: 228 S. Laredo St., San Antonio, Texas 78207. Phone: 210-226-4801. E-mail: casa-navarro@thc.state.tx.us. Operated by the Texas Historical Commission. Park hours: Tuesday–Sunday, 9 a.m.–4 p.m.

Casa Navarro was the home of the Texas Revolutionary leader José Antonio Navarro (1795–1871). When Texas was a part of Mexico, Navarro served as a state representative to the Mexican government. He was one of two men born in Texas who signed the Texas Declaration of Independence in 1836. As one of the writers of the Texas constitution, he championed the rights of the Mexican settlers in Texas. Navarro and his family moved to the house in San Antonio in about 1856. The three stone and adobe buildings have been restored and furnished with period antiques.

CONFEDERATE REUNION GROUNDS STATE HISTORIC SITE

Limestone County. From Mexia take U.S. 84 west to FM 2705, then 3 miles south. Mailing address: Rt. 3, Box 95, Mexia, Texas 76667. Phone: 254/716-3730. E-mail: crg@thc.state.tx.us. Operated by the Texas Historical Commission.

This 77-acre day-use park preserves an 1872 house, an 1893 dance pavilion, and a two-story log house. Besides shaded picnic tables and a pavilion, the park offers a hiking trail that leads alongside the Navasota River and Jacks Creek. Hours: daily, 8:00 a.m. to 5:00 p.m. Entrance fee charged.

After the Civil War, a strong sense of brotherhood persisted among the veterans of the Confederacy for decades. In 1889, veterans in Limestone and Freestone counties established an encampment where they could meet to "perpetuate the memories of fallen comrades, aid disabled survivors and indigent widows and orphans of deceased Confederate soldiers, preserve the fraternity that grew out of the war." The festive annual meetings continued for 57 years. In 1983, the nonprofit group donated the Reunion Grounds to the State of Texas.

COPANO BAY FISHING PIER

Aransas County. 5 miles north of Rockport on State Highway 35. Concession operated. Mailing address: P.O. Box 39, Fulton , TX 78358. Phone: Copano Causeway North, 361-425-8325; Copano Causeway South, 361-425-8326. Operated by the Aransas County Navigation District.

The lighted fishing pier, an old causeway cut to allow boat traffic, has 2,500 feet on the north side and 6,190 feet on the south side for saltwater fishing in Copano Bay. Facilities at each pier: store with fishing supplies, bait, and snack bar; boat ramp; fish-cleaning facilities. No camping or picnic facilities. Fees charged.

EISENHOWER BIRTHPLACE STATE HISTORIC SITE

Grayson County. Located at 609 S. Lamar, Denison, Texas 75021. 903-465-8908. E-mail: eisenhower-birthplace@thc.state.tx.us.

Directions: From U.S. Highway 75, exit Morton Street (FM 120 East), turn right on U.S. Highway 69 (Austin Avenue) to Main Street. Turn left on Main to Crockett Avenue; turn right on Crockett Avenue to Nelson Street, turn right on Nelson to Lamar Avenue and go left at the park entrance. Operated by the Texas Historical Commission.

The park surrounds the two-story frame house where Dwight Eisenhower was born on October 14, 1890. The house is furnished with Eisenhower family belongings and period antiques. Visitors can take an "Ike hike" through the wooded six acres surrounding the house and explore the woods, railroad tracks, and creeks where Ike grew up. The visitor's center includes a bookstore and a viewing library with videos depicting Ike's role in World War II and his presidency. Hours: Tuesday–Saturday, 9 a.m.–5 p.m.; Sunday, 1–5 p.m. Tours available.

FANNIN BATTLEGROUND STATE HISTORIC SITE

Goliad County. 9 miles east of Goliad on U.S. Highway 59 to City of Fannin, then south on Park Road 27 for 1 mile. Mailing address: P.O. Box 66, Fannin, Texas 77960. Phone: 512-463-6323. E-mail: fanning-bg@thc.state.tx.us. Operated by the Texas Historical Commission.

On March 20, 1836, at this site, Colonel J. W. Fannin and 284 men lost the Battle of Coleto and surrendered to Mexican General José Urrea. Though told they would be treated as prisoners of war, 7 days later they were executed as traitors by General Santa Anna. Fannin and 342 other prisoners were massacred near what is now Goliad State Historical Park. The 13-acre, day-use park has picnic sites, restrooms, and an interpretive center. Open daily 8 a.m. to 5 p.m.

FANTHORP INN STATE HISTORIC SITE

Grimes County. 10 miles east of Navasota on TX 90 in Anderson. Mailing address: P.O. Box 296, Anderson, Texas 77830. Phone: 936-873-2633.

Fanthorp Inn, a double-pen, cedar-log dogtrot house, served as an early stagecoach stop and the family home of English immigrant Henry Fanthorp. In 1832, while Texas was still a part of Mexico, Fanthorp petitioned Stephen F. Austin for permission to settle in the original Austin Colony. He bought 1,100 acres and built his house on the road that crossed his land. Fanthorp was appointed postmaster by the Provisional Texas Government in 1835 and saw the advantage of offering services and goods to his frequent visitors. Within time, Fanthorp's became a well-known stopping place for both travelers and the community.

The 1834 house is open for tours on Saturday and Sunday from 9 a.m. to 3:30 p.m. Fees charged.

FORT DAVIS NATIONAL HISTORIC SITE

Jeff Davis County. Within city of Fort Davis. Mailing address: P.O. Box 1379, Fort Davis, TX 79734. Phone: Visitor information, 432-426-3224, ext. 20. Internet: www.nps.gov/foda. Operating hours: 8 a.m.–5 p.m. daily. Closed: Thanksgiving, Christmas, New Year's Day, Martin Luther King Jr. Holiday. Fees charged.

Fort Davis is the finest surviving example of the frontier forts that stretched across the West during the epic, nation-building era following the Civil War. From 1854 to 1891, the fort protected settlers traveling west, mail coaches, and freight wagons on the San Antonio to El Paso Road from raiding Comanches and Mescalero Apaches. Eighteen residences on officer's row, two troop barracks, a warehouse, and hospital stand as they originally did.

A trail behind the fort leads into a wooded canyon, up a steep hill, and into Davis Mountains State Park. The hiking trail meanders along ridgetops with vistas that stretch miles across desert grasslands to the distant mountains. The path follows Skyline Drive and leads into Keesey Canyon at the heart of the 1,900 acre park.

One of the most scenic drives in Texas loops 75 miles through the Davis Mountains from the town of Fort Davis. The road winds along wooded Madera Canyon and Limpia Creek, crosses grasslands, and passes the University of Texas McDonald Observatory. The ranch land along the loop is the easiest place in the state to see the graceful pronghorn antelope. Herds of this once-abundant animal regularly graze within camera range of the highway. When alarmed, pronghorns, one of the fastest creatures in the world, can race away at speeds of 55 mph.

FORT LANCASTER STATE HISTORIC SITE

Crockett County. East of Sheffield on U.S. 290. Mailing address: box 306, Sheffield, Texas 79781. Phone: 432-836-4391. E-mail: ft-lancaster@thc.state.tx.us. Operated by the Texas Historical commission. Open daily, 9 a.m.–5 p.m.

Operated from 1855 to 1861, this fort was one of the string of forts stretching across West Texas established to combat hostile Indians. It was near the Pecos River crossing on the road connecting El Paso and San Antonio. At its peak, the fort housed 72 soldiers in 25 stone and wooden buildings. Today, only a few of the hewn limestone chimneys remain. Open 8 a.m. to 5 p.m. daily except Christmas.

FORT LEATON STATE HISTORIC SITE

Fort Leaton sits high on a hill above the Rio Grande.

Presidio County. South of Presidio on TX 170. Mailing address: PO Box 2319, Presidio, TX 79845. Phone: 432-229-3613.

This private fort was built by Benjamin Leaton on a bluff overlooking the Rio Grande in 1848. Leaton made his living collecting Indian scalps for bounty, terrorizing Mexican settlements, and operating a farming enterprise in the rich floodplains. The beautiful white-washed adobe structure with massive walls, 25 rooms, high ceilings, and vaulted doorways remains in excellent condition. Fort Leaton is located 4 miles south of Presidio on the scenic River Road, TX 170, and serves as the western visitor center for Big Bend Ranch State Park. Open 8 a.m. to 4:30 p.m. daily except Christmas.

FORT MCKAVETT STATE HISTORIC SITE

Menard County. From Menard, west on U.S. 190 17 miles, then south on FM 864 for 6 miles to park.
Mailing address: Box 867, Fort McKavett, Texas 76841. Phone: 325-396-2358. E-mail: ft-mckavett@thc.state.tx.us. Operated by the Texas Historical Commission. Fees charged.

Facilities include picnic tables, grills, drinking water, ½-mile nature/interpretive trail to Government Springs and a historic lime kiln, and Texas State Park Store. Established on the San Saba River in 1852, this frontier fort was located on the Upper El Paso Road. It protected immigrants to the California goldfields and local settlers from hostile Indians. The fort was abandoned during the Civil War and reestablished in 1868 because of increased Indian warfare. Finally, it was no longer needed and was abandoned in 1883.

Civilians moved in and lived in the fort, keeping the buildings in good condition. Today, more than 25 historical buildings including the 1870 hospital which houses the interpretive center and restrooms, an officers' quarters, schoolhouse, barracks, post headquarters, and bakery.

The park hosts an annual living history event in March. Past reenactments have included Fort Concho's Cavalry, Infantry, and Laundresses groups; Fort Stockton's Infantry and Laundresses groups; Fort Griffin's Topographical Engineers; Lubbock's Memorial Fourth Cavalry; as well as Texas Rangers and buffalo hunters. Contact the park for information.

FREDERICKSBURG: NATIONAL MUSEUM OF THE PACIFIC WAR

Gillespie County. Downtown Fredericksburg on U.S. 290. Mailing address: 328 E. Main Street, Fredericksburg, TX 78624. Phone: 830-997-4379. E-mail: nimitz@thc.state.tx.us. Internet: www.nimitz-museum.org. Operated by the Texas Historical Commission.

Located in the old Steamboat Hotel in downtown Fredericksburg, this museum and Peace Gardens are dedicated to the soldiers on both sides of the conflict who died in the Pacific during World War II. As commander-in-chief of the Pacific, Admiral Chester W. Nimitz, a native of Fredericksburg, commanded more men and military power than anyone in history. After the war, Admiral Nimitz honored the Japanese by returning Admiral Togo's samurai swords and initiating a fund drive to restore his flagship, the Mikasa, now a Japanese national memorial. In an act of friendship, the Japanese built the Garden of Peace in the museum, incorporating classic Japanese architecture.

The museum also includes the National Museum of the Pacific War George Bush Gallery, the History Walk of the Pacific War, the Plaza of the Presidents, the Surface Warfare Plaza, the Memorial and Victory Walls, the Veterans Walk of Honor and the Center for Pacific War Studies. Nearly 24,000 square feet of indoor exhibits document the war in the Pacific and the horrendous cost of lives required to secure the islands for the Allies. The outdoor plaza displays American and Japanese attack planes and dive bombers, tanks, artillery, a Japanese submarine, and other large artifacts from the war in the Pacific.

FULTON MANSION STATE HISTORIC SITE

Aransas County. 3.5 miles north of Rockport on TX 35, east on Henderson Street for 7 blocks. Mailing address: 317 South Fulton

Beach Rd., Fulton, Texas 78358. Phone: 361-729-0386. E-mail: fulton-mansion@thc.state.tx.us. Operated by the Texas Historical Commission.

Facilities: guided mansion tours, interpretive heritage garden, picnic area. Wear flat, soft-soled shoes to prevent damage to the carpets and floors. Only the first floor is ADA accessible. Open to guided tours that start on the hour Tuesday–Saturday, 10 a.m.–3 p.m., Sunday, 1–3 p.m. Fee charged. Open Wednesday through Sunday, closed Monday and Tuesday, Thanksgiving, Christmas, and New Year's Day.

The Fulton Mansion, completed in 1877, was the home of cattle baron George Ware Fulton and his wife Harriet. The three-story mansion represents one of the earliest French Second Empire buildings constructed in Texas and one of the few that embodied all of the major characteristics of the Second Empire style. The first floor opens into a vestibule, conservatory, parlor, library, and dining room, and the upper two floors have six bedrooms and two bathrooms. A central ventilation shaft, hot air heating system, dumbwaiter, clothes drying apparatus, food chilling troughs, and gas and plumbing systems were incorporated into the mansion. Harriet's interpretive garden is maintained in the rear with heritage plants and wildflowers.

JIM HOGG STATE HISTORIC SITE

Cherokee County. 2 miles northeast of Rusk off U.S. 84. Mailing address: RR 5, Box 80, Rusk, Texas 75785. Phone: 903-683-4850. Operated by the City of Rusk. Open Friday–Sunday. Hours: June–August 8 a.m. to 8 p.m., September–May 8 a.m. to 5 p.m.

This wooded 175-acre park preserves the homesite of the state's first native Texas governor. He was known as the people's governor and is considered, along with Stephen F. Austin, Sam Houston, and John H. Reagan, one of Texas' four greatest statesmen. He was one of the founders of Texaco. When he died in 1906, he told his daughter, Ima, that he desired no monument of stone. "Let my children plant at the head of my grave a pecan tree and at my feet an old-fashioned walnut. And when the trees shall bear, let the pecans and fruit be given out among the plain people so that they may plant them and make Texas a land of trees." The park includes a museum, historic structures, picnic tables, and nature trails through the scenic Piney Woods. The Governor Hogg Shrine Historic Site in Quitman features three renovated homes that belonged to Governor Hogg and his daughter, Ima, as well as RV/tent camping.

LANDMARK INN STATE HISTORIC SITE AND BED & BREAKFAST

Medina County. In Castroville on Florence and Florella streets just off U.S. 90. Mailing address: 402 Florence St., Castroville, Texas

78009. Phone: 830-931-2133. E-mail: landmark-inn@thc.state.tx.us. Call for B&B reservations or see www.landmarkinntx.com. Operated by the Texas Historical Commission.

Built in 1849 as a store and expanded into a hotel in the 1870s, the Landmark Inn served stagecoach passengers heading west from San Antonio. Sitting on the bank of the Medina River, the building was converted into a grist mill in the 1920s and used to produce electricity for the city until 1935. In 1940 the main building was renovated and named the Landmark Inn. Now, restored to the 1940's era, the inn offers travelers a relaxed atmosphere with rocking chairs instead of telephones and televisions. The park includes an interpretive center that displays artifacts, a water-powered grist mill, and landscaped grounds. The inn has 10 air-conditioned rooms with private and shared bathrooms. The rates include continental breakfast with fresh Alsatian pastries, bicycles for exploring historic Castroville, settled by immigrants from the Alsatian region of France, indoor pet kennels, gardens, and trails along the cypress-lined Medina River.

LONGHORN CAVERNS STATE PARK

Burnet County. 6 miles south of Burnet on U.S. 281 to Park Road 4, then 6 miles west. Mailing address: P.O. Box 732, Burnet, Texas 78611. Phone, tour information: 877-441-CAVE or 830-598-CAVE.

Recreation: hourly cave tours, picnicking, nature trails, gift shop, snack bar. Indian artifacts indicate that human use of the extensive caverns beneath the 637-acre park dates back to prehistoric times. The Confederates stored gunpowder in the cave during the Civil War, and outlaws sought its darkness for safety. Later, local residents dined and danced in the cool, 64° Hall of Marble. Though not as decorated with flowstone formations as some central Texas caves, the huge rooms and sculpted hallways reflect the exquisite beauty of nature's handiwork. The labyrinth passageways reach 130 feet below the surface, making the cave one of the longest ever discovered. Admission charged. Open daily, except December 24 and 25.

LUBBOCK LAKE LANDMARK

Lubbock County. Northwest Lubbock, near intersection of Loop 289 and Clovis Road (U.S. 84). Mailing address: Museum of Texas Tech University, Box 43191, Lubbock, Texas 79409-3191. Phone: 807-742-1116. E-mail: lubbock.lake@ttu.edu. Internet: www.depts .ttu.edu/museumttu/lll/.

The perennial springs in Yellowhouse Draw have attracted humans for 12,000 years. When irrigation lowered the water table and decreased flow in the 1930s, the springs were dredged. Excavation revealed one of the richest archaeological sites in North America. The 336-acre site is the only location with artifacts from all the cultures known to have existed on the Southern Plains. Facilities include picnicking areas, an interpretive center and exhibit gallery, and a one-mile self-guided trail of the excavations with wayside exhibits. A four-mile trail through the natural area offers opportunities to see wildflowers, prairie dogs, burrowing owls, and small mammals such as foxes and coyotes. Open Tuesday through Saturday, 9:00 a.m. to 5:00 p.m., Sundays, 1:00 to 5:00 p.m. Admission charged.

LYNDON B. JOHNSON NATIONAL HISTORICAL PARK

Blanco County. In Johnson City. Mailing address: P.O. Box 329 Johnson City, Texas 78636. Phone: 830-868-7128. Internet: www.nps.gov/lyjo. Open daily except Christmas and New Year's Day.

Reconstructed period buildings demonstrate life in early Texas at the LBJ National Historic Site.

This park preserves the boyhood home and mementos from the early life of President Johnson and gives a perspective on the roots that influenced him. In addition, it includes a living-history pioneer ranch with exhibits, a longhorn herd, log cabin, rock barn, and a museum documenting the rise to glory of the cowboy and trail drive.

The park is open daily except Thanksgiving, Christmas, and New Year's Day. The Visitor Center is open from 8:45 a.m. to 5 p.m. Guided tours of the LBJ Boyhood Home in Johnson City are offered 7 days a week. Self-guided tours of the Johnson Settlement, also in Johnson City, are available from 9 a.m. until sunset 7 days a week. Costumed or ranger-guided interpretive tours of the Johnson Settlement are offered as staffing permits.

LYNDON B. JOHNSON STATE PARK AND HISTORIC SITE

Gillespie County. 14 miles west of Johnson City on U.S. 290. Mailing address: Box 238, Stonewall, Texas 78671. Phone: 830-644-2252.

Facilities: restrooms, picnic sites with and without shelters, dining hall (capacity 80), group picnic area (capacity 200), playgrounds, museum, interpretive center with programs, swimming pool, 1.25-mile nature trail, historic structures, tennis courts, baseball field, narrated bus tours of the LBJ ranch, pioneer farm, animal enclosure with buffalo, longhorn, and white-tailed deer, Texas State Park Store.

Created to honor President Johnson, the park occupies 733 acres across the Pedernales River from the president's ranch. The Visitor Center displays memorabilia from President Johnson's boyhood and photographs from his presidential years. The park also commemorates the early pioneers who settled in the Hill Country. Two period log houses are displayed near the Visitor Center. The Behrens Cabin, a two-room dogtrot cabin built in the 1870s, contains furnishings typical of the period. In the spring, a luxuriant display of wildflowers surrounds the 1840s Danz log cabin west of the Visitor Center. In the spring, bluebonnets, paintbrushes, and a medley of other wildflowers blanket the roadsides and fields of the park.

A nature trail leads from the Visitor Center past an enclosure with bison, deer, turkey, and longhorns to the Sauer-Beckmann Farmstead. The living history farm presents life as it was on a German-American family farm in the early 1900s. Park interpreters wear period clothing, demonstrate farm and household chores, and conduct tours.

Bus tours of the LBJ Ranch conducted by the National Park Service start at the State Park Visitor Center. The tour passes by the one-room Junction School first attended by the four-year-old Lyndon B. Johnson in 1912, stops at his reconstructed birthplace and the Johnson family cemetery where the President is buried, and drives through the LBJ Ranch where cattle still are raised. Fees charged.

MAGOFFIN HOME STATE HISTORIC SITE

El Paso County. Located east of the intersection of Octavia Street and Magoffin Avenue, the home is eight blocks east of downtown El Paso and south of IH 10. Westbound traffic on IH 10 exit at Cotton Street and turn left. Follow the brown directional signs. Eastbound traffic should take the downtown exit to Kansas Street and follow the brown directional signs. Mailing address: 1120 Magoffin Avenue, El Paso, TX 79901. Phone: 915-533-5147 E-mail: Magoffin-home@ thc.state.texas.us. Operated by the Texas Historical Commission.

The nineteen room, adobe Magoffin Home, built in 1875 by pioneer Joseph Magoffin, is a prime example of Territorial style architecture. This style developed in the southwest in the mid-1800s and combined local materials (adobe) and then fashionable mid-Victorian wood trim. The home is filled with the original family furnishings and decorative arts. Docents conduct guided tours with information about the three generations of Magoffins that occupied the house for 110 years. Open Tuesday–Sunday, 9 a.m.–5 p.m. Guided tours on the hour, fees charged.

MONUMENT HILL AND KREISCHE BREWERY STATE HISTORIC SITE

Fayette County. 1 mile south of La Grange on U.S. 77, west on Spur 92. Mailing address: 414 State Loop 92, La Grange, Texas 78945-5733. Phone: 979-968-5658. E-mail: monument.hill@tpwd .state.tx.us.

Recreation: picnicking, interpretive and nature trails, historic buildings. Open daily 8 a.m. to 5 p.m. Closed on Christmas Day. Fees charged.

Twice in 1842, six years after Texas won its independence from Mexico, Mexican forces captured and looted San Antonio. After the second attack, a group of volunteers originating in La Grange marched toward San Antonio. The group intercepted the Mexican army, and after a hard battle, the fifteen surviving Texans were taken to Mexico. An army was raised to rescue the prisoners, but they too were captured and taken into Mexico. As punishment for an attempted escape, one prisoner in ten was shot. The men drew beans from a pot, with a black bean meaning death and a white bean meaning life. After the United States defeated Mexico in 1847, the bones of the slain prisoners were returned and interred at Monument Hill.

In 1849, Heinrich Kreisch purchased the property and constructed the first brewery in the state. His descendants lived in his original stone house until 1952. Guided brewery tours October–May, Saturday, Sunday 2 p.m. and 3:30 p.m.; June–September, Saturday 10 a.m. Tours of the Kreische house, first and second Sundays, between 1:30 p.m. and 4 p.m. if docent volunteers are available.

OLD TUNNEL WILDLIFE MANAGEMENT AREA

Kendall County. 2 miles east of Fredericksburg on U.S. Highway 290 to Grapetown Road, south 11 miles through Grapetown to the WMA. Mailing address: 102 E. San Antonio, Suite B, Fredericksburg, TX 78624. Phone: 866-978-2287 for bat flight information. Open year-round from sunrise to sunset.

Ironically, the smallest wildlife management area in Texas, 16 acres, has the largest number of animals. From April to October, 3 million Brazilian free-tailed bats roost in an abandoned railroad tunnel near Fredericksburg. The WMA is open sunrise to sunset year-round for hiking the nature trail and bird-watching. The trail to the lower viewing platform is closed at sunset during bat flights except for evening programs (fees charged). TPWD conducts nightly bat flight programs Thursday–Sunday from May to October. The programs begins ½–1 hour before sunset and seating often sells out, so arrive early. As a general guideline, bat flights begin in May–July between 8–9 p.m. and August–October between 6–8 p.m. Call for tour schedules and bat emergence time. Bring binoculars for spectacular views of the hoards of bats leaving to forage for insects.

PORT ISABEL LIGHTHOUSE STATE HISTORIC SITE

Cameron County. In Port Isabel near the South Padre Island Causeway. Mailing address: 421 Queen Isabella Blvd., Port Isabel, Texas 78578. Phone: 965-943-2262; 1-800-527-6102.

Constructed in 1853, the 72-foot lighthouse operated until 1905. Of the 16 lighthouses originally constructed along the Texas coast, Port Isabel is the only one open to the public. A winding staircase with 75 steps and three ladders leads to the top with expansive views of the causeway and South Padre Island. A replica of the lighthouse keeper's cottage serves as the Port Isabel Chamber of Commerce office with interpretive exhibits. Picnicking available on the grounds. Summer hours: Sunday through Thursday, 10 a.m.–6 p.m. Friday and Saturday, 11 a.m.–8 p.m. Winter hours: 9 a.m.–5 p.m., 7 days a week. Admission charged.

Port Isabel Lighthouse

SABINE PASS BATTLEGROUND STATE HISTORIC SITE

LOCATION

Jefferson County. Operated by Texas Historical Commission. 15 miles south of Port Arthur on TX 87 to Sabine Pass, then 1.5 miles south on FM 3322.
Physical address: 6100 Dowling Rd., Port Arthur, TX 77640.
Mailing address: PO Box 12276, Austin, TX 78711-2276. Phone: 512-463-6323. E-mail: sites@thc.state.tx.us. Note: Hurricane Ike in September 2008 did considerable damage. Check for condition of park facilities.

FACILITIES

In 2008, Texas Parks & Wildlife transferred operation of this site to the Texas Historical Commission. Due to hurricane damage, the campgrounds were removed.

Recreation: fishing and crabbing along one-fourth-mile shore, fish cleaning shelter, boat launch, covered picnic tables.

WEATHER

July high averages 93 degrees, January low 42 degrees.

HISTORY

During the Civil War, Sabine Pass was a strategic port for the Confederacy. Though the Union navy patrolled the Gulf coast from Florida to Texas, Rebel ships boldly ran the blockade. They traded cotton from the plantations of east Texas for arms and commerce vital to the war efforts. In 1863, an armada of 22 Union gunboats convoying soldiers attempted a landing at Sabine Pass near Port Arthur. Lt. Richard W. Dowling, with only 46 Texans and 6 cannons, successfully repelled the invasion and won his place in Texas history. Every year around September 8, Dick Dowling Days, a living history reenactment, commemorates the engagement. The 56-acre park encompasses a point of land at the mouth of Sabine Lake.

SAM BELL MAXEY HOUSE STATE HISTORIC SITE

Lamar County. City of Paris on the corner of South Church and Washington Streets. Mailing address: 812 South Church Street, Paris, Texas 75460. Phone: 903-785-5716. E-mail: sam-bell-maxey@ thc.state.tx.us. Operated by the Texas Historical Commission.
Samuel Bell Maxey and his wife Marilda moved to Paris, Texas, in 1867 and built their High Victorian Italianate style house the following year. Maxey served in the Mexican War, Civil War, and two terms as a U.S. senator. Members of the Maxey family lived in the house until 1966. The house has been restored and furnished to reflect almost 100 years of continuous use by the Maxey family. Open daily 8 a.m.–5 p.m. Admission free.

SAN ANTONIO MISSIONS NATIONAL HISTORICAL PARK

San Antonio. Mailing address: 2202 Roosevelt, San Antonio, Texas 78210. Phone: headquarters 210-534-8833, visitor information 210-932-1001. Internet: www.nps.gov/saan.
Four missions built by Franciscan friars in the early 1700s. Admission charged. All the missions are open daily 9 a.m. to 5 p.m., closed January 1, Thanksgiving Day, and December 25.

The San Antonio Missions National Historical Park visitor center, 210-932-1001, is located at Mission San Jose and has a book store, interpretive exhibits, and a movie dramatizing the efforts of the missions to Christianize the Indians and how the Indian culture evolved into the modern Tejano culture.

Mission Nuestra Senora de la Purisima Concepcion, 807 Mission Rd. Oldest unrestored stone church still in use in the United States, and the best preserved. Some original frescoes still can be seen.

Mission San Francisco de la Espada, 10040 Espada. Has an ornate triple bell tower and is still used as a church.

Mission San José y San Miguel de Agauyo, 6539 San Jose Dr. at Mission Rd. The entire compound of this "Queen of the Missions" has been restored. Some original art remains, including the famous Rose Window. The chapel is still used for church services.

Mission San Juan Capistrano, 9101 Graf Rd. off Mission Rd. The small chapel is still used as a church.

SAN JACINTO BATTLEGROUND STATE HISTORIC SITE

Harris County. From Houston, east on La Porte Freeway, TX 225, north on Battleground Rd. Mailing address: 3523 Battleground Rd. (Highway 134), La Porte, Texas 77571. Phone: 281-479-2431. Internet: www.sanjacinto-museum.org. Hurricane Ike in 2008 caused considerable damage. Check for condition of park facilities.

On April 21, 1836, Sam Houston and a ragtag group of 927 Texans surprised and attacked the Mexican General Santa Anna and his army of 1,600 soldiers. Hemmed in by waterways, the Mexicans suffered 630 casualties and 208 wounded and surrendered in 18 minutes. The Texans lost 9 men. After numerous defeats, the Texans finally won their independence and became a sovereign republic with Sam Houston as the first president. The 570-foot San Jacinto monument, 15 feet taller than the Washington Monument, was opened in 1939 to commemorate the battle. The monument and museum are open daily 9 a.m.–6 p.m., closed Thanksgiving, Christmas Eve, Christmas Day. Admission fees charged for park entry, elevator to the top (or you can climb the stairs), and entry to the observation deck. The Battleship Texas adjacent to the battleground (see separate entry) offers tours 10 a.m.–5 p.m.

SEBASTOPOL STATE HISTORIC SITE

Guadalupe County. City of Seguin, 704 Zorn Street off Alternate Route 90 (Court Street). Mailing address: P.O. Box 900, Seguin, Texas 78156. Phone: 830-379-4833.

Built by Col. Joshua W. Young between 1854 and 1856, Sebastopol is architecturally and technologically significant as one of the best surviving examples of early concrete construction in the southwest. Limecrete was made inexpensively from local limestone rock. Joseph Zorn, Jr. purchased the house in 1874. Zorn served as mayor from 1890 to 1910. Zorn family members lived in the house until 1952. Park programs focus on the natural, cultural, and built environments of 19th century south central Texas. Park hours: Friday–Sunday, 9 a.m. to 4 p.m., closed Thanksgiving, Christmas, Easter, New Year's Day. Tours Friday–Sunday, 9 a.m.–4 p.m. No fees.

SHELDON LAKE STATE PARK AND ENVIRONMENTAL EDUCATION CENTER

LOCATION

Harris County. In the Houston metro area, 2 miles east of Beltway 8 on Garrett Rd. (Lake unit), and on Beaumont Hwy (Education Center). Mailing address: 15315 Beaumont Highway, Houston, TX 77049. Phone: 281-456-2800. E-mail: sheldonlake@tpwd.state. tx.us. Hurricane Ike in 2008 caused considerable damage. Check for condition of park facilities.

FACILITIES

Day-use only.

Fees: entrance, facility, activity use; subject to change.

Recreation: Primary activities at the Sheldon Lake Unit are fishing, canoeing, and wildlife observation. Motorboats restricted to 10 hp, south boat ramp on Pineland Road, north boat ramp on Garrett Road. No boats between November 1 and February 28 to limit disturbance to migratory waterfowl. Bank fishing from four T-piers on west and south levees and parking lot on Garrett Road. Reservoir stocked with Florida bass, crappie, sunfish, catfish.

Environmental Education Center: Open Monday–Friday, 8 a.m.–5 p.m.; Saturday–Sunday, 8 a.m.–7 p.m. Birding, nature study, ½-mile self-guided nature trail that passes 28 naturalized ponds with alligators. Free catch-and-release "Family Fishing" on Sundays for children accompanied by adults. Wildscape gardens illustrate how to attract wildlife by landscaping with native plants that help restore the habitat destroyed by urban sprawl. Programs for organized groups include nature/ecology, nature walks, catch-and-release fishing in two stocked ponds (poles provided), canoeing, archery, pond ecology, native plant gardening, hunter education, composting, and recycling.

WEATHER

July high averages 93 degrees, January low 46 degrees.

MAIN ATTRACTIONS

The 2,500-acre park provides fishing, canoeing, hiking, bird-watching, wildlife viewing, and family nature activities in the urban setting of greater metropolitan Houston. From November through March, thousands of waterfowl overwinter in the reservoir and marshes of the park. TPWD maintains 800 acres of flooded habitat and 400 acres of marshland. Migrating songbirds flock to the woodlands during spring and fall, and herons and egrets nest on rookery islands from March through June. Sheldon Lake, located on Carpenter's Bayou, a tributary of Buffalo Bayou, originally was impounded in 1942 to provide water for the war industries along the Houston Ship Channel. TPWD acquired the reservoir in 1952 as a wildlife management area.

STARR FAMILY STATE HISTORIC SITE

Harrison County. In Marshall, take U.S. Highway 59 north, then west on Travis Street to South Grove Street. Mailing address: 407 West Travis St., Marshall, Texas 75670. Phone: 903-935-3044. E-mail: starr-family-home@thc.state.tx.us. Operated by the Texas Historical Commission.

The Starr Family Home State Historic Site preserves the 150-year-old Starr-Blake Home and two other period houses and a schoolhouse. Dr. James Harper Starr, a prominent official during the Republic and statehood periods, built the house. His son, James Franklin Starr, was a leading land developer later in the 19th century. Guided and self-guided tours of the three homes, the schoolhouse, and gardens are available. Candlelight dinner tours are offered during the Wonderland of Lights Festival in Marshall from Thanksgiving to Christmas.

The Rosemont Cottage Bed and Breakfast, with fully furnished kitchenette, can accommodate four people on one queen size bed and a hide-a-bed sofa. The four-room cottage offers a sample of a luxurious family home in the Victorian era. The room rate includes a continental breakfast.

Open for guided tours only Tuesday–Sunday, 10 a.m.–4 p.m. Admission charged.

VARNER-HOGG PLANTATION STATE HISTORIC SITE

Brazoria County. From Angleton, 15 miles west on TX 35 to West Columbia, north on FM 2852. Mailing address: 1702 N. 13th

Street, West Columbia, TX 77486. Phone: 979-345-4656. E-mail: varner-hogg@thc.state.tx.us. Operated by the Texas Historical Commission.

The first native-born governor of Texas, James Hogg, purchased the land and two-story plantation home in 1901. As one of the founders of Texaco, he believed oil lay under the property. His conviction proved true. After his death the West Columbia oil field was discovered. Hogg's daughter and renowned philanthropist, Ima, filled the mansion with antebellum furnishings in the Empire and Rococo Revival style. She donated the mansion and accompanying buildings to the state in 1958. Day use only. Open Tuesday–Sunday, 8 a.m.–5 p.m. House open for guided tours only (none on Sunday). Fees charged.

WASHINGTON-ON-THE-BRAZOS STATE HISTORIC SITE

LOCATION

Washington County. 21 miles northeast of Brenham on TX 105, northeast on FM 1155. Mailing address: Box 305, Washington, Texas 77880. Phone: 936-878-2214. E-mail: Washington.Brazos@ tpwd.state.tx.us.

FACILITIES

Historic buildings and living history farm with activities and tours, picnic area with pavilions, museum, nature trails. Hours: Gates open 8 a.m. until sundown. Barrington Farm open daily 10 a.m. to 4:30 p.m. Limited WiFi available (user fee).

On March 2, 1836, while the Alamo was under siege, representatives from across Texas met in the town of Washington to declare Texas free from Mexico. They wrote a constitution and established an interim government. Then they fled from the advancing Mexican army. After San Antonio was invaded by Mexico, President Sam Houston moved the capital from Austin to Washington, where it remained until 1845.

Today, the 154-acre park on the banks of the Brazos River features a reconstructed Independence Hall, period buildings, interpretive signs, and a Visitors Center with an excellent timeline exhibit of the tumultuous events that led to the Texas revolution and eventual victory as an independent republic.

The Star of Texas Museum contains more than 20,000 artifacts from the period surrounding the Texas struggle for independence from Mexico. Exhibits, model replicas, audiovisual displays, and a 1,000-square-foot Discovery Room with interactive displays explain life in early Texas. Seasonal exhibitions, special events, and interpretive demonstrations are

Barrington Farm recreates life in pioneer Texas.

regularly scheduled. The research library consists of over 3,000 volumes, journals, and magazines.

Both the homestead of Anson Jones, the fourth and last president of the Republic of Texas, and the Barrington Living History Farm are displayed in the park. Costumed staff and period livestock demonstrate life on a 19th-century farm. Seasonal special events illustrate farm life in the 1850s.

WYLER AERIAL TRAMWAY

El Paso County. From El Paso take U.S. Highway 54 north from Interstate 10 and exit Fred Wilson Boulevard; left on Fred Wilson, which turns into Alabama Street; follow Alabama to McKinley Avenue and take a right. McKinley ends at the park. Mailing address: 1700 McKinley, El Paso, Texas 79930. Phone: 915-566-6622.

The tram ride to the top of Ranger Peak offers an unencumbered and unexcelled view of El Paso, the Franklin Mountains, and the surrounding Chihuahuan Desert. The 4-minute ride in a Swiss-made gondola travels from the base station at 4,692 feet to the top of Ranger Peak at 5,632 feet in elevation. A 2,600-foot-long, 1⅜-inch-diameter steel cable carries the gondola as high as 240 feet above the rugged mountain slopes and canyons. The view from the peak encompasses 7,000 square miles of west Texas, New Mexico, and Mexico.

The station at the top has accessible ramps and paved trails to the observation deck with a 360-degree view. Take your binoculars. Summer Hours (Memorial Day to Labor Day): Monday and Thursday: 12 noon to 6 p.m. Friday, Saturday, and Sunday: 12 noon to 9 p.m. Closed on Tuesday and Wednesday. Winter hours (Labor Day to Memorial Day): Monday, Thursday, and Sunday, 12 noon to 6 p.m. Friday, Saturday, and holidays: 12 noon to 8 p.m. Closed Tuesday and Wednesday. Ticket sales end one hour before closing. Fees charged.

Appendix 1

In addition, private concessionaires at many Corps of Engineers reservoirs operate motels and cabins.

MOTELS AND COTTAGES

Balmorhea SP: San Soloman Courts
Big Bend National Park
Cooper Lake State Park, Doctors Creek Unit
Davis Mountains SP: Indian Lodge
E. V. Spence Reservoir, Wildcat Point
Fossil Rim Wildlife Center Lodge, Glen Rose
Lake Buchanan: Canyon of the Eagles Lodge and Nature Park
Landmark Inn SHP B&B, Castroville
Martin Creek Lake State Park
O. H. Ivie Reservoir, Kennedy Park
Ray Roberts Lake State Park, Lantana Lodge
Starr Family SHP (Rosemont Cottage)

CABINS

State Parks
Bastrop SP
Caddo Lake SP
Cooper Lake SP–South Sulphur Unit
Daingerfield SP
Garner SP
Lake Brownwood SP
Martin Creek Lake SP
Palo Duro Canyon SP
Possum Kingdom SP

Other Parks

Alabama-Coushatta Indian Reservation

Caddo National Grasslands, Lake Fannin

Fossil Rim Wildlife Center, Foothills Safari Camp

Freeport: Quintana Beach County Park

Freeport: San Luis Pass County Park

Kerrville-Schreiner Park

Lake Bastrop Recreation Area

Lake Brady Park

Lake Buchanan (LCRA): Black Rock Park

Lake Fannin (concessionaire)

Lake Fayette (LCRA): Oak Thicket Park

Lake Lewisville, Hidden Cove Park

Lake Sam Rayburn (COE): Jackson Hill Park and Marina,

Lake Sam Rayburn Marina Resort, Powell Marina, Shirley Creek

Lake Tawakoni: Wind Point Park

Lake Texoma (COE): Big Mineral, Grandpappy Point Marina, Lighthouse Marina, Cedar Mills, Paradise Cove, Paw Paw Creek, Rock Creek, Walnut Creek, Cedar Bayou Marina

Lake Whitney (COE): McCown Valley Park

O. H. Ivie Reservoir: Kennedy Park

Silverton: Lake Mackenzie Park, Mackenzie Bait & Tackle Marina

Victoria: Coleto Creek Park and Reservoir

MINI-CABINS AND LIMITED-USE CABINS

Fridge, microwave, bunk beds, no linens, ac/heat, outside table and grill.

Fort Travis Seashore Park (cabanas)

Inks Lake SP

Lake Brady Park (cabanas)

Lake Colorado City SP

Lake Bob Sandlin SP

Martin Dies, Jr. SP

San Angelo SP

South Padre Island: Isla Blanca RV Park (cabanas)

SCREENED SHELTERS

Single shelter with table, electricity, outside grill or fire ring, water (no indoor plumbing), paved or gravel parking for two vehicles. Maximum of eight persons per shelter.

State Parks

Abilene SP

Blanco SP

Brazos Bend SP

Buescher SP

Caddo Lake SP

Choke Canyon SP: Calliham Unit (winterized)

Cleburne SP

Cooper Lake SP

Eisenhower SP

Falcon SP (winterized)

Fort Griffin SHP (winterized)

Fort Parker SP (winterized))

Fort Richardson SHP

Galveston Island SP
Garner SP
Goliad SHP
Huntsville SP
Lake Bob Sandlin SP (winterized)
Lake Brownwood SP
Lake Corpus Christi SP
Lake Livingston SP

Lake Mineral Wells SP
Lake Whitney SP
Martin Creek Lake SP
Martin Dies, Jr. SP
McKinney Falls SP
Meridian SP
Stephen F. Austin SHP
Tyler SP

Other Parks with Screened Shelters

Alabama-Coushatta Indian Reservation
Big Spring: Moss Creek Lake Park
Bowie: Selma Park (Lake Amon G. Carter)
Canyon Lake, Potter's Creek
Freeport: Quitana Beach County Park
Kerrville-Schreiner Park
Lake Bastrop: North Shore Park
Lake Brady Park
Lake B. A. Steinhagen: Magnolia Ridge Park, Sandy Creek Park
Lake Belton: Cedar Ridge Park
Lake Benbrook: Holiday Park
Lake Cyress Springs: Walleye Park

Lake Fayette: Oak Thicket Park, Park Prairie Park
Lake Granger, Wilson H. Fox Park
Lake Hords Creek: Flatrock Park, Lakeside Park
Lake Jacksonville Park
Lake Lewisville: Hidden Cove Park, Oakland Park, Pilot Knoll Park
Lake Proctor: Promontory Park, Sowell Creek Park
Lake Sam Rayburn: Twin Dikes Park, Hanks Creek Park
Lake Tawakoni: Wind Point Park
Lake Waco: Speegleville Park
Lake Whitney: McCown Valley
Navarro Mills Lake: Liberty Hill Park

APPENDIX 2

PARKS WITH GROUP FACILITIES

GROUP LODGES

Big Bend Ranch SP
Caddo National Grasslands, Lake Fannin
Daingerfield SP
Hill Country SNA
Lake Brownwood SP
Lake Houston Park

GROUP BARRACKS AND BUNKHOUSES

Bastrop SP
Big Bend Ranch SP
Bonham SP
Cleburne SP
Devils River SNA
Old Fort Parker
Lake Brownwood SP
Matagorda Island SP

OTHER OVERNIGHT FACILITIES

Abilene SP (2 recreation halls)
Buescher SP (recreation hall)
Garner SP (Cypress Springs, dining hall)
Kerrville-Schreiner SP (recreation hall)
Lake Houston Park (group cabin)
Lake Whitney SP (recreation hall)
Lockhart SP (recreation hall)
Village Creek SP (group cabin)

KITCHENS AND DINING HALLS

Abilene SP
Bastrop SP
Bonham SP
Bridgeport: Wise County Park
Buescher SP
Caddo Lake SP

Choke Canyon SP, Calliham Unit
Cleburne SP
Daingerfield SP
Devils River SNA
Eisenhower SP
Fort Parker SP
Garner SP
Goose Island SP
Kerrville-Schreiner Park
Lake Brownwood SP
Lake Colorado City SP
Lake Cyprus Springs, Twin Oaks
 Park
Lake Houston Park
Lake Lewisville SP
Lake Mineral Wells SP
Lake Somerville SP, Birch Creek
 Unit
Lake Whitney SP
Martin Dies, Jr. SP
McKinney Falls SP
Meridian SP
Stephen F. Austin SP and San
 Felipe State Historic Site
Tyler SP
Village Creek SP

APPENDIX 3

PARKS WITH BICYCLE AND HORSE TRAILS

BIKE TRAILS

The national parks, forests, grasslands, and seashores have many roads suitable for mountain biking. The parks shown here have maintained trails. The mileage and ratings are listed.

Bastrop SP, 12.5 miles, paved road

Big Bend Ranch SP, 49 miles, 1–3

Big Thicket National Preserve, 18 miles, 1–3

Bonham SP, 11 miles, 1–2

Brazos Bend SP, 21 miles, 1–2

Buescher SP, 12.5 miles, paved road

Canyon Lake, 8.2 miles, 2–3

Caprock Canyons SP, 16 miles, 1–3

Caprock Canyons State TW, 64 miles, 1–2 (rails-to-trail)

Cedar Hill SP, 12.5 miles, 2–4

Choke Canyon SP (Calliham), 1 mile, 1

Choke Canyon SP (North Shore), 12 miles, 1

Cleburne SP, 7 miles, 1–3

Colorado Bend SP, 9 miles, 1–2

Cooper Lake SP (South Sulphur), 5 miles, 2

Copper Breaks SP, 9.5 miles, 2

Davis Mountains SP, 75 miles, paved highway loop

Davy Crockett National Forest

Devils River SNA, 12-mile loop

Dinosaur Valley SP, 5.5 miles, 1–2

Eisenhower SP, 4 miles, 1–2

Fairfield Lake SP, 9 miles, 1

Falcon SP, 2 miles, 1

Ft. Boggy SP, 2 miles, 1

Ft. Parker SP, 2 miles, 1

Ft. Richardson SHP & Lost Creek Reservoir State TW, 12 miles, 1–2

Franklin Mountains SP, 51 miles, 1–3

Galveston Island SP, 4 miles, 1

Government Canyon SNA, 7 loops .6–4 miles long

Guadalupe River SP, 10 miles, 2–3

Hill Country SNA, 36 miles, 1–3

Huntsville SP, 11 miles, 1–2

Kerrville-Schreiner Park, 6 miles, 1–3

Kickapoo Cavern SP, 14 miles, 1–2

Lake Benbrook, 14 miles multi-use

Lake Bob Sandlin SP, 5 miles, 1–2

Lake Casa Blanca International SP, 2 miles, 1

Lake Fayette, 3 miles, multi-use

Lake Grapevine (COE), 9 miles, 1–2 (Northshore Trail)

Lake Joe Pool: Loyd Park, 6 miles, 1

Lake Houston SP, 12 miles, 1

Lake Lewisville/Ray Roberts Lake Greenbelt Corridor, 12 miles, 1

Lake Livingston SP, 5 miles, 1

Lake Meredith National Recreation Area, Devil's Canyon multi-use trail, 1

Lake Mineral Wells SP, 8 miles, 1–2

Lake Mineral Wells State TW, 20 miles, 1–2 (rails-to-trail)

Lake Rita Blanca City Park, 9 miles, 1–2

Lake Somerville SP & TW (Birch Creek), 19 miles, 1

Lake Somerville SP & TW (Nails Creek), 17 miles, 1–2

Lake Waco, Speegleville II Park, 6 miles, multi-use

Lake Whitney, 12.5 miles, multi-use

Lubbock: Buffalo Springs Lake, 6 miles, multi-use

Martin Creek Lake SP, 6 miles, 1–2

Martin Dies, Jr. SP, 4 miles, 1

Matagorda Island SP, 70 miles, 1 (beach)

McKinney Falls SP, 4 miles, 1

Mustang Island SP, 5 miles, 1 (beach)

Palo Duro Canyon SP, 10 miles, 1–3

Pedernales Falls SP, 20 miles, 1–2

Ray Roberts Lake SP (Isla Du Bois), 16.5 miles, 1–2

Ray Roberts Lake SP (Johnson Branch), 7 miles, 1–2

Ray Roberts Lake SP (Greenbelt Corridor), 10 miles, 1

Sam Houston National Forest, 85 miles multi-use

San Angelo SP, 50 miles, 1–3

Seminole Canyon SHP, 8 miles, 1–2

South Llano River SP, 4 miles, 1 (closed October–March)

Tyler SP, 13 miles, 1–3

Village Creek SP, 7 miles, 1–2

Bicycle Trail Ratings

Beginner Level [L1]: An easy trail requiring basic riding skills. Terrain may be varied in composition but will have no steep grades, ledges, or ruts. Example: unpaved jeep road.

Intermediate Level [L2]: A trail requiring off-road riding experience and more advanced technical skill. Terrain may have steeper grades with ruts and small ledges that may require dismounts, depending on skill level. Example: single- or double-track trail in rolling terrain with water bars or ruts.

Difficult Level [L3]: A trail requiring expert-level riding skills to traverse potentially hazardous conditions. Steep grades, water crossings, and blind dropoffs may exist over a variety of terrain composition. Example: single-track trail with steep climbs, rocky terrain, unexpected dropoffs.

PARKS WITH EQUESTRAIN TRAILS

All horses entering state parks must have written proof that they tested negative for Coggins disease. Form VS 10-11, less than 12 months old, is acceptable proof.

Day-Use Only

Beaumont: Cattail Marsh
Choke Canyon State Park, North Shore Equestrian Area
Fairfield Lake State Park
Guadalupe River SP
Huntsville SP (rentals only)
Lake Granger, Willis Creek Park
Lake Joe Pool: Loyd Park

Lake Lewisville
Lake Livingston SP (rentals only)
Lake Proctor
Lake Rita Blanca City Park
Lake Waco, Speegleville II Park
Monahans Sandhills SP
Pedernales SP

Overnight and Day-Use

Anahuac: Whites Park
Big Bend State Park
Brazos Bend State Park
Caddo National Grasslands
Caprock Canyon SP
Cooper Lake SP, South Sulphur Unit
Copper Breaks SP
Davis Mountain SP, Limpia Canyon Primitive Area
Davy Crockett National Forest: Piney Creek Horse Trail
Dinosaur Valley SP
Fort Griffin State Historic Site
Government Canyon SNA (planned, call for status)
Hill Country SNA
Lake Arrowhead SP

Lake Benbrook
Lake Houston Park
Lake Meredith National Recreation Area
Lake Mineral Wells SP and Trailway
Lake Sam Rayburn, Ebenzer
Lake Somerville SP, Birch Creek, Nails Creek, and Trailway
Lake Texoma, Oklahoma side
Lake Whitney, McCown Valley
Palo Duro Canyon SP
Ray Roberts Lake SP, Isla Du Bois Unit, Lantana Lodge, and Greenbelt Corridor
Sam Houston National Forest
San Angelo SP

Horse Rental Available

Caprock Canyon SP
Hill Country SNA
Huntsville SP

Lake Livingston SP
Palo Duro Canyon SP

APPENDIX 4

STATE PARK REGULATIONS

The state park regulations, available from any state park headquarters, should be carefully read. The following is an abbreviated list of the major items:

1. Unauthorized removal of rock, earth, or other materials constitutes theft.
2. Archaeological sites, features, and artifacts are protected.
3. Wildlife may not be harmed, captured, or harassed.
4. Firewood may not be gathered. All plants, trees, and deadwood are protected.
5. Fires may be built only in camp stoves or designated fireplaces.
6. Pets must be kept on leash and attended at all times.
7. No alcoholic beverages may be consumed in any place to which the public has access.
8. Noise may not be broadcast into the camp of another visitor between 10 P.M. and 6 A.M.
9. Trash and sewage must be disposed of properly.
10. Two- and three-wheeled vehicles must be equipped with street-legal muffler and spark arrester-exhaust system. They may be operated only in areas designated for their use.
11. Use of motor vehicle or bicycle on a pedestrian trail is prohibited.
12. Campers must obtain a camping permit.
13. Camping is limited to 14 consecutive days and 2 vehicles and 8 people per site.
14. Waste water or sewage may not be deposited on the surface of the ground or in bodies of water.

BIBLIOGRAPHY

Note: Some titles are out of print but may be available in libraries.

Ajilvsgi, Geyata. 1979. *Wild Flowers of the Big Thicket, East Texas, and Western Louisiana*. College Station: Texas A&M University Press.
———. 1984. *Wildflowers of Texas*. Fredricksburg, Texas: Shearer Press.
Correll, D. S., and M. C. Johnston. 1970. *Manual of the Vascular Plants of Texas*. Renner: Texas Research Foundation.
Cox, Paul W., and Patty Leslie. 1988. *Texas Trees: A Friendly Guide* (3rd edition). San Antonio, Texas: Corona Publishing.
Crow, Melinda. 1998. *Rockhounding Texas*. Helena, Mont.: Falcon Publishing.
Dixon, James Ray. *Amphibians and Reptiles of Texas*. 2000. College Station: Texas A&M University Press.
Enquist, Marshall. (1987). *Wildflowers of the Texas Hill Country*. Austin: Lone Star Botanical.
Evans, Douglas B. 1998. *Cactuses of Big Bend National Park*. Austin: University of Texas Press.
Finsley, Charles E. 1999. *A Field Guide to Fossils of Texas*. Houston: Gulf Publishing.
Jackman, J. 1997. *Field Guide to Spiders and Scorpions of Texas*. Houston: Gulf Publishing.
Kutac, Edward A. 1998. *Birder's Guide to Texas* (2nd edition). Houston: Gulf Publishing.
Maxwell, Ross A. 1990. *The Big Bend of the Rio Grande*. Austin: Bureau of Economic Geology, University of Texas.
Miller, George Oxford. 1991. *Texas Hill Country*. Stillwater, Minn.:Voyageur Press.
———. 1986. *Texas Photo Safaris*. Austin: Texas Monthly Press.
———. 1988. *A Field Guide to Wildlife of Texas and the Southwest*. Austin: Texas Monthly Press.
National Geographic Society. 2002. *Field Guide to the Birds of North America* (4th edition). Washington, D.C.: National Geographic Society.
Parent, Laurence. 1996. *Hiking Big Bend National Park*. Helena, Mont.: Falcon Publishing.

————. 1996. *Hiking Texas*. Helena, Mont.: Falcon Publishing.

Rehder, Harald A. 1981. *National Audubon Society Field Guide to North American Seashells*. New York: Knopf.

Sibley, David Allen. 2000. *The Sibley Guide to Birds*. New York: Knopf.

Spearing, Darwin. 1991. *Roadside Geology of Texas*. Missouls, Mont.: Mountain Press.

Tennant, Alan. 2006. *Lone Star Field Guide to Texas Snakes* (revised edition). Lanham, Md.: Taylor Trade.

Tull, Delena. 1987. *Edible and Useful Plants of Texas and the Southwest: A Practical Guide*. Austin: University of Texas Press.

Tull, Delena and George O. Miller. 2003. *A Guide to Wildflowers, Trees, and Shrubs of Texas* (2nd edition). Austin: Lone Star Books.

Woodall's 2008 North American Campground Directory. Woodall's Publishing, published annually. Online at www.woodalls.com.

INDEX

ABOUT THE AUTHOR

George Oxford Miller, an environmental photojournalist, has been writing nature and travel-oriented books and articles for more than two decades. He regularly contributes travel articles and photography to magazines and newspapers across the nation. He has published in *Texas Highways, Texas Parks and Wildlife, Wildlife Conservation, Sierra Club Magazine* and books, *Living Bird, Hooked on the Outdoors, Endless Vacation*, Southwest Airlines *Spirit*, and *Travel Holiday*. He received the National Audubon Society's Annual Conservation Award for his column Austin Au Natural, which ran for five years in the *Austin American Statesman*. He taught photography at the University of Texas, Austin, and currently leads nature and photography tours throughout North and Central America. He is a member of the Society of American Travel Writers.

Also by George Oxford Miller:

> *A Field Guide to Wildflowers, Trees, and Shrubs of Texas*
> *The Texas Hill Country*
> *The Ozarks: The People, the Mountains, the Magic*
> *Landscaping with Native Plants of Texas*
> *Landscaping with Native Plants of the Southwest*
> *Landscaping with Native Plants of Southern California*
> *A Field Guide to Wildlife of Texas and the Southwest*
> *Texas Photo Safaris*